WOMEN CRITICS
1660–1820

Members of the Folger Collective on Early Women Critics

Virginia Walcott Beauchamp

Matthew Bray

Susan Green

Susan Sniader Lanser

Katherine Larsen

Judith Pascoe

Katharine M. Rogers

Ruth Salvaggio

Amy Cohen Simowitz

Tara Ghoshal Wallace

WOMEN CRITICS 1660–1820

An Anthology

**edited by
the Folger Collective
on Early Women Critics**

Indiana University Press
Bloomington and Indianapolis

The paper used in this publication meets the minimum
requirements of American National Standard for Information
Sciences—Permanence of Paper for Printed Library Materials,
ANSI Z39.48-1984.

Manufactured in the United States of America

Library of Congress Cataloging-in-Publication Data

Women critics 1660–1820 : an anthology / edited by the Folger
Collective on Early Women Critics.
p.   cm.
Includes bibliographical references and index.
ISBN 0-253-32872-1 (alk. paper).—ISBN 0-253-20963-3 (pbk. :
alk. paper)
1. Criticism—Europe—History—Sources.   2. Women and literature—
Europe—History—Sources.   I. Folger Collective on Early Women
Critics (Scholarly group)
PN99.E9W66   1995
801'.95'082—dc20   94-40962
1 2 3 4 5   00 99 98 97 96 95

CONTENTS

Acknowledgments   *xi*
Introduction   *xiii*
Note on the Text   *xxvi*

Madeleine de Scudéry (1607–1701)   1
From *Clelia* (1654–1661)   *2*

Margaret Cavendish, Duchess of Newcastle (1623–1673)   9
Preface to *The Worlds Olio* (1655)   *10*
Letter CXXIII from *CCXI Sociable Letters* (1664)   *11*
Preface to *Observations upon Experimental Philosophy* (1666)   *13*
Preface and Epilogue to *The Description of a New World,
called the Blazing-World* (1668)   *14*

Aphra Behn (1640?–1689)   17
Epistle to the Reader from *The Dutch Lover* (1673)   *18*
Preface to *The Lucky Chance* (1687)   *21*
Translator's Preface to *A Discovery of New Worlds* (1688)   *25*

Jane Barker (1652–1727?)   29
From *A Patchwork Screen for the Ladies* (1723)   *30*

Anne Lefèvre Dacier (1654–1720)   34
Translator's Preface to *The Odyssey* (1716)   *35*

Contents

Anne Finch, Countess of Winchilsea (1661–1720)   45
The Introduction (c. 1702)   *46*
The Preface (c. 1702)   *47*
To the Nightingale (1713)   *52*

Catherine Trotter Cockburn (1679–1749)   54
Dedication to *The Unhappy Penitent A Tragedy* (1701)   *55*

Elizabeth Elstob (1683–1756)   58
From *The Rudiments of Grammar for the English-Saxon Tongue* (1715)   *59*

Eliza Haywood (1693?–1756)   67
From *The Female Spectator* (1744, 1746)   *68*

Elizabeth Cooper (fl. 1735–1740)   72
Preface to *The Muses Library* (1737)   *73*

Sarah Fielding (1710–1768)   80
From *The Adventures of David Simple* (1744)   *81*
From *Remarks on Clarissa* (1749)   *84*
From *The Cry* (with Jane Collier, 1754)   *88*
From Preface to *The History of the Countess of Dellwyn* (1759)   *93*

Elizabeth Robinson Montagu (1720–1800)   96
Dialogue III from *Dialogues of the Dead* (1760)   *97*
From *An Essay on the Writings and Genius of Shakespear* (1769)   *103*

Louise d'Epinay (1726–1783)   111
Review of Diderot's *Le Fils naturel* from
the *Correspondance littéraire* (1771)   *112*

Contents

Elizabeth Griffith (1727?–1793)   116
From *The Morality of Shakespeare's Drama Illustrated* (1775)   *117*

Charlotte Ramsay Lennox (1729?–1804)   125
From *Shakespear Illustrated* (1753–1754)   *126*

Clara Reeve (1729–1807)   134
From *The Progress of Romance* (1785)   *135*

Sophie Guntermann von LaRoche (1730–1807)   144
On Reading (1783)   *145*

Isabelle van Tuyll de Zuylen de Charrière (1740–1805)   148
Is Genius Above All Rules? (1788)   *149*
Camilla, or, The New Novel (1796) [fragment]   *158*

Mary Alcock (c. 1742–1798)   161
A Receipt for Writing a Novel (1799)   *162*

Anna Seward (1742–1809)   165
Correspondence between Anna Seward and Clara Reeve from the
Gentleman's Magazine (1786)   *166*

Anna Laetitia Aiken Barbauld (1743–1825)   174
From "On the Origin and Progress of Novel-Writing" (1810)   *175*
From Preface to Richardson, in *The British Novelists* (1810)   *186*
From Preface to Fielding, in *The British Novelists* (1810)   *193*

Hannah Parkhouse Cowley (1743–1809)   199
"An Address" from *A School for Greybeards* (1786)   *200*

Contents

Hannah More (1745–1833)   203

From *Strictures on the Modern System of Female Education* (1799)   *204*

Stéphanie-Félicité Ducrest, Comtesse de Genlis (1746–1830) 207

From "Preliminary Reflections" to *The Influence of Women on French Literature* (1811)   *208*

Reflections on Comedies of Character (1813)   *212*

Charlotte Turner Smith (1749–1806)   216

Preface to *Desmond* (1792)   *217*

From *Marchmont* (1796)   *219*

Judith Sargent Murray (1751–1820)   221

From *The Gleaner* (1798)   *222*

Frances Burney d'Arblay (1752–1840)   231

From *Journal* (1768)   *232*

Author's Preface to *Evelina* (1778)   *233*

Letter to Samuel Crisp (1782)   *235*

From Dedication to *The Wanderer* (1814)   *236*

Phillis Wheatley (1753?–1784)   241

On Recollection (1773)   *241*

On Imagination (1773)   *243*

To S. M. a young *African* Painter, on seeing his Works (1773)   *244*

Elizabeth Simpson Inchbald (1753–1821)   246

Selected *Remarks* from *The British Theatre* (1808)   *247*

Letter to George Colman, the Younger (1818)   *263*

Contents

Mary Robinson (1758–1800) 267
Preface to *Sappho and Phaon* (1796) *268*

Elizabeth Hamilton (1758–1816) 273
From "The Breakfast Table" (1818) *274*

Hannah Webster Foster (1758–1840) 279
From *The Boarding School* (1798) *279*

Mary Wollstonecraft (1759–1797) 284
Advertisement to *Mary, a Fiction* (1788) *285*
Selected Reviews from *The Analytical Review* (1790) *285*
From Letter to Mary Hays (1792) *289*
On Poetry and our Relish for the Beauties of Nature (1797) *290*
Preface to *The Wrongs of Woman: or, Maria* (1798) *293*

Mary Hays (1760–1843) 296
From *Letters and Essays, Moral, and Miscellaneous* (1793) *297*

Joanna Baillie (1762–1851) 301
From "Introductory Discourse," *Plays on the Passions* (1798) *302*
From "To the Reader," from *A Series of Plays* (1812) *322*

Ann Ward Radcliffe (1764–1823) 330
On the Supernatural in Poetry (1826) *331*

Dorothea Mendelssohn Veit Schlegel (1764–1839) 339
From "A Conversation about the Latest Novels by French Women
Writers" (1803) *340*

Contents

Anne-Louise Germaine Necker de Staël (1766–1817) 343
Essay on Fictions (1795) *344*
From *On Literature* (1800) *360*

Maria Edgeworth (1768–1849) 375
From Letter to Miss Ruxton (1809) *375*
From Letter to Elizabeth Inchbald (1810) *376*

Jane Austen (1775–1817) 379
Selected Letters (1809–1816) *380*
From *Northanger Abbey* (1818) *385*
From *Persuasion* (1818) *388*

Rachel Mordecai Lazarus (1788–1838) 391
From Correspondence with Maria Edgeworth (1815–1821) *392*

Biographical and Bibliographical Sources *399*
Members of the Folger Collective on Early Women Critics *402*
Index *405*

ACKNOWLEDGMENTS

A COLLABORATIVE WORK of this scope necessarily accrues multiple debts, which we happily acknowledge. We are particularly grateful to William Rasch, who undertook extensive archival research on German women critics; to Simon Richter, who assisted in choosing the German texts and translated one of the selections; and to Lisa Bernstein and Jack Undank, who also translated texts. For help with research and manuscript preparation, we thank Sharon Groves, Leigh Anna Eicke, and Caroline Eisner.

We have benefited from the support of a number of institutions and the people who make them work. The Comparative Literature Program at the University of Maryland at College Park offered essential support with reproduction, mailing, and other material needs; Mary Ann Hines at the Library Company of Philadelphia provided assistance in researching texts; and the Research Council and College of Arts and Sciences at the University of Oklahoma funded a portion of the research. We gratefully acknowledge their help.

The Folger Evening Colloquium on Women in the Eighteenth Century, which had its genesis in 1989, provided the inspiration for this project. We thank Werner Gundersheimer, Director of the Folger Library, for permission to use the Folger's name in constituting our editorial collective. We are grateful for the consistent support of Lena Cowen Orlin, Executive Director of the Folger Institute, and of the Institute staff. Finally, we thank Joan Catapano of the Indiana University Press for her commitment to the project and for her editorial advice, and her assistant LuAnne Clark Holladay for dedicated and expert assistance.

Perhaps the most crucial debt is to those we cannot acknowledge individually: the many scholars who, during the past few decades, have returned to us the buried or neglected work of early modern women. We hope that this contribution to the scholarly, editorial, and critical project of recovery will speak our thanks.

For permission to quote from the correspondence of Mary Wollstonecraft to Mary Hays, dated November 12, 1792, we gratefully acknowledge

Acknowledgments

The Carl H. Pforzheimer Collection of Shelly and His Circle, The New York Public Library, Astor, Lenox and Tilden Foundations. We also thank Columbia University Press for permission to reprint the *Essay on Fictions* from *An Extraordinary Woman: Selected Writings of Germaine de Staël*, translated and edited by Vivian Folkenflik, copyright 1987. For permission to quote excerpts from Lars Troide, ed., *Early Journals and Letters of Fanny Burney, Vol. II*, we thank McGill-Queen's University Press, Montreal. Finally, we acknowledge the use of extracts from *Jane Austen's Letters to Her Sister Cassandra and Others*, ed. R. W. Chapman, 2nd ed., 1952, by permission of Oxford University Press, London.

INTRODUCTION

IN THE "Preliminary Reflections" to *The Influence of Women on French Literature*, Stéphanie-Félicité de Genlis berates male critics who give "celebrity to talents which are quite mediocre." After listing some egregious errors of taste committed by the French Academy, she boldly concludes that "if there existed an academy of women, one ventures to guess that it could, without trouble, better conduct itself and judge more sanely." Whether or not they judged more sanely than their male counterparts, women practiced criticism virtually from its establishment as a separate discourse in modern Europe. Yet nearly all anthologies and histories of criticism exclude early women, and nearly all anthologies and histories of early women's writings exclude criticism.[1] The critical writing that we have uncovered vividly demonstrates the need to revise the genealogy of criticism.

To make visible the contexts and dimensions of this neglected work, we have selected a range of critical writings by forty-one of the nearly one hundred women we have identified who were producing criticism between 1660 and 1820.[2] The breadth and depth of these women's thought demonstrate not only their participation in diverse critical traditions but also the distinctive insights they brought to critical theory and practice. While the selections that follow are drawn primarily from England, we have also included a sample of selections from France, Germany, and the United States and have recognized the continual cross-cultural exchange that marks this cosmopolitan period. We present this collection of primary texts as a means by which students and scholars may explore new visions of women, literature, and criticism in ways that may reshape our understanding of the 160-year period that coincides with the development both of print culture and of modern configurations of gender identity.

Our purpose is not to forge from this diverse group of writers a distinctly female critical tradition, nor to suggest that women's writing in this period exists apart from the complex developments that have been recognized in the criticism of men. Like their male counterparts, women critics attend, often through similar methodologies, to issues raised by the emergence of criticism as a distinct and privileged form. As individuals, they write from their own historical moments: Cavendish, for example, evokes the scientific spirit of the 1660s by attaching medical terminology to her desire to write, while Wollstonecraft incorporates the tropes of the French

Revolution in her arguments for representing women as rational creatures. At the same time, women's contributions alter the critical map. We hope that the debates about literature, art, and culture which engaged women's talents and energies can be incorporated into our sense of the past, inform our understanding of the present, and suggest directions for future critical inquiry.

While some of our selections are necessarily drawn from better-known (though hardly well-known) works—Aphra Behn's prefaces, Charlotte Lennox's *Shakespear Illustrated*, Clara Reeve's *Progress of Romance*, the essays of Germaine de Staël—this collection consists mostly of newly recovered material representing a spectrum of topics, theories, and critical practices. The variety of ways in which women engaged in critical and cultural debate becomes apparent when one compares Elizabeth Cooper's assumption that poetry is progressing toward "the highest Perfection" with Mary Robinson's complaint that the sonnet form has decayed beyond recognition, or Hannah More's condemnation of novels as "mischievous and dangerous" with Judith Sargent Murray's defense of their pedagogical value, or Joanna Baillie's generalized theories about the workings of drama upon its audience with Elizabeth Inchbald's study of particular performances. These divergent perspectives and practices support Anna Barbauld's caution that "different sentiments and connections separate [literary women] much more than the joint interest of their sex would unite them."[3]

This material has also challenged several of our own assumptions about early women writers and their critical practices. For example, we have come to recognize that even feminist reconstructions of the eighteenth century ally women with novels and novel criticism in a way that has obscured the wealth of their attention to other genres. Initially surprised at the number of women who theorized about dramatic literature and performance, we now associate this involvement with the licensing agreements enacted in England after 1660 which required that only women play female roles. These stipulations gave women new access to the stage as a space for public identity and professional reward and enabled women such as Griffith, Haywood, Inchbald, and Robinson to move from acting to writing careers. Similarly, while we expected women to be concerned with writing as an educational and social process, we discovered that they also show a keen interest in the psychodynamics of reading. And although even so international a celebrity as Germaine de Staël understood that for a woman writer, "the best behavior in the world can scarcely obtain forgiveness for real superiority,"[4] we found that women created intricate, often subversive strategies for circumventing the dichotomies between the moral and the writing woman.

In the search for criticism by early women, we explored writings in a wide spectrum of genres. Some of the criticism presented in this collection is embedded in plays, novels, and poems. Other selections take the form of dialogues between fictional characters rather than emerging directly from the authorial voice. Still others are confined to the private vehicles of letters and diaries, and many more women than men protected their authorship through anonymous publication. Given women's tenuous position in the intellectual life of patriarchal societies, such practices did not surprise us; rather, we were surprised that so much of the material we discovered takes conventional critical forms—substantive introductions and prefaces, periodical essays, and book-length treatises. Early women's critical writings thus invite us to expand the generic boundaries with which criticism has traditionally been identified and to explore the relationship between critical content and critical form.

The women represented in this volume entered the domain of criticism at a particularly privileged moment— the very moment of its formation as a genre. In the eighteenth century for the first time, as Jürgen Habermas puts it, the institution of criticism organized "the lay judgment of a public that had come of age."[5] Criticism of the arts—literature, theater, painting, music —is closely connected to the rise of a bourgeois public sphere and to the burgeoning print culture it produced. The physical spaces of coffeehouses, literary clubs, theaters, and cultural festivals, as well as the discursive spaces of periodicals, pamphlets, prefaces, and reviews, altered the very concepts of author, canon, critic, and text, helping to create a body of literary criticism that became distinct from cultural commentary in the more general sense.

From the very start, women were active participants in the construction of critical discourse. Indeed, perhaps the earliest institution of criticism on the European continent was created as the province of women. A border space between private and public life, the salon culture that first developed in seventeenth-century France constituted women as arbiters of taste and enablers of literary fortune and provided in mid-eighteenth-century England an alternative to such men-only spaces as the coffeehouses.[6] Similarly, women frequently contributed to mainstream periodicals, but they also sometimes founded publications specifically for themselves, such as Eliza Haywood's *Female Spectator* and Charlotte Lennox's *Lady's Museum* in England and Sophie von LaRoche's *Pomona* in Germany. These spatial and discursive institutions gave women unprecedented opportunities to participate in shaping a critical discourse while this discourse was developing its very identity.

In spite of this engagement in the critical enterprise, however, the long association of women with the private spheres of society and culture made their entrance into these public and textual spaces both conspicuous and precarious. Women still faced long-established hierarchies, reinforced by centuries of religious and secular ideology—or what Anne Finch called "mistaken rules" that "Debarr'd" women "from all improvements of the mind"—which established judgment and intellect as masculine preserves. Throughout our period, women who entered the public world of critical discourse recognized and exposed the contradictory social positions in which their critical activities placed them: Finch's lament that an intellectual woman is considered "an intruder on the rights of men" who neglects "the dull manage of a servile house" is not substantially different from Charlotte Smith's accusation nearly a century later that "knowledge, which qualifies women to speak or to write on any other than the most common and trivial subjects, is supposed to be of so difficult attainment, that it cannot be acquired but by the sacrifice of domestic virtues, or the neglect of domestic duties." Mary Wollstonecraft warns Mary Hays about a different kind of domestication when she objects to Hays's publishing men's laudatory comments on her work, for "your male friends will still treat you like a woman. . . . An author, especially a woman, should be cautious lest she too hastily swallows the crude praises which partial friend and polite acquaintance bestow." Mary Robinson celebrates the persistence of women against male indifference when she extols "my illustrious country-women; who, unpatronized by courts, and unprotected by the powerful, persevere in the paths of literature, and ennoble themselves by the unperishable lustre of mental pre-eminence!"

Pressured by gendered critical conventions, women in turn exerted pressure upon these conventions through their own practices. Perhaps because women were entering a domain potentially unsettling both to their traditional subordination and to the construction of letters as a male preserve, their discourse shows a marked investment in the importance of the critical voice. Aphra Behn makes vivid the impossibility for women to claim a neutral voice when she asks ironically to be accorded

the Priviledge for my Masculine Part the Poet in me, (if any such you will allow me) to tread in those successful Paths my Predecessors have so long thriv'd in, to take those Measures both the Ancient and Modern Writers have set me, and by which they have pleas'd the World so well: If I must not, because of my Sex, have this Freedom, but that you will usurp all to your selves; I lay down my Quill, and you shall hear no more of me, no not so much as to make Comparisons, because I will be kinder to my Brothers of the Pen, than they have been to a defenceless Woman; for I am not content to write for a Third day only. I value Fame as much as if I had been born a Hero; and if you rob me of that, I can retire from the ungrateful World, and scorn its fickle Favours.

Here Behn cannily exposes the cultural contradictions among three subject positions from which she might operate: as a man, in her fame-seeking intellectual ambition; as an ungendered subject, in her claim for human freedoms and general rights; as a woman, in her superior virtue and in her threat to leave the public sphere for private retirement.

Behn's consciousness of her gender and its attendant social contradictions is shared by many of the women in this anthology. It is therefore not surprising that these women seem to give significantly more attention than do their male colleagues to women writers, as individuals or as a group. Such attention, however, by no means precluded harsh judgments. Wollstonecraft turned Charlotte Lennox's attack on chivalric romances in *The Female Quixote* against Lennox's own *Euphemia*, and Isabelle de Charrière began a parody of Frances Burney's *Camilla* by introducing a heroine who would be "as ugly as the night" in response to novels that make their heroines "as lovely as the day." Women sometimes even parodied women who practiced criticism, as in chapter 2 of Sarah Fielding's *David Simple*, in which women critics are made to articulate classist and racist judgments; in Charlotte Smith's *The Old Manor House* (1793), which ridicules Hannah Cowley; and in Burney's unproduced play *The Witlings* (1779), in which Lady Smatter proclaims herself "among the Critics" and proceeds to denounce "errors" in Shakespeare and Pope, but admits "I have not, yet, read above half their Works."[7] Anna Seward's response to Reeve's critique of Richardson is so hostile that Reeve "cannot conceive it possible that so much malevolence, with so little delicacy, could proceed from the pen of one of my own sex."

More characteristically, however, women support other women's work. Austen makes a point of listing novels by women when she defends the genre; Genlis insists that no man has surpassed the letters of Madame de Sévigné or the fictions of Madame Cottin; and Maria Edgeworth writes to Elizabeth Inchbald that *A Simple Story* makes her want to tear up her own *Belinda*. A more complex model of critical dialogue occurs when Rachel Mordecai Lazarus challenges Edgeworth's anti-Semitic representation of Jews, eliciting Edgeworth's commitment to make "reparation" by writing the pro-Semitic novel *Harrington*. This occasion marks a particularly generative exchange between a woman critic and a woman writer.

At the same time, women critics clearly felt authorized to examine and evaluate the canonical writings of men. Lennox, Montagu, and Griffith are among many women who took Shakespeare as their object of inquiry; others turned their attention to Homer, Pope, Richardson, or Rousseau. Elizabeth Cooper, concerned to preserve a canon of early English literature, offers a "Poetical Chronicle" so that, "in Spite of Difficulties, and Discouragements, it may be hardly possible for us to recede into our first Barbarism." And Elizabeth Elstob attends at once to women and to tradition: her chief reason for writing the first Anglo-Saxon grammar, she explains, is to make it accessible to women; and she counters Swift's proposal to improve upon English by presenting a formidable array of "our greatest and noblest Poets" who employed Swift's despised monosyllables.

The strength of these commitments points to the extent to which women critics were engaged in the literary and cultural life of their time, integrating their concerns for women and women's writings with more traditional concerns. Using protest or apology to resist marginalization, these women took seriously their critical projects and claimed the right to judge men's work. If Elizabeth Inchbald justifies the critical prefaces gathered in *The British Theatre* by noting the inconsequentiality of a "female observer's" remarks about works that "our learned Reviews" have already pronounced upon, still she embraces the name "critic" and only half refuses comparison to the renowned classicist Anne Dacier.

In turning to specific issues which engaged early women critics, we find that they locate themselves in dialogue with male critics around topics of general concern. Like men of the period, women critics are preoccupied with questions of genre. Sometimes they inaugurate woman-centered inquiries, particularly in their criticism of the novel: as a form not yet sanctioned by tradition, the novel offered a place for women to participate in the very definition of a genre. Even the earliest of women romancers, Madeleine de Scudéry, defined the "true art of Fiction" as "handsomely to resemble truth." Ironically, Scudéry's romances came to be discredited precisely for their lack of "Truth," as Clara Reeve suggests in what became the standard distinction between the improbable romance and the novel:

Introduction

The Novel gives a familiar relation of such things, as pass every day before our eyes, such as may happen to our friend, or to ourselves; and the perfection of it, is to represent every scene, in so easy and natural a manner, and to make them appear so probable, as to deceive us into a persuasion (at least while we are reading) that all is real, until we are affected by the joys or distresses, of the persons in the story, as if they were our own.

This engagement with "real life" led many to consider novels stronger in moral influence, for good or ill, than other genres, as Johnson's *Rambler* number 4 typifies. Critics of both sexes worried about this influence, perhaps all the more because women predominated among novel writers and readers. Apart from a few exceptions such as Mary Alcock and Hannah More, however, women generally insisted on the artistic and moral value of the novel despite fluctuations throughout the eighteenth century in the estimation of the genre. Jane Austen playfully argues in *Northanger Abbey* that novels have "only genius, wit, and taste to recommend them"; Frances Burney in her dedication to *The Wanderer* asserts that the novel is the best genre for "conveying useful precepts," because it portrays the "natural and probable."

Women critics were particularly interested in the relationship between representations of women in fiction and what they believed to be true of women's lives. In her introduction to *The British Novelists*, Anna Barbauld points out that good novels could give inexperienced young women useful vicarious knowledge of the world but that such novels could also arouse inflated expectations. Since novels tended to exaggerate the centrality of romantic love, they would not prepare a young woman for the "neglect and tedium of life which she is perhaps doomed to encounter." Germaine de Staël agreed that the moral influence of novels was weakened by their overemphasis on romantic love, but she nevertheless asserted that "we can glean a morality purer and higher from novels than from any didactic work on virtue" because lifelike fictional characters move us to sympathy.

A few women continued to champion the romance, which had come to assume the status of a degraded genre. Politically radical Mary Hays, for example, argues in her *Letters and Essays* that young people's taste for the romantic ought to be gratified: "the love of the marvellous . . . is natural to young minds, that have any degree of energy and fancy." Dorothea Schlegel goes even further in critiquing the realistic social novel for failing to inspire heroic virtue and insists that a novel is "art" only when it is both romantic and poetic. And the usually conservative Reeve startlingly anticipates modern cultural criticism when she traces privileged forms such as history and epic to the same sources which produce romance: "there is frequently a striking resemblance between works of high and low estimation, which prejudice only, hinders us from discerning, and which when seen, we do not care to acknowledge."

Although women were associated most closely with the novel, many women wrote and criticized drama and poetry, which were of course still considered more prestigious forms. Charlotte Lennox produced a ground-breaking study of Shakespeare's sources in which she did not hesitate to argue that *Measure for Measure* is less rationally plotted than the Italian tale from which Shakespeare took it. Aphra Behn boldly exposed the absurdity of the common assumption that the primary purpose of drama was to provide moral instruction: in her preface to *The Dutch Lover*, she denies that plays are written to amend morals, although she affirms that a play is "the best divertissement that wise men have."

Later women critics, perhaps responding to the conservative backlash after the French Revolution, may have been less ready to flout venerable assumptions, but they brought distinctive insights to their analyses of drama's moral effects. While critics of novels assumed that realistic literature was most likely to influence behavior, Joanna Baillie carefully examined the ways in which the grand heroes, extreme situations, and overwhelming passions of tragedy operate on our minds in order to demonstrate that it has a stronger emotional effect than any other genre (Introductory Discourse to *Plays on the Passions*). Taking a position similar to Schlegel's toward fiction, Baillie argues that the very greatness of tragic characters and the extraordinary stress to which they are subjected enlarge our views of the capacity of human nature; she also maintains that visual representation of tragic action, intensely engaging our interest, forcefully impels us to moral inquiry. Indeed, Baillie's writings not only resemble but precede the Romantic "manifestos" of such writers as Wordsworth and Coleridge.

Other women critics also link staged representation to social reality. Thus Elizabeth Griffith, arguing in *The Morality of Shakespeare's Drama Illustrated* that drama's moral effectiveness stems from its concrete presentation of situation and character, rejects abstract principles in favor of a moral apprehension that replicates the nuances of actual life. Several of Elizabeth Inchbald's prefaces make marital constancy a critical criterion: in her remarks on Thomas Otway's *Venice Preserved*, for example, she claims that married love "has a deeper interest in the bosom of every auditor, than any other affection." Louise d'Epinay too is mindful of audiences' responses when she criticizes Diderot's *Le Fils naturel* on the grounds that the author fails to meet criteria of psychological consistency and "theatrical effect."

While women from Behn to Baillie wrote oppositionally about drama, early women critics, though lamenting woman's marginal place in poetry, engage issues with which eighteenth-century male critics were also concerned. This criticism sometimes placed women writers in a revitalizing role in the wake of a neoclassicism that had come to seem unnatural. Echoing Pope's critique of schools where "As Fancy opens the quick springs of Sense, / We ply the memory, we load the brain" (*Dunciad* 4. 156–157), Mary Wollstonecraft blames the overinstitutionalized aesthetics of boys' education for perpetuating the stiff and derivative verses of her time: "The silken wings of fancy are shrivelled by rules." Radcliffe also favors fancy when she opposes "high talents, wit, genius, judgment" to "the soul of poetry," which is "the spirit of all these, and also something wonderfully higher."

To these female critics, the very acts of reading and writing held powerful cultural messages. A particularly sharp awareness of the power of readers to interpret texts seems to characterize women's critical writings, which often acknowledge the legitimacy of reader response and encourage readers to engage in interpretive dialogue. Margaret Cavendish prescribes a method for reading *The Worlds Olio* but then authorizes her reader to ignore it; Jane Barker offers to "correct and amend" what her readers do not find enjoyable. Sophie von LaRoche invites her readers to write responses to her work and provides detailed instructions about the reading process: she cautions, for example, that reading aloud is an interpretive project that provides listeners with an already-inflected text and that women should perhaps allow only those with whom they are in strong sympathy to read to them.

Such acknowledgments of the real stakes involved in the reading and writing of literature appear frequently in this anthology. Perhaps because of the complex cultural position of women within the institutions of literature and criticism, much of their writing is marked by an acute sense of the author in the text. We see this in Hannah Cowley's strictures against conflating the author with the "low" characters she represents, in Edgeworth's appreciation of Inchbald's unobtrusive narrative presence, in Elizabeth Hamilton's disquisition on the personalities versus the writings of Addison and Johnson, in Eliza Haywood's parody of the anonymous Spectator figure, and in Lazarus's pleasure in finding that Edgeworth confutes the truism "that authors at home and authors on our shelves are quite different persons." These remarks suggest that women may be especially aware of the complex relationship between author and textual voice, perhaps because they know that these are frequently conflated where women writers are concerned.

Many of the women represented here are also vocal about the relationship of literature and criticism to social and national history. Some women, most notably Cooper and Elstob, are concerned with the development of a specifically national or nationalist canon, while women from Montagu to Radcliffe participate with men in the ongoing construction of Shakespeare as a specifically English commodity whose supremacy is challenged repeatedly by critics on the Continent. Postrevolutionary American critics frequently point to their nation's commitment to liberty and equality: Foster extols "this land of liberty, where the female mind is unshackled by the restraints of tyrannical custom," and Judith Sargent Murray, addressing laws against theaters in Massachusetts, warns that "in the present enlightened era and administration of liberty, the citizen would hardly consent to an abridgment of those amusements, the evil tendency of which could not be unequivocally demonstrated to his understanding."

Women critics alert us to the connections between aesthetic process and material life. Just a year before the French Revolution, Isabelle de Charrière argues for particular attention to architecture because it gives pleasure not only to the wealthy but to the "poor Citizen," and urges that asylums for the poor be especially beautiful so that they arrest more privileged passersby and force them to contemplate and alleviate others' sufferings. Germaine de Staël advances an early materialist literary theory when she argues that political systems, whether among the Greeks and Romans or in Revolutionary France, create the conditions for literary production and hence shape the kind of literature that is produced. Barbauld argues that the connection works the other way as well: "Let me make the novels of a country, and let who will make the systems!"

Perhaps because many women critics were conscious of their own denigrated social status, they are often led to question hierarchies of race and ethnicity. In the context of translation from French to English, for example, Aphra Behn recognizes the temptations of ethnocentrism, though without entirely transcending them herself:

> If one follows [the] Flourishes and Embroideries [of the original language] it is worse than French Tinsel. But these defects are only comparatively, in respect of English: And I do not say this so much, to condemn the French, as to praise our own Mother-Tongue, for what we think a Deformity, they may think a Perfection: as the Negroes of Guinney think us as ugly, as we think them.

In a similar expression of conscious protest, Sarah Fielding pillories critics who condemn Desdemona "because she was such a Fool as to marry a

Filthy Black" or who assert of Lear's confrontation with Goneril's servant Oswald that "it was a great Oversight in the Poet, when he was writing the Character of a King, to take notice of the Behaviour of such *vulgar Wretches*." Even as we recognize some women's alertness to cultural prejudice, however, we must acknowledge other women's complicity: both Inchbald and Seward perpetuate the notion of Mahomet as false prophet; Catherine Trotter Cockburn begs for Lord Halifax's "approbation, without which I esteem'd the Suffrages of the People, as the Votes of our Representatives, of no force till the Royal Assent Stamps them into a Law"; and Maria Edgeworth, while championing the Irish, writes disparagingly of both Jews and blacks.[8] Still, the remarkable correspondence between Lazarus and Edgeworth in 1815, or Elizabeth Inchbald's recognition of the damage wrought by anti-Semitic stereotypes in her preface to Cumberland's *The Jew*, or, most notably, Phillis Wheatley's constant negotiation of her complicated positioning as woman, poet, American, and slave, provide glimpses into women's efforts to inform literary criticism, and hence literature, with racial consciousness.

In the eighteenth century, literary criticism inevitably overlaps with political commentary: *Mac Flecknoe* and the *Dunciad* consistently conflate political and literary decay, and the metaphor of political conflict informs the whole of Swift's *Battel of the Books*. Refusing exclusion from political life, women critics also visibly engage in the debates of the period. At times this engagement is explicit, as when Charlotte Smith in the preface to her novel *Desmond* (1792) defends the propriety of "making a book of entertainment the vehicle of political discussion." At other times it is covert and allusive, as in Elstob's decision in 1715, the year of the Jacobite Rebellion in Scotland, to use Scottish citations "since we are a united Nation." Even Burney, who at the time she published *Camilla* primly remarked that politics was "not a feminine subject for discussion,"[9] makes the following declaration in her dedication to *The Wanderer*:

> To attempt to delineate, in whatever form, any picture of actual human life, without reference to the French Revolution, would be as little possible, as to give an idea of the English government, without reference to our own: for not more unavoidably is the last blended with the history of our nation, than the first, with every intellectual survey of the present times.

To a large extent, our anthology also attempts to present an intellectual survey of the writings of these early women critics, and to delineate, in whatever form, a picture of the energies and talents of those women who struggled with and contributed to some of the most pressing literary and cultural concerns of their time. As we near the end of the twentieth century, when feminism, theory, and cultural studies have once again begun to re-define the institutions of literature and criticism, we may find that the writings of these neglected women can teach us as much about our own practices as about theirs. The work of early women critics is serious, extensive, and passionate. In the preface to *Observations upon Experimental Philosophy*, Margaret Cavendish proclaimed that "were I sure no body did read my Works, yet I would not quit my pastime for all this; for although they should not delight others, yet they delight me." We hope that as this volume opens new intellectual connections and contexts, it will also give these eigh-teenth-century critics the audience they have so long deserved.

Notes

1. Among current anthologies of early criticism, only Robert Con Davis and Laurie Finke's *Literary Criticism and Theory* (White Plains: Longman, 1989) presents more than one woman critic; it includes selections by Behn, Finch, and Haywood. Germaine de Staël is virtually the only other woman of the early period whose critical writings are sometimes anthologized. Anthologies of eighteenth-century women's writing, by the same token, rarely include criticism; Katharine M. Rogers and William McCarthy's *Meridian Anthology of Early Women Writers* (New York: New American Li-brary, 1987), Vivian Jones's *Women in the Eighteenth Century* (London: Routledge, 1990), and Robert Uphaus and Gretchen Foster's *The "Other" Eighteenth Century: English Women of Letters* (East Lansing: Colleagues Press, 1991) are typical in featuring only one or two brief examples. Literary histories that include women critics are similarly rare. René Wellek's monumental *History of Modern Criticism*, which discusses hundreds of critics, gives only one eighteenth-century woman (Staël) more than a sentence of attention, and such a recent endeavor as James Engell's *Forming the Critical Mind: Dryden to Coleridge* (Cambridge: Harvard University Press, 1989) entirely omits criticism by women.

For essays specifically on early women critics, see Susan Sniader Lanser and Evelyn Torton Beck, "[Why] Are There No Great Women Critics?" in *The Prism of Sex: Essays in the Sociology of Knowledge*, ed. Julia A. Sherman and Evelyn Torton Beck (Madison: University of Wisconsin Press, 1979), 79–91; Lawrence Lipking, "Aristotle's Sister: A Poetics of Abandonment," *Critical Inquiry* 10 (September 1983): 61–81; Temma Berg, "Louise Rosenblatt: A Woman in Theory," in her *Engendering the Word: Feminist Essays on Psychosexual Poetics* (Urbana: University of Illinois Press, 1989), 177–195; Kristina Straub, "Women, Gender, and Criticism," in *Literary Criticism and Theory*, ed. Davis and Finke, 855–876; and Terry Castle's entry "Women and Literary Criticism" in the forth-coming *Cambridge History of Literary Criticism*, vol. 4, ed. Claude Rowson and H. B. Nisbet.

2. The following women are among those whose critical writings we found valu-

able but were unable to include: Penelope Aubin, Elizabeth Benger, Frances Brooke, Elizabeth Carter, Mary Davys, Ann Donellan, Laetitia Hawkins, Mary Leapor, Delarivier Manley, Elizabeth Rowe, Mary Scott, Frances Sheridan, Catherine Talbot, Ann Taylor, Jane Taylor, Hester Thrale, Jane West, Helen Maria Williams, and Ann Yearsley in England; Sophie Cottin, Marie-Jeanne Riccoboni, and Madame de Sévigné in France; Helmina von Chezy, Betty Gleim, Luise Gottsched, Henriette Herz, Anna Karsch, and Caroline Schlegel-Schelling in Germany; and Sor Juana de la Cruz, Susanna Rowson, and Mercy Otis Warren in the Americas.

   3. Quoted in Betsy Rodgers, *Georgian Chronicle: Mrs. Barbauld and Her Family* (London: Methuen, 1958), 133.

   4. Germaine de Staël, *On Literature* (1800); trans. Vivian Folkenflick, in *An Extraordinary Woman: Selected Writings of Germaine de Staël* (New York: Columbia University Press, 1987), 201.

   5. Jürgen Habermas, *The Structural Transformation of the Public Sphere: An Inquiry into a Category of Bourgeois Society*, trans. Thomas Burger and Frederick Lawrence (Cambridge: MIT Press, 1989). See also Terry Eagleton, *The Function of Criticism* (London: Verso, 1984), and Joan B. Landes, *Women and the Public Sphere in the Age of the French Revolution* (Ithaca: Cornell University Press, 1988).

   6. Landes, *Women and the Public Sphere*, 54, notes the influence of the French *salonnières* "over publication and over the academic careers of talented men. It was women who were reputed to be the real powers behind an election to the Academy."

   7. Burney, "The Witlings," unpublished manuscript in the Berg Collection, New York Public Library, Act II, pp. 28–29.

   8. See, for example, the novels *Belinda* and *The Absentee* and the story "The Grateful Negro."

   9. Frances Burney, *Journals and Letters*, vol. 3, 186.

NOTE ON THE TEXT

To minimize editorial intervention, we have arranged the entries chronologically according to the authors' dates of birth. Each author's entry begins with a brief bio-bibliographical introduction followed by an identification of the edition or editions from which the texts are excerpted. The selections for each author are arranged chronologically, and editorial notations appear at the end of the entry. Sources consulted for the preparation of the authorial introductions are listed together at the end of the anthology.

We have made alterations in eighteenth-century typography for the convenience of the reader while leaving other conventional practices intact. Where we make use of eighteenth-century editions, we do not alter spelling or punctuation but have usually omitted the routine italicization of proper names. Except where indicated, line citations for works of Shakespeare are taken from the Folger Shakespeare editions. We have followed the practice in our annotations of using B.C.E. (Before Common Era) and C.E. (Common Era) instead of B.C. and A.D.

WOMEN CRITICS
1660–1820

MADELEINE DE SCUDÉRY
(1607–1701)

Aᴌᴛʜᴏᴜɢʜ Aᴘʜʀᴀ Bᴇʜɴ is often considered to be the first woman to earn a living by her pen, that status might more properly belong to Madeleine de Scudéry. Orphaned in early childhood and raised by an uncle, Scudéry and her brother Georges made their way in Parisian society primarily through their literary knowledge and accomplishments. Both frequented the famous salon of the Marquise de Rambouillet, which was associated particularly with the movement for female autonomy and "feminine" taste that became known as *préciosité*. In 1652 or 1653, Scudéry inaugurated her own salon, which dominated French culture for the next half-century. Scudéry was one of the most famous and successful writers of her day and the only woman of her century to be acknowledged by the Académie Française, which awarded her its first prize for a discourse on glory in 1671. She was also elected to the Academia dei Ricovrati of Padua and was one of only two women of her time to receive (in 1683) a royal pension. Never married, she had a long and intimate friendship with the historian Paul Pellison.

Scudéry is known principally for her novels, the first two of which were published under the name of her brother and written partly in collaboration with him. Her most famous works, widely reprinted and translated, were the ten-volume *Artamène ou le grand Cyrus* (1649–1653) and *Clélie, histoire romaine* (1654–1661). Her novels are characterized by ancient settings; multiple plots blending adventure, war, and love; a focus on the lovers' fidelity; and lengthy self-analyses in dialogic form. In later years, Scudéry turned to a form she called *conversations*, which she created by extracting dialogues from her novels and publishing them as separate texts. Her work emphasizes the kind of love she called *galanterie*, in which sexual desire is sublimated to spiritual and intellectual fulfillment as an alternative to both arranged marriages and dangerous liaisons.

The present text is taken from an early English translation of Scudéry's historical romance *Clélie*, which invokes the Roman legend of adventure and love in which Cloelia, given as a hostage to the Etruscan king, swims the Tiber to save herself. In the novel, Clélie's suitor Aronce ultimately rescues and marries her. The episodic and digressive narrative features many

I

conversations, one of which is excerpted here. It explores the relationship between truth and fiction, history and poetry, giving a high place to the writer of fiction, who is described as a creator who nevertheless must rely upon history. Although Scudéry's own works would later be criticized for their lack of verisimilitude, she argues that the work of imagination must be rendered believable.

Clelia, trans. George Havers (London: Dorman Newman and Thomas Cockerel, 1678) Part IV, Book II.

From *Clelia* (1654–1661)

Nothing more commends a well-invented Fable than those historical foundations which are interweav'd throughout in it, and cause the Fiction to be receiv'd together with the truth. But to speak unfeignedly, 'tis more difficult than is believ'd, to mingle those two together aright: for they must be so handsomely blended, as not to be discerned one from another, and that which is invented, must generally seem more likely than the true: for Chance indeed may bring such things about as are incredible, but it is not lawful for a man to invent such as cannot be believ'd.[1]

If all that I have heard (said Plotina) be not true, I require Amilcar to restore me the tears which I have shed, or invent some other History as delightful as this is melancholly, or at least to describe how an invented History ought to be made, so as to be good: for, as for my part (added she agreeably) were I to invent a History, I think I should make things much more perfect than they are. All Women should be admirably fair, and all Men should be as valiant as Hector, all my Heroes should slay at least a hundred men in every battel, I would build Palaces of precious stones, I would make Prodigies fall out every moment, and without troubling my self to invent with judgement, I should suffer my fancy to act as it pleased; so that seeking out only surprising events without examining whether they were consistent to reason or not, I should certainly make very extraordinary things, [as] continual Shipwracks, burning of Cities, and a thousand other like accidents, which occasion handsome lamentations and descriptions; Plotina spoke this with a certain sprightly air which made it apparent, she knew sufficiently, what she said, was not that which ought to be done, and that she only design'd to draw Anacreon, Herminius, and Amilcar to speak, who no doubt were able to speak excellently upon this Subject. And accordingly she obtain'd the end she propos'd to her self: for Anacreon not

Madeleine de Scudéry (1607–1701)

knowing her yet sufficiently to be acquainted with all the ingenious subtilty she made profession of, turning towards her, and beholding her with a smile; Should you invent a History after the manner you speak of, amiable Plotina, (said he) you would do a thing no doubt sufficiently strange; for with rare Events, wonderful Descriptions, heroical Actions, extraordinary Matters, and Palaces of precious Stones, you would make one of the lewdest[2] Fables that can possibly be invented; there being without doubt nothing worse, than to see things of this nature made without order and reason: Is there any thing imaginable more strange, than when 'tis in ones power to make such events fall out as he pleases, yet to introduce such as can never possibly arrive?

But yet (said Plotina) how comes it to be so, and wherein is my opinion so absurd? Because (answer'd Anacreon) when you invent a Fable, your purpose is to be believ'd, and the true art of Fiction is handsomely to resemble truth. For when this rule is deserted there is no longer any difficulty in any thing whatsoever; and there is no more proper occasion to display the wit, than to invent without judgement. For my part (said Clelia) I well understand what Anacreon speaks; for certainly things which have resemblance with truth, and seem possible to happen, affect far more, than those which cannot either be believ'd or fear'd: But if an Historian of this kind (answer'd Valeria) never relates things but such as appear to be true, and are of easie belief, methinks his composures will be extream vulgar, and not much delightful. You are upon a tender point, Valeria (reply'd Amilcar) for in disallowing things incredible and impossible, it is not intended to imploy only such as are mean and common; there is a third way to be taken, which is the most delightful of all, and most reasonable. Wonderful accidents are so far from being forbidden, that they are necessary, provided they do not happen too often, and produce handsome effects; only odd and impossible things are absolutely condemned. For 'tis the occasion of disparaging the credit of the whole, when one thing is presented that surpasses belief. When any Slave of mine has told me a lye but once, I afterwards suspect all that he tells me; judge then if I can believe a man who should recount extraordinary adventures to me, which my reason cannot consider as possible. So that impossible things, and such as are low and common must almost equally be avoided, and such ways of invention follow'd, as are at once both strange and natural; for without this last quality, no wonder can please a reasonable person.

I conceive (answer'd Herminius) whosoever will invent such kind of adventures, as may both instruct and delight, he ought to consider all the World in general, as a Painter beholds his Pattern when he is at work. And as diversity or variety is the Soul of the World, he ought to take heed of making all men Heroes, all Women equally fair, the dispositions and humors of all particular persons alike and correspondent, and Love, Anger, Jealousie, Hatred, to produce always the same effects. On the contrary, he must imitate that admirable variety, which is seen in all men, according to the example of Homer. Which is not unknown to two Ladies I see here present; for there is so great a variety of representations in his Works, that 'tis not one of the things which makes me most admire him. Those two Lovers, who, in the beginning of their contest with one another, about a captive Virgin, being of different tempers, act also after different manners; and though they are possess'd with the same passion, do not take the same course. There is seen in Paris, a representation of disorderly love, in which Virtue has no part; in Hector and Andromache, an Idea of virtuous love; in Patroclus and Achilles, one of Heroical friendship, and the better to understand this variety of characters wherewith Homer has adorn'd his Works, it needs only to take notice in general, of Agamemnon, Nestor, Achilles, Ulysses, Ajax, Menelaus, Diomedes, Paris, Helen, Hector, Andromache, Priam, Penelope,[3] and of so many others, even to the pleasant Characters,[4] as that of Thirsites,[5] which is so particularly excellent. But 'tis moreover worth observation that the persons which Homer introduces, are presently known and familiar to the Readers, because they always act according to the temper he attributes to them. Wherefore heed must be taken not to confound these different Characters: but above all things, the nature of the passions ought necessarily to be understood, and what they work in the hearts of those who are possess'd with them, after having describ'd them for such and such persons: for every one has his manner of loving according to his own humor.

You have reason (answer'd Plotina) and I begin to conceive well what you say: but since any one may invent a History, why is it not lawful to invent all things, and to suppose such Countreys as are no where in the World; for it would spare much pains. 'Tis true (replied Anacreon) but it would also diminish much of the pleasure for, if such places and persons only were us'd as were never heard of, there would be the less curiosity in the minds of the Readers to know them: and the imagination finding all things new, would be inclin'd to doubt of all; whereas on the contrary, when an Age is made choice of, which is not so remote, but that some particularities of it are known, not so near, as that all the passages of it be too well understood, which notwithstanding is so between both, that events may be introduc'd in it, which an Historian may probably have been ignorant of, or ought not to have related; there is more conveniency to make handsomer things than if all were invented. For when names of Countreys are employed, which all the World hears of, and wherewith Geography is exactly acquainted; and when great events are made use of, which are sufficiently known, the mind is wholly dispos'd to suffer it self to be seduc'd, and to receive the fiction together with the truth, provided it be handsomely interwoven, and the Writer take pains to study the Age well he makes choice of, to improve all the rarities of it, and to conform to the customs of places he treats of, not to mention Laurels in Countreys where there was never any seen, not to confound the Religions or Customs of Nations that are introduc'd; though they may with judgement be a little drawn to the usage of the present age, to the end they may be the more delightful; I am confident if this be observ'd, and they which are introduc'd in a Fable of this nature, speak well, the passions be well painted out, the adventures be natural and prudently invented, all the little matters which discover the bottom of mens hearts, be pertinently plac'd; Vice be blam'd, Virtue rewarded, and Variety dispers'd through the whole, without confusion, if the fancy be always subject to the judgement, extraordinary events be rationally grounded; if there be knowledge, without affectation, delight, ornament, and pleasantness, wherever it is necessary; if the style be neither too high nor too low, and no violence offer'd to decency and good manners; I am confident, I say, such a Work will please all that read it, be more delightful to them than a History, and withal be more profitable. For a person who writes the History of a Prince, can blame only the vices of him whose life he writes: but he that undertakes to compose an ingenious Fable, may take occasion, if he please, to condemn all Vices, and teach all Virtues. And therefore I wish, with all my heart, Herminius and Amilcar would set about a composition of this nature.

As for Amilcar (answer'd Clelia) I must disswade him from it; for according to the humor he is of, he will never be able to resolve to blame inconstancy: but for Herminius, who makes profession of being constant and knows all virtues, I wish he would take the pains to do it. I assure you (reply'd he) I should gladly undertake it, if I believ'd I could do it as well as I apprehend it might be done; for I am perswaded a Map of the World, and that a little embellish't, would be a very delightful thing, and withal very profitable, But to speak freely, the undertaking is more difficult than it seems, and I believe it is easier to write a handsome History, than to compose an accurate Fable, after the manner I apprehend it may be made. Yet it is requisite an Historian have great accomplishments; he must have a wit of great extent which his fancy must adorn when it is needful, both which his judgement must guide and restrain, when 'tis convenient, and his memory ought never to be unfaithful to him. He must have an universal knowledge of the World, of the interest of Princes, and the humors of Nations; policy must not be unknown to him, nor the art of War; he must understand to describe battels; and, which is most necessary, he must be able perfectly to represent those wars of the closet, which are met with in all Courts, which consist in intrigues, delusions, and negotiations, true or feign'd, and which notwithstanding are of such importance, that 'tis in them the seeds are sown of the most considerable Wars, and on which the ruin or felicity of Nations, as well as the verity of History depends. It is requisite also to be skilful, how to represent the different passions of Princes, as those which govern; not to say too much, or too little of them, and never to write any thing, but what instructs or delights, and is either good or pleasant. However when a man is provided with faithful memorials, has liv'd himself in the world, and has part of the qualities necessary to an Historian, 'tis easie to make a History not wholly bad.

But to compose an accurate Fable, adorn'd with all that can render it agreeable or profitable, I conceive it necessary, not only to have all that I said was requisite to an Historian, but to have a hundred knowledges more comprehensive and particular. Such a writer must be (as I may so speak) the Creator of his Works; he must understand the art of setting forth Virtue, and exhibiting it as a thing not difficult to be practis'd. He must know the World, not only as the Author of a History ought, but he must understand the handsome mode of the World perfectly, politeness of conversation, the art of ingenious raillery, and that of making innocent Satyrs; nor must he be ignorant of that composing of Verses, writing Letters, and making Orations. He must also know (as I may so speak) the secrets of all hearts, and be ignorant of not one of all the commendable Sciences; of which occasion may be sometimes offer'd to speak by the way. But above all things, he must know how to take away plainness and driness from Morality, and set it off in a dress so natural and so agreeable, that it may divert all those to whom it gives instruction; and as Ladies break not their Looking-glasses which show them the defects which they amend when they know; so they may not hate a Work wherein they oftentimes see things which none durst speak to them of, and which they would never speak of to themselves, Whence it is easie to judge, that it is much more difficult to make a Work of this nature, than to write a History.

You discourse admirably well (answer'd Anacreon). I am of your opinion (added Amilcar): but that which seems strange to me, is, that if it were possible to find one that had compos'd a Fable of this nature, yet there would also be found a great number of people, who would speak of it but as a meer trifle, and an unprofitable amusement: and I know divers antient Sena-

Madeleine de Scudéry (1607–1701)

tors here, and also several Roman Matrons, who would be so affrighted with a Love-story, that they would absolutely forbid their Children from casting their eye upon any such. That conceit, (answer'd Herminius) seems very unjust; for Love is not learnt in Books, nature teaches it all men; and in all places through which I have travell'd I have found love every where: But I have found it more gross, brutish, and criminal, amongst people of no politeness, and such as are wholly ignorant of handsome gallantry, than amongst persons of worth and civil education. And besides, if it were unfit to read Books wherein Love is treated of, we must forbear reading Histories, in which we find examples of all crimes, and wherein oftentimes the Criminals are happy, and cause desire in some to imitate them. One day, History will record the abominable action of Sextus,[6] the miserable death of Servius Tullus, the unjust Loves of Turquin and Tullia,[7] and a thousand other things of ungenerous example; which need not be in a Fable according to the way I understand; for therein modesty may always be joyn'd with love, and no criminal loves be ever related, which prove not in the end unhappy. For my part (said Clelia) I think it more important than is believ'd, to shew that there may be innocent loves and delightful together, for there are but too many who think this can never be.

No doubt Madam, you have reason (answer'd Herminius) wherefore those good Senators, and severe Matrons are to blame for hindering their Children from reading a Work wherein they might find wherewith to understand the practice of all Virtues, and by the advantages of which they might spare the pains of travelling, to become persons of worth and accomplisht; since there may be made so handsome a Map of the World, that it might be seen in Epitome, without going forth of their Closet. And as for Ladies, I conceive likewise that the reading of such a Work as I am speaking of, would rather hinder them from admitting of Gallants, than induce them to entertain them; for if they would compare the love pretended to them, with that they found describ'd in a Book of this Nature, they would apprehend so much difference between them, that they would never suffer themselves to be mov'd with it. I add moreover confidently, that such a Book might not only teach all Virtues, blame all Vices, and reprove all the little defects the World is full of, but it might also teach to reverence the gods, by the example given in the persons of Heroes, propos'd for a pattern, and that of whatever Nation or Religion the Reader be of, he might be profited by it, For when I behold a Roman adore the gods of his Countrey, I am not backward to improve by the example, (though I am an African) and thereby to remember I ought to worship those of my Countrey. Therefore I do not weigh the morosity of some unreasonable people, who blame a Work of this nature; but at the venture of undergoing their injustice, I wish I were the Author of one. For I, being contented with my own intention, should comfort my self against the severity of a few persons with the general applause of the World, and the peculiar knowledge I had of the profitableness of this kind of Work in which may be had experience without the assistance of old age, precepts without severity, innocent Satyrs, judgement which costs nothing, and the means to learn that art of the World, without which it is unpossible ever to be acceptable.

If you make one (said Plotina) I promise you to read it with pleasure: For my part (added Clelia) I promise my admiration to Herminius. I promise him more than you (added Valeria) for I promise him to reform many defects which I have. For what concerns me (said Anacreon) I engage my self to sing his glory. And for my part (answer'd Amilcar) I promise him to read it with delight, to esteem it highly, to commend it in all places, and to do nothing which he shall say, for I never do any thing but what I say to my self. And besides, he has such an inclination to constant love, that I should never conform to it.

Notes

1. The translation has no paragraphs; these have been provided here for the convenience of the reader.

2. Lewdest: most ignorant or foolish.

3. Characters from Homer's *Iliad* and *Odyssey*, each representing different dominant characteristics. Penelope is patient and loyal, Helen beautiful, Nestor old and wise, etc.

4. Pleasant: humorous; laughable.

5. Thirsites was the ugliest and most impudent of the Greeks at Troy.

6. Scudéry probably has in mind Sextus Tarquinius, rapist of Lucretia, but she might also be referring to Sextus Naso, one of the conspirators against Caesar, or to Sextius Paconianus, the unscrupulous agent of Sejanus, who was involved in his downfall.

7. Servius Tullus, sixth king of Rome, was a kind ruler who was popular with the people and eventually incurred the resentment of the patricians. His daughter Tullia conspired with her brother-in-law, Lucius Tarquinius (Turquin), to murder their respective spouses, hastily marry each other, and usurp the throne from her father. With the patricians' support, Turquin seized power, had Servius Tullus murdered, and allowed his body to rot in the street.

MARGARET CAVENDISH, DUCHESS OF NEWCASTLE (1623–1673)

THE YOUNGEST of eight children, Margaret Cavendish claimed the love and protection of a close-knit and talented family. Perhaps her audacity in publishing her voluminous writings—fourteen works in fifteen years, some over seven hundred pages long—arose from the example of her widowed mother's ruthless expansion of the family fortunes after her husband's death when Margaret was two. Elizabeth Lucas did not dissuade her awkward and precocious daughter from becoming at nineteen a lady-in-waiting to Queen Henrietta Maria. Residing in Oxford during the early years of the Civil Wars, Margaret eventually spent fifteen years on the Continent in exile with the English court. During this time she became the second wife of the much older and extremely wealthy William Cavendish, Duke of Newcastle, leader of Charles I's forces at the time of their crucial defeat at Marston Moor in 1644. The Duke's ostentatious hospitality attracted such notable intellectuals as Hobbes, Descartes, Mersenne, Gassendi, John Pell, Sir Kenelm Digby, William Perry, and Sir Charles Cavendish—William's older brother, a renowned mathematician who, like her husband, encouraged Margaret's writing.

Cavendish's *Poems and Fancies* (1653) inaugurated her copious and influential literary production. She wrote in almost every genre—drama, poetry, prose narrative, essay, epistle, biography, autobiography, oration, and fable. Dubbed "Mad Madge" by some contemporaries, Cavendish maintained that her desire for fame was justification enough for her imaginative writing. The only woman of her time to write extensively on issues of scientific theory, she insisted on attending a special meeting of the all-male Royal Society, which did not elect a woman member until 1945.

Cavendish's critical sensibility blends with her fanciful writing, especially in her feminist science fiction utopia, *The Description of a New Blazing World*, which was appended to her much longer *Observations upon Experimental Philosophy* (1666). We include the prefaces to both works and the epilogue to the *Description* (1668 edition), in which Cavendish accounts for her desire to write. The preface to *The Worlds Olio* (1655) speculates about the role of the reader in creating meaning. The excerpt from *CCXI Sociable Letters* (1664) offers original insights about the nature of Shakespeare's imagination, anticipating Dryden and Coleridge in her description of Shakespeare's self-effacement in authorship and character development.

The Worlds Olio (London: Martin and Allestrye, 1655); *CCXI Sociable Letters* (London: William Wilson, 1664); *Observations upon Experimental Philosophy. To which is added, the Description of a New Blazing World* (London: A. Maxwell, 1666); *The Description of a New World, called the Blazing-World* (London: A. Maxwell, 1668).

Preface to *The Worlds Olio* (1655)

To the Reader—

I Desire those that read any of this Book, that every Chapter may be read clearly, without long stops and staies; for it is with Writers as it is with men; for an ill affected Fashion or Garb, takes away the Natural and grace-full Form of the Person; So Writings if they be read lamely, or crookedly, and not evenly, smoothly & throughly, insnarle the Sense; Nay the very sound of the Voice will seem to alter the sense of the Theme; though the Sense will be there in despight of the ill Voice or Reader, but it will be concealed, or discovered to its disadvantage; for like an ill Musician, or in-deed one that cannot play at all, who instead of playing he puts the Fiddle out of tune, and causeth a Discord, which if well plaid upon would sound Harmoniously; or is like one that can play but one Tune on all sorts of Instruments; so some will read with one Tone or Sound of Voice, though the Passions and Numbers are different; and some again in reading wind up their Voices to such a passionate scrue, that they whine or squeal rather than speak or read; others, fold up their Voices with that distinction, that they make that three square that is four square, and narrow that should be broad, and high that should be low, and low that should be high; and some again so fast, that the Sense is lost in the Race: So that Writings, though they are not so, yet they sound good or bad according to the Readers, and not according to their Authors; and indeed such advantage a good or ill Reader gives, as those that read well, shall give a grace to a foolish Author, and those that read ill, disgrace a wise and a witty Author. But there are two sorts of Readers, the one that reads to himself and for his own benefit, the other to benefit another by hearing it; in the first, there is required a good Judgement, and a ready Understanding; in the other, a good Voice, and a gracefull Delivery; so that a Writer hath a double desire, the one that he may write well, the other, that he may be read well; And my desire is the more earnest, because I know my Writings are not strong enough to bear an ill Reader; wherefore I intreat so much favour, as to give it its own Countenance, wherein you will oblige the Writer to be

Yours,

M. N.

Letter CXXIII from *CCXI Sociable Letters* (1664)

Madam,

I wonder how that Person you mention in your Letter, could either have the Conscience, or Confidence to Dispraise Shakespear's Playes, as to say they were made up onely with Clowns, Fools, Watchmen, and the like; But to Answer that Person, though Shakespear's Wit will Answer for himself, I say, that it seems by his Judging, or Censuring, he Understands not Playes, or Wit; for to Express Properly, Rightly, Usually, and Naturally, a Clown's, or Fool's Humour, Expressions, Phrases, Garbs, Manners, Actions, Words, and Course of Life, is as Witty, Wise, Judicious, Ingenious, and Observing, as to Write and Express the Expressions, Phrases, Garbs, Manners, Actions, Words, and Course of Life, of Kings and Princes; and to Express Naturally, to the Life, a Mean Country Wench, as a Great Lady, a Courtesan, as a Chast Woman, a Mad man, as a Man in his right Reason and Senses, a Drunkard, as a Sober man, a Knave, as an Honest man, and so a Clown, as a Well-bred man, and a Fool, as a Wise man; nay, it Expresses and Declares a Greater Wit, to Express, and Deliver to Posterity, the Extravagancies of Madness, the Subtilty of Knaves, the Ignorance of Clowns, and the Simplicity of Naturals, or the Craft of Feigned Fools, than to Express Regularities, Plain Honesty, Courtly Garbs, or Sensible Discourses, for 'tis harder to Express Nonsense than Sense, and Ordinary Conversations, than that which is Unusual; and 'tis Harder, and Requires more Wit to Express a Jester, than a Grave Statesman; yet Shakespear did not want Wit, to Express to the Life all Sorts of Persons, of what Quality, Profession, Degree, Breeding, or Birth soever; nor did he want Wit to Express the Divers, and Different Humours, or Natures, or Several Passions in Mankind; and so Well he hath Express'd in his

Playes all Sorts of Persons, as one would think he had been Transformed into every one of those Persons he hath Described; and as sometimes one would think he was Really himself the Clown or Jester he Feigns, so one would think, he was also the King, and Privy Counsellor; also as one would think he were Really the Coward he Feigns, so one would think he were the most Valiant, and Experienced Souldier; Who would not think he had been such a man as his Sir John Falstaff? and who would not think he had been Harry the Fifth? & certainly Julius Caesar, Augustus Caesar, and Antonius, did never Really Act their parts Better, if so Well, as he hath Described them, and I believe that Antonius and Brutus did not Speak Better to the People, than he hath Feign'd them; nay, one would think that he had been Metamorphosed from a Man to a Woman, for who could Describe Cleopatra Better than he hath done, and many other Females of his own Creating, as Nan Page, Mrs. Page, Mrs. Ford, the Doctors Maid, Bettrice, Mrs. Quickly, Doll Tearsheet, and others, too many to Relate? and in his Tragick Vein, he Presents Passions so Naturally, and Misfortunes so Probably, as he Peirces the Souls of his Readers with such a True Sense and Feeling thereof, that it Forces Tears through their Eyes, and almost Perswades them, they are Really Actors, or at least Present at those Tragedies. Who would not Swear he had been a Noble Lover, that could Woo so well? and there is not any person he hath Described in his Book, but his Readers might think they were Well acquainted with them; indeed Shakespear had a Clear Judgment, a Quick Wit, a Spreading Fancy, a Subtil Observation, a Deep Apprehension, and a most Eloquent Elocution; truly, he was a Natural Orator, as well as a Natural Poet, and he was not an Orator to Speak Well only on some Subjects, as Lawyers, who can make Eloquent Orations at the Bar, and Plead Subtilly and Wittily in Law-Cases, or Divines, that can Preach Eloquent Sermons, or Dispute Subtilly and Wittily in Theology, but take them from that, and put them to other Subjects, and they will be to seek; but Shakespear's Wit and Eloquence was General, for, and upon all Subjects, he rather wanted Subjects for his Wit and Eloquence to Work on, for which he was Forced to take some of his Plots out of History, where he only took the Bare Designs, the Wit and Language being all his Own; and so much he had above others, that those, who Writ after him, were Forced to Borrow of him, or rather to Steal from him; I could mention Divers Places, that others of our Famous Poets have Borrow'd, or Stoln, but lest I should Discover the Persons, I will not Mention the Places, or Parts, but leave it to those that Read his Playes, and others, to find them out. I should not have needed to Write this to you, for his Works would have Declared the same

Margaret Cavendish, Duchess of Newcastle (1623–1673)

Truth: But I believe, those that Dispraised his Playes, Dispraised them more out of Envy, than Simplicity or Ignorance, for those that could Read his Playes, could not be so Foolish to Condemn them, only the Excellency of them caused an Envy to them. By this we may perceive, Envy doth not Leave a man in the Grave, it Follows him after Death, unless a man be Buried in Oblivion, but if he Leave any thing to be Remembred, Envy and Malice will be still throwing Aspersion upon it, or striving to Pull it down by Detraction. But leaving Shakespear's Works to their own Defence, and his Detractors to their Envy, and you to your better Imployments, than Reading my Letter, I rest,

Madam,

Your faithful Friend
and humble Servant.

Preface to *Observations upon Experimental Philosophy* (1666)

It is probable, some will say, that my much writing is a disease; but what disease they will judg it to be, I cannot tell; I do verily believe they will take it to be a disease of the Brain, but surely they cannot call it an Apoplexical or Lethargical disease: Perhaps they will say, it is an extravagant, or at least a Fantastical disease; but I hope they will rather call it a disease of wit. But, let them give it what name they please, yet of this I am sure, that if much writing be a disease, then the best philosophers, both Moral and Natural, as also the best Divines, Lawyers, Physitians, Poets, Historians, Orators, Mathematicians, Chymists, and many more have been grievously sick, and Seneca, Plinius, Aristotle, Cicero, Tacitus, Plutarch, Euclid, Homer, Virgil, Ovid, St. Augustin, St. Ambrose, Scotus, Hippocrates, Galen, Paracelsus, and hundreds more, have been at deaths door with the disease of writing; but to be infected with the same disease, which the devoutest, wisest, wittiest, subtilest, most learned and eloquent men have been troubled withal, is no disgrace, but the greatest honour, even to the most ambitious person in the world: and next to the honour of being thus infected, it is also a great delight and pleasure to me, as being the onely Pastime which imploys my idle hours; in so much, that, were I sure no body did read my Works, yet I would not quit my pastime for all this; for although they should not delight others, yet they delight me; and if all Women that have no imployment in worldly affairs, should but spend their time as harmlessly as I do, they would not commit such faults as many are accused of. . . .

Preface and Epilogue to *The Description of a New World, called the Blazing-World* (1668)

To the Reader.

. . . And this is the reason, why I added this Piece of Fancy to my Philo-sophical Observations,[1] and joined them as two Worlds at the ends of their Poles; both for my own sake, to divert my studious thoughts, which I Im-ployed in the Contemplation thereof, and to delight the Reader with va-riety, which is always pleasing. But lest my Fancy should stray too much, I chose such a Fiction as would be agreeable to the subject I treated of in the former parts; it is a Description of a New World, not such as Lucian's,[2] or the French-man's World in the Moon; but a World of my own Creating, which I call the Blazing-World: The first part whereof is Romancical, the second Philosophical, and the third is meerly Fancy, or (as I may call it) Fantastical; which if it add any satisfaction to you, I shall account my Self a Happy Creatoress; If not, I must be content to live a melancholy Life in my own World. I cannot call it a poor World, if poverty be onely want of Gold, Silver, and Jewels; for there is more Gold in it then all the Chymists ever did, and (as I verily believe) will ever be able to make. As for the Rocks of Diamonds, I wish with all my soul they might be shared amongst my noble Female Friends, and upon that condition, I would willingly quit my part; and of the Gold I should onely desire so much as might suffice to repair my Noble Lord and Husbands Losses:[3] For I am not Covetous, but as Ambitious as ever any of my Sex was, is, or can be; which makes, that though I cannot be Henry the Fifth, or Charles the Second, yet I endeavour to be Margaret the First. And although I have neither power, time nor oc-casion to Conquer the World as Alexander and Caesar did; yet rather then not to be Mistress of one, since Fortune and the Fates would give me none, I have made a World of my own: for which no body, I hope, will blame me, since it is in every ones power to do the like.

The Epilogue to the Reader.

By this Poetical Description, you may perceive, that my ambition is not onely to be Empress, but Authoress of a whole World; and that the Worlds I have made, both the Blazing-and the other Philosophical World, men-tioned in the first part of this Description, are framed and composed of the most pure, that is, the Rational parts of Matter, which are the parts of my Mind; which Creation was more easily and suddenly effected, than the Conquests of the two famous Monarchs of the World, Alexander and Cesar. Neither have I made such disturbances, and caused so many dissolutions of particulars, otherwise named deaths, as they did; for I have destroyed but some few men in a little Boat, which dyed through the extremity of cold, and that by the hand of Justice, which was necessitated to punish their crime of stealing away a young and beauteous Lady. And in the formation of those Worlds, I take more delight and glory, than ever Alexander or Cesar did in conquering this terrestrial world; and though I have made my Blazing-world a Peaceable World allowing it but one Religion, one Language, and one Government; yet could I make another World, as full of Factions, Divisions, and Warrs, as this is of Peace and Tranquility; and the Rational figures of my Mind might express as much courage to fight, as Hector and Achilles had; and be as wise as Nestor, as Eloquent as Ulysses, and as beautiful as Hellen. But I esteeming Peace before Warr, Wit before Policy, Honesty before Beauty; instead of the figures of Alexander, Cesar, Hector, Achilles, Nestor, Ulysses, Hellen, &c. chose rather the figure of Honest Margaret Newcastle, which now I would not change for all this Terrestrial World; and if any should like the World I have made, and be willing to be my Subjects, they may imagine themselves such, and they are such, I mean in their Minds, Fancies or Imaginations; but if they cannot endure to be Subjects, they may create Worlds of their own, and Govern themselves as they please: But yet let them have a care, not to prove unjust Usurpers, and to rob me of mine: for, concerning the Philosophical World, I am Empress of it my self; and as for the Blazing-world, it having an Empress already, who rules it with great Wisdom and Conduct, which Empress is my dear Platonick Friend; I shall never prove so unjust, treacherous and unworthy to her, as to disturb her Government, much less to depose her from her Imperial Throne, for the sake of any other, but rather chuse to create another World for another Friend.

Notes

1. Cavendish had originally added the *Description* to her *Observations on Experimental Philosophy* (1666).
2. Lucian (c. 120–c. 180): Greek rhetorician and satirist who influenced the sixteenth-century French comic and satirical writer François Rabelais. He wrote a fan-

tastical description of the moon as a country of lights—a place called Lamptown where the inhabitants were lamps.

    3. William Cavendish, Duke of Newcastle, the leader of Charles I's defeated forces at Marston Moor and head of one of the twenty richest families in England, lost nearly all his property when he fled, on the day of the defeat, into exile in France, where he met and married Margaret, who was exiled with Queen Henrietta Maria's court in Paris. At the Restoration, a portion of his property was returned to him.

APHRA BEHN (1640?–1689)

Nothing is known with certainty of Aphra Behn's early life, not even her original name; but it does seem that she lived in Surinam, a South American colony of the Dutch and the English, for some months, as she claims in her novella *Oroonoko* (1688). After an apparently brief marriage to Mr. Behn, she went to Antwerp as a spy during the second Dutch War (1666), returning to London penniless. Possibly influenced by her acquaintance with Thomas Killigrew, manager of one of the two licensed theaters in London, and doubtless encouraged by the voracious demand for new plays after the theaters reopened in 1660, Behn turned to playwriting to support herself. She wrote two conventional tragicomedies that were modestly successful but found her style with the comedy *The Dutch Lover* (1673). Nevertheless, this work was not well received, partly because of poor acting and costuming but mostly because of prejudice against a woman author. The female playwright had become a serious competitor instead of an entertaining novelty. Provoked, Behn added a vigorously feminist preface to the published play.

She went on to write fifteen (or possibly eighteen) more plays, most of which were successful and many published with her name. They feature ingenious intrigue, amusing characters, witty courtship scenes, and the bawdy humor that was characteristic of Restoration comedy. They include *Sir Patient Fancy* (1678), *The Lucky Chance, or An Alderman's Bargain* (1687), *The Rover* (1677), and *The Emperor of the Moon* (1687); the latter two held the stage well into the eighteenth century. Behn also wrote poems, translations, novellas, and an early epistolary novel, *Love Letters between a Nobleman and His Sister* (1684, 1687).

Behn's Epistle to the Reader, prefixed to *The Dutch Lover*, not only defends a woman's right to write plays but also challenges fundamental critical assumptions of her time about the purpose of comedy and the connection between creative writing and classical education. Her Preface to *The Lucky Chance* offers an even stronger assertion of a woman's claim to the "masculine" prerogatives of poetry. In the preface to her translation of Bernard Le Bovier de Fontenelle's *Discovery of New Worlds* (1688), Behn considers the problems of translation and differences between French and English.

The Dutch Lover a comedy acted at the Dukes theatre (London: Thomas Dring, 1673); *The lucky chance, or, An Alderman's bargain* (London: William Canning, 1687); *A discovery of new worlds from the French, made English by A. Behn* (London: William Canning, 1688).

Epistle to the Reader from *The Dutch Lover* (1673)

Good, Sweet, Honey, Sugar-candied READER.

Which I think is more than any one has call'd you yet.) I must have a word or two with you before you do advance into the Treatise; but 'tis not to beg your pardon for diverting you from your affairs, by such an idle Pamphlet as this is, for I presume you have not much to do, and therefore are to be obliged to me for keeping you from worse imployment, and if you have a better, you may get you gone about your business: but if you will misspend your time, pray lay the fault upon your self; for I have dealt pretty fairly in the matter, and told you in the Title Page what you are to expect within. Indeed, had I hung out a sign of the Immortality of the Soul, of the Mystery of Godliness, or of Ecclesiastical Policie, and then had treated you with Indiscerpibility, and Essential Spissitude (words, which though I am no competent Judge of, for want of Languages,[1] yet I fancy strangly ought to mean just nothing) with a company of Apocryphal midnight tales cull'd out of the choicest insignificant Authors; If I had only prov'd in Folio that Apollonius[2] was a naughty Knave, or had presented you with two or three of the worst principles transcrib'd out of the peremptory and ill natur'd, (though prettily ingenious) Doctor of Malmsbury[3] undigested, and ill manag'd by a silly, saucy, ignorant, impertinent, ill educated Chaplain, I were then indeed sufficiently in fault; but having inscrib'd Comedy on the beginning of my Book, you may guess pretty near what penyworths you are like to have, and ware your money and your time accordingly.

I would not yet be understood to lessen the dignity of Playes, for surely they deserve a place among the middle if not the better sort of Books; for I have heard that most of that which bears the name of Learning, and which has abus'd such quantities of Ink and Paper, and continually imploys so many ignorant, unhappy souls for ten, twelve, twenty years in the University (who yet poor wretches think they are doing something all the while) as Logick, &c. and several other things (that shall be nameless, lest I should mispel them) are much more absolutely nothing than the errantest Play that e're was writ. . . .

And therefore to return to that which I before was speaking of, I will have leave to say that in my judgement the increasing number of our latter Plays have not done much more towards the amending of mens Morals, or their Wit, than hath the frequent Preaching, which this last age hath been pester'd with, (indeed without all Controversie they have done less harm) nor can I once imagine what temptation any one can have to expect it from them: for, sure I am, no Play was ever writ with that design. If you consider Tragedy, you'l find their best of characters unlikely patterns for a wise man to pursue: For he that is the Knight of the Play, no sublunary feats must serve his Dulcinea; for if he can't bestrid the Moon, he'l ne'er make good his business to the end, and if he chance to be offended, he must without considering right or wrong confound all things he meets, and put you half a score likely tall fellows into each pocket;[4] and truly if he come not something near this pitch, I think the Tragedies not worth a farthing; for Playes were certainly intended for the exercising of mens passions, not their understandings, and he is infinitely far from wise, that will bestow one moments private meditation on such things: And as for Comedie, the finest folks you meet with there, are still unfitter for your imitation, for though within a leaf or two of the Prologue, you are told that they are people of Wit, good Humour, good Manners, and all that: yet if the Authors did not kindly add their proper names, you'd never know them by their characters; for whatsoe'er's the matter, it hath happen'd so spightfully in several Playes, which have been prettie well receiv'd of late, that even those persons that were meant to be the ingenious Censors of the Play, have either prov'd the most debauch'd, or most unwittie people in the Companie: nor is this error very lamentable, since as I take it Comedie was never meant, either for a converting or confirming Ordinance: In short, I think a Play the best divertisement that wise men have; but I do also think them nothing so, who do discourse as formallie about the rules of it, as if 'twere the grand affair of humane life. This being my opinion of Plays, I studied only to make this as entertaining as I could, which whether I have been successful in, my gentle Reader, you may for your shilling judge.[5] To tell you my thoughts of it, were to little purpose, for were they very ill, you may be sure I would not have expos'd it; nor did I so till I had first consulted most of those who have a reputation for judgement of this kind; who were at least so civil (if not kind) to it as did incourage me to venture it upon the Stage, and in the

Press: Nor did I take their single word for it, but used their reasons as a confirmation of my own.

Indeed that day 'twas Acted first there comes me into the Pit, a long, lither, phlegmatick,[6] white, ill-favour'd, wretched Fop, an officer in Masquerade newly transported with a Scarfe & Feather out of France, a sorry Animal that has nought else to shield it from the uttermost contempt of all mankind, but that respect which we afford to Rats and Toads, which though we do not well allow to love, yet when considered as a part of Gods Creation, we make honourable mention of them. A thing, Reader—but no more of such a Smelt: This thing, I tell ye, opening that which serves it for a mouth, out issued such a noise as this to those that sate about it, that they were to expect a woful Play, God damn him, for it was a womans. Now how this came about I am not sure, but I suppose he brought it piping hot from some, who had with him the reputation of villanous Wit: for Creatures of his size of sence talk without all imagination, such scraps as they pick up from other folks. I would not for a world be taken arguing with such a propertie[7] as this, but if I thought there were a man of any tolerable parts, who could upon mature deliberation distinguish well his right-hand from his left, and justly state the difference between the number of sixteen and two, yet had this prejudice upon him; I would take a little pains to make him know how much he errs. For waving the examination, why women having equal education with men, were not as capable of knowledge, of whatever sort as well as they: I'l only say as I have touch'd before, that Plays have no great room for that which is mens great advantage over women, that is Learning: We all well know that the immortal Shakespears Playes (who was not guilty of much more of this than often falls to womens share) have better pleas'd the World than Johnsons works, though by the way 'tis said that Benjamin was no such Rabbi[8] neither, for I am inform'd his Learning was but Grammer high; (sufficient indeed to rob poor Salust of his best Orations) and it hath been observ'd, that they are apt to admire him most confoundedly, who have just such a scantling of it as he had; and I have seen a man the most severe of Johnsons Sect, sit with his Hat remov'd less than a hairs breadth from one sullen posture for almost three hours at the Alchymist; who at that excellent Play of Harry the Fourth (which yet I hope is far enough from Farce) hath very hardly kept his Doublet whole;[9] but affectation hath always had a greater share both in the actions and discourse of men than truth and judgement have: and for our Modern ones, except our most unimitable Laureat,[10] I dare to say I know of none that write at such a formidable rate, but that a woman may well hope to reach their greatest hights. Then for their musty rules of Unity,[11] and God knows what besides, if they meant any thing, they are enough intelligable, and as practible by a woman; but really methinks they that disturb their heads with any other rules of Playes besides the making them pleasant, and avoiding of scurrility, might much better be imploy'd in studying how to improve mens too imperfect knowledge of that ancient English Game, which hight long Laurence:[12] And if Comedy should be the Picture of ridiculous mankind, I wonder any one should think it such a sturdy task, whilst we are furnish'd with such precious Originals as him, I lately told you of; if at least that Character do not dwindle into Farce, and so become too mean an entertainment for those persons who are us'd to think. Reader, I have a complaint or two to make to you, and I have done; Know then this Play was hugely injur'd in the Acting, for 'twas done so imperfectly as never any was before, which did more harm to this than it could have done to any of another sort; the Plot being busie (though I think not intricate) and so requiring a continual attention, which being interrupted by the intolerable negligence of some that acted in it, must needs much spoil the beauty on't. My Dutch Lover spoke but little of what I intended for him, but supply'd it with a deal of idle stuff, which I was wholly unacquainted with, till I had heard it first from him; so that Jack pudding[13] ever us'd to do: which though I knew before, I gave him yet the part, because I knew him so acceptable to most o'th'lighter Periwigs[14] about the Town, and he indeed did vex me so, I could almost be angry: Yet, but Reader, you remember, I suppose, a fusty piece of Latine that has past from hand to hand this thousand years they say (and how much longer I can't tell) in favour of the dead.[15] I intended him a habit much more notably ridiculous, which if it can ever be important was so here, for many of the Scenes in the three last Acts depended upon the mistakes of the Colonel for Haunce, which the ill-favour'd likeness of their Habits is suppos'd to cause.[16] Lastly, my Epilogue was promis'd me by a Person who had surely made it good, if any, but he failing of his word, deputed one, who has made it as you see, and to make out your penyworth you have it here. The Prologue is by misfortune lost. Now, Reader, I have eas'd my mind of all I had to say, and so sans farther complyment, Adieu.

Preface to *The Lucky Chance* (1687)

The little Obligation I have to some of the witty Sparks and Poets of the Town, has put me on a Vindication of this Comedy from those Censures that Malice, and ill Nature have thrown upon it, tho in vain: The Poets, I heartily excuse, since there is a sort of Self-Interest in their Malice, which

I shou'd rather call a witty Way they have in this Age, of Railing at every thing they find with pain successful, and never to shew good Nature and speak well of any thing; but when they are sure 'tis damn'd, then they afford it that worse Scandal, their Pity. And nothing makes them so thorough-stitcht an Enemy as a full Third Day,[1] that's Crime enough to load it with all manner of infamy; and when they can no other way prevail with the Town, they charge it with the old never failing Scandal—That 'tis not fit for the Ladys: As if (if it were as they falsly give it out) the Ladys were oblig'd to hear Indecencys only from their Pens and Plays, and some of them have ventur'd to treat 'em as Coursely as 'twas possible, without the least Reproach from them; and in some of their most Celebrated Plays have entertained 'em with things, that if I should here strip from their Wit and Occasion that conducts 'em in and makes them proper, their fair Cheeks would perhaps wear a natural Colour at the reading them: yet are never taken Notice of because a Man writ them, and they may hear that from them, they blush at from a Woman—But I make a Challenge to any Person of common Sense and Reason—that is not wilfully bent on ill Nature, and will in spight of Sense wrest a double Entendre from every thing, lying upon the Catch for a Jest or a Quibble, like a Rook for a Cully;[2] but any inprejudic'd Person that knows not the Author, to read any of my Comedys and compare 'em with others of this Age, and if they find one Word that can offend the chastest Ear, I will submit to all their peevish Cavills; but Right or Wrong they must be Criminal because a Woman's; condemning them without having the Christian Charity, to examine whether it be guilty or not, with reading, comparing, or thinking; the Ladies taking up any Scandal on Trust from some conceited Sparks, who will in spight of Nature be Wits and Beaus; then scatter it for Authentick all over the Town and Court, poysoning of others Judgments with their false Notions, condemning it to worse than Death, Loss of Fame. And to fortifie their Detraction, charge me with all the Plays that have ever been offensive; though I wish with all their Faults I had been the Author of some of those they have honour'd me with.

For the farther Justification of this Play; it being a Comedy of Intrigue, Dr. Davenought[3] out of Respect to the Commands he had from Court, to take great Care that no Indecency should be in Plays, sent for it and nicely look't it over, putting out any thing he but imagin'd the Criticks would play with. After that, Sir Roger L'Estrange[4] read it and licens'd it, and found no such Faults as 'tis charg'd with: Then Mr. Killigrew,[5] who more severe than any, from the strict Order he had, perus'd it with great Circumspection; and lastly the Master Players, who you will I hope in some Measure esteem

Judges of Decency and their own interest, having been so many Years Prentice to the Trade of Judging.

I say, after all these Supervisors the Ladys may be convinc'd, they left nothing that cou'd offend, and the Men of their unjust Reflections on so many Judges of Wit and Decencys. When it happens that I challenge any one, to point me out the least Expression of what some have made their Discourse, they cry, That Mr. Leigh opens his Night Gown,[6] when he comes into the Bride-chamber; if he do, which is a jest of his own making, and which I never saw, I hope he has his Cloaths on underneath? And if so, where is the Indecency? I have seen in that admirable Play of Oedipus,[7] the Gown open'd wide, and the Man shown in his Drawers and Waistcoat, and never thought it an Offence before. Another crys, Why we know not what they mean, when the Man takes a Woman off the Stage, and another is thereby cuckolded; is that any more than you see in the most Celebrated of your Plays? as the City Politicks,[8] the Lady Mayoress, and the Old Lawyers Wife, who goes with a Man she never saw before, and comes out again the joyfull'st Women alive, for having made her Husband a Cuckold with such Dexterity, and yet I see nothing unnatural nor obscene: 'tis proper for the Characters. So in that lucky Play of the London Cuckolds,[9] not to recite Particulars. And in that good Comedy of Sir Courtly Nice,[10] the Taylor to the young Lady—in the fam'd Sir Fopling Dorimont and Bellinda, see the very Words[11] in Valentianian, see the Scene between the Court Bawds. And Valentianian[12] all loose and ruffl'd a Moment after the Rape, and all this you see without scandal, and a thousand others. The Moor of Venice in many places.[13] The Maids Tragedy—see the Scene of undressing the Bride, and between the King and Amintor, and after between the King and Evadne[14]—All these I Name as some of the best Plays I know; If I should repeat the Words exprest in these Scenes I mention, I might justly be charg'd with course ill Manners, and very little Modesty, and yet they so naturally fall into the places they are designed for, and so are proper for the Business, that there is not the least Fault to be found with them; though I say those things in any of mine wou'd damn the whole Peice, and alarm the Town. Had I a Day or two's time, as I have scarce so many Hours to write this in (the Play, being all printed off and the Press waiting,) I would sum up all your Beloved Plays, and all the things in them that are past with such Silence by; because written by Men: such Masculine Strokes in me, must not be allow'd. I must conclude those Women (if there be any such) greater Criticks in that sort of Conversation than my self, who find any of that sort in mine, or any thing that can justly be reproach't. But 'tis in vain by dint of Reason or Comparison to consider the Obstinate Criticks, whose Business is to find Fault, if not by a loose and gross Imagination to create them, for they must either find the Jest, or make it; and those of this sort fall to my share, they find Faults of another kind for the Men Writers. And this one thing I will venture to say, though against my Nature, because it has a Vanity in it; That had the Plays I have writ come forth under any Mans Name, and never known to have been mine; I appeal to all unbyast Judges of Sense, if they had not said that Person had made as many good Comedies, as any one Man that has writ in our Age; but a Devil on't the Woman damns the Poet.

Ladies, for its further Justification to you, be pleas'd to know, that the first Copy of this Play was read by several Ladys of very great Quality, and unquestioned Fame, and received their most favorable Opinion, not one charging it with the Crime, that some have been pleas'd to find in the Acting. Other Ladys who saw it more than once, whose Quality and Vertue can sufficiently justifie any thing they design to favour, were pleas'd to say, they found an Entertainment in it very far from scandalous; and for the Generality of the Town; I found by my Receipts it was not thought so Criminal. However, that shall not be an Incouragement to me to trouble the Criticks with new Occasion of affronting me, for endeavouring at least to divert; and at this rate, both the few Poets that are left, and the Players who toil in vain, will be weary of their Trade.

I cannot omit to tell you, that a Wit of the Town, a Friend of mine at Wills Coffee House, the first Night of the Play, cry'd it down as much as in him lay, who before had read it and assured me he never saw a prettier Comedy. So complaisant one pestilent Wit will be to another, and in the full Cry make his Noise too; but since 'tis to the witty Few I speak, I hope the better Judges will take no Offence, to whom I am oblig'd for better Judgments; and those I hope will be so kind to me, knowing my Conversation not at all addicted to the Indecencys alledged, that I would much less practice it in a Play, that must stand the Test of the censuring World. And I must want common Sense, and all the Degrees of good Manners, renouncing my Fame, all Modesty and Interest for a silly Sawcy fruitless Jest, to make Fools laugh, and Women blush, and wise Men asham'd; My self all the while, if I had been guilty of this Crime charg'd to me, remaining the only stupid, insensible. Is this likely, is this reasonable to be believ'd by any body, but the wilfully blind? All I ask is the Priviledge for my Masculine Part the Poet in me, (if any such you will allow me) to tread in those successful Paths my Predecessors have so long thriv'd in, to take those Measures that both the Ancient and Modern Writers have set me, and by which they have pleas'd the World so well. If I must not, because of my Sex, have this Freedom, but that you will usurp all to your selves; I lay down my Quill, and you shall hear no more of me, no not so much as to make Comparisons, because I will be kinder to my Brothers of the Pen, than they have been to a defenceless Woman; for I am not content to write for a Third day only. I value Fame as much as if I had been born a Hero; and if you rob me of that, I can retire from the ungrateful World, and scorn its fickle Favours.

Translator's Preface to *A Discovery of New Worlds* (1688)

The General Applause this little Book of the Plurality of Worlds has met with, both in France and England in the Original, made me attempt to translate it into English.[1] The Reputation of the Author, (who is the same, who writ the Dialogues of the Dead) the Novelty of the Subject in vulgar Languages, and the Authors introducing a Woman as one of the speakers in these five Discourses, were further Motives for me to undertake this little work; for I thought an English Woman might adventure to translate any thing, a French Woman may be supposed to have spoken: But when I had made a Tryal, I found the Task not so easie as I believed at first. Therefore, before I say any thing, either of the Design of the Author, or of the Book it self, give me leave to say something of Translation of Prose in general: . . .

In translating French into English, most People are very cautious and unwilling to print a French Word at first out of a new Book, till Use has rendered it more familiar to us; and therefore it runs a little rough in English, to express one French Word, by two or three of ours; and thus much, as to the Ease and Difficulty of translating these Languages in general: But, as to the French in particular, it has as many Advantages of the English, as to the Sounds, as ours has of the French, as to the Signification; which is another Argument of the different Genius of the two Nations. . . . [Behn analyzes the advantanges and disadvantages of French and English. She considers the history of the development of European languages and their relative affinities.]

But as the French do not value a plain Suit without a Garniture, they are not satisfied with the Advantages they have, but confound their own Language with needless Repetitions and Tautologies; and by a certain Rhetorical Figure, peculiar to themselves, imply twenty Lines, to express what an English Man would say, with more Ease and Sense in five; and this is the great Misfortune of translating French into English: If one endeavours to make it English Standard, it is no Translation. If one follows their Flourishes and Embroideries, it is worse than French Tinsel. But these defects are only comparatively, in respect of English: And I do not say this so much, to condemn the French, as to praise our own Mother-Tongue, for what we think a Deformity, they may think a Perfection; as the Negroes of Guinney think us as ugly, as we think them: But to return to my present Translation.

I have endeavored to give you the true meaning of the Author, and have kept as near his Words as was possible; I was necessitated to add a little in some places, otherwise the Book could not have been understood. . . .

I know a Character of the Book will be expected from me, and I am obliged to give it to satisfie my self for being at the pains to translate it, but I wish with all my heart I could forbear it; for I have that Value for the ingenious French Author, that I am sorry I must write what some may understand to be a Satyr against him. The Design of the Author is to treat of this part of Natural Philosophy in a more familiar Way than any other hath done, and to make every body understand him: For this End, he introduceth a Woman of Quality as one of the Speakers in these five Discourses, whom he feigns never to have heard of any such thing as Philosophy before. How well he hath performed his Undertaking you will best judge when you have perused the Book: But if you would know beforehand my Thoughts, I must tell you freely, he hath failed in his Design; for endeavouring to render this part of Natural Philosophy familiar, he hath turned it into Ridicule; he hath pushed his wild Notion of the Plurality of Worlds to that heighth of Extravagancy, that he most certainly will confound those Readers, who have not Judgment and Wit to distinguish between what is truly solid (or, at least, probable) and what is trifling and airy: and there is no less Skill and Understanding required in this, than in comprehending the whole Subject he treats of. And for his Lady Marquiese, he makes her say a great many very silly things, tho' sometimes she makes Observation so learned, that the greatest Philosophers in Europe could make no better. . . .

I have laid the Scene at Paris, where the Original was writ; and have translated the Book near the Words of the Author. . . . And I resolv'd either to give you the French Book into English, or to give you the subject quite changed and made my own; but having neither health nor leisure for the last I offer you the first such as it is.

Notes

Epistle to the Reader from *The Dutch Lover*

1. Greek and Latin, prominent in the education of upper-class men and very rarely taught to women. Behn derisively contrasts the significance of an entertaining

comedy with that of more highly esteemed works, tomes on theology or church politics. *Indiscerpibility*, or indestructibility because indivisible into parts, and *spissitude*, or density, were theoretical attributes of the soul.

2. Apollonius of Tyana (first century), a Neo-Pythagorean, became a mythical figure during the Roman Empire when Empress Julia Domna had a biography of him written which inspired a religious devotion rivaling that of the early Christians.

3. Thomas Hobbes, called the Doctor of Malmsbury, was a witty philosopher (1588–1679) whose materialism and anticlericalism verged on atheism. Hence he was constantly attacked by the clergy.

4. The hero of the most prominent type of contemporary tragedy, the heroic play, was like Cervantes' knight Don Quixote in his uncompromising pursuit of glory, his devotion to his lady (Dulcinea was Don Quixote's love), and his touchy honor.

5. The printed play would sell for a shilling.

6. Impotent, dull.

7. Tool, catspaw.

8. Learned man.

9. Ben Jonson had more classical learning than his contemporary William Shakespeare and commented on Shakespeare's "small Latin and less Greek." But Behn says that Jonson had only the basic Latin and Greek he would have learned in Elizabethan grammar school. Jonson's Roman plays, such as *Catiline*, include long passages translated from Latin authors, including the historian Sallust. *The Alchemist* (1610) is a comedy by Jonson; Shakespeare's history play *Henry IV* (1596–98) contains many comic scenes.

10. John Dryden, the leading writer of the age, was poet laureate.

11. Renaissance critics had formalized Aristotle's critical principles into rules, including the unities of time, place, and action; a play must be limited to one plot, which must take place during one day and within one city. Contemporary French playwrights followed these rules, but the English debated their importance.

12. To "play at Lawrence" meant to do nothing, to laze.

13. Buffoon.

14. All upper-class men wore wigs; light periwigs, being particularly fashionable, would suggest fops.

15. Edward Angel, who played Haunce, died a few months after the play's premiere. The fusty Latin is "De mortuis nil nisi bonum," "Of the dead [speak] nothing but good."

16. The Colonel (Alonzo) is a romantic lead in *The Dutch Lover*; he causes confusion by dressing in ridiculous clothing like that of the buffoon Haunce.

Preface to *The Lucky Chance*

1. Playwrights were paid by the net proceeds of the third night of performance.

2. A rook is a cheat, and a cully is his or her dupe.

3. Sir William Davenant (1612–1683) reopened the stage at the Restoration in 1660 when he was licensed by Charles II to form the Duke's Company.

4. Sir Roger L'Estrange (1606–1668) was a Tory journalist and pamphleteer who became licenser of the press in 1663.

5. Thomas Killigrew (1612–1683) was a dramatist who built a playhouse in Drury Lane in 1663.

6. Dressing gown.

7. *Oedipus, King of Thebes*, adapted from Sophocles' play by John Dryden and Nathaniel Lee (1678).

8. A play by John Crowne first performed in 1682, in which the Lady Mayoress and the Old Lawyer's Wife are characters.

9. Edward Ravenscroft's play first performed in 1681.

10. A play by John Crowne first performed in 1683, in which the Taylor and the young Lady are characters.

11. Dorimant is the hero of George Etherege's *The Man of Mode; or Sir Fopling Flutter* (1676) who seduces Bellinda.

12. A play by John Fletcher performed in 1669.

13. Shakespeare's *Othello* was performed in the first season of the reopening of the theaters in 1660.

14. John Fletcher's play performed in 1660.

Translator's Preface to *A Discovery of New Worlds*

1. Behn here translates *Entretiens sur la pluralité des modes* published in 1686 by Bernard Le Bovier de Fontenelle (1657–1757), in which he lucidly explains new discoveries in astronomy to a lady and speculates about life on other planets.

JANE BARKER (1652–1727?)

Most of the available information about Jane Barker's life derives from her partially autobiographical novel trilogy, *Love's Intrigues* (1713), *A Patchwork Screen for the Ladies* (1723) and *The Lining of the Patchwork Screen* (1726), and from her *Poetical Recreations* (1688). She was born in 1652 into a Royalist and probably Catholic family. Both her parents and her beloved brother were dead by 1688, when Barker followed James II into exile in France, returning to England only during Queen Anne's reign. Barker remained unmarried, probably living on her estate in Wiltsthorp, Lincolnshire. It is not known when or where she died.

Barker's works focus on the double bind presented by constricted avenues of expression for women: they can either conform to social conventions that require them to refrain from saying what they feel or boldly express their feelings and meet with disdain. In *Love's Intrigues* Galesia, Barker's autobiographical heroine, cannot with propriety reveal her feelings to her on-again, off-again suitor, Bosvil. She tries to indicate her love through "broken words, stollen sighs, suppressed tears, that the meerest Fresh-man in Love's Academy, could not but read and understand," but Bosvil fails to comprehend. A subsequent dream emphasizes that by choosing poetry over love, Galesia has also chosen "Cassandra's Fate" of being misunderstood.

A Patchwork Screen seeks to resolve this dilemma. Galesia weaves her story with those of other women, good, bad and "unaccountable." The text is likened to the screen which a lady whom Galesia meets on her travels is constructing. With Galesia's assistance this screen becomes a departure from the "rich silks and silver and gold brocades" of the rest of the lady's furnishings. Galesia's material consists instead of "pieces of romances, poems, love-letters" and even an occasional recipe in verse, which tumble out of her trunk instead of clothing. Thus the very structure of the book becomes a comment on how women might construct literature as a piecemeal and communal effort allowing for bold expression within a "feminine" framework.

A Patchwork Screen for the Ladies (London: E. Curll, 1723).

From *A Patchwork Screen for the Ladies* (1723)

To The Reader.

My Two former Volumes of *Novels* having met with a favourable Reception, (much beyond their Desert) encourages me to perform my Promise in pursuing *The Sequel of Galesia's Story*.★

But I doubt my *Reader* will say, Why so long about it? And why a *History* reduc'd into *Patches*? especially since *Histories* at *Large* are so Fashionable in this Age; viz. *Robinson Crusoe*, and *Moll Flanders*; *Colonel Jack*, and *Sally Salisbury*;[1] with many other *Heroes* and *Heroines*? Why, truly, as to the *First*, I had left my Galesia, she being gone from St. Germains, and I retir'd into an obscure Corner of the World. As to the *Second,* you'll find in the following Pages, by what Steps and Means it was fram'd into this Method. And now, having given you this Account, I think I ought to say something in Favour of *Patch-Work,* the better to recommend it to my Female Readers, as well in their Discourse, as their Needle-Work: Which I might do with Justice, if my Genius were capable: But indeed, I am not much of an *Historian*; but in the little I have read, I do not remember any thing recorded relating to *Patch-Work,* since the Patriarch Joseph, (whose Garment was of sundry Colours) by which means it has not been *common* in all Ages; and 'tis certain, the *Uncommonness* of any *Fashion,* renders it acceptable to the *Ladies.*

And I do not know but this may have been the chief Reason why our *Ladies*, in this latter Age, have pleas'd themselves with this sort of Entertainment; for, whenever one sees a Set of Ladies together, their *Sentiments* are as differently mix'd as the *Patches* in their Work: To wit, *Whigs* and *Tories*, *High-Church* and *Low-Church, Jacobites* and *Williamites*,[2] and many more Distinctions, which they *divide* and *sub-divide*, 'till at last they make this *Disunion* meet in an harmonious *Tea-Table* Entertainment. This puts me in mind of what I have heard some *Philosophers* assert, about the *Clashing of Atoms*, which at last *united* to compose this glorious Fabrick of the *UNIVERSE*.

Forgive me, kind Reader, for carrying the Metaphor too high; by which means I am out of my Sphere, and so can say nothing of the *Male Patch-Workers*; for my high Flight in Favour of the Ladies, made a mere Icarus of me, melted my Wings, and tumbled me Headlong down, I know not where.

★The last NOVEL in Mrs. Barker's 2d. Volume.

Nevertheless my *Fall* was amongst a joyful Throng of People of all Ages, Sexes, and Conditions! who were rejoycing at a wonderful *Piece* of *Patch-Work* they had in Hand;[3] the Nature of which was such, as was to compose (as it were) a *New Creation*; where all Sorts of People were to be *Happy*, as if they had never been the *Off-spring* of fallen Adam.

I was greatly rejoyc'd at this my *Fall*, when I found my self amongst these happy Undertakers, and hop'd to unite my-self in their Confraternity; but they finding some Manuscript *Ballads* in my Pocket, rejected me as one of that Race of Mortals who live on a certain barren Mountain 'till they are turn'd into *Camelions*; so I was forc'd to get away, every one hunching and pushing me, with Scorn and Derision. However, as the Sequel prov'd, I had no small Reason to rejoice at being thus used; for soon after, their *Patch-Work Scheme*, by carrying the Point too high, was blown up about their Ears, and vanish'd into Smoke and Confusion; to the utter Ruin of many Thousands of the Unhappy Creatures therein concern'd.[4]

When I was got out of this Throng into the open Field, I met with the poor Galesia, walking to stretch her Legs, having been long sitting at her Work. With her I renew'd my Old Acquaintance; and so came to know all this Story of her *Patch-Work*: Which if you like, I will get the remaining Part of the *Screen;* for they are still at Work: And, upon my Word, I am glad to find the Ladies of *This Age,* wiser than *Those* of the *Former;* when the working of *Point* and curious *Embroidery,* was so troublesome, that *they* cou'd not take *Snuff* in Repose, for fear of soiling their Work: But in *Patch-Work* there is no Harm done; a smear'd Finger does but add a *Spot* to a *Patch,* or a *Shade* to a *Light-Colour:* Besides, those curious Works were pernicious to the Eyes; *they* cou'd not see the *Danger themselves* and *their Posterity might be in, a Thousand Years hence, about I know not what*—But I will inquire against the next Edition; therefore, be sure to buy *these Patches* up quickly, if you intend to know the *Secret;* thereby you'll greatly oblige the *Bookseller,* and, in some degree, the *Author.* Who is,

> Your humble Servant,
> Jane Barker.

[After a series of mishaps on her journey, Galesia finds herself seated on a bench in a secluded park. A lady who has been hunting is on her way home through the park when she finds Galesia.]

Galesia, in few and respectful Words, inform'd the Lady of her Disaster of being overthrown into the River the Day before, and her bad Lodging at Night, and her losing her Way that Morning, all which made her betake herself to that Seat. The Lady most courteously and charitably took her along with her to her House, which was a Noble Structure, situate in the midst of that Park. Here she entertain'd her very kindly; assuring her of all Assistance to convey her to the Place to which she was design'd, when she had rested and recover'd her Fatigue. In the mean Time, she diverted her, by shewing Galesia her Gardens, House, and glorious Appartments, adorn'd with rich Furniture of all Sorts; some were the Work of hers and her Husband's Ancestors, who delighted to imploy poor Gentlewomen, thereby to keep them from Distress, and evil Company, 'till Time and Friends could dispose Things for their better Settlement.

At last, the Lady shew'd her an Appartment embellish'd with Furniture of her own making, which was PATCH-WORK, most curiously compos'd of rich Silks, and Silver and Gold Brocades: The whole Furniture was compleated excepting a SCREEN, which the Lady and her Maids were going about. Her Ladyship told Galesia, She would take it kindly if her Affairs would permit her to stay with her some time, and assist her in her SCREEN. Which Invitation Galesia most gladly accepted, begging the Lady to send to the next Stage of the Coach and Carrier, for her Trunks and Boxes, which contained her Wearing-Cloaths. The Lady forthwith sent for the Things, hoping that therein they might find some Bits of one thing or other, that might be useful to place in the SCREEN. But when the Trunks and Boxes came, and were opened, alas! they found nothing but Pieces of *Romances, Poems, Love-Letters,* and the like: At which the good Lady smil'd, saying, She would not have her Fancy balk'd, and therefore resolved to have these ranged and mixed in due Order, and thereof compose a SCREEN.

Notes

1. *Robinson Crusoe* (1719), *Moll Flanders* (1722), and *Colonel Jack* (1722) are all novels by Daniel Defoe. *The Authentick Memoires of the Life, Intrigues and Adventures of the Celebrated Sally Salisbury,* by Capt. C. Walker (London, 1723), is a lascivious book chronicling the life of an independent, highly successful, and thoroughly unprincipled whore.

2. Jacobites supported the old Stuart monarchy, represented by the exiled James II, and Williamites supported William of Orange, later William III, who was invited to take over the country by a group of English leaders in what became known as the Glorious Revolution.

3. The South Sea Company and the fever of speculation engendered by a bill passed in 1720 enabled individuals to whom the government owed money to convert their claims into stock, causing a precipitous rise in its value. In 1721 the South Sea Company failed, leaving many financially ruined. The incident was known as the South Sea Bubble.

4. See n. 3.

ANNE LEFÈVRE DACIER
(1654–1720)

Anne Lefèvre Dacier was well known and respected throughout Europe as a scholar of classical literature. She was the only daughter of Tanneguy Lefèvre, an eminent professor of classics at the Protestant Academy of Saumur. Anne married early but soon left her printer husband to return to her father's house and continue her studies with him. Under his tutelage she soon became proficient enough to publish on her own, and at twenty-eight began a lifelong career of scholarly production, which included many editions and translations of ancient texts, both Latin and Greek. Several of them appeared as part of the Delphin Series, commissioned by the representatives of Louis XIV and designed to further the education of his first son. This much-admired series caused her gifts to be recognized.

After the death of her husband, Anne married a fellow scholar and Protestant, André Dacier, who had also been her father's pupil. She worked closely with him for forty years. When the persecution of French Protestants became intense, they converted to Catholicism and moved to Paris, where they became a part of the brilliant courtly life of their era. They attended the literary salon of Anne-Thérèse de Lambert who, though not herself a scholar, very much respected Anne Dacier and remarked that she was proof of the value of education for women. André Dacier became a member of the French Academy and held the post of Keeper of the King's Books at the Louvre, which brought him both an income and an apartment in the Louvre. Louis XIV chose to honor André's wife as well by declaring that should she outlive her husband, she would retain his post with all its privileges. Anne remained active in scholarly work throughout her long life, her crowning achievement coming toward the end of her career with her translations into French of the *Iliad* (1711) and the *Odyssey* (1716). Alexander Pope relied upon these works for his own translations of Homer.

Anne Dacier was at the center of the controversy over the Ancients and the Moderns, in which she defended Homer against attackers. She believed strongly in the moral and aesthetic beauty of Homer's poetry and derided the Moderns who sought to evaluate him as though he were a contemporary. In her translator's preface to the *Odyssey*, she compares Homer's poetry to a romance of her own day, the *Cassandre* of La Calprenède, which had been hailed by the Moderns as an epic poem in prose.

L'Odysée d'Homère traduite en françois avec des remarques par Madame Dacier (Paris: Rigaud, 1716).

Translator's Preface to *The Odyssey* (1716)

Let us apply the rules (for epic poetry) to one of our own Romances, and we will see if we are right to call them Epic Poems in prose. I have chosen one of the most successful, *Cassandre* of M. de la Calprenède.[1] It cannot be denied that the author has a lively mind, a happy and fertile imagination and a great facility of expression. I would praise his talents with great pleasure if he had used them to better effect.

The first rule of the Epic Poem demands that the subject be a Fable which applies to everyone, and from which all can profit. Let us examine the subject of *Cassandre*, to see if we find in it that Fable which is the soul of the Poem.[2] Orondate, the son of Mathée, King of the Scythians, in a battle fought by his father against Darius the King of Persia—mortal enemy of his people—succeeds so well that he arrives at the tents which house the mother, wife and daughters of Darius. He has these Princesses in his power, he can make them his prisoners and carry them off, but he is so struck by the beauty of Statira that in an act of extraordinary generosity, very inappropriate and even against his own best interests as a lover, he lets them go free. In the next moment he saves the life of Prince Artaxerce, Darius' only son, and instead of taking him prisoner sets him free also. The following winter, his love having grown to a violent passion, he is moved to leave his father's Court for that of his enemy. He goes to Persepolis under a false name: he is recognized as the warrior who freed the Queens and spared the Prince, and he becomes Darius' favorite. He sees Statira as often as he wishes, courts her and declares his passion for her. Statira is somewhat offended, as decorum requires, but once Orondate has revealed himself to Artaxerce as Prince of the Scythians, Artaxerce pleads his cause with Statira, and finally she responds to the passion of the Prince. His happiness is frustrated by various obstacles, which the makers of Romances may easily imagine. The Princesses become the prisoners of Alexander, who lacking Orondate's generosity retains them, then falls madly in love with Statira and marries her. Alexander dies after a time, and other obstacles arise to Orondate's love, but after infinite adventures, all incredible and entirely unlikely, at the end of the tenth volume *Alexander's widow gives herself to her first lover.*[3]

Can anyone find the least idea of a Fable in this story? Can we dare claim that it is a discourse in prose, invented to influence morality through instruction disguised in an allegory? What is the moral teaching in this tale of *Cassandre*? Where is that instruction which is the heart of Fable? Can we consider this anything other than a very false story, or rather an unworthy corruption of history told without Fable, in which morality itself is grossly violated?

What I have said of *Cassandre* must also be said of all other Romances. The stories of *Cléopâtre, Cyrus,* or *Clélie* are no more Fables of morality than *Cassandre*: they are all alike in this respect as in many others.[4] The only characteristic of the Epic Poem which they retain, is that they do not portray ordinary people, but rather those of high station, Princes and Kings.

It is easy to see that the authors of these works have followed a path which is quite opposed to that of the Poets. Aristotle teaches that Poets must first lay out the plan of their Fable, which should be general. Then they give names to the characters and attach the Fable to a known History, in order to draw from those names and History the circumstances needed to amplify the action and give it the necessary breadth, which we call Episodes. These Authors have done just the opposite. They have taken names in History and added others of their own invention, given them actions which are extravagant and strange, and made not an Epic Poem but a tissue of adventures governed only by caprice and which fail to develop out of any sense of necessity or truthfulness; also this kind of action, far from being general, is as particular as any individual action of Caesar, Alcibiades, Pompey, etc. As far as true grandeur is concerned, the Author has certainly not observed the proper limitations which Aristotle has prescribed for Homeric poetry. One may say of this romance *Cassandre*, and of most of the others, that it really is the animal whose length measures ten thousand stadia,[5] as described by Aristotle. If it is true that nothing too large can be beautiful, can we describe as beautiful these monstrous works which stretch out their frivolous fictions to ten volumes' length, and require at least ten days' reading, without teaching anything worthwhile?

The other rules of Epic Poetry require that the action be unified, creating a perfect and regular whole. That is what the action of *Cassandre* does not do; all its parts do not combine to create a single action. It is impossible to make of them anything which is whole and simple, because the central incidents are mixed with an infinite number of others which destroy their unity. The plot falls into the same weakness as afflicts the Poems *Heracleïde* and *Théseïde*, which if they do not contain the entire lives of these heroes, do include most of those lives. We cannot describe an action as whole because it recounts throughout the love of Orondate, or say that it is regular and perfect because it explores this passion from beginning to end. That would be quite ridiculous.

Not only do these Romances sin against the rules of Epic Poetry when they describe several incidents in the lives of their heroes which cannot be made to form a unified action, but they also sin by mixing in the adventures of other heroes which are completely unrelated to the central story, and which are equally striking. The love and the adventures of Artaxerce and of Bérénice have no relation to the adventures of Orondate, and are no less important. There are several other such stories, and this multiplication of independent adventures is very detrimental, for it ruins entirely that unity of action which is the essence of an Epic Poem. One can introduce several Fables, several different adventures, but they must each be only an incomplete part of a single action, which is the principal action.

We have seen that truth must be mixed with falsehood throughout the Poem. This the authors of Romances have so poorly understood, that in their works one never finds truth mixed with fiction. There is no moral truth in the action of a Romance; how could there be, as there is no Fable? But even in all its other aspects, we find nothing truthful. We do sometimes find historical truths; the Author of *Cassandre* has taken many things from the Historians of Alexander. Apart from the fact that these are almost always truths which he has altered and corrupted, they are never truths mixed with fiction in order to render it more believable, they are truths added to fiction which only make its falsehood more obvious, more dreary and more unappealing.

I would be truly amazed to hear a Romance praised as Aristotle has praised Epic Poetry, when he called it more serious and moral than History. Nor can we say of the Romance what Horace has said of the Epic, elaborating on Aristotle, calling it more philosophical than Philosophy itself. He claims that it teaches better than Philosophers how to flee vice and practice virtue.

Homer introduces pious maxims into his Poetry, and everywhere he produces Gods to instruct his Readers and to make the prodigious credible. The Romancers do not amuse themselves with such trivialities. Not only are pious maxims banned from their works, but often we find in them great blasphemies pronounced by maddened lovers. As for the divinity, he counts for nothing in any of this work. The Authors would believe their hero dishonored if he were aided by a God. These heroes do the most prodigious and incredible things quite on their own. The Historians of Alexander note that in his time Alexander was believed capable of such great things only through the special assistance of the gods. That might have suited the Pagans, but our Romancers are careful never to suggest such things for their heroes. And perhaps that is one of the strongest marks of their judgment and prudence. It would have been truly ridiculous to make the Divinity intervene in order to fortify men who are solely possessed by love, and who think, speak and act only for love; this would be unlikely to move the Divinity and elicit his aid. In a word, the Romances sin no less in the domain of Theology than in that of Morality.

If these Authors have so openly violated all the rules of Fable, even though the Fable is the basis of Epic Poetry, they have no better observed the rules of the representation of thoughts and feelings which are the source of actions. Everything they touch becomes unrecognizable; they seem to have Circe's magic wand, or an even more powerful sort of wand, for they transform not only men but whole peoples, and alter the whole face of nature.[6] It is a precept of the Art of Poetry to study the manners and morals of each country, or period in time. The Romancers have studied them poorly: they have wished only to alter them or to change them completely. For example, in *Cassandre* the Author portrays the Scythians as a people just as polite and grand as the Persians, and of both he makes, not Barbarians, but Frenchmen. This fault is all the more strange, especially for the Scythians, as everyone can see how the Author contradicts everything which such ancient Historians as Herodotus, Strabo and others reported with respect to the simple way of life and the frugality of these peoples; he clearly contradicts what the Historian of the life of Alexander has written, and which the ambassadors of the Scythians and Persians themselves related to Alexander, telling how each person counted among his earthly goods no more than a yoke for cattle, an arrow, a lance, and a drinking cup, but that their poverty was useful in dealing with their enemies. The Author did not believe that such poor and savage peoples could enhance his Romance. Thus through his magic, known only to Romancers, he has made them civilized, polite, magnificent. When I think of the pleasure we find in *Quinte Curse*,[7] when we read of the poor and simple Scythians by contrast with the luxury and pomp of the Persians, I do not understand how this writer has failed to perceive the beauty of the contrast, nor how he has dared to change it.

The character of individuals is no better preserved. The Author has brought into his Romance all the greatest and best-known men who were involved in the History of Alexander, yet there is virtually none who has not been changed, and who resembles the portrait which History made of him. Alexander himself, valorous and great as the Author must acknowledge him to have been, becomes a bewitched lover, and quite ridiculous. As for the hero of the Poem, the brave Orondate, he is completely invented so that the Author can do as he likes with him. But even then he is obligated to portray the true character of such a person, as I have described it to be. At first he does show a true Scythian quite well, but that soon changes, and Orondate's behavior is neither appropriate, realistic nor consistent.

There are only three ways to portray morals and character: we can show men as they are, as they are reputed to be, or as they should be. That is not the habit of Romancers. They do not show people either as they were, or as Reputation claimed they were. Instead, their characters become quite other than what they were. Nor can we say that these people have been made better, that is to say more beautiful, because they are shown as they should have been, for they have been given so many weaknesses of which they were incapable, and which are entirely out of character, that we can be sure they have been made much worse, uglier and more wicked. For example, the characters of Orondate and of his friend Prince Artaxerce— both invented, for History does not mention a Scythian Prince, and the son of Darius was still a child when his father was conquered by Alexander— these two, as I was saying, are quite wicked. Orondate is at Darius' court when his father enters Persia with an army of two hundred thousand men. Darius sends out to meet him an equally strong army led by Artabase and by his own son Artaxerce. How does Orondate respond to this? Ruled by love, he goes out with his friend Artaxerce and fights against his father and his country. Artaxerce imitates this generosity, wild and unnatural as it is. He commands a reserve corps of four thousand horses, but instead of fighting, he is motionless, and holds back the ardor and impatience of his troops. He is furiously attacked, and still cannot resolve to defend himself, lest his sword spill the blood of his friend's army. Finally he is wounded by two blows, and fights to save his life and to stay with Orondate. Orondate for his part has performed prodigies of valor, and thus each Prince has betrayed his father and his country, one out of friendship and the other for love. Is it possible to imagine two acts of greater madness? And does this not clearly violate the precept expressed by Horace in his *Ars Poetica*

> Qui didicit patriae quid debeat, & quid amicis
> Quo fit amore parens, quo frater amandus & hospes.[8]

Does this not violate one's duty to country and friends? What are the different degrees of love which we should feel for a father and for a brother? How far is a guest obligated to his host? It is true that Horace has not shown what is owed a beloved woman. He was quite wrong not to teach that for her we must suppress all other natural and legitimate feelings.

In any case, Orondate is mad. He stabs himself twice upon hearing a false report of Statira's death, and he tries to do the same again when that Princess has become Alexander's wife, and through duty and delicacy refuses to see him. Nothing could be more ridiculous than to make one's hero a madman, or to make him a blasphemer and a weakling, even in the eyes of Pagans. A blasphemer because, as Socrates has so plainly proven, *To commit suicide is to usurp a right which belongs only to God*. A weakling because, as Aristotle formally declares, *To commit suicide*, defeated by poverty, love or another passion, is the action, not of a valiant man, but of a cowardly one. For only cowardice leads us to succumb in the face of difficulty. The Pagan Poets have been much wiser. In the *Iliad*, when Achilles learns of the Death of Patroclus, a mortal pain seizes him and he throws himself down on the ground, covering his head with burning cinders. But in this extreme affliction, violent and wild as it is, he gives no sign that he is thinking of suicide. Homer contented himself with saying that the young Antilochus holds his hands, lest the violence of his grief move him to attempt suicide. When Sophocles showed an Ajax committing suicide on the Athenian stage, he makes clear that Ajax is mad. Dido kills herself in the *Aeneid*, but apart from the fact that she is not the heroine of the Poem—she is a woman, and one whose passion has driven her mad—this is an example of suicide which Virgil offers to make us hate the act, and to teach us how such criminal passions ordinarily come to an unhappy end. The Romans had one among them who was thought wise, but who nevertheless killed himself: that was Cato.[9] But a Poet could never make him the hero of a Poem, unless he wished to make horror its central theme. Otherwise the Epic Poem would be debased according to Aristotle's rules, which on this subject are the same as those on social custom. Thus we see that the Author of *Cassandre* is far from having made his hero better according to Aristotle's precept, and that he has made him worse than necessary. One might say that Orondate was a Scythian, and that a Scythian can commit suicide, but that is false; the Scythians of those times were still so upright and so grandly simple in their way of life that the act of suicide was unknown among them.

Another rule of the Epic Poem is that the hero must have a superior nature which stands out from the others, as though he were the principal figure in a Painting. This rule is ignored in *Cassandre*, as in the other Romances; all the characters are the same. There are twenty men, all the most valiant in the world; Orondate, Artaxerce, Lysymachus, Demetrius, Memnon, etc. All perform the same prodigies of valor, and nothing sets them apart from one another but their arms and their names. Homer is quite different: Achilles in the *Iliad*, and Ulysses in the *Odyssey* are the dominant figures to whom all others are subordinate. Nor do any of Homer's characters resemble either Achilles or Ulysses, for each has a particular quality which distinguishes him from the others, which never changes and which makes itself felt throughout. That is what the character of Orondate does not have. He is simply in love and he is brave, but the others are also. He has nothing special which distinguishes him, and all the other characters are as central and dominant as he is.

This prodigious valor which the Romancers freely give their heroes is another considerable defect which makes all the characters seem false, for what is absent in nature does seem false in poetry. The Epic Poem is the imitation of an action; to be imitated, an action must be possible, and thus the impossible cannot be imitated. This excess in the Romance, the result of poor judgment and ignorance, takes it outside the realm of imitation. Consequently it is no longer an Epic Poem. Everything Achilles does in the *Iliad* which is prodigious becomes possible with the help of the Gods whom the Poet causes to intervene.

Feelings are the expression of moral and social custom, and it is a virtual necessity that the feelings of characters in Romances correspond to the social customs which the author has given them. We cannot say that the Author of *Cassandre* does not show much spirit and imagination in this regard; he is what Longinus calls *inventive*,[10] and he finds everything which his subject can provide, but the feelings he portrays are more affected than natural. He relies less on common usage than on Rhetoric; thus he so often falls into either a horrible affectation, or an outrageous exaggeration. His characters are always Gascon French, and never Persian, Macedonian, or Scythian. However, these different peoples should each think and speak in a different manner, as in Horace's precept:

> Intererit multum Diuus ne nutritus an heros;
> Colchus an Assyrius. Thebis nutritus an Argis.[11]

Just as feelings are the expression of custom, language is the expression of feelings. The Epic Poem has the most noble and figured language, because it brings into play everything which is most great in the world. The language of Kings and Gods cannot be too elevated. Since the Romance is written in prose, and treats only Princes and Kings, it should stay within the bounds of a noble style, but it should be simple and not too much ornamented. That is what the Romance does not do; usually its style is like the feelings it expresses, either full of affectation, or ridiculously overblown. How astonishing that Homer and Virgil, who wrote so many centuries before us, are still models to be followed for feeling and expression, and that so many works written in our own time are merely, if I may say so, models of that which is to be avoided. There is not a wise man who could fail to be delighted were he able to think and write as Homer and Virgil do. Nor could he fail to be ashamed were he to think and write in the manner of Romancers. If Achilles, Ulysses and Aeneas were to come alive again, they would be pleased to acknowledge all that Homer and Virgil have made them say and think. And if the heroes of Antiquity which the Romancers introduce were to return, I doubt they would forgive those who have so disfigured them. Alexander, who forbade any painter but Apelles to paint him or any sculptor but Lysippus to cast him in bronze,[12] would have been furious to see himself so changed and foolish. He would have torn up the letters that he is made to write in *Cassandre*, and he would have been the first to mock the speeches he is made to give. Even the Scythian king would demand the return of his hard and savage nature, and would loudly complain of the gentle and gallant temper which he had been given. He would find all that a too shameful mask of his true self. To be frank, I would not advise the Author, Gascon though he be, to appear in the presence of these great men whom he has so strangely disguised.

Homer wrote two Epic Poems, and they are quite different, yet we have a great number of Romances which are all alike. They all have the same tone, all speak of love, and all tell the same tale—for after many frustrations, all the lovers are happy.

Another very considerable defect is the fact that these turns of plot often involve several characters in the same way. *Cassandre* ends with the marriage of six princes and their ladies. Thus it is clear that the Romance is not like the Epic Poem, the imitation of the action of a single hero, but rather the adventures of several, which completely ruins the idea which it is meant to convey. If it is impossible to make of the life of one man something which is whole and unified, as Aristotle has shown to be the case, how could it be possible to reduce to such a perfect unity the various adventures of several heroes which are all moving in the same direction?

If the conclusion of *Cassandre* and of almost all the other Romances is so contrary to the rules of Epic Poetry, the beginning is equally so. Homer and Virgil quickly acquaint us not only with their heroes, but also with almost all the characters who take part in the action; the Romancers do not do that at all. We must read three or four volumes of *Cassandre*, each as large as the *Iliad* and the *Odyssey*, before we meet Cassandre and know that she is the Princess Statira.

Since the Romances violate in every way the rules of Epic Poetry; since they offer neither Fable, and thus no moral truth, nor proper presentation of manners, morals or feelings, I was right to say in my Preface to the *Iliad* that they are very different from the Epic Poem, both in their ends and their manner of imitation—in fact, in every aspect of their making. They are frivolous works which Ignorance and Love have produced, created to elevate weaknesses into virtues. In them good sense and reason are set aside, and decorum scorned. Instead of a Fiction both ingenious and useful, we are given merely a flat falsehood which flouts the truth, even the known truth. The greatest people of Antiquity are transformed into weak lovers— they who were furthest from such extravagance. In truth, we would have to be as simple as children to enjoy reading such frivolous and foolish works. They only fill the young with vain thoughts, and distract them from anything good or solid. The Romance is so little an Epic Poem that to show its nature well, we must make a definition quite opposed to that which describes the Poem. The Romance is a prose discourse invented to spoil morals, or at the very least to amuse the young without profit through the telling of several false adventures lacking fiction or allegory. Heroes are said to possess weaknesses and foolish ideas which are quite false, according to all the historical truths of time, place, custom and character.

Translated by Amy Simowitz

Notes

1. *Cassandre* (1642–1645) by La Calprenède was one of a number of "heroic" novels written between 1625 and 1655 that tell of great acts and describe great feelings. The best-known authors of these works were Gomberville, La Calprenède, and Scudéry.

2. Dacier's definition of fable and some of her rules for epic poetry derive from her belief in the moral function of poetry. Earlier in the preface, she maintains that poetry was invented as a form of philosophy, to teach through pleasure. Here she is following the contemporary critic Le Bossu, whose work she admired.

3. The italicized passage is from *Cassandre*.

4. *Cléopâtre* (1647–1658) is by La Calprenède; *Artamène ou le grand Cyrus* (1649–1653) and *Clélie, histoire romaine* (1654–1661) are both by Mademoiselle de Scudéry.

5. Stadium, from the Greek, was a measure that varied between 147 and 192 meters, or about 600 feet.

6. Circe, an enchantress, plays an important role in the *Odyssey*. When Ulysses landed on her island, she transformed his men into swine.

7. Quintus Curtius, a Roman historian of the first century, author of a history of Alexander which contains many errors.

8. English translation (Loeb); with the complete sentence:

He who has learned what he owes his country and his friends, what love is due a parent, a brother and a guest, what is imposed on senator and judge, what is the function of a general sent to war, he surely knows how to give each character his fitting part.

9. Cato committed suicide to avoid capture by the forces of Julius Caesar.

10. Longinus, Greek rhetorician of the third century B.C.E., is thought to have written *On the Sublime*.

11. English translation (Loeb):

Vast difference will it make
Whether a god be speaking or a hero
A Cochian or an Assyrian,
One bred at Thebes or in Argos.

12. Apelles was the most famous of the Greek painters. He lived at the court of Alexander the Great and painted his portrait. Lysippus was a Greek sculptor, also of the fourth century B.C.E.

ANNE FINCH, COUNTESS OF WINCHILSEA (1661–1720)

ANNE FINCH was fortunate in her social position, her loving and appreciative husband, and the political chance that removed the couple from public life. Born into the county aristocracy, she lost her father when she was five months old, her mother when she was three, and her stepfather when she was ten. In 1683 she became a maid of honor to Mary of Modena, wife of James, Duke of York, and met the wits of the brilliant but cynical Restoration court. Heneage Finch, a gentleman of the bedchamber to the Duke, fell in love with her and they married in 1684. The marriage was childless but blissfully happy and congenial; far from disparaging his wife's intellectual interests as would the average Restoration husband, Heneage actively encouraged her to write poetry.

When James was exiled in 1688, the Finches lost their public positions and for several years had no settled home. Anne, moreover, was personally grief-stricken because of her devotion to Mary of Modena; this triggered her most serious bout with depression, which afflicted her periodically throughout her life. When Heneage's nephew became Earl of Winchilsea in 1690, he invited the Finches to reside at Eastwell, the family seat in Kent. There they lived in happy retirement, enjoying nature and a congenial circle of friends. Anne continued to write poetry and, about 1702, began to collect her work in a handsome folio volume, which remained in manuscript until 1903.

In 1712 the Earl died, and Heneage succeeded to the title. In the following year, Anne published a volume of her poems, originally without and then with her name; it did not include her more personal and feminist works: "To the Nightingale" was published; "The Introduction" and "The Preface" to her folio volume of poems were not. These two pieces show that even though Finch wrote under favorable and protected circumstances, she anticipated criticism for aspiring beyond her sphere. Finch was angered by such narrowness, but it seems to have undermined her self-confidence and caused her to curb her ambition and shrink from publicity. The three works presented here articulate her premises about both women poets and poetic practice in general.

The Poems of Anne Countess of Winchilsea, ed. Myra Reynolds (Chicago: University of Chicago Press, 1903).

The Introduction (c. 1702)

Did I, my lines intend for publick view,
How many censures, wou'd their faults persue,
Some wou'd, because such words they do affect,
Cry they're insipid, empty, uncorrect.
And many, have attain'd, dull and untaught
The name of Witt, only by finding fault.
True judges, might condemn their want of witt,
And all might say, they're by a Woman writt.
Alas! a woman that attempts the pen,
Such an intruder on the rights of men,   10
Such a presumptuous Creature, is esteem'd,
The fault, can by no vertue be redeem'd.
They tell us, we mistake our sex and way;
Good breeding, fassion, dancing, dressing, play
Are the accomplishments we shou'd desire;
To write, or read, or think, or to enquire
Wou'd cloud our beauty, and exaust our time,
And interrupt the Conquests of our prime;
Whilst the dull mannage, of a servile house
Is held by some, our outmost art, and use.   20
      Sure 'twas not ever thus, nor are we told
Fables, of Women that excell'd of old;
To whom, by the diffusive hand of Heaven
Some share of witt, and poetry was given.
On that glad day, on which the Ark return'd,
The holy pledge, for which the Land had mourn'd,
The joyfull Tribes, attend itt on the way,
The Levites do the sacred Charge convey,
Whilst various Instruments, before itt play;
Here, holy Virgins in the Concert joyn,   30
The louder notes, to soften, and refine,
And with alternate verse, compleat the Hymn Devine.
Loe! the yong Poet, after Gods own heart,
By Him inspired, and taught the Muses Art,

Anne Finch, Countess of Winchilsea (1661–1720)

Return'd from Conquest, a bright Chorus meets,
That sing his slayn ten thousand in the streets.
In such loud numbers they his acts declare,
Proclaim the wonders, of his early war,
That Saul upon the vast applause does frown,
And feels, itts mighty thunder shake the Crown.   40
What, can the threat'n'd Judgment now prolong?
Half of the Kingdom is already gone;
The fairest half, whose influence guides the rest,
Have David's Empire, o're their hearts confess't.
    A Woman here, leads fainting Israel on,
She fights, she wins, she tryumphs with a song,
Devout, Majestick, for the subject fitt,
And far above her arms, exalts her witt,
Then, to the peacefull, shady Palm withdraws,
And rules the rescu'd Nation, with her Laws.¹   50
How are we fal'n, fal'n by mistaken rules?
And Education's, more then Nature's fools,
Debarr'd from all improve-ments of the mind,
And to be dull, expected and dessigned;
And if some one, wou'd Soar above the rest,
With warmer fancy, and ambition press't,
So strong, th' opposing faction still appears,
The hopes to thrive, can ne're outweigh the fears,
Be caution'd then my Muse, and still retir'd;
Nor be dispis'd, aiming to be admir'd;   60
Conscious of wants, still with contracted wing,
To some few freinds, and to thy sorrows sing;
For groves of Lawrell, thou wert never meant;
Be dark enough thy shades, and be thou there content.

The Preface (c. 1702)

Beaumont in the beginni[n]g of a Coppy of Verses to his freind Fletcher
(upon the ill successe of his Faithfull Shepheardesse) tells him,

I know too well! that no more, then the man
That travells throo' the burning Deserts, can
When he is beaten with the raging Sun,
Half smother'd in the dust, have power to run
From a cool River, which himself doth find,
E're he be slack'd; no more can he, whose mind

Joys in the Muses, hold from that delight,
When Nature, and his full thoughts, bid him write.

And this indeed, I not only find true by my own experience, but have also
too many wittnesses of itt against me, under my own hand in the following
Poems; which tho' never meritting more then to be once read, and then
carlessly scatter'd or consum'd; are grown by the partiality of some of my
friends, to the formidable appearance of a Volume; tho' but in Manuscript,
and have been solicited to a more daring manefestation, which I shall ever
resist, both from the knowledge of their incapassity, of bearing a publick
tryal; and also, upon recalling to my memory, some of the first lines I ever
writt, which were part of an invocation of Apollo, whose wise and limitted
answer to me, I did there suppose to be

I grant thee no pretence to Bays,
    Nor in bold print do thou appear.
Nor shalt thou reatch Orinda's[1] prayse,
    Tho' all thy aim, be fixt on Her.

And tho' I have still avoided the confident producing anything of mine in
thatt manner, yett have I come too neer itt, and been like those imperfect
penitents, who are ever relenting, and yett ever returning to the same offences. For I have writt, and expos'd my uncorrect Rimes, and immediatly
repented; and yett have writt again, and again suffer'd them to be seen; tho'
att the expence of more uneasy reflections, till at last (like them) wearied
with uncertainty, and irresolution, I rather chuse to be harden'd in an errour,
then to be still att the trouble of endeavering to over come itt: and now,
neither deny myself the pleasure of writing, or any longer make a mistery
of that to my freinds and acquaintance, which does so little deserve itt; tho'
itt is still a great satisfaction to me, that I was not so far abandon'd by my
prudence, as out of a mistaken vanity, to lett any attempts of mine in Poetry,
shew themselves whilst I liv'd in such a publick place as the Court, where
every one wou'd have made their remarks upon a Versifying Maid of Honour; and far the greater number with prejudice, if not contempt. And indeed,
the apprehension of this, had so much wean'd me from the practice and
inclination to itt; that had nott an utter change in my Condition, and Circumstances, remov'd me into the solitude, & security of the Country, and
the generous kindnesse of one that possest the most delightfull seat in itt;
envited him, from whom I was inseparable, to partake of the pleasures of
itt, I think I might have stopp'd ere it was too late, and suffer'd those few
compositions I had then by me, to have sunk into that oblivion, which I

ought to wish might be the lott of all that have succeeded them. But when I came to Eastwell, and cou'd fix my eyes only upon objects naturally inspiring soft and Poeticall immaginations, and found the Owner of itt, so indulgent to that Art, so knowing in all the rules of itt, and att his pleasure, so capable of putting them in practice; and also most obligingly favorable to some lines of mine, that had fall'n under his Lordship's perusal, I cou'd no longer keep within the limmitts I had prescrib'd myself, nor be wisely reserv'd, in spite of inclination, and such powerfull temptations to the contrary. Again I engage my self in the service of the Muses, as eagerly as if

> From their new Worlds, I know not where,
> Their golden Indies in the air—[2]

they cou'd have supply'd the material losses, which I had lately sustain'd in this. And now, whenever I contemplate all the several beautys of this Park, allow'd to be (if not of the Universal yett) of our British World infinitely the finest,

> A pleasing wonder throo' my fancy moves,
> Smooth as her lawnes, and lofty as her Groves.
> Boundlesse my Genius seems, when my free sight,
> Finds only distant skys to stop her flight.
> Like mighty Denhams, then, methinks my hand,
> Might bid the Landskip, in strong numbers stand,
> Fix all itts charms, with a Poetick skill,
> And raise itts Fame, above his Cooper's hill.[3]

This, I confesse, is whatt in itts self itt deserves, but the unhappy difference is, that he by being a real Poet, cou'd make that place (as he sais) a Parnassus to him; whilst I, that behold a real Parnassus here, in that lovely Hill, which in this Park bears that name, find in my self, so little of the Poet, that I am still restrain'd from attempting a description of itt in verse, tho' the agreeablenesse of the subject, has often prompted me most strongly to itt.

But now, having pleaded an irresistable impulse, as my excuse for writing, which was the cheif design of this Preface, I must also expresse my hopes of excaping all suspition of vanity, or affectation of applause from itt; since I have in my introduction, deliver'd my sincere opinion that when a Woman meddles with things of this nature,

> So strong, th' opposing faction still appears,
> The hopes to thrive, can ne're outweigh the fears.

And, I am besides sensible, that Poetry has been of late so explain'd, the laws of itt being putt into familiar languages, that even those of my sex, (if they will be so presumptuous as to write) are very accountable for their transgressions against them. For what rule of Aristotle, or Horace is there, that has not been given us by Rapin, Despreaux, D'acier, my Lord Roscomon, etc.? What has Mr. Dryden omitted, that may lay open the very misteries of this Art? and can there any where be found a more delightsome, or more usefull piece of Poetry, then that,

> correct Essay,
> Which so repairs, our old Horatian way."[4]

If then, after the perusal of these, we fail, we cannott plead any want, but that of capacity, or care, in both of which I own myself so very defective, y^t whenever any things of mine, escape a censure, I allways attribute itt, to the good nature or civility of the Reader; and not to any meritt in the Poems, which I am satisfy'd are so very imperfect, and uncorrect, that I shall not attempt their justifycation.

For the subjects, I hope they are att least innofensive; tho' sometimes of Love; for keeping within those limmitts which I have observ'd, I know not why itt shou'd be more faulty, to treat of that passion, then of any other violent excursion, or transport of the mind. Tho' I must confesse, the great reservednesse of Mrs. Philips in this particular, and the prayses I have heard given her upon that account, together with my desire not to give scandal to the most severe, has often discourag'd me from making use of itt, and given me some regrett for what I had writt of that kind, and wholy prevented me from putting the Aminta of Tasso[5] into English verse, from the verbal translation that I procured out of the Italian, after I had finish'd the first act extreamly to my satisfaction; and was convinc'd, that in the original, itt must be as soft and full of beautys, as ever anything of that nature was; but there being nothing mixt with itt, of a serious morality, or usefullnesse, I sacrafis'd the pleasure I took in itt, to the more sollid reasonings of my own mind; and hope by so doing to have made an attonement, to my gravest readers, for the two short pieces of that Pastoral, taken from the French, the Songs, and other few lighter things, which yett remain in the following sheetts.

As to Lampoons, and all sorts of abusive verses, I ever so much detested, both the underhand dealing and uncharitablenesse which accompanys them, that I never suffer'd my small talent, to be that way employ'd; tho' the facility of doing itt, is too well known to many, who can but make two words rime; and there wants not some provocation often, either from one's own resentments, or those of others, to put such upon itt, as are any way capable of that mean sort of revenge. The only coppy of mine that tends towards this, is the letter to Ephelia, in answer to an invitation to the Town;[6] but, as that appears to have been long written, by the mention made of my Lord Roscommon, under the name of Piso, given to him first, in a Panegerick, of Mr. Wallers, before his Art of Poetry; so I do declare, that att the time of composing itt, there was no particular person meant by any of the disadvantageous Caracters; and the whole intention of itt, was in general to expose the Censorious humour, foppishnesse and coquetterie that then prevail'd. And I am so far from thinking there is any ill in this, that I wish itt oftener done, by such hands as might sufficiently ridicule, and wean us from those mistakes in our manners, and conversation.

Plays, were translated by our most vertuous Orinda; and mine, tho' originals, I hope are not lesse reserv'd. The Queen of Cyprus, I once thought to have call'd the Triumphs of Love and Innocence; and doubted not but the latter part of the Title, wou'd have been as aptly apply'd as the former. Aristomenes is wholy Tragicall, and, if itt answer my intention, moral and inciting to Vertue. What they are as to the performance, I leave to the judgment of those who shall read them; and if any one can find more faults then I think to be in y'''; I am much mistaken. I will only add, that when they were compos'd, itt was far from my intention ever to own them, the first was for my own private satisfaction, only an Essay wheither I cou'd go throo' with such a peice of Poetry. The other, I was led to, by the strong impressions, which some wonderfull circumstances in the life of Aristomenes, made upon my fancy;[7] and cheifly the sweetnesse of his temper, observable in itt, wrought upon me; for which reason tho' itt may be I did not so Poetically, I chose rather to represent him Good, then Great; and pitch'd upon such parts of the relation, and introduc'd such additional circumstances of my own, as might most illustrate that, and shew him to be (as declared by the Oracle) the best of Men. I know not what effect they will have upon others, but I must acknowledge, that the giving some interruption to those melancholy thoughts, which posesst me, not only for my own, but much more for the misfortunes of those to whom I owe all immaginable duty, and gratitude,[8] was so great a benefitt; that I have reason to be satisfy'd with the undertaking, be the performance never so inconsiderable. And indeed, an absolute solitude (which often was my lott) under such dejection of mind, cou'd not have been supported, had I indulg'd myself (as was too natural to me) only in the contemplation of present and real afflictions, which I hope will plead my excuse, for turning them for releif, upon such as were immaginary, & relating to Persons no more in being. I had my end in the writing, and if they please not those who will take the pains to peruse them, itt will be a just accusation to my weaknesse, for letting them escape out of their concealment; but if attended with a better successe, the satisfaction any freind of mine, may take in them, will make me think my time past, not so unprofitably bestowed, as otherwise I might; and which I shall now endeavour to redeem, by applying myself to better employments, and when I do write to chuse, my subjects generally out of Devinity, or from moral and serious occasions; which made me place them last, as capable of addition; For when we have run throo' all the amusements of life, itt will be found, that there is but one thing necessary; and they only Wise, who chuse the better part. But since there must be also, some relaxation, some entertaining of the spiritts,

> Whilst Life by Fate is lent to me,
> Whilst here below, I stay,
> Religion, my sole businesse be,
> And Poetry, my play.

To the Nightingale (1713)

Exert thy Voice, sweet Harbinger of Spring!
    This Moment is thy Time to sing,
    This Moment I attend to Praise,
And set my Numbers to thy Layes.
    Free as thine shall be my Song;
    As thy Musick, short, or long.
Poets, wild as thee, were born,
    Pleasing best when unconfin'd,
    When to Please is least design'd,
Soothing but their Cares to rest;   10
    Cares do still their Thoughts molest,
    And still th' unhappy Poet's Breast,
Like thine, when best he sings, is plac'd against a Thorn.
She begins, Let all be still!
    Muse, thy Promise now fulfill!
Sweet, oh! sweet, still sweeter yet
Can thy Words such Accents fit,
Canst thou Syllables refine,
Melt a Sense that shall retain
Still some Spirit of the Brain,   20
Till with Sounds like these it join.
    'Twill not be! then change thy Note;
    Let division[1] shake thy Throat.

Anne Finch, Countess of Winchilsea (1661–1720)

Hark! Division now she tries;
Yet as far the Muse outflies.
    Cease then, prithee, cease thy Tune;
    Trifler, wilt thou sing till *June?*
Till thy Bus'ness all lies waste,
And the Time of Building's past!
    Thus we Poets that have Speech,   30
Unlike what thy Forests teach,
    If a fluent Vein be shown
    That's transcendent to our own,
Criticize, reform, or preach,
Or censure what we cannot reach.

Notes

The Introduction

    1. Lines 25–50 refer to three episodes in the Hebrew Bible. (1) The Israelites sang and played instruments to celebrate bringing the Ark of the Covenant into Jerusalem (I Chronicles 15); the "holy virgins," however, appear to be Finch's addition. (2) The women of Israel, greeting the victorious David ("the young poet, after God's own heart") with songs, praised his achievement over King Saul's (I Samuel 18). (3) The judge Deborah led the Israelites to victory and then composed a triumphal song (Judges 4, 5).

The Preface

    1. Katherine Philips (1632–1664), who used the pen name of Orinda, was extolled as the model of a female poet because of the modesty of her manners and the purity of her works.
    2. Abraham Cowley, "The Complaint," stanza 6 (slightly adapted).
    3. John Denham's descriptive poem "Cooper's Hill" (1642), widely admired in the seventeenth and eighteenth centuries.
    4. The "correct Essay" is the "Essay upon Poetry" (1682) of John Sheffield, Earl of Mulgrave; the quotation is from the "Essay on Translated Verse" (1684) of Wentworth Dillon, Earl of Roscommon, who also wrote a blank verse translation of Horace's "Ars Poetica" (1680).
    5. Torquato Tasso's *Aminta* (1573) is a joyous, uninhibited pastoral drama.
    6. "Ardelia's Answer to Ephelia, who had invited her to come to her in town," probably written ten years before this preface.
    7. Aristomenes led a long, heroic, but hopeless uprising of the Messenians against Sparta. The Oracle of Delphi referred to him as "the noblest of the Greeks."
    8. King James II and his Queen, Mary of Modena, deposed and exiled in 1688.

To the Nightingale

    1. Florid variation on a melody, featuring runs and trills.

CATHERINE TROTTER COCKBURN
(1679–1749)

AN ACCOMPLISHED playwright, philosopher, and theologian, Catherine Trotter Cockburn enjoyed both popularity and professional respect during her fifty-two-year career as a writer. She was the daughter of Sarah Ballenden and Captain David Trotter, a Scotsman who assumed the command of the Royal Navy under Charles II. She converted to Catholicism in her youth but reconverted to Anglicanism in 1707. One year later, she married the Rev. Patrick Cockburn. Because he refused to renounce his allegiance to the exiled heir to the Stuart line (James III), Cockburn could not advance beyond his humble curacy. As a result, the couple lived an austere existence until 1726, when Cockburn took the oath of allegiance to George I.

Trotter's eleven-year career as a playwright began in 1695, when her tragedy *Agnes de Castro* was produced at the Theatre Royal. She wrote three more tragedies—*The Fatal Friendship* (1698), *The Unhappy Penitents* (1701), and *The Revolution of Sweden* (1706)—and a comedy, *Love at a Loss; or the most votes carry it* (1701). During this time, she maintained a professional correspondence with Congreve, who at her request critiqued an early draft of *The Revolution of Sweden*.

Partly due to an increasing frustration at having to mold her plays to popular taste, which she expresses in the dedication to *The Unhappy Penitent*, and partly owing to the demands of maintaining a household on a constrained budget, Trotter ended her career as a playwright when she became engaged to Patrick Cockburn. Her second career, as a theologian and philosopher, continued until her death. In 1702, she published *A Defense of Mr Locke's Essay Concerning Human Understanding*, which supported the empiricist against the charge of materialism leveled by Thomas Burnet. This cogently argued treatise earned her an effusive letter of appreciation and a gift of books from Locke. Her second defense of Locke, in 1726, was directed against Dr. Winch Holdsworth, who attacked what he believed to be Locke's views on Christ's resurrection.

The Unhappy Penitent A Tragedy (London: William Turner, 1701).

Catherine Trotter Cockburn (1679–1749)

Dedication to *The Unhappy Penitent A Tragedy* (1701)

To the Right Honourable
Charles
Lord Hallifax[1]

My Lord,

Since I first ventur'd into the World to stand the Test of Publick Censure, I have ever had in my aim as the highest Point of Ambition, to produce something worthy of your Lordships approbation, without which I esteem'd the Suffrages of the People, as the Votes of our Representatives, of no force until the Royal Assent Stamps them into a Law, which after none dare contradict: But conscious how far short of that Merit I have hitherto fall'n, and yet impatient to offer my intended Homage, I thus address you not as the Sovereign Judge of perfection, but as the Patron and Encourager of all who aspire to it, the no less God-like, tho' less awful Character; which how eminently your Lordships, the many who Flourish under your auspicious Influence are a prooff: for if we allow a Congreve to owe your Favour to your Strictest Justice, there are not Numbers who cou'd find their Safety but with me, in appealing to your Goodness; tho' I am apt to think more of our Poets wou'd arrive at perfection, if they observ'd their particular Talent, and confin'd themselves to it.

The most Universal Genius this Nation ever bred, Dryden himself did not excel in every part, through most of what he has writ there appears a distinguishing greatness, that Elevation of Thought, that Sublime which transports the Soul; he commands our Admiration of himself, but little moves our concern for those he represents; his Genius seems not turn'd to work upon the softer Passions, tho' some of his last Translations are excellent in that kind, nothing more lively, more tender, or more moving, but there the *Words*, alone are his, of which it must be confess'd he had on all Subjects the exactest *Propriety*, the most *Expressive*, and dispos'd into the sweetest Numbers.[2]

Otway[3] besides his judicious Choice of the *Fable*, had a peculiar Art to move Compassion, which as it is one of the chief *Ends* of *Tragedy*, he found most adapted to his Genius, and never venturing where that did not lead him, excell'd in the Pathetick.

Had Lee[4] consulted his strength as well, he might have giv'n us most perfect Pieces, but aiming at the sublime, instead of being Great he is extravagant; his Stile too swelling, and if we pursue him in his flights, he often carries us out of Nature: Had he restrain'd that vain Ambition, and intirely apply'd himself to describe the softest of the Passions (for Love of all the rest he seems best to have understood, if that be allow'd a proper subject for *Tragedy*) he had certainly had fewer defects.

The inimitable Shakespeare seems alone secure on every side from an attack, (for I speak not here of Faults against the Rules of Poetry, but against the natural genius) he had all the Images of nature present to him, Study'd her throughly, and boldly copy'd all her various Features, for tho' he has chiefly exerted himself on the more Masculine *Passions*, 'tis as the choice of his Judgment not the restraint of his Genius, and he seems to have de-sign'd those few tender moving Scenes he has giv'n us, as a prooff he cou'd be every way equally Admirable.

I know not how, my Lord, in designing only to hint an Obstacle to perfection in our Poets, I have unawares launch'd into a subject which I fear your Lordship will think unbecoming me to touch; but if Presidents may be admitted as a Plea, several wretched Poets before me have had the advantage of passing their Censure on the best; however I may be allow'd to urge that the Fault which I have caution'd against, is not mine. I know too well the Bounds of my stinted Talent, and I fear may rather be accused of not having exerted the little strength I have, than of aiming beyond it in this weak Performance, which I presume not to offer your Lordship but as an object of your mercy; and like some City Ladies, who are content to be the jest at Court rather than not appear there, I feel a Satisfaction in the Honour of being known to your Lordship, tho' only by my Faults. The knowledge of our Transgressions may be a considerable Step towards amending them for the future, but 'tis certainly a great aggravation of them in the Committing, which I must confess my self guilty of in Writing this *Play*, being sensible before I began it of a defect in the Plot, the only one I shall mention as the foundation of all the rest; the Distress is not great enough, the Subject of it only the misfortune of Lovers, which I partly design'd in Compliance with the effiminate taste of the Age; notwithstand-ing which, and the right of Possession, it has long held on the Modern Stage, I have ventur'd to propose a Doubt whether Love be a proper Subject for it; it seems to me not Noble, not solemn enough for *Tragedy*, but I have a much greater Objection against it, at least as 'tis generally represented, which the best of the *French Poets* has made before me, and gives as a Rule,

—que Lamour Souvent de remors combattu
Pariosse une foiblesse, & non une vertu.

Boileau in his *Art Poetique*.[5]

Catherine Trotter Cockburn (1679–1749)

The most that can be allow'd that Passion is to be the Noblest frailty of the Mind, but 'tis a Frailty, and becomes a Vice, when cherish'd as an exalted Vertue: A Passion which contracts the Mind, by fixing it intirely on one object, and sets all our happiness at Stake on so great hazard as the caprice, or fidelity of another, which if there were no greater is sure sufficient reason, not to Arm it with more Power than its own insinuating Nature; yet this is made the shining Vertue of our Heroes, we are to rejoice in their success, or pitty their Disappointments, as Noble Lovers, Patterns for our imitation, not as Instances of humane Frailty, and I fear this has not been so constantly done without ill consequence; not but Love will maintain his Dominion in the World how muchsoever oppos'd, but if we resign him the heart, let us not give him up the Judgment too. On these Reflections I compos'd this *Tragedy*, in which the principal Characters are indeed doting Lovers, but hurry'd by their Passion into a Fault of which their immediate punishment makes them conscious, and at once deserve their Sufferings and our Pitty. This (I cannot forbear taking notice by the way) tho' giv'n by our great Master as an inviolable Law in this sort of Poem, is yet observ'd by few without which tho' they may give Delight, they can rarely attain that End to which the other shou'd only be Subservient of forming an Instructive Moral.

Notes

1. Charles Montagu, Earl of Hallifax (1661–1715), president of the Royal Society (1695–1698) and patron of numerous authors, including Addison, Congreve, and Newton.

2. "Numbers" here refers to measured rhythm in verse.

3. Thomas Otway, author of the moving pathetic tragedies *The Orphan* (1680) and *Venice Preserved* (1682).

4. Nathaniel Lee, author of bombastic heroic tragedies such as *The Rival Queens* (1677).

5. "When love emerges from a struggle with remorse, it seems a fault, not a virtue." *L'Art poétique* (The Art of Poetry) (1674) by Nicholas Boileau-Despréaux (1636–1711) had a great influence on English and French writers, becoming an authoritative text for the neoclassical movement.

ELIZABETH ELSTOB (1683–1756)

Eᴌɪᴢᴀʙᴇᴛʜ Eʟꜱᴛᴏʙ's strong intellectual interests were encouraged by her mother, who died when she was eight. She and her brother, William, became wards of an uncle, Dr. Charles Elstob, Canon of Canterbury. When Elizabeth asked her uncle to let her learn French, he told her that "one Tongue was enough for a woman." Her reaction against this pronouncement seems to have shaped her life. She accompanied her brother to Oxford, where he studied under the great Anglo-Saxon scholar George Hickes, who encouraged Elizabeth's interest in languages. She went on to learn French, Latin, German, Old English, Old Germanic, Icelandic, and probably Greek and Hebrew.

Her first published translation was the anonymous 1708 *Essay upon Glory*, from the French of Madeleine de Scudéry. In 1709 Elstob published *An English-Saxon Homily on the Birthday of St. Gregory*, which was printed in facing columns with the Old English text on the left and her modern English translation on the right. The illuminated capital letter G, with which both began, matched a portrait of St. Gregory with her own self-portrait. Her preface to this work is a strong argument for women's education.

In 1715 Elstob published *The Rudiments of Grammar for the English-Saxon Tongue*, designed specifically for women, the first Old English grammar written in English rather than in the Latin of male scholarship. For this work Elstob oversaw the creation of a special Old English alphabet, a font called the Elstob Type, which is still a standard for Old English texts. Her preface attacked Jonathan Swift's *Proposal for Correcting, Improving and Ascertaining the English Tongue* (1712), which called for establishing an English Academy, like that in France, to perfect and fix the language. From her knowledge of comparative philology, Elstob argued against Swift's view, at that time conventional, that earlier forms of language were "barbarous"; instead, she showed how they had evolved. In the excerpt included here, she answers his charge that languages with many monosyllabic words were harsh and grating to the ear. Elstob marshals counterexamples of monosyllabic lines from the world's great poets, from Homer and Virgil to Chaucer and later English poets, concluding, ironically, with Swift himself. Although her argument was unacknowledged, Swift's proposal died away.

Elizabeth Elstob (1683–1756)

Both George Hickes and William Elstob died in 1715. Unmarried and without financial resources, Elstob moved to the village of Evesham, living in poverty as proprietress of a dame school. Finally, in 1739, the dowager Duchess of Portland offered her a post as governess, which she held for nearly two decades until her death.

The Rudiments of Grammar for the English-Saxon Tongue (London: W. Bowyer, 1715).

From *The Rudiments of Grammar for the English-Saxon Tongue* (1715)

. . . . To give greater Probability to what I have said concerning Monosyllables, I will give some Instances, as well from such Poets as have gone before him,[1] as those which have succeeded him. It will not be taken amiss by those who value the Judgment of Sir Philip Sydney, and that of Mr. Dryden, if I begin with Father Chaucer.

Er it was Day, as was her won to do.

Again,

And but I have her Mercy and her Grace,
That I may seen her at the leste way;
I nam but deed there nis no more to say.

Again,

Alas, what is this wonder Maladye?
For heate of colde, for colde of heate I dye.
   Chaucer's first Book of *Troylus*, fol. 159. b.[2]

And since we are a united Nation, and he as great a Poet, considering his time, as this Island hath produced, I will with due Veneration for his Memory, beg leave to cite the learned and noble Prelate, Gawen Douglas,[3] Bishop of Dankeld in Scotland, who in his Preface to his judicious and accurate Translation of Virgil, p. 4. says,

Nane is, nor was, nor zit sal be, trowe I,
Had, has, or sal have, sic craft in Poetry:

. . . .

But before, at least contemporary with Chaucer, we find Sir John Gower,[4] not baulking Monosyllables;

Myne herte is well the more glad
To write so as me bad,
And eke my Fear is well the lasse.[5]

. . . .

Again,

Peace is the chefe of al the Worldes Welth,
And to the Heven it ledeth eke the way,
Peace is of Soule and Lyfe the Mannes helth,
Of Pestylence, and doth the Warre away,
My Liege Lord take hede of that I say,
If Warre may be lefte, take Peace on Hande
Which may not be without Goddes Sande★.

. . . .

Let Lydgate,[6] Chaucer's Scholar also be brought in for a Voucher;

For Chaucer that my Master was and knew
What did belong to writing Verse and Prose,
Ne'er stumbled at small faults, nor yet did view
With scornful Eye the Works and Books of those
That in his time did write, nor yet would taunt
At any Man, to fear him or to daunt.

Tho' the Verse is somewhat antiquated, yet the Example ought not to be despised by our modern Criticks, especially those who have any Respect for Chaucer. . . . I will hasten to the Times of greater Politeness, and desire that room may be made, and attention given to a Person of no less Wit than Honour, the Earl of Surrey,[7] who at least had all the Elegancy of a gentle Muse, that may deserve the Praises of our Sex,

Her Praise I tune whose Tongue doth tune the Spheres,[8]
And gets new Muses in her Hearers Ears.
Stars fall to fetch fresh Light from her rich Eyes,
Her bright Brow drives the Sun to Clouds beneath.

★Besides the Purpose for which these Verses are here cited, it may not be amiss to observe from some Instances of Words contain'd in them, how necessary, at least useful, the Knowledge of the Saxon Tongue is, to the right understanding our Old English Poets, and other Writers. For example, . . . Sande, this is a pure Saxon Word, signifying Mission, or being sent. . . .

Elizabeth Elstob (1683–1756)

Again,

O Glass! with too much Joy my Thoughts thou greets.

. . . .

And Michael Drayton,[9] who had a Talent fit to imitate, and to celebrate so great a Genius, of all our English Poets, seems best to have understood the sweet and harmonious placing of Monosyllables, and has practised it with so great a Variety, as discovers in him a peculiar Delight, even to Fondness; for which however, I cannot blame him, notwithstanding this may be reputed the Vice of our Sex, and in him be thought effeminate. But let the Reader judge for himself;

Care draws on Care, Woe comforts Woe again,
Sorrow breeds Sorrow, one Griefe brings forth twaine,
If live or dye, as thou doost, so do I,
If live, I live, and if you dye, I dye;
One Hart, one Love, one Joy, one Griefe, one Troth,
One Good, one Ill, one Life, one Death to both.

. . . .

And to the Countess of Bedford, one of his great Patronesses;

Sweet Lady yet, grace this poore Muse of mine,
Whose Faith, whose Zeal, whose life, whose All is thine.

. . . .

I come now to the incomparable Spencer,[10] against whose Judgment and Practice, I believe scarce any Man will be so bold as to oppose himself;

Assure your self, it fell not all to Ground;
For all so dear as Life is to my Heart,
I deem your Love, and hold me to you bound.

Again,

Go say his Foe thy Shielde with his doth bear.

Afterwards,

More old than Jove, whom thou at first didst breed.

And,

And now the Prey of Fowls in Field he lies.

Nor must Ben. Johnson[11] be forgotten;

Thy Praise or Dispraise is to me alike;
One doth not stroke me, nor the other strike.

Again,

Curst be his Muse, that could lye dumb, or hid
To so true Worth, though thou thy self forbid.

In this Train of Voters for Monosyllables, the inimitable Cowley[12] marches next, whom we must not refuse to hear;

Yet I must on; what Sound is't strikes mine Ear?
    Sure I Fames Trumpet hear.

And a little after,

Come my best Friends, my Books, and lead me on;
    'Tis time that I were gone.
                    . . . .

And in the beginning of the next Ode, he wou'd not certainly have apply'd himself to WIT in the harsh Cadence of Monosyllables, had he thought them so very harsh;

Tell me, O tell, what kind of thing is Wit,
    Thou who Master art of it.
                    . . . .

But did he believe such Concord to be inconsistent with the use of Monosyllables, he had surely banished them from these two Lines; and were I to fetch Testimonies out of his Writings, I might pick a Jury of Twelve out of every Page.

And now comes Mr. Waller,[13] and what does he with his Monosyllables, but,

Give us new Rules, and set our Harp in Tune.

And that honourable Peer whom he commends, the Lord Roscommon thus keeps him in Countenance;

Be what you will, so you be still the same.

And again,

In her full Flight, and when she shou'd be curb'd.
                    . . . .

The next I shall mention is my Lord Orrery,[14] who, as Mr. Anthony Wood says, was a great Poet, Statesman, Soldier, and great every thing which merits the Name of Great and Good. In his Poem to Mrs. Philips, he writes thus;

> For they imperfect Trophies to you raise,
> You deserve Wonder, and they pay but Praise;
> A Praise which is as short of your great due,
> As all which yet have writ come short of you.
>
> . . . .

But having thank'd these noble Lords for their Suffrage, we will proceed to some other Witnesses of Quality: And first I beg leave to appeal to my Lord Duke of Buckinghamshire,[15] in his Translation of The Temple of Death;

> Her Chains were Marks of Honour to the Brave,
> She made a Prince when e'er she made a Slave.

Again,

> By wounding me, she learnt the fatal Art,
> And the first Sigh she had, was from my Heart.

My Lord Hallifax's[16] Muse hath been very indulgent to Monosyllables, and no Son of Apollo will dare to dispute his Authority in this Matter. Speaking of the Death of King Charles the Second, and his Improvement of Navigation, and Shipping; he says,

> To ev'ry Coast, with ready Sails are hurl'd,
> Fill us with Wealth, and with our Fame the World.

Again,

> . . . .

> In Charles, so good a Man and King, we see,
> A double Image of the Deity.
> Oh! Had he more resembled it! Oh why
> Was he not still more like; and cou'd not die?

My Lord Landsdown's[17] Muse, which may claim her Seat in the highest Point of Parnassus, gives us these Instances of her Sentiments in our Favour;

> So own'd by Heaven, less glorious far was he,
> Great God of Verse, than I, thus prais'd by thee.
>
> . . . .

In such noble Company, I imagin Mr. Addison[18] will not be ashamed to appear, thus speaking of Mr. Cowley;

His Turns too closely on the Reader press;
He more had pleas'd us, had he pleas'd us less.

And of Mr. Waller,

Oh had thy Muse not come an Age too soon.

And of Mr. Dryden's Muse,

Whether in Comick Sounds or Tragick Airs
She forms her Voice, she moves our Smiles or Tears.

. . . .

To these let me add the Testimony of that Darling of the Muses, Mr.
Prior,[19] with whom all the Poets of ancient and modern Times of other
Nations, or our own, might seem to have intrusted the chief Secrets, and
greatest Treasures of their Art. I shall speak only concerning our own Island,
where his Imitation of Chaucer, of Spencer, and of the old Scotch Poem,
inscribed the Nut-Brown Maid, shew how great a Master he is. . . .

Me all too mean for such a Task I weet.

Again,

Grasps he the Bolt? we ask, when he has hurl'd the
    Flame.

And,

Nor found they lagg'd too slow, nor slew too fast.

. . . .

The only farther Example of Monosyllabick Verses I shall insert here,
and which I cannot well omit, is what I wou'd desire the Author to apply
to his own Censure of Monosyllables. . . . ;

Then since you now have done your worst,
Pray leave me where you found me first.

*Part of the seventh Epistle of the first Book of Horace imitated, and address'd
to a noble Peer, p. ult.*[20]

After so many Authorities of the Gentlemen, these few Instances from
some of our Female Poets, may I hope be permitted to take place. I will
begin with Mrs. Philips on the Death of the Queen of Bohemia;[21]

Over all Hearts and her own Griefs she reign'd.

And on the Marriage of the Lord Dungannon,

Elizabeth Elstob (1683–1756)

May the vast Sea for your sake quit his Pride,
And grow so smooth, while on his Breast you ride,
As may not only bring you to your Port,
But shew how all things do your Virtues court.

To Gilbert Lord Archbishop of Canterbury,

That the same Wing may over her be cast,
Where the best Church of all the World is plac'd.

Mrs Wharton[22] upon the *Lamentations* of Jeremiah;

Behold those Griefs which no one can repeat,
Her Fall is steep, and all her Foes are great.

And my Lady Winchelsea[23] in her Poem entituled, The Poor Man's
Lamb;

Thus wash'd in Tears, thy Soul as fair does show
As the first Fleece, which on the Lamb does grow.

Sir, from these numerous Instances, out of the Writings of our greatest
and noblest Poets, it is apparent, That had the Enmity against Monosyllables,
with which there are some who make so great a Clamour, been so great in
all Times, we must have been deprived of some of the best Lines, and finest
Flowers, that are to be met with in the beautiful Garden of our English
Posie.

. . . .

Notes

1. That is, Swift.
2. Geoffrey Chaucer, *Troilus and Creseyde*, a narrative poem probably written after
1387.
3. Gavin Douglas (1475?–1522), Scottish translator of Virgil's *Aeneid* as *The XIII
Bukes of the Eneados*. The earliest extant manuscripts date from about 1525.
4. John Gower, author of the English poem *Confessio Amantis* (1390), died in
1408.
5. "And moreover my fear is well the less." The deletions here represent additional
examples from Elstob's copious selections of monosyllabic lines.
6. John Lydgate (1370?–1450?), author of numerous long, moralistic poems.
7. Henry Howard, Earl of Surrey (1517?–1547).
8. In ancient astronomy, spheres were the concentric, transparent globes which
held the sun, the moon, and the planets; as they turned, they were said to make beautiful
music.

9. Michael Drayton (1563–1630) wrote manly lyric, pastoral, and narrative poems, some of which he dedicated to Lucy Harrington Russell, Countess of Bedford (1580?–1627). A favorite of Queen Anne, consort of James I, the Countess was a major literary patron.

10. Edmund Spenser (1552?–1599). The first quotation occurs in Book I, Canto I, stanza 54 of *The Faerie Queen* (1590). Sources of the others have not been located.

11. Ben Jonson, poet and playwright (1573–1637). Elstob quotes from his Epigrams 61 and 63, published in *Works* (1616).

12. Abraham Cowley (1618–1667). The first two quotations are taken from "The Motto," the last from "To Wit," both collected in *Miscellanies* (1656).

13. Edmund Waller (1606–1687), "Upon the Earl of Roscommon's Translation of Horace" (1680), published together with a translation of the "Ars Poetica" by Wentworth Dillon, Fourth Earl of Roscommon (1633?–1685). Lord Roscommon was, ironically, an advocate for an English Academy, whose purpose Elstob's preface attacks. Possibly she cites him to undermine his position, as later she also quotes Swift.

14. Roger Boyle, First Earl of Orrery (1621–1679), who introduced rhymed heroic drama into England with his tragicomedy, *The Generall*, or *Altemira*. Anthony Wood (1632–1695), an English antiquarian and historian of Oxford, published a biographical dictionary of Oxford writers, *Athenae Oxonienses* (1691–1692). Katharine Philips (1631–1664), English poet known as "the Matchless Orinda" (see also n. 21). The Earl of Orrery's eulogy of Philips was published in a 1710 edition of her poems.

15. John Sheffield, First Duke of Buckingham and Normandy (1648–1721). His translation, as "The Temple of Death," of a work by Philippe Habert was published in 1695 with poems by other noblemen. On the title page he is listed as the Duke of Buckinghamshire. "The Temple of Death" was first published in 1673 in *A Collection of Poems Written Upon Several Occasions By Several Persons*.

16. Charles Montagu, Earl of Halifax (1661–1715), "On the Death of His Most Sacred Majesty King Charles II," in *Poems on Several Occasions* (1715).

17. George Granville or Grenville (1667–1735), a poet and dramatist who became the First Baron Lansdowne. His *Poems upon Several Occasions* was published in 1712.

18. Joseph Addison (1672–1719), from "An Account of the Greatest English Poets" (1694).

19. Matthew Prior (1664–1721), diplomat and poet. The first quotation is from "An Ode, Humbly Inscribed to the Queen on the Glorious Success of Her Majesty's Arms, 1706. Written in Imitation of Spencer's Stile." The others are from "Henry and Emma, A Poem, Upon the Model of The Nut-Brown Maid."

20. Swift himself was the author of "Horace Book I. Ode XI. Imitated," later printed in *A New Miscellany In Prose and Verse* (1742).

21. Katharine Philips's poem "On the Death of the Queen of Bohemia" was published in *Poems* by Mrs. K. P., 1664. The two others appeared in the 1667 edition.

22. Anne Wharton (1632–1685), a poet, wrote a metrical paraphrase of the lamentations of Jeremiah, a prophet in the Old Testament; see Jeremiah 4: 19–6:30. The only published version of her works seems to have been included in *Whartoniana; or Miscellanies, in Verse and Prose*. Either Wharton's "Lamentations of Jeremiah" was published anonymously or Elstob knew it in manuscript.

23. Anne Finch, Countess of Winchelsea (1661–1720), whose only collection of poems published in her lifetime came out in 1713.

ELIZA HAYWOOD (1693?–1756)

Eliza Haywood's long, varied and successful literary career began in 1719 with the publication of her erotic novel *Love in Excess; or, the Fatal Inquiry.* Over the next forty years she produced nearly eighty works, including fiction, translations, plays, periodicals, conduct books, and political pamphlets. Her short novels of the 1720s combined the overflowing, rich texture of French romance with a sharp political analysis of everyday problems and dangers for English women in the early eighteenth century. Having begun her public life as a not-so-successful actress in Dublin's Smock Alley Theater, she later wrote and performed in Henry Fielding's Little Theater in the Haymarket.

After Pope lampooned her for her scandal writing in *The Dunciad* (1728), claiming without foundation that her two children were "babes of love," Haywood began to publish anonymously. She began her own publishing company in the 1740s in order to publish her *Anti-Pamela,* a critique of Richardson's *Pamela* emphasizing both the genuine resources and the real dangers facing a servant girl who has conscious class aspirations. In the same decade, Haywood published a monthly periodical for women, *The Female Spectator,* ostensibly written by a committee of female editors but no doubt written entirely by herself. Using as her model Addison and Steele's *Spectator,* Haywood addressed the issue of proper female conduct by interweaving moral essays with elaborate and often scandalous and erotic narratives illustrating the sexual-political dimensions of women's lives. *The History of Miss Betsy Thoughtless* (1751), written late in her career, was reprinted in 1986, but all of Haywood's vast, innovative, sympathetic, and politically engaged work deserves to be reprinted and read seriously today. These excerpts from the first and final issues of *The Female Spectator* place the objectives of this periodical in the contexts of Haywood's career, the dynamics of publishing, and the politics of contemporary taste.

The Female Spectator. In Four Volumes (London: A. Miller, W. Law, and R. Cater, 1775).

From *The Female Spectator* (1744, 1746)

It is very much by the choice we make of subjects for our entertainment, that the refined taste distinguishes itself from the vulgar and more gross. Reading is universally allowed to be one of the most improving as well as agreeable amusements; but then to render it so, one should, among the number of books which are perpetually issuing from the press, endeavour to single out such as promise to be most conducive to those ends. In order to be as little deceived as possible, I, for my own part, love to get as well acquainted as I can with an author, before I run the risk of losing my time in perusing his work; and as I doubt not but most people are of this way of thinking, I shall, in imitation of my learned Brother,[1] of ever precious memory, give some account of what I am, and those concerned with me in this undertaking; and likewise of the chief intent of the Lucubrations hereafter communicated, that the reader, on casting his eye over the four or five first pages, may judge how far the book may, or may not be qualified to entertain him, and either accept, or throw it aside as he thinks proper: And here I promise, that in the pictures I shall give of myself and associates, I will draw no flattering lines, assume no perfection that we are not in reality possessed of, nor attempt to shadow over any defect with an artificial gloss.

As proof of my sincerity, I shall, in the first place, assure him, that for my own part I never was a beauty, and am now very far from being young; (a confession he will find few of my sex ready to make:) I shall also acknowledge, that I have run through as many scenes of vanity and folly as the greatest coquet of them all.—Dress, equipage, and flattery, were the idols of my heart.—I should have thought that day lost, which did not present me with some new opportunity of shewing myself. My life, for some years, was a continued round of what I then called pleasure, and my whole time engrossed by a hurry of promiscuous diversions. But whatever inconveniencies such a manner of conduct has brought upon myself, I have this consolation, to think that the public may reap some benefit from it:—The company I kept was not, indeed, always so well chosen as it ought to have been, for the sake of my own interest or reputation; but then it was general, and by consequence furnished me, not only with the knowledge of many occurrences, which otherwise I had been ignorant of; but also enabled me, when the too great vivacity of my nature became tempered with reflection, to see into the secret springs which gave rise to the actions I had either heard or been witness of;—to judge of the various passions of the human mind, and distinguish those imperceptible degrees by which thcy become masters of the heart, and attain the dominion over reason.—A thousand odd adventures, which, at the time they happened, made slight impression on me, and seemed to dwell no longer on my mind than the wonder they occasioned, now rise forth to my remembrance; with this advantage, that the mystery I then, for want of attention, imagined they contained, is entirely vanished, and I find it easy to account for the cause by the consequence.

With this experience, added to a genius tolerably extensive, and an education more liberal than is ordinarily allowed to persons of my sex, I flattered myself that it might be in my power to be in some measure both useful and entertaining to the public; and this thought was so soothing to those remains of vanity, not yet wholly extinguished in me, that I resolved to pursue it, and immediately began to consider by what method I should be most likely to succeed. To confine myself to any one subject, I knew could please but one kind of taste, and my ambition was to be as universally read as possible. From my observation of human nature, I found that curiosity had more or less a share in every breast; and my business therefore, was to hit this reigning humour in such a manner, as that the gratification it should receive from being made acquainted with other people's affairs, might at the same time teach every one to regulate their own.

Having agreed within myself on this important point, I commenced author, by setting down many things, which being pleasing to myself, I imagined would be so to others; but on examining them the next day, I found an infinite deficiency both in matter and style, and that there was an absolute necessity for me to call in to my assistance such of my acquaintance as were qualified for that purpose. . . .

These three [women] approved my design, assured me of all the help they could afford, and soon gave a proof of it in bringing their several essays; but as the reader, provided the entertainment be agreeable, will not be interested from which quarter it comes, whatever productions I shall be favoured with from these ladies, or any others, I may hereafter correspond with, will be exhibited under the general title of THE FEMALE SPECTATOR. . . .

I would, by no means, however, have what I say be construed into a design of gratifying a vicious propensity of propagating scandal: whoever sits down to read me with this view, will find themselves mistaken; for though I shall bring real facts on the stage, I shall conceal the actors names under such as will be conformable to their characters; my intention being only to expose the vice, not the person. . . .

And now, having said as much as I think needful of this undertaking,

I shall, without being either too greatly confident, or too anxious for the success, submit it to the public censure.

> Of all the passions given us from above,
> The noblest, softest, and the best, is love,

says a justly celebrated poet; and I readily agree that love in itself, when under the direction of reason, harmonizes the soul, and gives it a gentle, generous turn; but I can by no means approve of such definitions of that passion as we find in plays, novels, and romances. In most of these writings, the authors seem to lay out all their art in rendering that character most interesting, which most sets at defiance all the obligations, by the strict observance of which, love alone can become a virtue. They dress their Cupid up in roses, call him the god of soft desires and ever-springing joys, yet at the same time give him the vindictive fury, and the rage of Mars; shew him impatient of controul, and trampling over all the ties of duty, friendship, or natural affection, yet make the motive sanctify the crime. How fatal, how pernicious to a young and unexperienced mind must be such maxims, especially when dressed up in all the pomp of words! The beauty of the expression steals upon the senses, and every mischief, every woe that love occasions, appears a charm.—Those who feel the passion are so far from endeavouring to repel its force, or being ashamed of their attachment, however opposite to reason, that they indulge, and take a pride in turning into ridicule the remonstrances of their most discerning friends. But what is yet more preposterous, and more evidently shews the ill effects of writing in this manner, is, that we often see girls too young either to be addressed to on the score of love, or even to know what is meant by the passion, affect the languishment they read of,—roll their eyes, sigh, fold their arms, neglect every useful learning, and attend to nothing but acquiring the reputation of being enough a woman to know all the pains and delicacies of love. . . .

. . . Many of the subscribers to this undertaking, I am told, complain that I have deviated from the entertaining method I set out with at first;—that since the second or third book I have become more serious;—that I moralize too much, and that I give them too few tales. . . . In the first place, it was necessary to engage the attention of those I endeavoured to reform, by giving them such things as I knew would please them: tales and little stories, to which every one might flatter themselves with being able to find a key, seemed to me the most effectual method, and therefore I began that way, and proceeded by degrees to more grave admonitions. . . .

Eliza Haywood (1693?–1756)

I was obliged to treat them [her readers] with the tenderness of a mother, but not like some mothers, to continue my indulgence to their ruin. The examples I gave of good and bad behaviour, were not merely to divert them, but to inspire them with an ambition of imitating the one, and care to avoid the other.

For this end it was that I chose to assume the name of the FEMALE SPECTATOR, rather than that of Monitor, as thinking the latter, by discovering too plainly my design, might, in a great measure, have frustrated it with the gay and unreflecting, who are indeed those for whom this work was chiefly intended, as standing most in need of it. . . .

But now it is time to quit the spectatorial function, and thank the public for the extraordinary encouragement these lucubrations have received. To those who have favoured us with their correspondence, and who express a desire of having the work continued yet a longer time, our gratitude is particularly due: though on a consultation of our members, it is judged more for the advantage of our reputation to break off while we are in the good graces of the town, than become tedious to any part of it. . . .

Close as we endeavoured to keep the mystery of our little cabal, some gentlemen have at last found means to make a full discovery of it. They will needs have us take up the pen again, and promise to furnish us with a variety of topics yet untouched upon, with this condition, that we admit them as members, and not pretend to the world, that what shall hereafter be produced is wholly of the feminine gender.

We have not yet quite agreed on the preliminaries of this league, but are very apt to believe we shall not differ with them on trifles, especially as one of them is the husband of Mira.[2]

In the mean time, should any one, from this hint, take it in their head, to publish either book or pamphlet, as wrote by the authors of the FEMALE SPECTATOR, it may be depended on, that, whether we do any thing ourselves or not, we shall advertise against whatever shall come out that way, and lay open the imposition.[3]

Notes

1. *The Female Spectator* was published in monthly installments beginning in April 1744 with this installment. Steele had had *The Spectator* characterize himself in number 2.

2. Mira is one of the group of fictional editors Haywood introduces in the first issue.

3. This final installment was published in May 1746.

ELIZABETH COOPER
(fl. 1735–1740)

Elizabeth Cooper compiled one of the first anthologies of English poetry and was the author of two plays. Little is known about her life. All three of her works appeared after she was widowed. She acted the lead role in her first play, *The Rival Widows: or, Fair Libertine* (1735). In her preface to this play, Cooper prided herself on "the Soul of the Piece," a character who "happens, indeed, to be a Woman . . . capable of thinking for herself, and acting on the Principles of Nature and Truth." Cooper's second play, *The Nobleman: or, The Family Quarrel,* was staged in 1736. In the following year Cooper published *The Muses Library,* issued again in 1738 and 1741. Described by Cooper as a "Poetical Chronicle," the anthology contains selections of poetry and biographical sketches of English poets from Langland and Gower to Spenser and Daniel.

Cooper's critical task was to show the progression and development of English poetry from the "Dawning of polite Literature in England" through its continuing pursuit of the "highest Perfection." Concerned as well about the value of a national literature and the progress of the English language, she was influenced by the critical writings of Sidney, Bacon, and Shaftesbury and acknowledged a particular debt to the "generous Assistance" of William Oldys. Cooper placed her work in the context of other scholars who had undertaken "Lives of the Poets," such as Edward Phillips, William Winstanly, and Giles Jacob, but claimed to have corrected some of their mistakes, to have added new material, and ultimately to have completed "one of the most valuable Collections, that ever was made publick." A woman of obvious critical acumen, Cooper had intended to write "some Account of the Progress of Criticism in England," but this volume seems never to have appeared. As one of the first anthologists of English poetry, she is responsible for helping to shape the canon of male writers who have subsequently been credited with the development of a distinctly national English literature.

The Muses Library; Or, A Series of English Poetry (London: James Hodges, 1737).

Elizabeth Cooper (fl. 1735–1740)

Preface to *The Muses Library* (1737)

We are all apt to make our own Opinions, the Standard of Excellency, and I must plead guilty to my Share of this general Weakness: What has given me Pleasure in my Closet, I have undertaken to recommend to the Publick; not presuming to inform the Judgment, but only awaken the Attention; and rather endeavouring to preserve what is valuable of others, than advance any thing of my own.—The mere Hint of a good-natur'd, and not unuseful Design, is all the Merit I can pretend to.—'Tis true I attempt to clear the Ground, and lay in the Materials, but leave the Building to be rais'd, and finish'd by more masterly Hands.

What is said of the Nightengle's singing with her Breast against a Thorn, may be justly apply'd to the Poets.—Their Harmony gives Pleasure to Others, but is compos'd with Pain to Themselves: And what is not to gratify a real Want, or fashionable Luxury, Few care to purchase: Thus Poetry has been, almost universally, a Drug, and its Authors have sacrific'd the *Substance* of present Life to the *Shadow* of future Fame. Fame, Fame alone they have fondly fancy'd an Equivalent for all they wanted beside, and the World has often been so malicious, or careless, as even to defeat them of that imaginary Good.—I am told, Time and Ignorance have devour'd many important Names which even the universal Languages flatter'd with a sure Immortality: 'Tis no Wonder, therefore, that Ours, rude, and barbarous, as it formerly was, should be so little able to defend its Authors from such incroaching Enemies.—Those, who read the ensuing Volume with Attention, will be convinc'd that Sense, and Genius have been of long standing in this Island; and 'tis not so much the Fault of our Writers, as the Language it self, that they are not read with Pleasure at this Day.—This, naturally, provokes an Enquiry, whether 'tis in the same Vagrant Condition still; or whether the Fame of our most admir'd Moderns, is not almost as precarious, as that of their now-obsolete Predecessors has prov'd to be; agreable to that Line in the celebrated *Essay on Criticism*.

And what now *Chaucer* is, shall *Dryden* be.[1]

If this is the Case, as, according to my little Knowledge, I think there is some Reason to fear, is it not high Time to think of some Expedient to cure this Evil; and secure the Poet in his Idol-Reputation however? I don't take upon me to say that Learning is of as much Importance here, as in *France;* or that we shou'd be at the Trouble, and Expence of a Publick Academy for the Improvement of our Language;[2] But, if any slight Essay can be made towards it, which, at a small Expence, may make a shift to supply that Defect, till a better Scheme shall be found, 'tis humbly hop'd that a moderate Encouragement will not be wanting.

Such, to the best of my poor Ability, is now presented to the Publick, a Sort of *Poetical Chronicle:* which begins with the first Dawning of polite Literature in England, and is propos'd to be continu'd to the highest Perfection, it has hitherto attain'd; That, in Spite of Difficulties, and Discouragements, it may be hardly possible for us to recede into our first Barbarism; or again lose sight of the true Point of Excellence, which Poetry, beyond all other Sciences, makes its peculiar Glory to aim at.

Of what real Value polite Literature is to a Nation, is too sublime a Task for me to meddle with; I therefore chuse to refer my Readers to their own Experience, and the admirable Writings of Sir Philip Sidney, Lord Bacon, Lord Shaftsbury, and innumerable other elegant Authors; the joint Sentiment of all the refin'd Spirits that ever had a Being, and the following excellent Rapture, in particular, of the ingenious Mr. Daniel, in his Poem call'd *Musophilus*.[3]

> Perhaps the Words, thou scornest now,
> May live, the speaking Picture of the Mind,
> The Extract of the Soul, that labour'd, how
> To leave the Image of herself behind;
> Wherein Posterity, that love to know,
> The just Proportion of our Spirits may find.
>   For these Lines are the Veins, the Arteries,
> And undecaying Life-Strings of those Hearts
> That still shall pant, and still shall exercise
> The Motion, Spirit and Nature both imparts
> And shall, with those alive so sympathize,
> As, nourisht with their Powers, injoy their parts.
>   O blessed Letters, that combine in One
> All Ages past, and make One live with All:
> By you, we doe conferr with who are gone,
> And the Dead-Living unto Council call:
> By you, th' Unborne shall have Communion
> Of what we feel, and what doth us befall.
>   Soul of the World! Knowledge! without thee,
> What hath the Earth, that truly glorious is?
> Why should our Pride make such a Stir to be,
> To be forgot? What good is like to this,
> To doe worthy the Writing, and to write
> Worthy the Reading, and the World's Delight?

Elizabeth Cooper (fl. 1735–1740)

And afterwards, alluding to *Stone-Henge* on Salisbury Plain.

And whereto serves that wondrous *Trophy* now,
That on the goodly Plaine, near *Wilton* stands?
That huge, dumb Heap, that cannot tell us how,
Nor what, nor whence it is, nor with whose Hands,
Nor for whose Glory, it was set to shew
How much our Pride mocks that of other Lands?
Whereon, when as the gazing Passenger
Hath greedy look't with Admiration,
And fain would know his Birth, and what he were,
How there erected, and how long agone;
Enquires, and asks his Fellow-Traveller,
What he hath heard, and his Opinion:
And he knowes nothing. Then he turns again,
And looks, and sighs, and then admires afresh,
And in himselfe, with Sorrow, doth complain
The Misery of dark Forgetfulness:
Angry with *Time* that nothing should remain,
Our greatest Wonder's Wonder to express!

But, to wave any farther Authorities, we need only look back to the Days of *Langland*, the first *English* Poet we can meet with, who employ'd his Muse for the Refinement of Manners, and, in the Rudeness of his Lines, we plainly discover the Rudeness of the Age he wrote in.—Chaucer, not the next Writer, tho' the next extraordinary Genius, encountered the Follies of Mankind, as well as their Vices, and blended the acutest Raillery, with the most insinuating Humour.—By his Writings, it plainly appears that Poetry, and Politeness grew up together; and had like to have been bury'd in his Grave; For War, and Faction, immediately after restor'd Ignorance, and Dulness almost to their antient Authority. Writers there were; but Tast, Judgment, and Manner were lost: Their Works were cloudy as the Times they liv'd in, and, till Barclay, and Skelton, there was scarce a Hope that Knowledge would ever favour us with a second Dawn.—But soon after these, Lord Surrey, having tasted of the Italian Delicacy, naturaliz'd it here, gave us an Idea of refin'd Gallantry, and taught Love to polish us into Virtue.—Before this Impression was worn off, Lord Buckhurst arose, and introduc'd the Charms of Allegory, and Fable, to allure Greatness, into a Love of Humanity, and make Power the Servant of Justice: Spencer made a Noble Use of so fine a Model, overflowing with Tenderness, Courtesy, and Benevolence, reconciling Magnificence and Decorum, Love and Fidelity; and, together with Fairfax, opening to us a new World of Ornament, Elegance, and Taste:

After these Lord Brook, and Sir John Davis corrected the Luxuriancy of Fable, inrich'd our Understandings with the deepest Knowledge, and distinguished Use from Ostentation, Learning from Pedantry—Donne, and Corbet added Wit to Satire, and restor'd the almost forgotten Way of making Reproof it self entertaining; Carew, and Waller taught Panegyrick to be delicate, Passion to be courtly, and rode the Pegasus of Wit, with the Curb of good Manners; D'Avenant blended Address and Politeness with the severest Lessons of Temperance, and Morality; and the divine Milton reconcil'd the Graces of them all, and added a Strength, Solidity, and Majesty of his own, that None can equal, Few can imitate, and All admire.[4]

So many and variously-accomplish'd Minds were necessary to remove the *Gothique* Rudeness that was handed down to us by our unpolish'd Fore-Fathers; and, I think, 'tis manifest all the Ornaments of Humanity, are owing to our Poetical Writers, if not our most shining Virtues. 'Tis not reasonable, therefore, that while the Work remains, the Artist should be forgot; and yet, 'tis certain, very Few of these great Men are generally known to the present Age: And tho' Chaucer, and Spencer are ever nam'd with much Respect, not many are intimately acquainted with their Beauties.—The Monumental Statues of the Dead have, in all Ages, and Nations, been esteem'd sacred; but the Writings of the Learned, of all others, deserve the highest Veneration; The Last bear the Resemblance of the Soul, the First only of the Body. The First are dumb, inanimate, and require the Historian to explain them; while the Last live, converse, reason, instruct, and afford to the Contemplative, one of their sincerest Pleasures. They are likewise to Authors, what Actions are to Heroes; In His Annals you must admire the one, in his Studies the other; and an elegant Poem should be as lasting a Memorial of the Scholar's Wit, as a pompous Trophy of the General's Conduct, or the Soldier's Valour. And yet, for want of certain periodical Reviews of the Learning of former Ages, not only many inestimable Pieces have been lost, but Science it self has been in the most imminent Danger.

I have often thought there is a Kind of Contagion in Minds, as well as Bodies; what we admire, we fondly wish to imitate; and, thus, while a Few excellent Authors throw a Glory on the Studies they pursue, Disciples will not be wanting to imitate them: But, when those Studies fall into Disesteem, and Neglect, instead of being profess'd, or encourag'd, 'tis more than probable they will not be understood. I have read 'twas thus in Greece, and Rome, and all the considerable Nations of Europe beside: In England 'tis notorious; and I wish our share of Reproach on this Head, may be confin'd to the Ignorance, and Inhumanity of former Times.

'Tis true, not only every Age, but every Year produces Numbers of new

Pieces, and 'twould be impossible to preserve them all; neither indeed, would all deserve it: But should we govern our Choice with Judgment, and Impartiality, the Task would be easy, and every good Author would receive the Benefit of it.—'Twill be in vain to object that Merit is its own Preservative; For, beside Numberless other Instances, most of the Poems in this Volume are a Proof to the contrary, and still many more that I have reserv'd for the next. Yet, let them be enquir'd for among the Booksellers, and the Difficulty of procuring them will be a sufficient Proof how little they are known, and how near they are to be lost in Oblivion.—This I am a Witness of my self, and 'tis with great Trouble and Charge, I have been able to collect a sufficient Number for my present Purpose: Nor, without the generous Assistance of the Candid Mr. Oldys,[5] would even this, have been in my Power: And, after all, there are still some omitted; which, if I can procure, shall be annex'd by way of Supplement, together with a Glossary, at the End of the Work.

Let me then, at least, be pardon'd for attempting to set up a Bulwark between Time, and Merit? I have heard that a certain modern Virtuoso, had a Project to discover the Age of the World, by the Saltness of the Sea, the Effect of which could not be known for Hundreds of Years after. I flatter my self, that the Success of mine need not be quite so far remov'd; nor is it more Romantick, or less Useful. The Alterations of a Language are of some Consequence to be known, tho' inferior to those of Nature; and 'tis some Satisfaction to be acquainted with the Lives of Authors, as well as their Works: This Undertaking includes all, nor is merely calculated for those which are already Obsolete; but, if it can be suppos'd that any of the Moderns would ever be in the same Danger, or any future Writer should do me the Honour to continue the Series, may prove some little Support even to Them. In a Word, it may serve as a perpetual Index to our Poetry, a Test of all foreign Innovations in our Language, a general Register of all the little, occasional Pieces, of our Holy-Day Writers (as Mr. Dryden prettily calls them) which might otherwise be lost; and a grateful Record of all the Patrons that, in *England*, have done Honour to the *Muses*.

Before I conclude, 'tis my Duty to acknowledge that no less than Three* Writers have undertaken, simply, the Lives of the Poets, beside Mr. Wood, who confines himself to those educated at Oxford; That Sir Thomas Pope Blunt, has wrote Remarks on a Few of them,[6] and Two or Three have had their Works republish'd in our own Times; what use I have made of all, or any of these Circumstances, will be obvious; as well as what is peculiarly my own.—This, however, I may, with Modesty, hint, that many Mistakes

*Mr. Phillips, Mr. Winstanly and Mr. Jacob.[7]

in Facts are rectify'd, several Lives are added, the Characters of the Authors are not taken on Content, or from Authority, but a serious Examination of their Works; and some of the most beautiful Passages, or entire Poems, I could chuse, are added to constitute a *Series of Poetry* (which has never been aim'd at any where else) and compleat one of the most valuable Collections, that ever was made publick.

How far I have succeeded, is submitted to the Understanding of every impartial, and sensible Reader: To which I the more cheerfully resign my self, as introducing more Beauties of others, to be my Advocates, than I can have Faults of my own to be forgiven.

To what has been said, on the Design of this Work in General, I, at first, intended to add some Account of the Progress of Criticism in *England*; from Sir Philip Sidney, the Art of *English* Poesy (written by Mr. Puttenham, a Gentleman Pensioner to Queen Elizabeth:) Sir John Harrington, Ben Johnson, &c.[8] But this part of my Task I am oblig'd to postpone, for want of Room, to my next Volume; and shall conclude with rectifying a Mistake of my own in the Life of Mr. Fairfax: Where 'tis said; that Author is crouded by Mr. Philips into his Supplement, which should have been said of Mr. Sacville:[9] And begging Pardon for the *Errata* which have escap'd me, not thro' neglect, but want of sufficient Experience in Affairs of this Nature.

Notes

1. Alexander Pope, *An Essay on Criticism* (1711), 1.483. The actual line reads: "And such as Chaucer is, shall Dryden be."

2. The Académie Française, founded in 1635, was established to preserve the highest linguistic and literary standards for the French language.

3. Sir Philip Sidney, poet and critic (1554–1586); Francis Bacon, philosopher, statesman, and writer (1561–1626); Anthony Ashley Cooper, Third Earl of Shaftesbury, philosopher and writer (1671–1713); Samuel Daniel, poet, dramatist, and critic (1563–1619). Daniel's "Musophilus: Containing a generall defence of learning" appeared in 1599.

4. The English writers mentioned in this paragraph include William Langland (fl. 1360–1387); Geoffrey Chaucer (c. 1343–1400); Alexander Barclay (1475?–1552); John Skelton (1460?–1529); Henry Howard, Earl of Surrey (1517?–1547); Thomas Sackville, First Earl of Dorset and Baron Buckhurst (1536–1608); Edmund Spenser (1552?–1599); Edward Fairfax (1568?–1635); Sir Fulke Greville, First Baron Brooke (1554–1628); Sir John Davies (1569–1626); John Donne (1572–1631); Richard Corbet (1582–1635); Thomas Carew (1595?–1640); Edmund Waller (1606–1687); Sir William D'Avenant (1606–1668); John Milton (1608–1674).

5. William Oldys (1696–1761), antiquary and editor, general editor of *Biographia Britannica* (6 vols., 1747–1766).

6. Anthony Wood (1632–1695), historian and antiquary, published *Athenae Oxonienses* (1691–1692), a biographical dictionary of Oxford writers and bishops; Sir Thomas Pope Blount (1649–1697), author, politician, compiler; published several volumes of bibliographical and literary works.

7. Edward Phillips (1630–1696?), editor, compiled *Theatrum Poetarum* (1675), a collection of literary biographies; William Winstanley (1628?–1698), compiler, published *Lives of the most famous English Poets* (1687); Giles Jacob (1686–1744), compiler, published the *Poetical Register, or Lives and Characters of the English Dramatic Poets* (2 vols., 1719–1720).

8. Sir John Harrington, translator and poet (c. 1561–1612); Ben Jonson, dramatist and poet (1572–1637).

9. Thomas Sackville, First Earl of Dorset, poet and statesman (1536–1608).

SARAH FIELDING (1710–1768)

SARAH FIELDING's mother died when she was eight years old. When her father was remarried to a Roman Catholic, Sarah and her five siblings were dispersed to various schools and relatives. In 1722, her maternal grandmother, Lady Gould, petitioned for custody of the children and control over their estate. It is through this court case and through the fame of her elder brother Henry that we know much of what we do about Sarah.

With her three sisters, Sarah Fielding grew up and attended boarding school in Salisbury, where she met Jane Collier, with whom she later collaborated on *The Cry* (1754). She taught herself Latin and Greek and was well read in a variety of subjects. In the 1740s she lived in London, where she became acquainted with many literary figures, including Samuel Richardson, Elizabeth Carter, and Sarah Scott. In poor health and with little money of her own, she stayed frequently with friends and family members, finally settling in Bath toward the end of her life; she died there in 1768.

Fielding was particularly concerned with the responses of readers; the possibility of misinterpretation and its consequences inform much of her work. The innocent hero of *The Adventures of David Simple* (1744) is methodically introduced to a string of social pretenders, including literary critics, and the novel is peppered with misread relationships. In the preface to *The History of the Countess of Dellwyn* (1759), Fielding lays out the responsibility not only of the writer but also of the audience. In *Remarks on Clarissa* (1749) she argues the importance of authorial intent and champions both the misunderstood Clarissa and her creator. And in *The Cry*, a mixture of allegory, philosophy, literary criticism, and romance, Fielding and Collier make an extended attempt to educate an ideal reader. *The Cry* depicts a narrow-minded reading public, such as the one described in the prologue to Part III, which is too envious of others' accomplishments to be able to benefit from them. These readers sit in judgment of Portia, who, in the course of relating her life, also tries, if unsuccessfully, to force them to be more discerning readers.

The Adventures of David Simple (London: A. Millar, 1744); *Remarks on Clarissa* (1749; rpt. Los Angeles: Augustan Reprint Society/William Andrews Clark Memorial Library, 1985); *The Cry* (1754; rpt. Delmar, N.Y.: Scholars' Facsimiles and Reprints, 1986); *The History of the Countess of Dellwyn* (1759; rpt. New York: Garland, 1974).

From *The Adventures of David Simple* (1744)

BOOK II, CHAPTER II
Which contains a Conversation, in which is proved, how high Taste may be carried by People who have fixed Resolutions of being Criticks

When David was alone, he began to reflect with himself, what could be the meaning that Mr. Spatter seemed to take such a Delight in *abusing* People; and yet as he observed, no one was more willing to oblige any Person, who stood in need of his Assistance: he concluded that he must be good at the Bottom, and that perhaps it was only his *Love of Mankind*, which made him have such a Hatred and Detestation of their Vices, as caused him to be eager in reproaching them; he therefore resolved to go on with him, till he knew more of his Disposition.

The next Day they went to visit a Lady, who was reputed to have a great deal of Wit, and was so *generous as to let all her Acquaintance partake of it, by omitting no Opportunity of displaying it.* There they found assembled a large Company of Ladies, and two or three Gentlemen; they were all busy in Discourse, but they rose up, paid the usual Compliments, and then proceeded as follows:

First Lady. "Indeed, Madam, I think you are quite in the right, as to your Opinion of Othello; for nothing provokes me so much, as to see Fools *pity a Fellow*, who could *murder* his *Wife*. For my part, I cannot help having some Compassion for *her*, though she does not deserve it, because she was such a Fool as to marry a *filthy Black*. Pray, did you ever hear any thing like what my Lady True-wit said the other Night, that the Part of the Play which chiefly affected her, was, that which inspired an Apprehension of what that *odious Wretch* must feel, when he found out that Desdemona was innocent; as if he could suffer too much, after being guilty of so barbarous an Action."

Second Lady. "Indeed, I am not at all surprized at any thing that Lady True-wit says; for I have heard her assert the most preposterous things in the World: Nay, she affirms, a Man may be very fond of a Woman, notwithstanding he is jealous of her, and *dares suspect her Virtue*."

Third Lady. "That Lady once said, that one of the most beautiful Incidents in all *King Lear* was, that the Impertinence of his Daughter's Servant, was the first Thing that made him uneasy; and after that, I think one can wonder at nothing: For certainly it was a great Oversight in the Poet, when he was writing the Character of a King, to take notice of the Behaviour of such *vulgar Wretches*; as if what they did was any thing to the purpose. But some People are very fond of turning the greatest Faults into Beauties, that they may be thought to have found out something extraordinary: And then they must admire every thing in Shakespear, as they think, to prove their own Judgment: But for my part, I am not afraid to give *my Opinion* freely of the greatest Men that ever wrote."

Fourth Lady. "There is nothing so surprizing to me, as the Absurdity of almost every body I meet with; they can't even laugh or cry in the right place. Perhaps it will be hardly believed, but I really saw People in the Boxes last Night, at the Tragedy of *Cato* set with dry Eyes, and show no kind of Emotion, when that *great Man* fell on his *Sword*; nor was it at all owing to any *Firmness of Mind*, that made them incapable of crying neither, for that I should have *admired*. But I have known those very *People* shed tears at *George Barnwell*."[1]

A good many Ladies speak at one time. "Oh intolerable! cry for an *odious Apprentice-Boy*, who murdered his Uncle, at the Instigation too of a common Woman, and yet be unmoved, *when even* Cato *bled for his Country*."

Old Lady. "That is no Wonder, I assure you Ladies, for I once heard my Lady Know-all, positively affirm *George Barnwell* to be one of the best Things that ever was wrote; for that Nature is Nature in whatever Station it is placed: And that she could be as much affected with the Distress of a Man in *low Life*, as if he was a *Lord* or a *Duke*. And what is yet more *amazing*, is, that the Time she chuses to weep most, is just as he has killed the Man who prays for him in the Agonies of Death: And then, only because he *whines over him*, and seems sensible of what he has done, she must shed tears for a *Wretch*, whom every body of either *Sense* or *Goodness*, would wish to crush, and make ten times more miserable than he is."

A Lady who had been silent, and was a particular Friend of Lady Know-all's, *speaks.* "Indeed that Lady is the most affected Creature that I ever knew, she and Lady True-wit think no one can equal them; they have taken a fancy to set up the Author of *George Barnwell* for a Writer, tho' certainly he writes the *worst Language* in the World: There is a little Thing of his, called, *The Fatal Curiosity*,[2] which, for my part, I know not what to make of; and they run about crying it up, as if Shakespear himself might have wrote it. Certainly that Fellow must be something very *low*, for his Distresses always arise from *Poverty*; and then he brings his wicked Wretches, who are to be tempted for Money to some monstrous Action, which he would have his Audience pity them for."

She would have talked on more in this Strain, but was interrupted by another Lady, who assured the Company, she had the most ridiculous Thing to tell them of the two Ladies they were talking of, in the World: "For, (continued she) I was once at *Don Sebastian*[3] with them, which is a favourite Play of their's; and they make a great Noise about the Scene between Dorax and Sebastian, in the fourth Act. I observed them more than the Play, to see in what manner they behaved: And what do you think they did? Why truly, all the time the Two Friends were quarrelling, they sat, indeed, with great Attention, altho' they were quite calm; but the Moment they were reconciled, and embraced each other, they both burst into a Flood of Tears, which they seemed unable to restrain. They certainly must have something very *odd* in their Heads, and the Author is very much obliged to them, for grieving most when his *Hero*, Don Sebastian, had most Reason to be pleased, in finding a true *Friend* in the Man he thought his *Enemy*."

Here the whole Company fell into a violent Fit of Laughter, and the Word *ridiculous* was the only Sound heard for some time; and then they fell back again to their Discourse on Authors, in which they were all so desirous to prove their own Judgment, that they would not give one another leave to speak.

And now, Reader, if ever you have lived in the Country, and heard the Cackling of Geese, or the Gobbling of Turkeys, you may have an Idea something adequate to this Scene; but if the Town has been mostly your Place of Abode, and you are a Stranger to every rural Scene, what will give you the best Idea of this Conversation is the 'Change at Noon, where every one has a particular Business of his own, but a *Spectator* would find it a very difficult matter to comprehend any thing distinctly. Addison, Prior, Otway, Congreve, Dryden, Pope, Shakespear, Tom Durfey[4] &c. &c. &c. were Names all heard between whiles, tho' no one could tell who spoke them, or whether they were mention'd with Approbation or Dislike. The words *Genius*,—and *no Genius*;—*Invention*,—*Poetry*,—*fine Things*,—*bad Language*,—*no Style*,— *charming Writing*,—*Imagery*—and *Diction* with many more Expressions which swim on the *Surface* of *Criticism*, seem'd to have been caught by those *Fishers for the Reputation of Wit*, tho' they were intirely ignorant what Use to make of them, or how to apply them properly: But as soon as the Noise grew loud, and the whole Company were engaged in admiring their own *Sentiments* so much, that they observed nothing else, David made a Sign to his Companion, and they left the Room, and went home; but were, for some

time, in the Condition of Men just escaped from a Shipwreck, who tho'
they rejoice in their Safety, yet is there such an Impression left on them by
the Bellowing of the Waves, the Cursing and Swearing of some of the Sail-
ors, the Crying and Praying of others, with the Roaring of the Winds, that
it is some time before they can come to their Senses. But as soon as David
could recover himself enough to speak coherently, he told the Gentleman,
"He had now shewn him what had surprized him more than any thing he
ever saw before; for he could comprehend what it was People pursued who
spent their time in Gaming, but he could not find out what were the
Schemes of this last Set of Company, nor what could possibly make so many
People eager about *nothing*; for what was it to them who writ best or worst,
or how could they make any Dispute about it, since the only Way of writing
well was to draw all the Characters from Nature, and to affect the Passions
in such a manner, as that the *Distresses* of the Good should move Compassion, and the Amiableness of their Actions incite Men to imitate them; while
the *Vices* of the Bad stirred up Indignation and Rage, and made Men fly
their Foot-steps: That this was the only kind of Writing useful to Mankind,
tho' there might be Embellishments, and Flights of Imagination, to amuse
and divert the Reader." His Companion was quite peevish with him, (*which
was no hard matter for him to be*) to find him always going on with his *Goodness—Usefulness,*—and *Morality.*—However, at last he fell a-laughing, and
told him, "He was much mistaken, if he thought any of them troubled their
Heads at all about the Authors, or ever took the least Pleasure in reading
them; nay, half of them *had not read* the Books they talk'd of; but they are
(said he) a Set of People, who place their whole *Happiness* in the *Reputation
of Wit and Sense*, and consequently all their Conversation turns on what
they think will establish that *Character*; and they are the most inveterate
Enemies to any Person they imagine has more Reputation that way than
themselves."

From *Remarks on Clarissa* (1749)

The next Scene of Criticism (if I may so call it) on *Clarissa* that I was
present at, was on the Publication of the two succeeding Volumes.

The same Company met, with the Addition only of one Gentleman,
whom I shall call Bellario; his known Taste and Impartiality made all those
who wished Reason instead of Prejudice might judge of the Subject before
them, rejoice at his Presence. The Objections now arose so fast, it was impossible to guess where they would end. Clarissa herself was a Prude—a

Coquet—all the Contradictions mentioned some Time ago in a printed Paper,[1] with the Addition of many more, were laid to her Charge. She was an undutiful Daughter—too strict in her Principles of Obedience to such Parents—too fond of a Rake and a Libertine—her Heart was as impenitrable and unsusceptible of Affection, as the hardest Marble. In short, the many contradictory Faults that she was at once accused of, is almost incredible: So many, that those who had attended enough to her Character, to have an Inclination to justify her, found it difficult to know where to begin to answer such a complicated Charge. But after a short Silence, Miss Gibson, with her usual Penetration, said;

"Whenever any Person is accused of a Variety of Faults, which are plainly impossible to dwell in the same Mind, I am immediately convinced the Person so accused is innocent of them all. A Prude cannot, by an observing Eye, be taken for a Coquet, nor a Coquet for a Prude, but a good Woman may be called either, or both, according to the Dispositions of her resolved Censurers; and hence I believe we may trace the Cause, why the Characters even of those Persons who do not endeavour to wear any Disguise are so very liable to be mistaken; for Partiality or Prejudice generally sit as Judges: If the former mount the Judgment-seat, how many different Terms do we make use of to express that Goodness in another, which our own fluctuating Imaginations only have erected? If the latter, how do we vary Expressions to paint that Wickedness which we are resolve to prove inhabits the Mind we think proper to condemn?" "Nay, but (said Mr. Dellincourt) how are we concerned either to justify or accuse Clarissa? we cannot be either partial to, or prejudised against her." "I know not how it is, (replyed Miss Gibson) but those who dread Censure, tho' Circumspection wait on every Step, will be censured, till there no longer remains in the World any of those Dispositions that delight in inflicting that Punishment on others they see they most fear. Now, tho' Clarissa was not so blameably fearful of Censure, but that her first Care was to preserve the Innocence of her own Mind, and do no wrong; yet it is plain, she would very gladly have avoided incurring, as well as deserving, Reproach; and that she is treated like an intimate Acquaintance by all her Readers, the Author may thank himself for. I dare say, the Authors of *Cassandra*, *Clelia*,[2] with numberless others I could name, were never in any Danger of having their Heroines thought on, or treated like human Creatures."

Bellario, who had hitherto been silent, said, "He thought Clarissa could not justly be accused of any material Fault, but that of wanting Affection for her Lover; for that he was sure, a Woman whose Mind was incapable of

Love, could not be amiable, nor have any of those gentle Qualities which chiefly adorn the female Character. And as to her whining after her Papa and Mamma, who had used her so cruelly, (added he) I think 'tis contemptible in her."

"But, Sir, (said Miss Gibson) please only to consider, first, Clarissa is accused of want of Love, and then in a Moment she is condemned for not being able suddenly to tear from her Bosom an Affection that had been daily growing and improving from the Time of her Birth, and this built on the greatest paternal Indulgence imaginable. Affections that have taken such deep Root, are little Treasures hoarded up in the good Mind, and cannot be torn thence without causing the strongest convulsive Pangs in the Heart, where they have been long nourished: And when they are so very easily given up as you now, Sir, seem to contend for, I confess I am very apt to suspect they have only been talked of by the Persons who can part with them with so little Pain, either from Hypocrisy, or from another very obvious Cause, namely, the using Words we are accustomed to hear, without so much as thinking of their Meaning. Such Hearts I think may be much more properly compared to the Hardness of Marble, than could that of the gentle Clarissa.

"There is in her Behaviour, I own, a good deal of apparent Indifference to Lovelace; but let her Situation and his manner of treating her be considered, and I fancy the whole will be seen in a different Light from what it may appear on the first View. She has confessed to Miss Howe, that she could prefer him to all the Men she ever saw; and that Friend of her Heart, to whom her very inmost Thoughts were laid open all along, pronounces her to be in Love with him. It is not from Hypocrisy that she does not confess the Charge, but from the Reason Miss Howe gives, when she says;

> I believe you did not intend Reserve to me, for two Reasons, I believe you did not; first, because you say you did not: Next, because you have not as yet been able to convince yourself how it is to be with you; and, persecuted as you are, how so to separate the Effects that spring from the two Causes (Persecution and Love) as to give to each its particular Due.

"That Clarissa positively did not intend to go off with Lovelace when she met him, to me is very plain; nor could he have prevailed on her, had not the Terrors raised in her Mind, by apprehended Murder, almost robbed her of her Senses, and hurried her away, not knowing what she did. For the Truth of this, I appeal to that charming painted Scene, where the Reader's Mind shares Clarissa's Terror, and is kept in one continued Tumult til.

Sarah Fielding (1710–1768)

*The Steeds are smote, the rapid Chariot flies,
The sudden Clouds of circuling Dust arise.

"She was vexed to her soul afterwards to find she was tricked, as she calls it, out of herself, when Lovelace, instead of comforting and assuring her Mind, begins such a Train of shufling artful Tricks, as no one but Lovelace could have thought on: And altho' she did not know all his Design, for if she had, she would certainly have left him, yet she sees enough of his *crooked ways*, to be convinced that he acted ungenerously by her, because she was in *his Power*. Does not Lovelace, in a Letter to Belford, writ in four Days after she was with him, say?

> And do I not see, that I shall want nothing but Patience, in order to have all Power with me? For what shall we say, if all these Complaints of a Character wounded, these Declarations of increasing Regrets of meeting me, of Resentments never to be got over for my seducing her away, these angry Commands to leave her,—what shall we say, if all were to mean nothing but Matrimony?—And what if my forbearing to enter upon that Subject comes out to be the true Cause of her Petulance and Uneasiness.

"And then he gives such an Account of his asking her Consent to marry him, and at the same Time artfully confusing her, so as to prevent her Consent, as perfectly paints his cunning vile Heart. How is her Behaviour altered to him from the Time she can write Miss Howe word that her Prospects are mended, till his returning Shufling convinces her there is no Confidence to be placed in him! But if, Sir, you cannot think Lovelace's Usage of Clarissa a full Justification of her in this Point, I think the Author has a just Right to be heard out before his Heroine is condemned in so heavy a Charge, as that of being void of all Affection. You know enough of my Sentiments, Sir, to be convinced that I do think this the heaviest Charge a Woman can be accused of; for Love is the only Passion I should wish to be harboured in the gentle Bosom of a good Woman. Ambition, with all the Train of turbulent Passions the World is infested with, I would leave to Men: And could I make my whole Sex of my Opinion, they would be resigned without the least Grudge or Envy; for Peace and Harmony dwell not with them, but on the contrary, Discord, Perturbation and Misery are their constant Companions. But tho' I speak thus with the utmost Sincerity of Love; yet I cannot think a Woman greatly the Object of Esteem, who, like Serina in the *Orphan*,[3] having such a Father as Acasto, and such

*Pope's Homer.

Brothers, affectionate to her, however blameable in other Respects; while she saw her whole Family distressed and confused, and Monimia, the gentle Companion of her Infancy, involved in that Confusion, her Lover too behaving like a Mad-man, yet still, could cry out,

> Chamont's the dearest thing I have on Earth;
> Give me Chamont, and let the World forsake me.

"Clarissa would have acted a different Part, I do confess; and yet, if I can guess any Thing of the Author's Intention by what is already published, I fancy, when we have read the Conclusion of this Story, we shall be convinced that Love was the strongest Characteristic of Clarissa's Mind."

Bellario answered, with that Candor, which is known to be one of the most distinguishing Marks of his Character by all who have the Pleasure of his Acquaintance, 'That if it proved so, he should 'have the greatest Esteem and highest Veneration for Clarissa, and would suspend his Judgment till he saw the remaining Part of the Story.'

From *The Cry* (with Jane Collier, 1754)

[Portia describes a girl consumed with the trappings of romance conventions, though not with love for any particular person.]

This young lady had taken a great fancy to shell-work, and was indulging that fancy by forming a little grotto at the end of the garden. She had always just finish'd something new whenever Philander paid his visits, and willing to entertain him with the sight of this agreeable grotto, thither she leads him.

And now behold the goddess seated on her throne, the work of her own fair hands, fill'd with the imagination of her own charms, receiving the adulation of her worshipper. Philander profusely pours forth his angels and his goddesses; makes himself the humblest of her slaves; petitions at the shrine of her altar for some distant hint of her favour, which by small degrees she grants him, 'till his task is done, 'till his number of flattering speeches are run out; and when the weather-glass of the lady's vanity is swell'd to the top, then is she persuaded into what she calls a rational affection. For she could not be *mean* enough to like a man before he had made use of such persuasion: but now is she perfectly satisfied to be most violently in love with him, and from that day forward, admits it reasonable to set no bounds to her fondness.

From the time that Portia began to describe the goddess on her throne, with her adoring lover at her feet, a sympathizing pleasure overspread the countenances of the female part of the Cry: but when she dropp'd the description and was proceeding with her own observations, their brows were again knit into their usual discontent, and Portia thus went on.

Strange absurdity! Strange language this of angel and of goddess! An adulation, which translated into plain *English*, means no more than an address of the following kind. "Madam, I like you (no matter whether from fortune, person, or any other motive) and it will conduce much to my pleasure and convenience, if you will become my wife: that is, if you will bind yourself before God and man to obey my commands as long as I shall live. And should you after marriage be forgetful of your duty, you will then have given me a legal power of exacting as rigid a performance of it as I please." But, as the adulating language is not thus translated 'till the ceremony of marriage is past, and is 'till then perfectly unintelligible; 'tis no wonder that the poor woman, who hath been thus egregiously imposed on, (or rather who hath so egregiously imposed on herself) should find it so difficult a language to learn; and very naturally will all her fancy'd love, which had no better a foundation than momentary flattery, when that ceases, fall to the ground. What a curse, under such circumstances, must attend a domestic life! The company of strangers, who are more likely to please her ears with some of her darling sounds, must be to such a wife her best relief from the dull company of her husband. Dull only will be the company of her husband, while he is indifferent to her; but she will not long stop here: for vanity disappointed, will always find an enemy on whom to bestow the utmost hatred and dislike; and the woman who hath been thus entangled in her own snares, will generally find that enemy in the person of her husband. As from him, when her lover, arose all her pleasure; so from him now flows all her disappointment. She will grow sour, and morose; every thing in her husband's house will become hateful to her sight. No indulgence on his side, (should he be willing to be an indulgent husband) can compensate the loss of adoration. She will not confess, even to herself, her own inferiority, enough to understand the language of indulgence, nor will she deign to accept it. The heart that is puffed up, and swelling with vanity, can never be fitted to receive real kindness, nor knows to beat with pleasure from gratitude, for gentle treatment. But I think a more ridiculous instance of female vanity cannot well be discovered, than that of a woman boasting that she scorns to love, without being persuaded, (that is, flattered out of her affections;) when by these means she robs herself of her greatest privilege, that of distinction and choice. She boasts of demanding to be used with insolence and contempt: she lays snares to entrap herself, and makes herself liable (as she insists on deceit) to fall to the share of the most worthless of mankind.

The female part of the Cry were so dull and melancholy, on Portia's mentioning a domestic life, that altho' they had many flying notions wandering in their brains, which they thought amounted to a proof of the absurdity of her sentiments, yet had they not spirit enough to contradict her: and as there were no men in that assembly, who durst avow the truth of Portia's translation of the adulating language, for fear of losing a mistress, or offending a wife, she met with neither approbation nor opposition, and without interruption thus proceeded.

Flattery in courtship is the highest insolence; for whilst it pretends to bestow on you more than you deserve, it is watching an opportunity to take from you what you really have. The bestower of it is laughing to think what a ridiculous figure you will make, when like the fox in the fable, he hath, by sounding your praises, robb'd you of your treasure; and you are indeed in a worse situation than the deluded crow, who only lost her piece of cheese; for you are fix'd for life the slave of your deluder.

The Cry now a little roused themselves from their lethargy, and affirm'd, that Portia from her discourse had intimated, that it was in no man's power to recommend himself to her favour; that her liking, if she could have any, (which indeed they scarcely allow'd, for they pronounced her totally incapable of that love, to which they join'd the epithets of generous and noble) must depend on caprice, and not on the merit of her lover; that she was above being courted, and in short, that she was the proudest of all her kind.

If the reader should chance to remember, that Spenser, in his allegory of the *house of pride,* makes all those who are enlisted in that numerous train, the most ready to complain of the pride of their leader; it may not appear strange, that the Cry should on all occasions be no less prompt to accuse others of a vice, to which they themselves are most prone.

"By invention (says an ingenious author) I believe is generally understood, a creative faculty; which would indeed prove romance writers to have the highest pretensions to it; whereas by invention is really meant no more (and so the word signifies) than discovery, or finding out; or to explain it at large, a quick and sagacious penetration into the true essence of all the objects of our contemplation."

Invention then is in truth pretty much the same with having eyes and opening them in order to discern the objects which are placed before us. But the eye here made use of must be the mind's eye (as Shakespear, with his peculiar aptness of expression, calls it) and so strictly just is this metaphor, that nothing is apparently more frequent than a perverse shutting of this mental eye when we have not an inclination to perceive the things offered to our internal view. I know not likewise, why a short-sighted mind's eye should not be as good an expression as a short-sighted body's eye. But in this we are much kinder to our sense than to our intellect; for in order to assist the former we use glasses and spectacles of all kinds adapted to our deficiency of sight, whereas in the latter we are so far from accepting the assistance of mental glasses or spectacles, that we often strain our mind's eye, even to blindness, and at the same time affirm that our sight is nothing less than perfect.

The poet who writes to the mind's eye, and collects his images through the same medium, lies under a great disadvantage in comparison with the painter. The original, from whence the latter draws his copy, is an outward object, and his picture, when finish'd, is address'd to the visual sense: whereas the original, from whence the former takes copy, is perceived by the mind's eye, and address'd also to the mental perception of his reader. In order, therefore, clearly and distinctly to convey his images, the poet is obliged to make use of allegories, metaphors, and illustrations from outward objects, and from things visible, to deduce the evidence of things not seen.

Thus, properly speaking, the works, which we call works of invention, ought to contain the history of the mind of man; and he is the best writer, who represents it most truly.

If invention then be only a capacity of finding, and not of creating, we must endeavour (if we would exercise this faculty) to keep our mind's eye open, and on the search, and not close it up by bending all our thoughts on the gratification of some present humour. The reader also may be said to partake of the invention of the author, when he finds his own acquaintance in the true representations of nature. Thus the reader who hath most truly considered and digested the sentiments which he reads, must be a man of the best taste, and must find most pleasure in the perusal of authors worth the reading. It is but to preserve candor enough to keep up an impartial attention, and instead of being actuated by a false shame of ignorance, to know when properly to confess myself a learner; and I have it in my power, as far as my capacity will reach, to command any knowledge that is extant in the whole universe.

Would mankind be but contented without the continual use of that little, but significant pronoun, *mine*, or *my own*, with what luxurious delight might they revel in the property of others! Every man possessed of a competency enough to obtain necessaries, without the task of hard labour, might, innocent of theft or pillage, reap enjoyment from all the productions of the industry and faculties of half mankind. He, like the queen of the bees, might partake in the fruit of the labours of all the hive. The works of nature and of art combine to delight his senses. To omit the ennumeration of all natural beauties, such as hills, dales, woods, rivers, the fragrance of flowering shrubs, the melody of birds, &c. which are all at the command of the poorest peasant; 'tis in my power with truth to declare, that to please my eyes the vain man builds magnificent palaces, and toils for riches in order to raise for my view a beautiful structure: for the same purpose serves the most finish'd pieces of the painter's art: the musician toils to gratify my sense of hearing, and the poet's pen is employ'd for my delight and entertainment: but if envy makes me sicken at the sight of every thing that is excellent out of my own possession; then will the sweetest food be sharp as vinegar, and every beauty will, in my depraved eyes, appear as deformity.

Men look on knowledge, which they learn, or might learn from others, as they do on the most beautiful structures, which are not their own: in outward objects they would rather behold their own hogsty than their neighbour's palace; and in mental ones, would prefer one grain of knowledge, gain'd by their own observation, to all the wisdom of a thousand Solomons.

It is the remark of a very ingenious French writer, that scarcely any man ever soared so high in knowledge as he might have done by more intense industry. And I believe the chief baulk to this industry is, the great aptitude of the human mind immediately to pronounce the perfection of all its own productions. We are inclined to do by the produce of our minds as by those of our bodies: namely, admire them for being ours; and instead of taking the proper pains to form our children into objects of esteem and admiration, we swear, although their deformity is apparent to all impartial eyes, that they are patterns of perfection: we are angry that others are not as blind as ourselves, and, knight-errant like, are at all times ready to defend the beauties of our own Dulcinea. . . .

The stamp of immortality, or rather of duration equal to mortality itself, which we have reason to believe is on some poems, must be made by a judgment directed by modesty and candor, which will not suffer the poet to think there is a magic in his touch which immediately brings all things to perfection. This modesty engages him, before he vents his thoughts, to examine and re-examine them; and not being partial to them as his own, he will awaken all his faculties, in order to cultivate and exalt his genius to the height, before he brings his productions into public view.

If modesty and candor are necessary to an author in his judgment of

Sarah Fielding (1710–1768)

his own works, no less are they in his reader. And, when I hear every pert boy and girl, just come from school, and who should not yet be out of the hands of their governors, admitted to sit in judgment on Milton, Shakespear, &c. the face of things seems reversed, the infant is become the master, and the master is forced to submit to be the scholar. . . .

I know not whether it would be too bold an assertion to say, that *candor* makes capacity; yet it is I believe indisputably true, that by this alone it hath the power of fully exerting all its vigour. But in order to try the truth of any observation relating to the mind, the easiest method is to illustrate it by outward objects. If, for instance, a man was to sweat and labour all the days of his life to fill a chest which was already full, the absurdity of his vain endeavour would be glaring: in the same manner, when the human mind is filled and stuffed with notions, brought thither by fallacious inclinations, there is no room for truth to enter; candor being banished, passions alone bear the sway.

> —— Function
> Is smother'd in surmise; and nothing is
> But what is not.

Truth is the very reverse of what is said of that fickle goddess Fortune;

> She flys those that sue,
> And those that fly pursue

For truth meets those who affectionately invite her, and is unattainable by none but those who detest her embraces, and fly her as their enemy.

After all that has been said in various shapes, by many various writers, concerning JUDGMENT, TASTE, INVENTION, &c. they all and severally mean no more than THE PERCEPTION OF TRUTH, which way soever it is offered to our view.

From Preface to
The History of the Countess of Dellwyn (1759)

Bossu[1] declares it to be the Opinion of both Aristotle and Horace, That Poets teach moral Philosophy; and that the latter even gives the Preference in this respect to Homer over the Philosophers themselves.

Then Bossu assigns the Cause why the Poets thus excel simple Philosophers, and says, that it arises from the Nature of the Poetry, which in every kind is wholly an Imitation; now Imitation, continues he, is extremely agreeable and natural to Man; for which Reason this Manner of treating any Subject is much more engageing, and more properly adapted to gain Attention. Besides Imitation gives Instruction by the Force of Examples; and Examples are so much the more powerful to persuade, as they prove the Possibility of following them; to all which Bossu also adds, that Imitation is so much of the intrinsic Nature of Poetry, that Aristotle declares the Art itself to that Cause owes its Birth.

Thus it is visibly the unanimous Opinion of those great Men, that Poets are, as it were, the Imitators, I had almost said the Mimicks, of Nature; an Appellation which, in its present Use, carries with it indeed very little Dignity, and seems to imply only a Capacity at catching at some Peculiarity of Gesture or Behaviour, in order to point out an Object of Derision. But the Poets were considered as Imitators of Nature in a very different Light from that narrow and confined Sense; as Searchers into the inmost Labyrinths of the human Mind; as penetrating the Force of the different characteristic Bent of the various Dispositions of Men towards their Conduct in Life, and then placing them in such Circumstances, as give an ample Field to display, by the Examples they bring into Action, the fatal Effects of indulged Passions, and the happy Result of restraining all Passions and Tumults of the human Breast within the proper Limits prescribed by Reason; for Monsieur Rochefocault[2] truly says, "It is difficult to conquer the Passions, but it is impossible to satisfy them;" that is, when they rebel against their proper Guide, and forcibly snatch the Reins out of the Hands of that Governor appointed to restrain and keep them within their own prescribed Bounds. Every Vice, by which a bad Man is actuated, as well as every Virtue which animates the Bosom of a good Character, tends, if properly managed, to produce the Moral, which is essentially necessary to render any Writing useful to the Reader.

The narrow-minded and illiberal Peruser of Books, who searches only for pointed Satire, and can relish no Character, but such as he finds, or imagines he finds, to partake of the Nature of an abusive Libel on some particular Person, is incapable of being pleased with general Pictures of Nature; but, like the Palate vitiated by habitual Luxury, he requires sharp and seasoned Sauce before he can relish any Food whatsoever; and it is more Matter of Triumph to such Readers to find out a Similitude in any Individual of their Acquaintance to some ridiculous Story, or bad Character, than if they could discover all the Verisimilitudes that were ever thought of. . . .

If an Author happens to live in an Age when a general Fashion of Dissipation banishes Reflexion, and the View in Reading at all is circumscribed within such narrow Limits, that the Pleasure thereby proposed seems to be no other than to discover some Reference to particular Objects, and universal Resemblances to human Nature are overlooked, he ought to content himself without such Applause as is only to be obtained by the Forfeiture of his own moral Character; and would make a very injudicious Bargain, if he so far adapted his Practice to their Taste, that he must necessarily be conscious of being a bad Man, in order to be accounted by such Readers a pleasing Writer.

Notes

The Adventures of David Simple

1. *Cato*, by Joseph Addison (1713), was an orthodox neoclassical tragedy filled with aristocratic characters and high-flown sentiments; *The History of George Barnwell, or, the London Merchent*, by George Lillo (1731), is a bourgeois drama in prose about the fall of an apprentice.

2. Lillo's *Fatal Curiosity* (1737) is another tragedy of lower-class characters who murder for money.

3. *Don Sebastian*, by John Dryden (1690). The ladies are weeping for joy and tenderness, a sign of virtuous sensibility.

4. Thomas Otway (1652–1685), playwright; Thomas D'Urfey (1653–1723), popular writer of songs, plays, and poetry.

Remarks on Clarissa

1. *The Jacobite's Journal*, no. 5, January 2, 1748.

2. Gautier de Costos de la Calprenède, *Cassandre*, 10 vols. (Paris 1642–1660), and Madeleine de Scudéry, *Clélie*, 5 vols. (Paris 1654–1661).

3. Thomas Otway, *The Orphan* (London 1680).

The History of the Countess of Dellwyn

1. René Le Bossu, *Treatise on the Epic Poem* (1675).

2. François, duc de La Rochefoucauld (1613–1680). His *Maxims* (1664) is a collection of pithy and cynical observations on human conduct.

ELIZABETH ROBINSON MONTAGU
(1720–1800)

MARRIED AT age twenty-two to Edward Montagu, a man of great wealth almost thirty years her senior, Elizabeth Robinson was assured of the means to carry out her intellectual interests. She had been educated at home along with her sister, novelist Sarah Scott, under a program largely directed by her stepgrandfather, the Cambridge scholar Dr. Conyers Middleton. In later life Elizabeth Montagu became a patron of artists and literary personalities. After her husband's death in 1775, she built a London townhouse, in part decorated by the painter Angelica Kauffman, and added extensively to a country seat at Sandleford. At both of these homes she held salons where the intellectual leaders of her day could carry on brilliant conversations. For this reason she became known as "Queen of the Bluestockings"—a term used to describe educated women with prominent scholarly interests. Among her guests were such figures as Elizabeth Carter, Hester Chapone, Hester Thrale, Samuel Johnson, David Garrick, Edmund Burke, and Sir Joshua Reynolds; she also became patron of, among others, the writers Anna Laetitia Barbauld, Hannah More, and Frances Burney.

Montagu was a writer of lively, entertaining letters which were published after her death as *The Letters of Elizabeth Montagu* (1809) and *Letters of Mrs. Elizabeth Carter to Mrs. Montagu* (1817). She is best known, however, as the author of *An Essay on the Writings and Genius of Shakespear* (1769), in which she answered charges brought against the playwright by the French author Voltaire by comparing Shakespeare favorably with Greek and French dramatists. The section excerpted here explores the functions of historical drama and the original qualities of Shakespeare's histories.

Earlier, Montagu had published anonymously three *Dialogues of the Dead* (1760) as part of a larger work conceived and carried out by her friend George, Baron Lyttleton. In the dialogue included here, which takes up the "Battle of the Books," a contemporary bookseller and the Greek historian Plutarch debate the merits of ancient and modern literature and discuss the tastes of current readers.

An Essay on the Writings and Genius of Shakespeare. To Which Are Added, Three Dialogues of the Dead (London: R. Priestly & R. Lea, 1810; rpt. New York: AMS Press, 1966).

Dialogue III from *Dialogues of the Dead* (1760)

Plutarch—Charon—and a
Modern Bookseller.

Charon.

Here is a fellow who is very unwilling to land in our territories. He says he is rich, has a great deal of business in the other world, and must needs return to it: He is so troublesome and obstreperous I know not what to do with him. Take him under your care therefore, good Plutarch; you will easily awe him into order and decency by the superiority an Author has over a Bookseller.

Bookseller.

Am I got into a world so absolutely the reverse of that I left, that here Authors domineer over Booksellers? Dear Charon, let me go back, and I will pay any price for my passage. But, if I must stay, leave me not with any of those who are styled Classical Authors. As to you, Plutarch, I have a particular animosity against you, for having almost occasioned my ruin. When I first set up shop, understanding but little of business, I unadvisedly bought an edition of your *Lives*; a pack of old Greeks and Romans, which cost me a great sum of money. I could never get off above twenty sets of them. I sold a few to the Universities, and some to Eaton and Westminster;[1] for it is reckoned a pretty book for boys and under-graduates; but, unless a man has the luck to light on a pedant, he shall not sell a set of them in twenty years.

Plutarch.

From the merit of the subjects, I had hoped another reception for my works. I will own indeed, that I am not always perfectly accurate in every circumstance, nor do I give so exact and circumstantial a detail of the actions of my heroes, as may be expected from a biographer who has confined himself to one or two characters. A zeal to preserve the memory of great men, and to extend the influence of such noble examples, made me undertake more than I could accomplish in the first degree of perfection: but surely the characters of my illustrious men are not so imperfectly sketched, that they will not stand forth to all ages as patterns of virtue, and incitements to glory. My reflections are allowed to be deep and sagacious; and what can be more useful to a reader, than a wise man's judgment on a great man's conduct? In my writings you will find no rash censures, no undeserved encomiums, no mean compliance with popular opinions, no vain ostentation of critical skill, nor any affected *finesse*. In my parallels, which used to be admired as pieces of excellent judgment, I compare with perfect impartiality one great man with another, and each with the rule of justice. If indeed latter ages have produced greater men and better writers, my heroes and my works ought to give place to them. As the world has now the advantage of much better rules of morality, than the unassisted reason of poor pagans could form, I do not wonder, that those vices, which appeared to us as mere blemishes in great characters, should seem most horrid deformities in the purer eyes of the present age: a delicacy I do not blame, but admire and commend. And . . . as I shall ever retain a high veneration for the illustrious men of every age, I should be glad you would give me some account of those persons, who in wisdom, justice, valour, patriotism, have eclipsed my Solon, Numa, Camillus,[2] and other boasts of Greece or Rome.

Bookseller.
Why, master Plutarch, you are talking Greek indeed. That work which repaired the loss I sustained by the costly edition of your books, was, *The Lives of the Highwaymen*: but I should never have grown rich, if it had not been by publishing the Lives of men that never lived. You must know, that though in all times it was possible to have a great deal of learning and very little wisdom, yet it is only by a modern improvement in the art of writing, that a man may read all his life and have no learning or knowledge at all; which begins to be an advantage of the greatest importance. There is as natural a war between your men of science and fools, as between the cranes and the pigmies of old.[3] Most of our young men having deserted to the fools, the party of the learned is near being beaten out of the field; and I hope in a little while they will not dare to peep out of their forts and fastnesses at Oxford and Cambridge. There let them stay and study old musty moralists, till one falls in love with the Greek, another with the Roman virtue: but our men of the world should read our new books, which teach them to have no virtue at all. No book is fit for a gentleman's reading, which is not void of facts and of doctrines, that he may not grow a pedant in his morals or conversation. I look upon history (I mean real history) to be one of the worst kinds of study. Whatever has happened, may happen again; and a well-bred man may unwarily mention a parallel instance he

had met with in history, and be betrayed into the awkwardness of introducing into his discourse a Greek, a Roman, or even a Gothic name. But
when a gentleman has spent his time in reading adventures that never occurred, exploits that never were achieved, and events that not only never
did, but never can happen, it is impossible that in life or in discourse he
should ever apply them. A secret history, in which there is no secret and no
history, cannot tempt indiscretion to blab or vanity to quote; and by this
means modern conversation flows gentle and easy, unencumbered with
matter and unburthened of instruction. As the present studies throw no
weight or gravity into discourse and manners, the women are not afraid to
read our books; which not only dispose to gallantry and coquetry, but give
rules for them. Caesar's Commentaries, and the account of Xenophon's Expedition,[4] are not more studied by military commanders, than our novels
are by the fair; to a different purpose indeed: for their military maxims
teach to conquer, our's to yield; those inflame the vain and idle love of glory,
these inculcate a noble contempt of reputation. The women have greater
obligations to our writers than the men. By the commerce of the world,
men might learn much of what they get from books; but the poor women,
who in their early youth are confined and restrained, if it were not for the
friendly assistance of books, would remain long in an insipid purity of mind,
with a discouraging reserve of behaviour.

Plutarch.

As to your men who have quitted the study of virtue for the study of
vice, useful truth for absurd fancy, and real history for monstrous fiction, I
have neither regard nor compassion for them: but I am concerned for the
women, who are betrayed into these dangerous studies: and I wish for their
sakes I had expatiated more on the character of Lucretia[5] and some other
heroines.

Bookseller.

I tell you, our women do not read in order to live or to die like Lucretia.
If you would inform us, that a *billet-doux* was found in her cabinet after her
death, or give a hint as if Tarquin really saw her in the arms of a slave, and
that she killed herself not to suffer the shame of a discovery, such anecdotes
would sell very well. Or if even by tradition, but better still, if by papers
in the Portian family, you could shew some probability that Portia[6] died of
dram-drinking; you would oblige the world very much; for you must know,
that next to new-invented characters, we are fond of new lights upon ancient characters; I mean such lights as shew a reputed honest man to have
been a concealed knave; an illustrious hero a pitiful coward, &c. Nay, we

are so fond of this kind of information, as to be pleased sometimes to see a character cleared from a vice or crime it has been charged with, provided the person concerned be actually dead. But in this case the evidence must be authentic, and amount to a demonstration; in the other a detection is not necessary; a slight suspicion will do, if it concerns a really good and great character.

Plutarch.

I am the more surprized at what you say of the taste of your contemporaries, as I met with a Frenchman who assured me, that less than a century ago he had written a much-admired life of Cyrus under the name of Artamenes,[7] in which he ascribed to him far greater actions than those recorded of him by Xenophon and Herodotus; and that many of the great heroes of history had been treated in the same manner; that empires were gained and battles decided by the valour of a single man; imagination bestowing what nature has denied, and the system of human affairs has rendered impossible.[8]

Bookseller.

I assure you these books were very useful to the Authors, and their Booksellers; and for whose benefit beside should a man write? These romances were very fashionable, and had a great sale: they fell in luckily with the humour of the age.

Plutarch.

Monsieur Scuderi tells me they were written in the times of vigour and spirit, in the evening of the gallant days of chivalry, which, though then declining, had left in the hearts of men a warm glow of courage and heroism; and they were to be called to books, as to battles, by the sound of the trumpet: he says too, that if writers had not accommodated themselves to the prejudices of the age, and written of bloody battles and desperate encounters, their works would have been esteemed too effeminate an amusement for gentlemen. Histories of chivalry, instead of enervating, tend to invigorate the mind, and endeavour to raise human nature above the condition, which is naturally prescribed to it; but as strict justice, patriot motives, prudent counsels, and a dispassionate choice of what upon the whole is fittest and best, do not direct these heroes of romance, they cannot serve for instruction and example, like the great characters of true history. It has ever been my opinion, that only the clear and steady light of truth can guide men to virtue, and that the lesson which is impracticable, must be unuseful. . . . Yet I confess it has been the practice of many nations to incite men to virtue by relating the deeds of fabulous heroes; but surely it is the custom only of yours to incite them to vice by the history of fabulous scoundrels. . . . Oh disgrace to letters! Oh shame to the Muses!

Bookseller.

You express great indignation at our present race of writers; but believe me, the fault lies chiefly on the side of the readers. As Monsieur Scuderi observed to you, authors must comply with the manners and disposition of those who are to read them. There must be a certain sympathy between the book and the reader, to create a good liking. Would you present a modern fine gentleman, who is negligently lolling in an easy-chair, with the Labours of Hercules for his recreation? or make him climb the Alps with Hannibal,[9] when he is expiring with the fatigue of last night's ball? . . .

Plutarch.

It should be the first object of writers to correct the vices and follies of the age. I will allow as much compliance with the mode of the times, as will make truth and good morals agreeable. Your love of fictitious characters might be turned to good purpose, if those presented to the public were to be formed on the rules of religion and morality. It must be confessed, that history, being employed only about illustrious persons, public events, and celebrated actions, does not supply us with such instances of domestic merit as one could wish: our heroes are great in the field and the senate, and act well in great scenes on the theatre of the world: but the idea of a man, who in the silent retired path of life never deviates into vice, who considers no spectator but the Omniscient Being, and solicits no applause but His approbation, is the noblest model that can be exhibited to mankind, and would be of the most general use. Examples of domestic virtue would be more particularly useful to women than those of great heroines. The virtues of women are blasted by the breath of public fame, as flowers that grow on an eminence are faded by the sun and wind, which expand them. But true female praise, like the music of the spheres, arises from a gentle, a constant, and an equal progress in the path marked out for them, by their great Creator; and, like the heavenly harmony, it is not adapted to the gross ear of mortals, but is reserved for the delight of higher beings, by whose wise laws they were ordained to give a silent light, and shed a mild benignant influence on the world.

Bookseller.

We have had some English and French writers who aimed at what you suggest. In the supposed character of Clarissa (said a clergymen to me a few days before I left the world) one finds the dignity of heroism tempered by the meekness and humility of religion, a perfect purity of mind and sanctity of manners; in that of Sir Charles Grandison, a noble pattern of every private virtue, with sentiments so exalted as to render him equal to every public duty.[10]

Plutarch.

Are there no other authors who write in this manner?

Bookseller.

Yes, we have another writer of these imaginary histories: one who has not long since descended to these regions: his name is Fielding; and his works, as I have heard the best judges say, have a true spirit of comedy, and an exact representation of nature, with fine moral touches. He has not indeed given lessons of pure and consummate virtue; but he has exposed vice and meanness with all the powers of ridicule. . . . Monsieur de Marivaux,[11] and some other French writers, have also proceeded much upon the same plan, with a spirit and elegance which give their works no mean rank among the *belles lettres*. I will own that, when there is wit and entertainment enough in a book to make it sell, it is not the worse for good morals.

Charon.

I think, Plutarch, you have made this gentleman a little more humble, and now I will carry him the rest of his journey. But he is too frivolous an animal to present to wise Minos.[12] I wish Mercury were here; he would damn him for his dulness. I have a good mind to carry him to the Danaïdes,[13] and leave him to pour water into their vessels, which, like his late readers, are destined to eternal emptiness. Or shall I chain him to the rock, side to side by Prometheus, not for having attempted to steal celestial fire, in order to animate human forms, but for having endeavoured to extinguish that which Jupiter had imparted? Or shall we constitute him *friseur* to Tisiphone,[14] and make him curl up her locks with his satires and libels?

Plutarch.

The supreme and righteous Judge does not esteem any thing frivolous, that affects the morals of mankind. By his final sentence Authors will be punished as guilty of every fault they have countenanced, and every crime they have encouraged; and vengeance will be denounced in proportion to the injuries, which virtue or the virtuous have suffered in consequence of their writings.

Elizabeth Robinson Montagu (1720–1800)

From *An Essay on the Writings and Genius of Shakespear* (1769)

Those Dramas of Shakspeare, which he distinguishes by the name of his Histories, being of an original kind and peculiar construction, cannot come within any rules, prior to their existence. The office of the Critic, in regard to Poetry, is like that of the Grammarian and Rhetorician in respect to Language: it is the business of both to shew why such and such modes of speech, are proper and graceful, others improper and ungraceful: but they pronounce on such words and expressions only, as are actually extant.

The rules of Aristotle were drawn from the tragedies of Æschylus, Sophocles, &c. Had that great critic seen a play so fashioned on the chronicles of his country, thus representative of the manners of the times, and of the characters of the most illustrious persons concerned in a series of important events, perhaps he would have esteemed such a sort of drama well worth his attention. . . . If it be the chief use of history, to teach philosophy by example, this species of history must be allowed to be the best preceptor. The catastrophe of these plays is not built on a vain and idle fable of the wrath of Juno, or of the revenge of slighted Bacchus; nor is a man represented entangled in the web of Fate, from which his Virtues and his Deities cannot extricate him: but here we are admonished to observe the effects of pride and ambition, the tyrant's dangers and traitor's fate. The sentiments and the manners, the passions and their consequences, are fully set before you; the force and lustre of poetical language join with the weight and authority of history, to impress the moral lesson on the heart. The poet collects, as it were, into a focus, those truths, which lie scattered in the diffuse volume of the historian, and kindles the flame of virtue, while he shews the miseries and calamities of vice.

The common interests of humanity make us attentive to every story that has an air of reality, but we are more affected if we know it to be true; and the interest is still heightened if we have any relation to the persons concerned. Our noble countryman, Percy,[1] engages us much more than Achilles, or any Grecian hero. The people, for whose use these public entertainments should be chiefly intended, know the battle of Shrewsbury[2] to be a fact; they are informed of what passed on the banks of the Severn: all that happened on the shore of the Scamander[3] has, to them, the appearance of a fiction. . . .

The nature of the Historical Play gave scope to the extensive talents of Shakspeare. He had an uncommon felicity in painting manners, and developing characters, which he could employ with peculiar grace and propriety, when he exhibited the chiefs in our civil wars. The great earl of Warwick, Cardinal Beaufort, Humphrey duke of Gloucester, the renowned Hotspur,[4] were very interesting objects to their countrymen. Whatever shewed them in a strong light, and represented them with sentiments and manners agreeable to their historical characters, and to those things which common fame had divulged of them, must have engaged the attention of the spectator, and assisted in that delusion of his imagination, whence his sympathy with the story must arise. We are affected by the catastrophe of a stranger, we lament the destiny of an Œdipus, and the misfortunes of an Hecuba; but the little peculiarities of a character touch us only where we have some nearer affinity to the person, than the common relation of humanity. . . .

We are apt to consider Shakspeare only as a poet; but he is certainly one of the greatest moral philosophers that ever lived.

Euripides was highly esteemed by the ancients for the moral sentences, with which he has interspersed the speeches in his tragedies; and certainly many general truths are expressed in them with a sententious brevity. But he rather collects general opinions into maxims, and gives them a form which is easily retained by memory, than extracts any new observations from the characters in action; which every reader of penetration will find the invariable practice of our author: and when he introduces a general maxim, it seems drawn from him by the occasion. As it arises out of the action, it loses itself again in it, and remains not, as in other writers, an ambitious ornament glittering alone, but is so connected as to be an useful passage very naturally united with the story. The examples of this are so frequent, as to occur almost in every scene of his best plays. But lest I should be misunderstood, I will cite one from the second part of Henry IV. where the general maxim is, that

> An habitation giddy and unsure
> Hath he that buildeth on the vulgar heart. . . .[5]

Moral reflections may be more frequent in this kind of drama, than in the other species of tragedy, where, if not very short, they teaze the spectator, whose mind is intent upon, and impatient for the catastrophe; and unless they arise necessarily out of the circumstances the person is in, they appear unnatural. For in the pressure of extreme distress, men are intent only on themselves and on the present exigence. The various interests and characters in these historical plays, and the mixture of the comic, weaken the operations of pity and terror, but introduce various opportunities of conveying moral instruction, as occasion is given to a variety of reflections and observations, more useful in common life than those drawn from the conditions of kings and heroes, and persons greatly superior to us by nature or fortune. . . .

To write a perfect tragedy, a poet must be possessed of the Pathetic or the Sublime; or perhaps, to attain the utmost excellence, must, by a more uncommon felicity, be able to give the Sublime the finest touches of passion and tenderness, and to the Pathetic the dignity of the Sublime. The straining a moderate or feeble genius to these arduous tasks, has produced the most absurd bombast, and the most pitiable nonsense that has ever been uttered. Aristotle's rules,[6] like Ulysses' bow, are held forth to all pretenders to Tragedy, who, as unfortunate as Penelope's suitors,[7] only betray their weakness by an attempt superior to their strength, or ill adapted to their faculties. Why should not Poetry, in all her different forms, claim the same indulgence as her sister art? The nicest connoisseurs in Painting have applauded every master, who has justly copied nature. Had Michael Angelo's bold pencil been dedicated to drawing the Graces, or Rembrandt's to trace the soft bewitching smile of Venus, their works had probably proved very contemptible. Fashion does not so easily impose on our sense, as it misleads our judgment. Truth of design, and natural colouring, will always please the eye: . . . in an imitative art we require only just imitation, with a certain freedom and energy, which is always necessary to form a complete resemblance to the pattern, which is borrowed from nature. . . .

Nothing great is to be expected from any set of artists, who are to give only copies of copies. The treasures of nature are inexhaustible, as well in moral as in physical subjects. The talents of Shakspeare were universal, his penetrating mind saw through all characters; and, as Mr. Pope says of him, he was not more a master of our strongest emotions, than of our idlest sensations.

One cannot wonder, that, endued with so great and various powers, he broke down the barriers that had before confined the dramatic writers to the regions of Comedy, or Tragedy. He perceived the fertility of the subjects that lay between the two extremes; he saw, that in the historical play he could represent the manners of the whole people, give the general temper of the times, and bring in view the incidents that affected the common fate of his country. . . . At the time he wrote, the wars of the Houses of York and Lancaster[8] were fresh in men's minds. They had received the tale from some Nestor in their family, or neigbourhood, who had fought in the battle, he related. Every spectator's affections were ranged under the white or red rose, in whose contentions some had lost their parents and friends, others had gained establishments and honours.

All the inducements which the Greek tragedians had to chuse their heroes from the works of the poets, who had sung the wars of Troy, and the Argonautic expedition, were still in greater force with our countryman to take his subjects from the history and traditions of those more recent transactions, in which the spectator was informed and interested more personally and locally. There was not a family so low, that had not had some of its branches torn off in the storms of these intestine commotions; nor a valley so happily retired, that, at some time, *the foot of hostile paces had not bruis'd her flow'rets*. In these characters the rudest peasant read the sad history of his country: while the better sort were informed of the most minute circumstances by our chronicles. The tragedians who took their subjects from Homer, had all the advantage a painter would have, who was to draw a picture from a statue of Phidias or Praxiteles. Poor Shakspeare from the wooden images in our mean chronicles was to form his portraits. What judgment was there in discovering, that by moulding them to an exact resemblance he should engage and please! And what discernment and penetration into characters, and what amazing skill in moral painting, to be able, from such uncouth models, to bring forth not only a perfect, but, when occasion required, a graceful likeness!

The patterns from which he drew, were not only void of poetical spirit and ornament, but also of all historical dignity. The histories of those times were a mere heap of rude undigested annals, coarse in their style, and crowded with trivial anecdotes. No Tacitus had investigated the obliquities of our statesmen, or, by diving into the profound secrets of policy, had dragged into light the latent motives, the secret machinations of our politicians: yet how does he enter into the deepest mysteries of state! There cannot be a stronger proof of the superiority of his genius over the historians of the times than the following instance.

The learned Sir Thomas More, in his history of Crook'd-Back Richard,[9] tells, with the garrulity of an old nurse, the current stories of this king's deformity, and the monstrous appearance of his infancy, which he seems with superstitious credulity to believe to have been the omens and prognostics of his future villainy. Shakspeare, with a more philosophic turn of mind, considers them, not as presaging, but as instigating his cruel ambition, and finely accounts . . . for the asperity of his temper, and his fierce and unmitigated desire of dominion, from his being by his person disqualified for the softer engagements of society. . . . [10]

Our author, by following minutely the chronicles of the times, has embarrassed his dramas with too great a number of persons and events. The hurley-burley of these plays recommended them to a rude illiterate audience, who, as he says, loved a noise of targets. His poverty, and the low condition of the stage (which at that time was not frequented by persons of rank), obliged him to this complaisance; and unfortunately he had not been tutored by any rules of art, or informed by acquaintance with just and regular dramas. Even the politer sort, by reading books of chivalry, which were the polite literature of the times, were accustomed to bold adventures and achievements. . . .

Shakspeare and Corneille are equally blameable for having complied with the bad taste of the age; and by doing so, they have both brought unmerited censures on their country. The French impute barbarity and cruelty, to a people that could delight in bloody skirmishes on the stage. The English, as unjustly but as excusably, accuse of effeminacy and frivolousness, those who could sit to hear the following address of a lover to his mistress's bodkin, with which she had just put out one of his eyes.[11] . . .

Our countryman was betrayed into his error, by want of judgment to discern what part of his story was not fit for representation. Corneille, for want of dramatic genius, was obliged to have recourse to points, conceits, cold and uninteresting declamations, to fill up his plays; and these heavily drag along his undramatical dramas to a fifth act.

The ignorance of the times passed over the defects of each author; and the bad taste then prevalent did more than endure, it even encouraged and approved, what should have been censured.

Mr. Voltaire has said, that the plots of Shakspeare's plays are as wild as that of the Clitandre just quoted; and it must be allowed, they are often exceptionable: but at the same time we must observe, that though crowded too much, they are not so perplexed as to be unintelligible, which Corneille confesses his Clitandre might be to those who saw it but once. There is still another more essential difference perhaps, which is, that the wildest and most incorrect pieces of our Poet contain some incomparable speeches; whereas the worst plays of Corneille have not a good stanza. The tragedy of King Lear is very far from being a regular piece; yet there are speeches in it, which perhaps excel any thing that has been written by any tragedian, ancient or modern. . . .

King Lear, whom age renders weak and querulous, and who is now beginning to grow mad, thus very naturally, in the general calamity of the storm, recurs to his own particular circumstances.

> Spit fire, spout rain;
> Nor rain, wind, thunder, fire, are my daughters;
> I tax you not, you elements, with unkindness,
> I never gave you kingdoms, call'd you children,

You owe me no submission. Then let fall
Your horrible pleasure: here I stand your slave,
A poor, infirm, weak, and despis'd old man!
And yet I call you servile ministers,
That have with two pernicious daughters join'd
Your high engender'd battles, 'gainst a head
So old and white as this. Oh! oh! 'tis foul.

They must have little feeling, that are not touched by this speech, so highly pathetic. . . .

Thus it is that Shakspeare redeems the nonsense, the indecorums, the irregularities of his plays: and whoever, for want of natural taste, or from ignorance of the English language, is insensible to the merit of these passages, is just as unfit to judge of his works, as a deaf man, who only perceived the blackness of the sky, and did not hear the deep-voiced thunder, and the roaring elements, would have been to describe the aweful horrors of this midnight storm.

The French critic apologizes for our persisting in the representation of Shakspeare's plays, by saying we have none of a more regular form. In this he is extremely mistaken; we have many plays written according to the rules of art; but nature, which speaks in Shakspeare, prevails over them all. If at one of our theatres there were a set of actors who gave the true force of every sentiment, seemed inspired with the passion they were to counterfeit, fell so naturally into the circumstances and situations the poet had appointed for them, that they never betrayed they were actors, but might sometimes have an awkward gesture, or for a moment a vicious pronunciation, should we not constantly resort thither?—If at another theatre there were a set of puppets regularly featured, whose proportions and movements were geometrically true, and the faces, the action, the pronunciation of these puppets had no fault, but that there was no expression in their countenance, no natural air in their motion, and that their speech had not the various inflections of the human voice; would a real connoisseur abandon the living actors for such lifeless images, because some nice and dainty critic pleaded, that the puppets were not subject to any human infirmities, would not cough, sneeze, or become hoarse in the midst of a fine period? Or could it avail much to urge, that their movements and tones, being directed by just mechanics, would never betray the awkwardness of rusticity, or a false accent caught from bad education?

The dramatis personae of Shakspeare are men, frail by constitution, hurt by ill habits, faulty and unequal: but they speak with human voices, are actuated by human passions, and are engaged in the common affairs of human life. We are interested in what they do, or say, by feeling, every moment, that they are of the same nature as ourselves. Their precepts therefore are an instruction, their fates and fortunes an experience, their testimony an authority, and their misfortunes a warning.

Love and ambition are the subjects of the French plays. From the first of these passions, many by age and temper are entirely exempted; and from the second, many more, by situation. Among a thousand spectators, there are not perhaps half a dozen, who ever were, or can be, in the circumstances of the persons represented: they cannot sympathize with them, unless they have some conception of a tender passion, combated by ambition, or of ambition struggling with love. The fable of the French plays is often taken from history, but then a romantic passion is superadded to it, and to that both events and characters are rendered subservient.

Shakspeare, *in various nature wise*, does not confine himself to any particular passion. When he writes from history, he attributes to the persons such sentiments, as agreed with their actions and characters. There is not a more sure way of judging of the merit of rival geniuses, than by bringing them to the test of comparison where they have attempted subjects of a similar nature.

Notes

Dialogues of the Dead

    1. Eton and Westminster were famous secondary schools for English boys of the upper class.

    2. Solon was an early Greek lawmaker (sixth century B.C.E.); Numa Pompilius (715–672 B.C.E.) succeeded Romulus as king of Rome; Marcus Furius Camilla (d. 365 B.C.E.), a dictator, was honored as second founder of Rome.

    3. Reference to an ancient folklore tradition, alluded to in the *Iliad*, that cranes during their migration to Africa would make war on the pygmies.

    4. The references are to Julius Caesar's accounts of his military experiences and to *The March Upcountry*, an account of the Greek military retreat from Mesopotamia written by Xenophon (c. 430 B.C.E.–after 355 B.C.E.), a Greek historian.

    5. Lucretia, a Roman woman who was raped by Sextus Tarquinius, stabbed herself to death because of the dishonor brought to herself and her family; in revenge the ruling Tarquins were driven out and a republic established. Through the centuries Lucretia has been seen as the ultimate example of the virtuous, chaste woman.

    6. Portia, wife of Marcus Brutus, assassin of Julius Caesar, killed herself after her husband's flight; she was the daughter of Marcus Cato. Montagu's reference to the Portian family is facetious, suggesting the ignorance of history of many readers of fiction.

    7. Cyrus the Great, founder of the Persian Empire, who ruled from 559 to 530

B.C.E., was the subject of many legendary accounts, including those by the ancient Greek historians Xenophon and Herodotus. In the years 1649–1653 a ten-volume heroic romance, *Artamène, ou le grand Cyrus*, was published in France by Madeleine de Scudéry, but under the name of her brother George.

8. Montagu is here satirizing the genre of long heroic romances popular in France in the seventeenth century and continuing in vogue in England well into the eighteenth.

9. The mythical figure Hercules carried out twelve prodigious feats, or labors. Hannibal, a Carthaginian general (247–183 B.C.E.), led an army, with elephants as pack animals, across the Alps toward Rome.

10. *Clarissa* (1747) and *Sir Charles Grandison* (1753–1754) were popular novels by Samuel Richardson (1689–1761).

11. Pierre Carlet de Chamblain de Marivaux (1688–1763), novelist and playwright, was the author of two especially influential and strongly moralistic novels, *La Vie de Marianne* (1731–1742) and *Le Paysan parvenu* (1735–1736).

12. In Greek mythology, Minos was judge of the souls of the dead in Hades.

13. The fifty daughters of Danaüs, condemned forever to carry water in a sieve.

14. One of the furies, whose heads were ringed with serpents.

Essay on Shakespear

1. Henry Percy, son of the Earl of Northumberland, called Hotspur in Shakespeare's *I Henry IV*.

2. Battle in 1403 near the Severn River between the forces of King Henry IV and those of the rebellious Earl of Northumberland and his allies.

3. River near Troy.

4. Historical figures appearing as characters in Shakespeare's plays on Henry IV or Henry VI.

5. Montagu here quotes the entire speech by the Archbishop of York about the people's shifting loyalty between Richard II and Bolingbroke (*II Henry IV* I.iii).

6. The Greek philosopher Aristotle in his *Poetics* discussed various forms of drama, the principles he set forth being taken in later ages as inviolable rules.

7. The faithful wife of Ulysses held many suitors at bay during his ten-year absence.

8. The Wars of the Roses, 1455–1485, were fought between two families, the House of York (white rose) and the House of Lancaster (red rose), both claimants to the throne of England.

9. More's *History of King Richard the Third* was a source for Shakespeare's characterization of Richard in *III Henry VI* and *Richard III*.

10. Montagu here quotes Richard's soliloquies from *III Henry VI* III.ii,146–171, and V.vi.74–83.

11. Pierre Corneille (1606–1684) was held forth by French critics as a dramatist superior to Shakespeare. Montagu here challenges that claim by quoting a speech of absurdly inappropriate gallantry from Corneille's *Clitandre*.

LOUISE D'EPINAY (1726-1783)

BORN INTO an aristocratic family of modest means, Louise d'Epinay was encouraged to study by her father, the baron d'Esclavelles. Upon his death in 1735, she was sent to live with a wealthy aunt and uncle in Paris. There she received a conventional young woman's education, which she was later to lament in these words (as translated by Francis Steegmuller):

> When I was a child it was not the custom to teach girls anything. They were more or less inoculated with their religious duties, to prepare them for their first communion: they were given a very good dancing-master, a very poor music teacher and in rare cases a mediocre teacher of drawing. Add to this a bit of history and geography, devoid of any incentive to further learning: it was merely a question of memorizing names and dates, which were forgotten as soon as the teacher was let go. Such was the extent of what was considered a superior education. Above all, we were never taught to think; and any study of science was scrupulously avoided as being inappropriate to our sex.

At twenty she made an unfortunate marriage to her cousin Denis-Joseph, with whom she had grown up. Later she lived more happily with Friedrich Melchoir Grimm, a German living in France who had become a member of the circle of Parisian *philosophes*. This circle, which included Denis Diderot, produced a cultural newsletter entitled *Correspondance littéraire* (1753–1790), which was distributed among enlightened aristocrats and intellectuals throughout Europe. Epinay's contributions were always anonymous by her own wish, although they were identified as having been written by a woman.

Over a period of many years Epinay kept a record of her life in fictional form, which was published after her death as the *Histoire de Madame de Montbrillant* (1951). During her lifetime she was well known for *Les Conversations d'Émilie* (1774), in which she recorded her attempts to guide and educate her granddaughter, Émilie de Belsunce. This work received the French Academy's *Prix d'Utilité*, an award given each year for the book most useful to society, in 1783.

Epinay's critical review in the *Correspondance littéraire* of her friend Denis Diderot's play *Le Fils naturel* (*The Natural Son*), produced by the Comédie Française in 1771, conveys some of the flavor of their friendship and of the spirit that must have prevailed among the *philosophes*, who lived and worked so closely together.

Correspondance littéraire, philosophique et critique par Grimm, Diderot, Raynal, Meister, etc., vol. 9 (Paris: Garnier frères, 1879).

Review of Diderot's *Le Fils naturel* from the *Correspondance littéraire* (1771)

Pleased with their success at having obtained the permission of M. Diderot to produce *le Père de famille [A Father and his Family]* in their theater, the members of the Comédie Française have just asked his consent to put on *le Fils naturel [The Natural Son]*.[1]

All the praise which might be showered on this drama would fall short of the honors which its reputation, so well earned in the fifteen years since its publication, has brought it from people of good taste. We have previously discussed the play itself, and everyone knows it well; therefore we will content ourselves with describing the impression made on the public by the theatrical production of the *Fils naturel*. It was offered for the first time on the 26th of September, without either promotion or opposition by M. Diderot. He let the Comédiens do as they liked with his work, and he did not hide from them his opinion that the play would fare poorly on the stage.

Without having achieved a decided success, it did quite well for a play devoid of all the pompous absurdities which the public applauds without knowing why. All the strongest parts, the best tableaux, the truest maxims were enthusiastically received. All the words of nature, of passion, all the work of genius, feeling and delicacy penetrated only to a few; what is called the public, and even the actors, were not aware of these things. But what went unapplauded nevertheless quietly touched the spectator, even though he was unaware. In fact, those things most praised were not, in my opinion, those which most deserved to be, and nothing has proved to me so clearly the decline of artistic taste in France, as the impression made on the public by the *Fils naturel*.

People of taste, that small number of spectators whom I like to consider and whom M. Diderot wishes to please, had a reaction different from that of the wider public. They found a great beauty in the details, the sublime words, the pathetic and touching tableaux; some of these, however, do not produce the expected effect, and if the reading of this drama leaves nothing to be desired, there are some observations to be made concerning the theatrical effect.

I am more convinced than ever that the conversations between Constance and Dorval will not appear too long when they are well played; they were not. Constance was cold, without the smallest nuance of enthusiasm. She should appear noble and even a little austere, but without any loss of graceful persuasiveness, and her expression must be that of one inspired. Mme Préville was very far from fulfilling her role, yet in spite of that the scenes were effective.[2]

Dorval's virtue and his manner of speaking are so elevated, that he seems to fall back into the class of ordinary men when circumstances force him to deceive Clairville, Constance and Rosalie. This failing is not evident in the reading, which is always faster than a stage presentation; in reading we are struck only by the profound moral character of Dorval, and by his fatalism; but on the stage, when we see these three people abused, there comes a moment when we are angry with Dorval for not confiding his true position to Constance, even at the risk of what might ensue. He does not, and Clairville, Constance and Rosalie no longer inspire interest, because they are fooled by appearances; we cannot feel sorry for them or laugh at them, yet in the theater we must be able to feel compassion for a person who is deceived, if we cannot laugh at him.

Here, I believe, is the reason for the failure of those scenes in which the characters are assembled in such violent circumstances.

The author answers these objections by claiming that interest can never come out of an absurdity, and that good sense can never spoil a work; that it would be absurd for a man so silent and strong as Dorval to reveal shameful feelings which he has promised himself to suppress; that he would mortify Constance unnecessarily, for she does not deserve it, and that he would humiliate both himself and Rosalie in the eyes of this woman. Does Dorval know Rosalie's secret? Supposing he did what I think he ought to have done; here is what Constance should have answered: "You have done wrong to speak thus to me, Monsieur Dorval, and you would have done much better to leave without speaking." Then let us consider what these three characters would have become after the departure or the confession of Dorval; they would have scorned and hated each other.[3]

And I answer the author that his reflections do not excuse the defect in theatrical effect; that, besides, the more the character of Dorval is strong, the more he should be honest and upright without concern for the opinion of the people involved. Keep in mind that the spectator knows the secret of the character's conscience, that he knows Dorval's awareness of the fact that he yielded for a moment to an inclination which his delicacy disapproves, and that when he is praised by his friends and honored with their confidence, he is uncomfortable. He makes his fault the greater in leaving his admirers unaware of the truth. Constance would be a prude and she would be out of character to be offended by a confession which reveals so much honesty, decency and nobility. I am well aware that if things were done as I suggest there would be no more play—that is quite true. But even though there would be no play if a defect were corrected, it is still true that if it is not corrected, a defect remains. Yet this only results in a momentary suspension of interest, and takes nothing away from the true beauties of this drama.

André's tale, which was so pleasing and appropriate when the work appeared, is not as interesting today. For the theater, it must be shortened. I would consent to this only if it could be done in such a way as to completely preserve Dorval's responses.[4] How profound his words are, and how true to his character! Sadly, they were barely expressed.

We could wish for no further changes in the rest of the play. The father's arrival, his words, caused tears to flow. If this play, so poorly acted and little understood by the public, had a much greater success than expected, I believe we can be certain it will do quite as well as *le Père de famille* when it is truly understood by the actors and audience.

The announcement of a second performance was met with very much applause. This never took place, because new religions are not established without controversy. The same division separating the spectators appeared among the actors, some defending, others criticizing the new genre. Molé is first among the defenders, Préville and his wife lead the other party. These last have little interest in the success of a kind of work which they dislike, and hardly study their roles. That is what happened in the case of Mme Préville. Molé reproached her, perhaps too strongly. She, already angry with Molé over another matter, answered him sharply. Préville, her husband, became involved in the quarrel, and wrote to Molé that his wife would play her role only one more time, because she had committed herself publicly. The author intervened, and feeling that Mme Préville would give a second performance even less satisfactory than the first had been, withdrew his play, which will reappear on the stage only when he can choose the actors himself.

Translated by Amy Simowitz

Louise d'Epinay (1726–1783)

Notes

1. *The Natural Son* was an example of the new bourgeois drama featuring middle-class characters and a simple prose style. Dorval falls in love with Rosalie, who is engaged to marry his friend Clairville. Dorval is profoundly troubled by his dilemma. Can he betray his friend and declare his love? Meanwhile, Clairville's sister Constance reveals to Dorval that she loves him. Rosalie also tells Dorval that she has ceased to love Clairville, and now loves him. At one point in the play, described by Mme. d'Epinay, Dorval remains silent while the other three characters are led to believe that he reciprocates Constance's affection and will marry her. Ultimately Dorval denies his love for Rosalie, embraces virtue and honor, and promotes the marriage of Rosalie to Clairville. The appearance of Rosalie's father reveals that Dorval and Rosalie are actually brother and sister, and the play ends with the unions of Rosalie with Clairville, Dorval with Constance. *Le Père de famille* had been performed by the Comédie Française in February 1761.

2. Constance and Dorval have a long discussion about the possibility of living a virtuous life, and of bringing children into a world which will be decent and rational.

3. Dorval does know Rosalie's secret, that she loves Dorval, but chooses not to reveal it. Madame d'Epinay seems to feel that he should have revealed to Constance that he could not love her, as he was already in love with Rosalie.

4. André is the faithful servant of Lysimond, Rosalie's father (he is Dorval's father also, although that is not known until the end of the play). Lysimond had been returning to France from Martinique in order to sanction the marriage of Rosalie to Clairville, when he and André endured a series of misfortunes. André's long tale recounts their capture at sea by the English, their torment as prisoners in England, and their fortunate release. Dorval's comments, praised by Madame d'Epinay, touch on the themes of morality (how the English showed both cruelty and kindness toward their captives), the shame of injustice, and the harshness of God, in whom Dorval appears to place little faith.

ELIZABETH GRIFFITH
(1727?–1793)

DAUGHTER OF the actor and entrepreneur Thomas Griffith, who managed Dublin's Theatre-Royal, Elizabeth Griffith turned from a stage career to writing from financial necessity after she became involved with Richard Griffith, a self-described "honourable libertine." The publication in 1757 of Elizabeth and Richard Griffith's correspondence as *A Series of Genuine Letters Between Henry and Francis* propelled her to literary celebrity; she subsequently published in several genres, and at least five of her plays were successfully staged. Her son Richard's success in India allowed her to retire from literary production some years before her death in 1793.

Griffith's large oeuvre includes numerous translations from such writers as Voltaire and Diderot. Of her three novels, the epistolary *History of Lady Barton* (1771) was the most popular. Themes of male inconstancy and sexual double standards recur both in the fictional writings and in the *Essays, Addressed to Young Married Women* (1782), which advises wives how to keep husbands from straying and how to respond if they do.

The Morality of Shakespeare's Drama Illustrated (1775), probably inspired by Griffith's friend Elizabeth Montagu's *Essay on the Writings and Genius of Shakespeare* (1769), rests its theoretical claim on the ground that for moral instruction, concrete situations are superior to abstract philosophy. Griffith thus presents morality in what might be called situational terms, arguing for an apprehension that rises "out of the action immediately before our eyes" and replicates the nuances of life. She is critical of categorical imperatives by which virtues are classified according to abstract principles, condemns the systematic approaches of metaphysics and Stoic philosophy in favor of intuition and nature, and warns against "wandering with the Schoolmen, through the pathless wilds of theory."

Griffith achieves this moral repositioning in part through a separation of story from discourse that enables her to evaluate a passage apart from its speaker's function as a good or bad character. While such a practice might be criticized as an extraction of content from context, it also constitutes a fruitful misreading that complicates the moral positioning of Shakespeare's characters and hence of Shakespeare as well.

The Morality of Shakespeare's Drama Illustrated (London: T. Cadell, 1775).

From *The Morality of Shakespeare's Drama Illustrated* (1775)

Among the many writers of our nation, who have by their talents contributed to entertain, inform, or improve our minds, no one has so happily or universally succeeded, as he whom we may justly stile our first, our greatest Poet, Shakespeare. For more than a century and a half, this Author has been the delight of the Ingenious, the text of the Moralist, and the study of the Philosopher. . . .

The learned and ingenious Doctor Johnson . . . is the only one who has considered Shakespeare's writings in a moral light;[1] and therefore I confess myself of opinion that he has best understood them, by thus pointing to their highest merit, and noblest excellence. And from several passages in the Doctor's Preface, particularly where he says, that "From his writings, indeed, a system of *social duties* may be selected; for he who thinks reasonably, must think *morally*;" as well as from frequent reflections of my own, respecting the œconomical conduct of life and manners, which have always arisen in my mind on the perusal of Shakespeare's works, I have ventured to assume the task of placing his Ethic merits in a more conspicuous point of view, than they have ever hitherto been presented in to the Public. . . .

Shakespeare is not only my Poet, but my Philosopher also. His anatomy of the human heart is delineated from *nature*, not from *metaphysics*; referring immediately to our intuitive sense, and not wandering with the schoolmen, through the pathless wilds of theory. We not only *see*, but *feel* his dissections just and scientific. . . .

Shakespeare seems to possess that happy and peculiar kind of Superiority over all other Dramatic Authors, that the ancient poets and historians confessedly bear above the modern ones, with regard to the genuine characters, manners, and sentiments, of the persons exhibited in their respective writings. In the first, we see the *men of Nature*; in the latter, but *the children of the Schools*.

The world at present is held more in trammels, than it formerly was.— From our modes of education, policies, and breeding, our conduct and demeanor are become more sophisticate, our minds less candid, and our actions more disguised. Our modern literary painters represent us such as we appear; but the genuine unadulterate heart can be moved by no affection, allied by no sympathy, with such factitious personages, such puppets of polity, such automata of modern refinement. Hence, love, friendship, patriotism, are long since become the obsolete sentiments of chivalry and romance. But in all the representations of Shakespeare, we are sensible of a connection; his whole Dramatis Personæ seem to be *our acquaintance and countrymen;* while in most other exhibitions, they appear to be *strangers and foreigners.* . . .

Our Author's poetical beauties have been already selected, though they needed it not, as they are undoubtedly so striking as scarcely to require the being particularly pointed out to any Reader capable of conceiving or relishing them; but a single line, sometimes a word, in many instances throughout his Works, may convey a hint, or impress a sentiment upon the heart, if properly marked, which might possibly be overlooked, while curiosity is attending to the fable, or the imagination transported with the splendor of diction, or sublimity of images.

There is a Moral sometimes couched in his Fable, which whenever I have been able to discover, I have pointed out to the Reader; and from those pieces where this excellence is deficient in the Argument, as particularly in his Historical Plays, where poetical justice cannot always obtain, human life not being the whole of our existence, I have given his moral and instruction in detail, by quoting the passages as they happen to lie detached, or referring to the scope and tenor of the dialogue.

In these remarks and observations I have not restricted myself to morals purely ethic, but have extended my observations and reflections to whatever has reference to the general œconomy of life and manners, respecting prudence, polity, decency, and decorum; or relative to the tender affections and fond endearments of human nature; more especially regarding those moral duties which are the truest source of mortal bliss—domestic ties, offices, and obligations.

This code of morality has an advantage over any other of the kind, on account of its not being conducted systematically. In all books that treat upon these subjects, the precepts are disposed methodically, under separate heads or chapters; as Ambition, Bravery, Constancy, Devotion, and so on to the end of the alphabet; which mode, though useful on account of references, or as a common-place book, cannot be near so entertaining, and consequently so well able to answer the *utile dulci,*[2] as a work of this sort, where the documents rise out of the action immediately before our eyes, and are constantly varying with the quick shifting of scenes, person, and subjects; where love sometimes follows war, jealousy succeeds friendship, parsimony liberality; and so proceeding throughout the intire *quicquid agunt homines*[3] of human life.

. . . The great principle of universal charity, which soars above the partial respects of nations or of sects, is srongly, though indirectly, inculcated, in the Jew's speech, here [in *The Merchant of Venice*]; which, according to this very principle, should be received without prejudice, though proceeding from the mouth of an Alien, and an Infidel.

Shylock, speaking of Anthonio,

> He hath disgraced me, and hindered me of half a million, laughed at my losses, mocked at my gains, scorned my nation, thwarted my bargains, cooled my friends, heated mine enemies; and what's his reason? I am a Jew. Hath not a Jew eyes? Hath not a Jew hands, organs, dimensions, senses, affections, passions? Fed with the same food, hurt by the same weapons, subject to the same diseases, healed by the same means, warmed and cooled by the same summer and winter, as a Christian is? If you prick us, do we not bleed? If you tickle us, do we not laugh? If you poison us, do we not die? [III.i.51–63]

As the remainder of the speech exceeds the moderation of Christian ethics, I think proper to stop the Jew's mouth, here. . . . [4]

Shakespeare has written three pieces on the subject of jealousy; the Winter's Tale, Cymbeline, and this one [*Othello*], besides the character of Ford, in the Merry Wives. But such was the richness of his genius, that he has not borrowed a single thought, image, or expression, from any one of them, to assist him in any of the others. The subject seems rather to have grown progressively out of itself, to have inspired its own sentiments, and have dictated its own language. This Play, in my opinion, is very justly considered as the last and greatest effort of our Author's genius, and may, therefore, be looked upon as the chef d'œuvre of dramatic composition.[5]

How perfectly does Othello's conduct throughout, correspond with Iago's description of it in the latter end of the First Act!

> The Moor is of a free and open nature,
> That thinks men honest, who but seem to be so. [I.iii.442–443]

Such a character is not uncommon in life; whose virtues, arising more from an excellence of nature, than an exertion of philosophy, is led to judge of others by itself, and of course become the dupe of art and villainy. . . .

The argument between philosophy and feeling, in cases of misfortune or grief, is well debated here [in scene iii].[6] The Duke, preaching patience to the father, upon his daughter's elopement with the Moor, says,

Good Brabantio,
Take up this mangled matter at the best.
Men do their broken weapons rather use,
Than their bare hands. [I.iii.198–201]

When remedies are past, the griefs are ended,
By seeing the worst, which late on hope depended;
To mourn a mischief that is lost and gone,
Is the next way to draw new mischief on.
What cannot be preserved, when fortune takes,
Patience her injury a mockery makes;
The robbed that smiles steals something from the thief;
He robs himself who spends a bootless grief.

Brabantio. So let the Turk of Cyprus us beguile,
We lose it not so long as we can smile.
He bears the sentence well, who nothing bears,
But the free comfort which from thence he hears★;
But he bears both the sentence and the sorrow,
That to pay grief must of poor patience borrow.
These sentences to sugar or to gall,
Being strong on both sides, are equivocal.
But words are words. I never yet did hear,
That the bruised heart was healed through the ear. [I.iii.232–250]

I may possibly be reprehended, by some severe moralists, for noting the equipoise of such an argument as this. In this instance, indeed, I confess that I act contrary to the usual tenor of document, which always takes part on the *wise* side of a question. But, as I have said before†, I do not think that ethic philosophy can ever be a gainer, by overstraining the sinews of the human mind. We ought neither to be votaries to the Cynic nor the Stoic sects. We should not, with Diogenes, *follow Nature* in the mere animal sense of the expression, nor with Zeno fly beyond it, in the metaphysical

★Alluding to the homily usually made by a judge, on passing sentence.
†Last Part of Postscript to Julius Cæsar, with other passages referred to in the Notes.

Elizabeth Griffith (1727?–1793)

one.[7] True virtue has no extremes. Its sphere extends not beyond the *Temperate* Zones. It sleeps in the Frozen, and but raves in the Torrid ones.

I have before observed upon the exuberance of Shakespeare's document and moral. He so much abounds in maxim and reflection, that he appears frequently at a loss to find proper characters, throughout even his own extensive drama, sufficient to parcel them out to; so that he is frequently obliged to make his fools talk sense, and set his knaves a-preaching. An instance of the latter impropriety may be seen in the following passage, which contains both sound philosophy, and useful admonition. But that it may have the better effect on my readers, I wish that whenever they remember the speech, they could contrive to forget the speaker.[8]

> *Rodorigo.* What should I do? I confess it is my shame to be so fond; but it is not in my *virtue* to amend it.
>
> *Iago.* Virtue? a fig. *'Tis in ourselves that we are thus, or thus.* Our bodies are our gardens, to the which our wills are gardeners. So that if we will plant nettles, or sow lettuce; set hyssop, and weed up thyme; supply it with one gender of herbs, or distract it with many; either have it sterile with idleness, or manured with industry; why, the power and corrigible authority of this lies in our will. If the ballance of our lives had not one scale of reason, to poise another of sensuality, the blood and baseness of our natures would conduct us to most preposterous conclusions. [I.iii.361–373]

The plea that Rodorigo offers above, for remaining still under the dominion of a lawless passion, is framed upon a fatal error, too prevalent in the world, that *virtue* is a peculiar gift from Heaven, granted *speciali gratia,*[9] as it were, to particular and chosen persons. Hence indolent minds are apt to conclude it a vain task to restrain their passions, or resist their temptations, without the supernatural aid of such an innate endowment. Iago, in his reply, reasons very justly against this dangerous and discouraging doctrine of *partial grace;* in support of which argument I shall here add a passage from a modern writer, who, speaking on this subject, says, "The difficulties we apprehend, more than those we find, in the strife with all our passions, is the only thing that prevents philosophy or virtue from being commonly attainable in general life. What makes the difference between a chaste woman, and a frail one? *The one had struggled, and the other not.* Between a brave man and a coward? *The one had struggled, and the other not.* An honest man and a knave? *One had struggled, the other not.*"* . . .

---

*The Posthumous Works of a late Celebrated Genius deceased.

It has often surprized me, to find the character of Desdemona so much mistaken and slighted, as it too generally is. It is simple, indeed, but that is one of its merits: for the simplicity of it is that of *innocence*, not of *folly*. In my opinion, she seems to be as perfect a model of a wife, as either this author, or any other writer, could possibly have framed. She speaks little; but whatever she says is sensible, pure, and chaste. The remark she makes in this place [scene iv], on the alteration of Othello's manners towards her, affords a very proper admonition to all women in her situation and circumstances.

> Something, sure, of state . . .
> Hath puddled his clear spirit; and, in such cases,
> Men's natures wrangle with inferior things,
> Though great ones are their object. 'Tis even so—
> For let our finger ake, and it endues
> Our other healthful members with a sense
> Of pain. *Nay, we must think men are not gods;*
> *Nor of them look for such observance always,*
> *As fits the bridal.* [Ill.iv.160–171]

She had said to himself before,

> Be't as your fancies teach you—
> *Whate'er you be, I am obedient.* [III.iii.98–99]

And afterwards, in confessing herself before Iago and Æmelia,

> Here I kneel—
> If e'er my will did trespass 'gainst his love,
> Or in discourse, or thought, or actual deed,
> Or that mine eyes, mine ears, or any sense
> Delighted them on any other form:
> Or that I do not yet, and ever did,
> And ever will, though he do shake me off
> To beggarly divorcement, love him dearly;
> Comfort forswear me! Unkindness may do much,
> *And his unkindness may defeat my life,*
> *But never taint my love.* [IV.ii.180–190]

And further on, where Æmelia says to her, of Othello,

> I wish you have never seen him!

She replies,

So would not I. *My love doth so approve him,*
That ev'n his stubbornness, his checks and frowns,
Have grace and favour in them. [IV.iii.20–22]

As the married state is both the dearest and most social connection of life, I think this a proper passage to conclude my observations with, on a work in which is comprehended the completest system of the œconomical and moral duties of human nature, that perhaps was ever framed by the wisdom, philosophy, or experience of *uninspired* man.

There are many favourite passages in Shakespeare, which most of my Readers have got by heart, and missing here, may possibly object to my having neglected to quote or observe upon them, in their proper places. But my intention, in this Work, was not to propound the beauties of the Poet, but to expound the document of the Moralist, throughout his writings. . . .

Example is better than precept. A dramatic moral affords us the benefit of both, at once. Plato wished that Virtue could assume a visible form. Dramatic exhibition gives one, both to Virtue and to Vice. The abstract idea is there materialized. The contrast of character, too, affords an additional strength to the moral; as we are led to love virtue, on a double account, by being made to abhor vice, at the same time. The dramatic moralist possesses a manifest advantage over the doctrinal one. Mere descriptions of virtue or vice do not strike us, so strongly, as the visible representations of them. Richard the Third's dream, Lady Macbeth's soliloquy in her sleep, the Dagger Scene in the same Play, Cardinal Beaufort's last moments,[10] with many other passages in our Author, of the same admonitory kind, avail us more than whole volumes of Tully's Offices, or Seneca's Morals.[11]

Notes

1. See Samuel Johnson's *Preface* to his edition of Shakespeare (1765).
2. I.e., the useful and agreeable (Horace).
3. I.e., whatever men do.
4. Shylock's next words call for revenge, a revenge he identifies as Christian.
5. Griffith is mistaken here. First performed in 1604 although not published until 1622, *Othello* is by no means Shakespeare's last work.
6. Throughout this excerpt, modern scene divisions are substituted for those given by Griffith. Italics are Griffith's throughout.
7. The Cynics, under the leadership of Diogenes (c. 430 B.C.E.), exalted virtue

as the only good and practiced a life of self-denial and self-sufficiency. Zeno, the founder of Stoicism (c. 300 B.C.E.), began as a Cynic but was also strongly influenced by Socratic philosophy. The Stoics also held virtue to be the highest good and professed indifference to physical suffering.

8. I.e., Iago. Here, as in her discussion of Shylock, Griffith separates the representation of the character from the character's discourse.

9. I.e., by special favor.

10. Henry Cardinal Beaufort is a character in Shakespeare's *Henry VI*, Parts I and II.

11. Tully is better known as Cicero (106 B.C.E.–43 B.C.E.). Considered the greatest Roman orator, Cicero was a philosopher and politician generally Stoical in bent. "Offices" refers to *De officiis*, Cicero's handbook on Stoic morality. Lucius Annaeus Seneca (4 B.C.E.?–65 C.E.) was a Roman playwright and Stoic philosopher whose tragedies considerably influenced European Renaissance drama. His prose work focuses heavily on moral exhortation.

CHARLOTTE RAMSAY LENNOX
(1729?–1804)

THE DAUGHTER of James Ramsay, captain of an infantry company, Charlotte Lennox spent four childhood years in the fort at Albany, New York. At about age fifteen, following the death of her father, she was sent to England. There she came under the patronage of Lady Isabella Finch, to whom Lennox dedicated her first work, *Poems on Several Occasions* (1747). Samuel Johnson, who unflaggingly encouraged her work, hosted a party marking the publication of her first novel, *The Life of Harriot Stuart* (1751); and under the word *talent* in his dictionary, he cited her best-selling novel, *The Female Quixote* (1752).

Soon after her marriage in 1747 to the profligate Alexander Lennox, Charlotte became through her writing the family's primary support. Among her works are the novels *Henrietta* (1758) and *Sophia* (1762) and several translations. She tried but failed at acting, and in 1760–1761 published a magazine, *The Lady's Museum*. A daughter of Lennox died young, and she later sent her son to America, away from the baleful influence of his father, from whom she had separated. In old age she wrote a final novel, *Euphemia* (1790), which, like her first, drew on life at the fort in Albany. The first had valorized romantic love; the last showed the misfortunes of a woman trapped by marriage to a man she no longer respected.

Lennox's three-volume *Shakespear Illustrated* (1753–1754) was the first of its kind to compare Shakespeare's plays with their sources, but its subtitle, *With Critical Remarks*, suggests a further purpose. Possibly in response to comments by critics like Henry Fielding that *The Female Quixote* was an inferior imitation of Cervantes' original, Lennox chides Shakespeare for lack of invention in creating plots. As evident in the excerpt here, she especially criticizes him for his female characters. So outraged were her contemporaries by this criticism of Shakespeare that they hissed off the stage her own subsequent play *The Sister* (1769), though *Old City Manners* (1775), her modernization of the Chapman, Jonson, and Marston comedy *Eastward Hoe* (1605), was well received.

Lennox died in poverty, having been sustained by the charity of friends.

A second edition of *Shakespeare Illustrated* (1809) was published posthumously in America.

Shakespear Illustrated (London, 1753; vol. 1 rpt. New York: AMS Press, 1973).

From *Shakespear Illustrated* (1753–1754)

. . . There are a greater Diversity of Characters, and more Intrigues in the Fable of the Play [*Measure for Measure*], than the Novel of Cinthio;[1] yet I think, wherever Shakespear has invented, he is greatly below the Novelist; since the Incidents he has added, are neither necessary nor probable.

The Story of Juriste and Epitia,[2] of itself, afforded a very affecting Fable for a Play; it is only faulty in the Catastrophe. The Reader, who cannot but be extremely enraged at the Deceit and Cruelty of Juriste, and very desirous of his meeting with a Punishment due to his Crime, is greatly disappointed, to find him in the End, not only pardoned, but made happy in the Possession of the beautiful Epitia.

Shakespear, though he has altered and added a good deal, yet has not mended the Moral; for he also shews Vice not only pardoned, but left in Tranquility.

The cruel, the vicious and hypocritical Angelo, marries a fair and virtuous Woman, who tenderly loved him, and is restored to the Favour of his Prince.

I said before, that the Story of Juriste and Epitia afforded an affecting Subject for a Play; and it is to be wished, since Shakespear thought proper to found one upon it, that he had left the Fable simple and entire as it was, without loading it with useless Incidents, unnecessary Characters, and absurd and improbable Intrigue.

Thus it would have stood by keeping close to the Novelist: A young Gentleman, vanquished by the Force of a too violent Passion, ravishes a Virgin, whom he is afterwards willing to marry, but is seiz'd and condemn'd to die for his Crime; his Sister a beautiful Maid, who tenderly loves the unfortunate Youth, solicits the rigid Governor for his Pardon, which he refuses, unless she sacrifices her Honour to him. The Lady rejects his Proposal with Disdain, but subdued by the affecting Tears and Prayers of a Brother, whose Life is dearer to her than her own, she reluctantly consents to the Governor's Proposal, on Condition, that he should give her Brother a free Pardon, and repair her Honour hereafter by Marriage.

The Governor binds himself by Oath, to perform both these Conditions; which Oath he breaks; after the unfortunate Lady had paid the Price of them, and sends an immediate Order for her Brother's Execution.

The Lady in the violence of her Grief and Rage, resolves to murder him with her own Hands, but reflecting that she could not take this Revenge on him, without subjecting herself to a second Violation, she complains of her Wrongs to her Sovereign, and demands Justice on the impious Perpetrator of them.

The Emperor in order to repair her Honour, obliges the perfidious Governor to marry her, and then commands him to be led to Execution, which she by an exalted Piece of Generosity opposes, and as his Wife kneels and solicits ardently for his Pardon; which the Emperor at last grants.

Here the Novelist should be dropt, and the Catastrophe, according to poetical Justice, might be thus wound up.

The Lady having performed her Duty, in saving the Life of a Man, who, however unworthy, was still her Husband, should devote herself to a Cloister, for the remainder of her Life; and the wretched Juriste, deprived of his Dignity, in Disgrace with his Prince, and the Object of Universal Contempt and Hatred, to compleat his Miseries, he should feel all his former Violence of Passion for Epitia renewed, and falling into an Excess of Grief, for her Loss, (since the Practice is allowed by Christian Authors) stab himself in Despair.

The Fable thus manag'd, takes in as great a Variety of Incidents, as with Propriety can be introduced in a Play, and those Incidents naturally rising out of one another, and all dependant on the principal Subject of the Drama, forms that Unity of Action, which the Laws of Criticism require.

This Fable also, would not be destitute of a Moral, which as Shakespear has managed it, is wholly wanting. The fatal Consequence of an irregular Passion in Claudio; the Danger of endeavouring to procure Good by indirect Means in Isabella, and the Punishment of lawless Tyranny in the Governor, convey Instruction equally useful and just.

Since the Fable in Cinthio is so much better contrived than that of *Measure for Measure*, on which it is founded, the Poet sure cannot be defended, for having altered it so much for the worse; and it would be but a poor Excuse, for his want of Judgment, to say, that had he followed the Novelist closer, his Play would have been a Tragedy, and to make a Comedy, he was under a Necessity of winding up the Catastrophe as he has done.

The comic Part of *Measure for Measure* is all Episode, and has no Dependance on the principal Subject, which even as Shakespear has managed it, has none of the Requisites of Comedy, great and flagrant Crimes, such as those of Angelo, in *Measure for Measure*, are properly the Subject of Tragedy, the Design of which is to shew the fatal Consequences of those Crimes, and the Punishment that never fails to attend them. The light Follies of a Lucio, may be exposed, ridiculed and corrected in Comedy.

That Shakespear made a wrong Choice of his Subject, since he was resolved to torture it into a Comedy, appears by the low Contrivance, absurd Intrigue, and improbable Incidents, he was obliged to introduce, in order to bring about three or four Weddings, instead of one good Beheading, which was the Consequence naturally expected.

The Duke, who it must be confess'd, has an excellent plotting Brain, gives it out that he is going *incog[nito]* to Poland, upon weighty Affairs of State, and substitutes Angelo to govern till his Return; to Friar Thomas his Confidant, however, he imparts his true Design, which is, in his Absence, to have some severe Laws revived, that had been long disused: Methinks this Conduct is very unworthy of a good Prince; if he thought it fit and necessary to revive those Laws, why does he commit that to another, which it was his Duty to perform?

The Friar's answer is very pertinent.

> It rested in your Grace
> T' unloose this tied-up Justice when you pleas'd;
> And it in you more dreadful would have seem'd
> Than in Lord Angelo.

The Duke replies,

> I do fear, too dreadful.

In short, the poor Duke is afraid to exert his own Authority, by enforcing those Laws, notwithstanding he thinks them absolutely necessary, and therefore as he says,

> I have on Angelo imposed the Office;
> Who may in the Ambush of my Name strike home.

However, in Fact, it is the Duke who strikes in the Ambush of Angelo's name; for it is he who causes Angelo to put those severe Laws in Execution, while he skulks in Concealment to observe how they are received; if ill, Angelo must stand the Consequence; if well he will enjoy the Merit of it. And in order to discover how Things are carried on in the Commonwealth, he makes the Friar procure him a Habit of the Order, and thus disguised, where does he go? Why, to the common Jail, among the condemned Malefactors. His Speculations are wholly confined to this Scene.

Charlotte Ramsay Lennox (1729?–1804)

Here, entirely taken up with the Affairs of the Prisoners, his Highness ambles backwards and forwards, from the Prison to Mariana's House, fetching and carrying Messages, contriving how to elude those very Laws he had been so desirous of having executed; corrupting one of the principal of his Magistrates, and teaching him how to deceive his Delegate in Power.

How comes it to pass, that the Duke is so well acquainted with the Story of Mariana, to whom Angelo was betrothed, but abandoned by him on Account of the Loss of her Fortune? She speaks of the Duke as of a Person she had been long acquainted with.

> *Mariana.* Here comes a Man of Comfort, whose Advice
> Hath often still'd my brawling Discontent.

Yet this could only happen while he assumed the Character of a Friar, which was but for two or three Days at most; he could not possibly have been acquainted with her Story before; if he had, the Character of Angelo would have been also known to him; and consequently it was unnecessary to make him his Deputy, in order to try him further, which was one of his Reasons, as he tells Friar Thomas, for concealing himself.

If it is granted, that the Duke could not know Mariana's Affair before his Disguise; what Opportunities had he of learning it afterwards? For, notwithstanding what Mariana says, which intimates a long Acquaintance, it is certain it could have been but a very short one; some extraordinary Accident therefore must have brought her Story to his Knowledge, which we find was known to no one else; for Angelo's Reputation for Sanctity was very high, and that could not have been, if his Wrongs to Mariana were publickly known.

But why does not the Poet acquaint us with this extraordinary Accident, which happens so conveniently for his Purpose? If he is accountable to our Eyes for what he makes us see, is he not also accountable to our Judgment for what he would have us believe? But, in short, without all this Jumble of Inconsistencies, the Comedy would have been a downright Tragedy; for Claudio's Head must have been cut off, if Isabella had not consented to redeem him; and the Duke would have wanted[3] a Wife, if such a convenient Person as Mariana had not been introduced to supply her Place, and save her Honour.

As the Character of the Duke is absurd and ridiculous, that of Angelo is inconsistent to the last Degree; his Baseness to Mariana, his wicked Attempts on the Chastity of Isabella, his villainous Breach of Promise, and Cruelty to Claudio, prove him to be a very bad Man, long practised in

Wickedness; yet when he finds himself struck with the Beauty of Isabella, he starts at the Temptation; reasons on his Frailty; asks Assistance from Heaven to overcome it; resolves against it, and seems carried away by the Violence of his Passion, to commit what his better Judgment abhors.

Are these the Manners of a sanctified Hypocrite, such as Angelo is represented to be? Are they not rather those of a good Man, overcome by a powerful Temptation? That Angelo was not a good Man, appears by his base Treatment of Mariana; for certainly nothing can be viler than to break his Contract with a Woman of Merit, because she had accidentally become poor; and, to excuse his own Conduct, load the unfortunate Innocent with base Aspersions, and add Infamy to her other Miseries: Yet this is the Man, who, when attacked by a Temptation, kneels, prays, expostulates with himself, and, while he scarce yields in Thought to do wrong, his Mind feels all the Remorse which attends actual Guilt.

It must be confessed indeed, that Angelo is a very extraordinary Hypocrite, and thinks in a Manner quite contrary from all others of his Order; for they, as it is natural, are more concerned for the Consequences of their Crimes, than the Crimes themselves, whereas he is only troubled about the Crime, and wholly regardless of the Consequences.

The Character of Isabella in the Play seems to be an Improvement upon that of Epitia in the Novel; for Isabella absolutely refuses, and persists in her Refusal, to give up her Honour to save her Brother's Life; whereas Epitia, overcome by her own Tenderness of Nature, and the affecting Prayers of the unhappy Youth, yields to what her Soul abhors, to redeem him from a shameful Death. It is certain however, that Isabella is a mere Vixen in her Virtue; how she rates her wretched Brother, who gently urges her to save him!

> *Isabella.* Oh, you Beast!
> Oh faithless Coward! Oh dishonest Wretch!
> Wilt thou be made a Man out of my Vice?
> Is't not a Kind of Incest, to take Life
> From thine own Sister's Shame? What shou'd I think?
> Heav'n grant my Mother play'd my Father fair:
> For such a warp'd Slip of Wilderness
> Ne'er issued from his Blood. Take my Defiance;
> Die; perish: Might my only bending down
> Reprieve thee from thy Fate, it should proceed.
> I'll pray a thousand Prayers for thy Death;
> No word to save thee.

Charlotte Ramsay Lennox (1729?–1804)

> *Claudio.* Nay, hear me, *Isabella.*
> *Isabella.* O fie! fie! fie!
> Thy Sin's not accidental, but a Trade;
> Mercy to thee wou'd prove itself a Bawd:
> 'Tis best that thou dy'st quickly.

Is this the Language of a modest tender Maid; one who had devoted herself to a religious Life, and was remarkable for an exalted Understanding, and unaffected Piety in the earliest Bloom of Life?

From her Character, her Profession, and Degree of Relation to the unhappy Youth, one might have expected mild Expostulations, wise Reasonings, and gentle Rebukes; his Desire of Life, though purchased by Methods he could not approve, was a natural Frailty, which a Sister might have pitied and excused, and have made use of her superior Understanding to reason down his Fears, recal nobler Ideas to his Mind, teach him what was due to her Honour and his own, and reconcile him to his approaching Death, by Arguments drawn from that Religion and Virtue of which she made so high a Profession; but that Torrent of abusive Language, those coarse and unwomanly Reflexions on the Virtue of her Mother, her exulting Cruelty to the dying Youth, are the Manners of an affected Prude, outragious in her seeming Virtue; not of a pious, innocent and tender Maid.

I cannot see the Use of all that juggling and Ambiguity at the winding up of the Catastrophe; Isabella comes and demands Justice of the Duke for the Wrongs she had received from his Deputy, declaring she had sacrificed her Innocence to save her Brother's Life, whom Angelo had, notwithstanding his Promise to the contrary, caused to be executed.

Upon the Duke's telling her, that he believed her Accusation to be false, she goes away in Discontent, without saying a Word more: Is this natural? Is it probable, that Isabella would thus publicly bring a false Imputation on her Honour, and, though innocent and unstained, suffer the World to believe her violated?—She knows not that the honest Friar who advised her to this extraordinary Action, is the Duke to whom she is speaking; she knows not how the Matter will be cleared up.

She who rather chose to let her Brother die by the Hands of an Executioner, than sacrifice her Virtue to save his Life, takes undeserved Shame to herself in public, without procuring the Revenge she seeks after.

Mariana's evasive Deposition; Friar Peter's enigmatical Accusation of Isabella; the Duke's winding Behaviour; what does it all serve for? but to perplex and embroil plain Facts, and make up a Riddle without a Solution.

The Reader can easily discover how the Plot will be unravelled at last; but the unnecessary Intricacies in unravelling it, still remain to be accounted for.

The Play sets out with the Moral in the Title, *Measure for Measure*; but how is this made out? the Duke speaking of Angelo to Isabella, says,

> _____but as a Judge,
> Being doubly Criminal, in Violation
> Of sacred Chastity, and of Promise Breach,
> Thereon dependant for your Brother's Life,
> The very Mercy of the Law cries out
> Most audible, even from his proper Tongue.
> An Angelo for Claudio; Death for Death.
> Haste still pays Haste, and Leisure answers Leisure;
> Like doth quit Like, and Measure still for Measure.

Thus it should have been, according to the Duke's own Judgment to have made it *Measure for Measure*; but when Angelo was pardoned, and restored to Favour, how then was it *Measure for Measure*?

The Case is not altered, because Claudio was not put to death, and Isabella not violated; it was not through Angelo's Repentance, that both these Things did not happen; a Woman he was engaged to, supplied the Place of Isabella, and the Head of another Man, was presented to him instead of Claudio's. Angelo therefore was intentionally guilty of perverting Justice, debauching a Virgin, and breaking his Promise, in putting her Brother to death, whose Life she had bought by that Sacrifice. Isabella when pleading for him, says,

> My Brother had but Justice,
> In that he did the Thing for which he dy'd;
> For Angelo, his Act did not o'ertake his bad Intent,
> And must be buried but as an Intent,
> That perish'd by the Way; Thoughts are no Subjects:
> Intents, but meerly Thoughts.

This is strange Reasoning of Isabella; her Brother deserved Death, she says, because *he did the Thing for which he died*; he intended to do it, and his doing it was the Consequence of his Intention.

Angelo likewise intended to debauch her, and murder her Brother, and he did both in Imagination; that it was only Imagination, was not his Fault, for so he would have had it, and so he thought it was. It is the Intention which constitutes Guilt, and Angelo was guilty in Intention, and for what he knew, in fact, therefore, as far as lay in his Power, he was as guilty as Claudio.

This Play therefore being absolutely defective in a due Distribution of Rewards and Punishments; *Measure for Measure* ought not to be the Title, since Justice is not the Virtue it inculcates; nor can Shakespear's Invention in the Fable be praised; for what he has altered from Cinthio, is altered greatly for the worse.

Notes

1. Giraldi Cinthio's *Hecatomithi*, Decade 8, Novella 5 (1565), has been summarized previously by Lennox as Shakespeare's source for *Measure for Measure*.

2. Juriste, the false judge, is the prototype for Shakespeare's Angelo; Epitia, the victimized heroine, is an earlier version of Isabella.

3. Lacked.

CLARA REEVE (1729–1807)

WHILE Clara Reeve is probably best known for her Gothic novel *The Old English Baron* (originally titled *The Champion of Virtue* [1777]), she belongs more squarely to the tradition of writers interested in pedagogical and moral reform. Her *School for Widows* (1791) and *Plans of Education* (1792) are devoted to the question of how best to educate young ladies. Reeve herself was a highly educated woman. Encouraged by her family to read at an early age, she was familiar with French, German, and Latin and had a lifelong interest in history and biography. She was born in Ipswich, in eastern England, the oldest daughter of eight children. Her father, William Reeve, was a clergyman who died in 1755, after which Reeve moved with her mother and two sisters to Colchester. There she began writing poetry and translations.

Reeve was caught between her dissatisfaction with the legal and educational status of women and her firm belief in keeping to one's place. The tension this created forced her into uneasy assertions that men and women were not created equal even while she was putting herself forward to be "admitted to the rank of authors, and amply rewarded by the public." It surfaces in the submissiveness of Mrs. Darnford and Mrs. Strictland in *School for Widows* even as they bristle at their husbands' respectively improvident and tyrannical ways. Reeve's critical writings are similarly poised between support for women's authority and a conservative moral stance.

In *The Progress of Romance* (1785), Euphrasia begins her discourse by asking her listeners to "divest yourselves of common prejudices" against both romances and women critics. Through Euphrasia, one of the two female voices, Reeve both defines and defends the novel. She is also careful to recommend only those novels of the highest moral value and leaves the defense of more questionable authors, such as Fielding and Rousseau, to Hortensius, the male voice of the dialogues.

The Progress of Romance Through Times, Countries, and Manners (Colchester: W. Keymer, 1785; rpt. New York: Garland, 1970), Evenings II and VII.

Clara Reeve (1729–1807)

From *The Progress of Romance* (1785)

Hortensius. Ladies, I rejoice to see you at my house on this occasion. Let us lay aside form and ceremony, and proceed to the business of our meeting.—I expect a pitch'd battle; for I see Euphrasia has brought her artillery and is placing them to advantage.

Euphrasia. You know your advantages, and that a woman is your opponent.

Hort. Whether you mean me a compliment or reproof, is not clear.—But I will not reply to it, lest it should hinder business.—It lies upon you Madam to proceed with your investigation.

Sophronia. You are to explain to us the word Romance, of which it seems we have no certain Idea.

Euph. Since our last meeting, I have not been idle.—I have consulted all the Dictionary writers upon the subject, and I do not find that any of them are clear and certain in their definition of it.

Ainsworth and Littleton speak in the following terms:—*Narratio ficta,—fabulosa heroicorum facinorum historia.—Scriptum eroticum—splendida fabula.*[1]

Boyer calls a Romance too concisely—*un fable—une conte—un mensonge.*[2]

Old Dyche and Bailey—a fiction, or feigned Story.

Dr. Johnson[3]—a military fable of the *middle ages:*—A tale of wild adventures of war and love.

With all respect to the Doctor's judgment,—I must affirm that this definition can only be proper to the Romances of the middle ages, but cannot extend to the whole Genus.

Hort. A proper distinction—but what use will you make of it?

Euph. The Origin of Romance is of much higher date, as I hope to convince you,—but first let us speak of the name.

Hort. How then would you define it?

Euph. By fixing a clear and certain meaning to it, not as of my own invention or judgment; but borrowing the idea of the Latinists, I would call it simply an *Heroic fable,*—a fabulous Story of such actions as are commonly ascribed to heroes, or men of extraordinary courage and abilities.—Or if you would allow of it, I would say an Epic in prose.[4]

Hort. I cannot allow of the last appellation, but to the first I make no objection. An Epic is a very superior composition.

Euph. We will speak of that hereafter. I do not despair of bringing you over to my definition; but let us first trace the Origin of our subject. Romances or Heroic fables are of very ancient, and I might say universal Origin. We find traces of them in all times, and in all countries: they have always been the favourite entertainment of the most savage, as well as the most civilized people. In the earliest accounts of all nations, we find they had traditional stories of their most eminent persons, that is of their *Heroes*, to which they listened in raptures, and found themselves excited to perform great actions, by hearing them recited;—they had their war-songs—and they had also their prose narratives.

Hort. This is indeed a truth that cannot be denied, I did not expect so ancient, nor so well authenticated an Origin, as you have given them.

Soph. I knew that Euphrasia would never advance, what she could not defend,—proceed Madam.

Euph. As a country became civilized, their narrations were methodized, and moderated to probability.—From the prose recitals sprung History,—from the war-songs Romance and Epic poetry.

Hort. History—Romance—and Epics all in a breath!

Euph. Let us first distinguish History from the others.—When a nation became acquainted with letters, they could record facts, and this is the Æra of true History. Before that time a story, that at first was founded on facts, by length of time and passing through many hands, lost many real circumstances, and acquired many fictitious ones. The heathen Mythology is an unanswerable proof of this truth;—what at first was the History of mortal men, and their actions, was at length ascribed to deities; and the veil of Allegory concealed and altered facts, till they could no longer be traced, and at last were lost in fable and obscurity. These Stories, though no longer believed by wise men as truths, yet continued to please as agreeable fictions; and in more enlightened times, men of Genius and fancy, perceiving the pleasure they gave and how willingly they were received, imitated those antient fables, and in process of time composed others of different kinds, following the track of their talents, and the temper of the times in which they lived.

Hort. All this I allow.—But will you involve History in this obscurity?

Euph. By no means.—Let us now leave History to her own strength and evidence, as the noblest and most useful of all studies; and let us proceed to Romance, and the Epic poem.

Hort. Romance and Epic again!—do you affirm that they are the same?

Euph. I do affirm it, and will endeavour to maintain it. They spring from the same root,—they describe the same actions and circumstances,—they produce the same effects, and they arc continually mistaken for each other.

Clara Reeve (1729–1807)

Hort. Your pardon Madam,—I must mention one material difference— The Epic poem is always derived from some Historical fact, though perhaps remote and obscure.

Euph. Remote and obscure indeed.—So perhaps are some of the stories in Ovid's *Metamorphoses*,—but I will bring a fairer comparison.—In the French Romances of the sixteenth Century, they had their foundation in real History; but the superstructure was pure fiction. I will not shelter myself under their authority, I will not speak of them as respectable works.— Let us compromise.—If you will permit me to go on in my own way, perhaps I may answer your objections when you least expect it, and I shall call upon you to make them, in due time.

Hort. I will hear you with attention and impartiality: but I wish you to come to the point directly.

Soph. The dispute waxes warm.—My dear Euphrasia, I expect you to answer all the scruples of Hortensius.

Euph. Well then, I will come to the point you wish to bring me.—Mankind willingly adopt the prejudices of their ancestors, they embrace them with affection, they quit them with reluctance. One of them is to decry Romance, and venerate Epic Poetry. I believe Hortensius has as few prejudices as any man living; but I must think this to be a strong one, and as such I shall treat it, and endeavour to cure him of it.

Hort. I hope I am open to conviction, and ready to acknowledge truth, whether it makes for or against me.—Proceed Madam.

Euph. The Romances of all countries are derived from the bards. All countries have had their bards of early times, and their prose Romances afterwards.—Lest my opinion should not be sufficient, I shall refer you to Dr. Percy's Essay on the old *Metrical Romances*,[5] in which he has treated this subject, in so clear and judicious a manner, that nothing I can say is worthy to come after it.—You shall take it home with you, and it will prepare you for our next conversation. You will there find that Romances have been written both in prose and verse, and that according to the different circumstances of the Author's genius and situation, they became Epics or Romances.

Hort. I will certainly read it, but I will not promise to receive it implicitly.—I cannot with any patience see Homer and Virgil degraded into writers of Romances.

Euph. I would not willingly degrade those great Poets: but I beg leave to distinguish them.——

Homer is universally acknowledged as the Prince of Epic poetry. If we may believe Dr. Blackwell,[6] there was a wonderful concurrence of circumstances, that elevated him to this high station; circumstances unlikely, perhaps impossible, to happen again to any other Poet, or at least as improbable, as to find another Poet equally capable of using the same advantages:—but with all this eclat that surrounds him, Homer was the parent of Romance; where ever his works have been known, they have been imitated by the Poets and Romance writers.—I look upon Virgil as the most successful of his Imitators.

Hort. This is what I call degrading both these divine men, which I did not expect from you, whom I reckoned among their admirers.

Euph. I am so still, as much as possible, on this side Idolatry.—I venerate Homer as much as one unlearned in his own language can do. From Pope's admired translation I can discern the strong paintings of his bold imagination, his knowledge and judgment in marking his characters; and above all things, the consideration that the world owes to him, in a great measure, the knowledge of the History and Manners of the times in which he wrote, and of some ages before him; on these and many other accounts, Homer must always claim our respect and even veneration.—But after all this can you forbear smiling at the extravagant sallies of his imagination, can you approve his violent machinery, in which he degrades his deities below his heroes, and makes deities of men. In a word, if you will not smile with me, I know many of his admirers that will; in spite of the labours of his commentators, who strive with all their strength, to allegorize away his absurdities.

Hort. Upon my word Madam, you have made a bold attack, I am not prepared to answer you of a sudden, but I shall do it hereafter.

Euph. In the mean time I am preparing to anticipate your answer, and to obviate your objections.—It is astonishing that men of sense, and of learning, should so strongly imbibe prejudices, and be so loth to part with them.—That they should despise and ridicule Romances, as the most contemptible of all kinds of writing, and yet expatiate in raptures, on the beauties of the fables of the old classic Poets,—on stories far more wild and extravagant, and infinitely more incredible.

Hort. It is because we pay due respect to works of true Genius, and disdain the comparison of such weak and paltry imitations, as those you have undertaken to support.

Euph. I am no stranger to the charms of Poetry, I have even felt a degree of its enthusiasm, yet I cannot sacrifice the convictions of truth at its shrine. I am of opinion that many of the fine old Historical ballads, are equally entitled to the name of Epic poems.

There are examples enough extant, of Romance in verse, and Epics in prose. I shall produce some of them in the course of our progress:—but at present I shall only mention the *Provencals*, or *Troubadours*,—and I refer you to Mrs. Dobson's[7] account of them.

Hort. You would engage me in a new course of reading, but I had rather you would give me your own arguments.

Euph. I am afraid they should not be sufficient, but I will try a shorter way with you. You think the divine Homer degraded by my comparisons, yet I will shew you a striking resemblance of him, in a work of much lower estimation:—Did you never read a book called the Arabian Nights Entertainments?

Hort. You cannot be in earnest in this comparison?

Euph. Indeed I am.—If you will take the trouble to read the Story of Sindbad the Sailor, in the first volume, you will think that either the genius of Homer was transfused into the writer, or else that he was well acquainted with his works; for he certainly resembles Homer in many particulars.—In the boldness of his imagination,—in the variety of his characters,—and in the marvellous adventures he relates.—In the history of Sindbad, we have most of those that Ulysses meets with in the Odyssey: insomuch that you must be convinced the likeness could not be accidental.

Soph. I can confirm your assertion by my testimony,—I have often been surprized at it.—But Hortensius must read the story in order to be convinced of the resemblance.

Euph. Above all other points the Arabian writer most resembles Homer in his Machinery: with this difference however, that he is by far the most modest in the use of it.—Homer takes the liberty of sending his deities perpetually on the most trifling errands,—it is true the Magicians of the Arabian perform very marvellous things, by the assistance of the good and evil Genii: but then they are all subordinate to the seal of the Sultan Solomon the son of David,—it is likewise worthy of observation; that throughout the whole work, the Supreme Being is never mentioned without the deepest marks of homage and veneration.

Give me leave to mention one more circumstance relating to this work. —That all doubts of its Origin and Authenticity are removed, by the testimony of several writers well acquainted with the original language: particularly by Lady M. W. Montague, and by Mr. Jones,[8] both of whom bear testimony to the fidelity of the English translation.

Hort. All that you have said, will only prove that this Arabian writer imitated Homer as many others have done.

Euph. If I am not mistaken, it will prove something more;—namely, that there is frequently a striking resemblance between works of high and low estimation, which prejudice only, hinders us from discerning, and which when seen, we do not care to acknowledge: for the defects of a favourite Author, are like those of a favourite friend; or perhaps still more like our own.

Soph. A palpable hit Hortensius!—confess it?

Hort. I confess that Euphrasia has thrown out many things that have surprized, if they have not convinced me, and that I am very desirous she should proceed.

Soph. You will then read the Story of Sindbad the Sailor, at our request.

Hort. I will,—but I will not promise to allow the comparison.

Euph. Not before you are convinced that it is just.

Hort. In what class will you place your Arabian writer?

Euph. In one of which he is the Original—Eastern Tales:—of which I shall say more in due time and place. In the mean time, I beg leave to lay down two points as certain; upon which I shall establish my system.

First, That Epic Poetry is the parent of Romance.

Secondly, That there is a certain degree of respect due to all the works of Genius, by whatever name distinguished.—Grant me these two postulata, and I shall proceed regularly.

Hort. I find you will take them for granted.—But I put in a caveat, in objection to your dogmas.

Euph. I will call upon you to make them, at a proper time.

Hart. Then I will not interrupt you unseasonably: but perhaps I may sometimes ask for explanation.

Euph. I will most willingly hear and answer you, and I beg your assistance as we go forward.

Soph. It appears to me that Euphrasia has advanced nothing that she has not proved, and I expect as she proceeds that she will explain herself still further.

Euph. You do me honour,—and I hope justice likewise.

Hort. Well Euphrasia,—I will follow you as closely as I can.

Euph. Having traced Romance to its Origin, I shall proceed with the progress of it: but this shall be the subject of our next conversation, it is now time to put an end to this.

Soph. Let us then adjourn to next Thursday, at my house.

Hort. I will not fail to meet you there.

Soph. What would your neighbour Ergastus say, if he should hear that you met weekly two women, to talk of Romances?

Hort. He would certainly indulge his splenetic humour at my expence.

Euph. If you are afraid of him, it will be best to give over our meetings, for I am meditating to tell the subject of them to all the world.

Hort. That is indeed enough to alarm one. I find I must take care of what I say before you.

Euph. Take courage my friend.—I promise you never to make our conversation public, without your consent and approbation.

Hort. On these conditions, I am satisfied; I dare say you will do nothing rashly, nor without due consideration.

Euph. I am honoured by your friendship and confidence.—Adieu 'till next Thursday.

Soph. I shall reckon the hours 'till our next meeting.—Adieu!

Euph. . . . . The word *Novel* in all languages signifies something new. It was first used to distinguish these works from Romance, though they have lately been confounded together and are frequently mistaken for each other.

Soph. But how will you draw the line of distinction, so as to separate them effectually, and prevent future mistakes?

Euph. I will attempt this distinction, and I presume if it is properly done it will be followed,—If not, you are but where you were before. The Romance is an heroic fable, which treats of fabulous persons and things.—The Novel is a picture of real life and manners, and of the times in which it is written. The Romance in lofty and elevated language, describes what never happened nor is likely to happen.—The Novel gives a familiar relation of such things, as pass every day before our eyes, such as may happen to our friend, or to ourselves; and the perfection of it, is to represent every scene, in so easy and natural a manner, and to make them appear so probable, as to deceive us into a persuasion (at least while we are reading) that all is real, until we are affected by the joys or distresses, of the persons in the story, as if they were our own.

Hort. You have well distinguished, and it is necessary to make this distinction.—I clearly perceive the difference between the Romance and Novel, and am surprized they should be confounded together.

Euph. I have sometimes thought it has been done insidiously, by those who endeavour to render all writings of both kinds contemptible.

Soph. I have generally observed that men of learning have spoken of them with the greatest disdain, especially collegians.

Euph. Take care what you say my friend, they are a set of men who are not to be offended with impunity. Yet they deal in Romances, though of a different kind.—Some have taken up an opinion upon trust in others whose judgment they prefer to their own.—Others having seen a few of the worst or dullest among them, have judged of all the rest by them;—just as some men affect to despise our sex, because they have only conversed with the worst part of it.

Hort. Your sex knows how to retort upon ours, and to punish us for our offences against you.—Proceed however. . . .

Euph. Among our early Novel-writers we must reckon Mrs. Behn.— There are strong marks of Genius in all this lady's works, but unhappily, there are some parts of them, very improper to be read by, or recommended to virtuous minds, and especially to youth.—She wrote in an age, and to a court of licentious manners, and perhaps we ought to ascribe to these causes the loose turn of her stories.—Let us do justice to her merits, and cast the veil of compassion over her faults.—She died in the year 1689, and lies buried in the cloisters of Westminster Abbey.—The inscription will shew how high she stood in estimation at that time.

Hort. Are you not partial to the sex of this Genius?—when you excuse in her, what you would not to a man?

Euph. Perhaps I may, and you must excuse me if I am so, especially as this lady had many fine and amiable qualities, besides her genius for writing.

Soph. Pray let her rest in peace,—you were speaking of the inscription on her monument, I do not remember it.

Euph. It is as follows:

Mrs. APHRA BEHN, 1689.

> Here lies a proof that wit can never be
> Defence enough against mortality.

Let me add that Mrs. Behn will not be forgotten, so long as the Tragedy of Oroonoko[9] is acted, it was from her story of that illustrious African, that Mr. Southern wrote that play, and the most affecting parts of it are taken almost literally from her.

Notes

1. I.e., a feigned narrative, a history of renowned heroic deeds, a composition of love, a splendid fable.
2. I.e., a fable, a fairy tale or false story, a lie.
3. The dictionary writers Reeve refers to take in a wide spectrum of practitioners. Robert Ainsworth's *Dictionary English and Latin* (1736), Adam Littleton's *Latin Dictionary*

in Four Parts (1673), Abel Boyer's French-English *Royal Dictionary* (1699), Thomas Dyche's *Guide to the English Tongue* (1707), and Nathaniel Bailey's *Universal Etymological English Dictionary* (1721) all ran to multiple editions throughout the century. Samuel Johnson's *Dictionary* was first published in 1755.

    4. A reference to Henry Fielding's preface to *Joseph Andrews*.

    5. Thomas Percy, Bishop of Dromore, best known for his *Reliques of Ancient English Poetry* (1765).

    6. Thomas Blackwell, *An Enquiry into the Life and Writings of Homer* (1736),

    7. Susannah (Dawson) Dobson, *The Literary History of the Troubadours* (1779).

    8. Mary Wortley Montagu learned Turkish as the wife of the ambassador to Constantinople. David Jones wrote *A Complete History of the Turks* (1701).

    9. *Oroonoko, or the History of the Royal Slave*, a novel written by Aphra Behn, published in 1688 and adapted for the stage by Thomas Southerne in 1695.

SOPHIE GUNTERMANN VON LAROCHE (1730–1807)

CONSIDERED GERMANY'S first woman novelist, Sophie von LaRoche was born Marie Sophie Guntermann, the eldest of thirteen children of a well-to-do physician and scholar who offered his daughter an exceptional education but expected of her a traditional wifely destiny. After two engagements opposed by her family (one to the poet and early feminist Christoph Wieland, with whom she maintained a lifelong literary connection), she bowed to her father's will and married Georg Michael Frank (later ennobled as von LaRoche), whose duties as private secretary to the Duke of Stadion involved the couple in the courtly life of Mainz. She bore eight children, of whom five survived infancy.

In 1771 LaRoche published her first work, *The History of Lady Sophie Sternheim*, an epistolary novel highly popular not only in Germany but also in England and France, manifestly influenced by *Clarissa* and as manifestly an influence upon Goethe's *Sorrows of Young Werther* (1774). LaRoche's literary projects took on economic urgency after 1780, when a political intrigue ended her husband's career. Her writings include not only novels—primarily in epistolary form—but also moral tales, essays, and travel literature, and she was an early initiator of French-style salons. She continued to write and publish until just before her death in 1807.

Always attempting to balance literary aspiration with pietist femininity, LaRoche was an advocate of a "women's sphere" in literature at a time in Germany when literacy for women in particular was still very limited. She promoted the works of younger women and encouraged women's intellectual activities while emphasizing the primacy of domestic responsibilities. During 1783 and 1784 she published a literary journal for women which she named *Pomona: For Germany's Daughters*, after the goddess of the autumn fruits. "On Reading" appeared in the *Pomona* of September 1783. Conventional in its wish to reconcile domesticity and reading, the essay is unconventional for its attention to reading as a material act over which women are encouraged to take control and for its understanding of reading and self-analysis as parallel dialogic practices. LaRoche considered *Pomona* itself

Sophie Guntermann von LaRoche (1730–1807)

to be a dialogic enterprise; she dubbed it a "paper salon" and encouraged her readers to become contributors.

Pomona: Für Teutschlands Töchter, vol. 2 (1783; rpt. Munich: Saur, 1987).

On Reading (1783)

I realize that I should have written about this sooner, because it would have promoted greater orderliness and usefulness in many of my women readers. But here I can make up for this omission, and the excerpts that I want to take from [my earlier] instructions on the useful life can be tried out right away in my *Pomona*.

I consider it extremely fortunate for my sex that our first reading exercises include all kinds of books that provide a foundation for our finest knowledge and virtue. Christian teachings and Bible stories together should have given us not only the ability to deal with life, but also a lasting standard of discrimination and judgment for all other books that come our way. The pure feelings of religion should have made us reject everything that could be damaging to our morals and beliefs, and biblical stories should remain our pointer to truly useful knowledge. Moses's description of the world's creation should have left in us seeds of desire for natural history; the Psalms of David, a love of beautiful and exalted poetry; the whole, a taste for the history of humankind, in order to know the ways in which the creatures of this earth utilize their lives and their gifts. This circle of knowledge is large enough, along with the everyday obligations of the good daughter, wife, and mother, to entertain us pleasantly and usefully.

To read silently is the most beneficial activity there is, because just as with solitary walks, one can linger—now in the meadow among the herbs, now on the hill with the pleasing prospect. So too with a book one pauses, reflects, repeats this or that passage, writes down excerpts, thinks about the writer's time and place: where these laws existed, where this custom still exists; that's how they thought then, this is how we think now; I can make this my own, I can put this into practice, etc. When I listen to someone read, I cannot do these things so easily, because I don't have the right to stop the reader whenever I want to reflect. Then, too, the reader's skill can make me find something good when it isn't. Only a like-minded friend or loving teacher should read to me, and teach me step by step to feel and consider everything.

A reasonable person should always read the preface of a book, first of all because she will always find the author's intention there, and will as a result be in a position to understand him correctly and to judge him according to his intent, and also because one can tell from the preface whether the book deserves to be read. After the preface, one reads the table of contents and selects several articles that seem the most important, and which are on topics about which one already knows something. For instance, each and every noble living soul knows the value of friendship and knowledge; and if she finds these subjects in the book's table of contents, then she shall read these parts first and test them against the knowledge and experience of her mind and heart. If the writer is telling us something new, if he says more beautifully and clearly something that is already known, then one writes down passages for oneself and reads the whole thing through with attention and orderliness. Only in this manner can one read usefully.

One should especially ask oneself: for what purpose am I reading this book? And if I answer myself, "To broaden my understanding," then after a few pages I look to see whether I really am finding nourishment for my mind. If I am reading for personal inspiration, then I soon notice whether I am heartened by the author's thoughts, just as I can answer the question: has only my imagination been moved, or also my heart? For no book can have any good in it that does not dispose me toward goodness.

Dear, beloved friends of *Pomona*! Allow me to hope that one of you will ask these questions of the first volume of *Pomona*, that you will examine yourself, write down your thoughts, and send them to me! It would be a splendid exercise, and such a woman could render me a genuine service if she would make me more conscious of everything I was sending to my female readers. In the process of posing these questions, I am reminded of several others which could also be very useful, ones which I found in the fragments of an anonymous source. He says:

> I enjoy talking to myself.—For example, when I come home dissatisfied from a social gathering, then I first go alone to my room and ask, what is wrong with you? Are you in a bad mood?—Yes. Are you sick? No.—I question myself more and more closely in order to get at the truth. Then it appears to me that I have one noble, benevolent soul which is interrogating another, weaker and more simple-minded one and which finally discovers that I have committed a folly; as a result, my ego is wounded because others now think less favorably of me. However, I set myself free in the end with the resolution to act more judiciously and intelligently the next time. If I find that others have abused my kindness and have caused me distress, I forgive them— and then I return happy, kind, and

Sophie Guntermann von LaRoche (1730–1807)

friendly to the company of my family, which would have suffered innocently from my bad mood without these solitary questions and their candid response.

There may always be many people who are plagued by such moods. Let
them make a habit of this laudable self-conversation! And note well that
this fragment was written by a man, who adds, "In this manner I have
remained a good husband, good father, friend, and gentleman." This recipe
will certainly also help a woman's bad moods, just as quinine relieves fever
in both sexes.

Translated by Lisa Ellen Bernstein

ISABELLE VAN TUYLL DE ZUYLEN DE CHARRIÈRE (1740–1805)

Cʟᴀɪᴍᴇᴅ ᴀs a distinguished woman of letters by the countries of her childhood (the Netherlands), her maturity (Switzerland), and her cultural affinity (France), Isabelle van Tuyll ("Belle de Zuylen") was raised in an upper-class Dutch Protestant family with the contradictory message to be both accomplished and suitably feminine. Her first story, published in 1763, caused such a stir for its satire on nobility that her parents had it withdrawn from circulation. Married to Charles-Emmanuel de Charrière in 1771, she associated with many literary figures of her time, including Boswell (who once proposed to her), Voltaire, Diderot, and Benjamin Constant, with whom she was long intimate.

An elusive and contradictory figure of radical and conservative, "enlightenment" and "romantic" tendencies, Charrière published novels, political pamphlets, tales, treatises, and plays and left hundreds of pages of unpublished work. The second part of her *Lettres écrites de Lausanne* (1785–1787), known by its subtitle, *Caliste*, has been her most admired work and is the obvious if unacknowledged source of her rival Germaine de Staël's *Corinne*. Many of her works provoked controversy for their bold satire and their avant-garde ideas: *Lettres de Mistriss Henley* (1784) portrayed the miseries of a "happily married" wife subjected to the will of an "ideal" husband, and the *Lettres neuchâteloises* (1784) exposed the plight of a working-class woman seduced by a social superior in a "righteous" Protestant town.

"Is Genius Above All Rules?" was written for the Besançon Academy of Science, Arts, and Letters, which published worthy entries and offered a prize for the most eloquent. Of fourteen published essays, four supported natural genius and six, including the winning entry, unequivocally supported adherence to rules. Charrière's stance is mixed; while she ultimately argues for an adherence to rules, she refuses the opposition between nature and convention by constructing the genius as one with a natural affinity for rules. Although its aesthetic position is more conservative than many of Charrière's political and fictional writings might lead one to expect, the essay ends with an implicit social critique and a call for a "happy revolution" in the arts. The scrap of a parody of Frances Burney's *Camilla* that Charrière wrote in 1796 embodies her criticism of conventional heroines and marriage plots.

Oeuvres complètes, vols. 9 and 10 (Amsterdam: G. A. Van Oorschot, 1980–1981).

Is Genius Above All Rules? (1788)

To speak of genius, to dare to decide what it is and what it can accomplish, is a bold act whose perils are clear to me. Anyone daring to say that genius, like mediocrity, must be governed by rules, risks being accused of not recognizing it, of being incapable of appreciating its sparks, its bursts of energy, its flights of imagination. But in proposing the question "Is Genius Above All Rules?" a learned Society has taken the position that it could be discussed without too much audacity—and why, good Sirs, should I not dare what you believed might be dared?

Besides, I am not afraid of offending men of genius with the response I have in mind. It is not they who show contempt for rules or who have to escape them. One of the gifts that characterize them is resourcefulness in difficult situations and the ability to draw forth great beauty from difficulty itself.

Let us begin by defining what we mean by rules in the various arts. If we did not try to be specific, we would get lost in generalities that the enlightened men we are addressing would scorn to follow.

Every art has its infancy. The earliest attempts to sketch an image of an absent loved one on canvas or on the walls of a dwelling, to preserve a memorable event in marble, to represent characters in a real or imagined action, all these attempts were imperfect and crude; and even the genius who created the arts from which our pleasures were to spring could not imagine all that would be needed to make our enjoyment complete and lasting. At first it was an achievement simply to draw the contour of objects that we would eventually succeed in painting not only in their true colors, but in depth and perspective, according to both the painter's conception and nature's laws. And to pass quickly from painting to the most seductive art to which poetry has been adapted, it was an achievement at first just for Thespis and his itinerant troupe to mix their songs either with some narration or with the representation of some heroic action fit for a *single* speaker.[1] It was an achievement indeed when Aeschylus made appear, speak, and act upon a stage—although in a rustic manner and somewhat artlessly—

those heroes whom Sophocles, Euripides, and Racine have since made at once our friends—so much have their misfortunes and passions become familiar to us—and demigods, so much has their very language become an object of respect and worship.[2]

So rules existed, even if they were not yet clearly set forth, just as property rights existed, were even protected and respected, before there were laws, codes, and tribunals. And just as in a quasi-civilized state, disorder made itself felt before order existed, so imperfection diminished the enjoyment of the arts before perfection existed: the rule, or regularity, was intimated by the existence of irregularity. But while something preceded property, and while man existed before he owned anything, the relative position, size, and hue of objects on canvas were determined from the moment that bodies and distance existed; and the discomfort we feel when an unfinished action is replaced by another, when, delighting in the illusion of a particular place and time, we are suddenly torn from it and transported to another time and place—this discomfort is as old as our origins, our soul, everything that constitutes us. He deserves our applause, then, who spares us these unpleasantnesses, who, pleasing us with his talents, does not spoil it by any negligence or peculiarity. It does not matter whether or not we are aware of what it cost him to submit to the rule—or rather to model himself on our nature both in the arrangement of the whole and in the execution of details. We rejoice in his submission and his care: it is because of his submission and care that our pleasure will be not only complete but repeatable, seeming always new.

To define rules in this way, to say that there are laws that, banishing irregularities from our plays, disharmony from our verses, and lack of proportion from our canvases, prescribe that the arts and those with talent present us only with what must please—is this not already to answer the question posed? And does this not imply that genius cannot even want to break free from the rules? Would genius try to change our being and make us love what it is not in our nature to love? "But," people will tell me, "what you claim that it cannot attempt, it does attempt, and it succeeds; it makes us admire its innovations and originality. Mistakenly basing the authority of rules on unchanging natural laws, you represent them as more respectable than they are. If the rhythm of our poetry, the construction of our plays, the composition of our paintings, the proportion of our buildings, were fixed by the very essence of things, we would not see architecture, painting, or poetry vary from country to country or from time to time. This should convince you of your error; and your error is dangerous. If a frightened, discouraged young man were to adopt your notion, he would not dare to try his talents; and the artist who dared to do so would feel intimidated, the cold, rigid arm of implacable rules blocking his every step. Fewer artists and among those remaining, less fire, courage, and verve: how many works of art, how many pleasures your doctrine would deny us!" I must answer, must try to prove that my principles are right and that, when understood, they do no injustice to the arts I love and cultivate, and to which my life owes its sweetest joys.

FIRST PART

Going back to the origin of the arts, it is in architecture that we first encounter the notion of beauty and elegance joined to that of utility. Man no doubt thought of shelter as soon as he had the idea of wearing clothes, and hardly had he kept himself safe from rain, sun, and wild animals, when he thought of making his dwelling place not only solid and lasting but spacious enough for him to move about unimpeded and high enough for him to have a sense of breathing freely; then he probably searched for a way of getting air to enter, and with the air, light. To these different needs there was soon joined the desire to look upon daily sights with pleasure and, among the notables of the nation, the longing to distinguish their homes from those of the common people—and among the citizens of the nation, the desire to display their country's grandeur and wealth in the ornamentation of temples and other public buildings. Man's stature had determined the height and width of the entrance to his home, and the eye, grown accustomed to these proportions, sought them out in everything else; they influenced the dimensions of arches and vaults and even the spacing between columns, whose model had originally been the trunks of trees. Rules were finally born from what proved pleasing in the eyes of neighbors and passersby, combined with what was suitable and pleasing to the inhabitants of a private dwelling, to a council assembled in a public place, or to a crowd worshipping the gods.

Have these rules varied? Never. In hot countries, it is from the sun especially that people seek protection. In cold countries, people guard against the snow. The inhabitant of one spot, fearing the tremors of a land given to frequent earthquakes or dreading the assault of brisk and impetuous winds, makes his home wider and weightier; in another spot, fearing the humidity of a marshy terrain and the flooding of rivers, he lifts it as much as possible off the ground. The Greeks, who were always wise and noble in their constructions, have been imitated by the ancient and modern Italians and continue to serve as models, with greater or lesser success, for all nations. The Goths were not so fortunate.[3] Prodigal with their strength and time, piling stone upon stone, they built enormous and astonishing masses in the midst of which a slender tower would sometimes thrust itself upward, like a rocket, sustained in the air by the lightness of its form. The Chinese decorate their temples and houses in a manner that seems to us capricious and bizarre; yet nowhere among them will you see the entrance of a building that is wider than it is high, or columns raised on a flying buttress, or a heavier order lifted above a lighter one and taking it as its base.* Did genius ever dream of violating rules that taste had drawn from convention? No, its daring lies elsewhere. But just as a skillful general, in arranging his troops, takes advantage of a wood or marsh that would have hindered an ordinary leader, or just as a nightingale hangs its nest in a crevice and conceals it beneath the debris of a roof in ruins, so the superior architect, without ever forgetting the principles of his art, varies its application in accordance with the setting and, daring all that he can, changes obstacles into blessings and seems unable to have done without what he had to overcome.

Should I pause to prove that in painting, the rules, once accepted, have not varied? This is only too evident. The grotesque, it is true, has been sometimes preferred to the imitation of nature, but only when skill or time was unavailable. Then people chose an art of pure fantasy rather than violate the rules of an art that no longer had anything arbitrary about it.

Sculpture, Music . . . But in setting forth the question now under consideration, the Academy undoubtedly had reflective labors principally in mind; it is the rules our predecessors recognized and respected that are of central concern here. Noticing that some people deplore the neglect of these rules while others find remnants of an obedience they consider too servile; noticing as well the paucity of contemporary masterpieces, which is attributed either to license or to constraint, you probably wanted, good Sirs, to provoke the partisans of both beliefs to enter in debate and to settle, if possible, the vacillating opinion of the public. Well then, it is of poetry, or rather of the theater, that I shall speak; for in poems not destined for the stage, who can complain about the severity of rules?

Given our freedom to choose among so many different forms through which the imagination may express itself—adorned by cadence and rhyme, in short or long lines, of equal or unequal length—is there any privilege or license left to ask for? If Epics are too heroic and require too lofty a tone, haven't we stories in verse where we may scale the heights, descend to the depths, and finally find equilibrium? Has anyone ever complained about

---

*Ignorance and haste may have made some blunders, but those blunders have not changed the general practice.

Isabelle van Tuyll de Zuylen de Charrière (1740–1805)

the unity of tone that must be preserved in the idyll or the romance, in an epigram or a madrigal?

The father of the stage was Aeschylus; through his own plays, imperfect as they were, he became its legislator. The three unities were established in the *Persae* and the *Oresteia*.[4] "It was thus ignorance and lack of experience" you will say, "that forced the legislator's hand and continues to force our own." It was difficult to set forth more than one action with two or three speakers; and without the necessary equipment, how could one move that action from place to place? They might have been able to enact isolated scenes in tiny theaters★ that probably did not give the viewer a distinct image of any particular place. In the end however, Aeschylus found favor by presenting a single action; he succeeded by focusing our interest. The Greeks flocked to plays, however imperfect, in which the three unities already reigned.

In the plays of Sophocles, whom the public surely supplied with greater assistance, greater resources, the setting remains no less fixed; the action, if more complicated, is not assumed to last any longer; the speakers, if more numerous, are no less subordinated to a single interest; they always have a reason for leaving the stage, they do not return without our knowing why; the exposition is clear; the interest continues to build until the denouement. Sophocles had undoubtedly witnessed Aeschylus's audience and recognized all the rules that had to be followed to achieve the effects he observed. Their rapt attention, their restlessness, tears, and terror, all told him what he must do; their distraction, boredom, or surprise mixed with impatience, signaled what he ought to avoid or add; and there you have the rules of the theater established for all time: for what Sophocles did is what every man, in his heart and by his very nature, asks of any playwright; that is what we all secretly but incontestably expect of him.

You English enthusiasts who worship Shakespeare, I speak to you neither of Aristotle nor Horace nor Boileau but of yourselves:[5] confess, if you dare, that Shakespeare would give you more pleasure, supply greater illusion and even more delight, if you did not have to follow his characters to different places and times, if his Desdemona were not suddenly transported from Venice to Cyprus. You will avoid my question by saying that you would not sacrifice a single thought, a single line of Shakespeare to the most perfect of unities. Perhaps you are right; but what if he did not have to sacrifice anything, if he could have maintained the unities without losing any-

★Pulpita (Horace).

thing . . . That would be impossible, you will interrupt; and if I made a case for Racine and Corneille over Shakespeare, you would embarrass me, I admit, by recalling the lack of verisimilitude that the exact observance of the unity of place sometimes produced in their finest plays.[6] You would embarrass me, as I said; I would feel how difficult it is to avoid the errors these great men fell into; but how can I forget the discomfort I always feel at the Opera when I see trees give way to columns, the seacoast metamorphose into a vestibule, a palace room become as tall as the entire building previously had been, and the actors, who have really not changed in size, change size in proportion to the set.* Pardon me that digressive comment: I agree that the Opera has not yet accepted definitive rules; let me return to my discussion of a theater where very precise rules are acknowledged, where the senses are less involved, and where the mind is therefore left more lucid, free, and demanding.

Perhaps by enlarging the theater as the great Voltaire suggested,[8] by making it more like those used by Sophocles and Euripides, we might do away with the annoyance that caused the authors of *Cinna* and *Brittanicus*[9] to slip into one or two mild errors—errors hardly noticed when, listening attentively and with our souls suspended, we no longer know where Cinna is or where we are. But suppose there is opposition to changing the theater or that the possible changes are insufficient: do we run the risk, in promoting a playwright's success, or in preventing the rejection of certain themes because they seem impossible to handle on the stage, of no longer having a single play without broken rules? And when will a change of setting be allowed? After the first act or before the last? Between each act? Or still more frequently? For if one is not made to remain with the original setting, and if one does not have to consider the fictive and poetic existence of the stage to be as unchanging as its actual physical existence, if Augustus's apartment is not as inalterable in Paris as it was in Rome, then one can as easily change settings twenty times as once. Then the actor would never have to leave the stage: why would Caesar go to the Capitol or the public square, since the Capitol and public square could come to him? I would, then, never feel that conflict I am complaining about, never experience the interruption of a fascinating illusion, the difficulty of getting adjusted to a new setting, of giving myself over to a new illusion; I would expect these changes and

---

*If I am to believe that the Opera is the domain of enchantment, even though it portrays supposedly true events, I would ask that Melusina and Merlin exercise their power more subtly and that Apollo's statue, for example, not present itself in so burlesque a manner to be worshipped by the wife of Admetus and her subjects.[7]

would watch cities, countrysides, and forests come and go as characters do now.

In this strange turnabout, what would become of dramatic art? And even if this imaginary revolution were not as sweeping, would not the essence of drama be altered nonetheless? Would we not have introduced a radical vice that would destroy its perfection? Yes, perfection—what makes for perfection throughout the world: in the eyes of the Englishman, who, in any case, has hardly been willing to hear me out and is far from convinced; the Italian, the Spaniard, the Frenchman; what makes for perfection even in the eyes of the sublime Shakespeare himself, who might never have been faulted had he not preferred a rich harvest of laurels to an even more glorious crown, but one bought with sleepless nights and painful effort. Just as the idea of unsurpassed beauty is somehow connected with the very imperfections of the object that bewitched our minds and enflamed our hearts, so that we cannot imagine being satisfied without them—so the Englishman rejects the laws that Shakespeare did not obey. But if we could get him to forget for a moment the vow he seems to have taken to judge only by what Shakespeare did; if we asked him to describe what he would consider a perfect play, if we asked this not only of him but of men of every nation, and if in describing their ideal tragedy or comedy they omitted none of the rules used by Sophocles, Racine, and Molière,[10] the victory is mine. The rules are eternal, unchangeable, and unchanging; in this first part at least my cause is won.

SECOND PART

Is genius above all rules? I believe I have answered that question and have served rather than harmed the arts by my answer. If someone had put forth an idea opposed to mine, but with more imagination and eloquence; if rules were presented as arbitrary laws that man could destroy as well as create; if someone were to say, "The path taken by those first artists, who managed (by chance or inclination) to please us, has been viewed, out of superstition or laziness, as the only path; and it has certainly been a good one, since it has so often led to excellent results. But there may, there must, be other paths, and it is the role of genius to open them; let us stop tying genius down with chains ill-suited to nature's greatest creation, the one most worthy not only of being free but of making the laws." If this is said and believed, you will witness lazy and overbearing mediocrity sit upon the throne that only genius was thought capable of winning.

Ah, genius, eternal and divine ray of light! Who is not filled with gratitude, trust, and respect at the sound of your name? How could we do without you? You created the arts and all human law; you set us on the path of invention; you gave us everything that makes for happiness; nations owe you their glory, and all men owe you their pleasures. But how can we be sure that it is you we are following when we declare that you can do anything? Do those whom you inspire most often (for in whose work do you preside all the time?) have a genuine and recognizable calling? I have sometimes thought I saw them tremble as they gave themselves up to you and followed your promptings. Like the Saints, they do not always know whether they are being tempted by an evil spirit or inspired by the divine one. In the arts, it has often been need, difficulty, an unforeseen obstacle that led them to their most glorious moment of inspiration, and I never saw them set about working with the conviction that they might change the very nature of the prescribed task or with the intention of daring all. No, I have witnessed only Icaruses preparing their wings and calmly undertaking so audacious a flight; I have only heard Phaetons saying, "I will drive the Sun chariot without paying attention to the route my father always took." [11]

Still, we cannot deny that genius has sometimes violated the rules. We have seen such great beauties born from this boldness that our admiration silenced any criticism, and envy was forced to be quiet out of fear of being revealed for what it was, or offered too much praise not to forgive. But when the man who vanquished the Curiatii killed his own sister, the Rome he had saved forgave him, but without declaring that every victorious hero could henceforth sacrifice similar victims.[12] And the victory of young Manlius did not excuse his disobedience, even in his own father's eyes.[13]

If there are future moments when the genius has to take liberties, is he likely to wait for our blessing before taking them? What would make him bow before laws whose authority he is challenging? Mediocrity dares to break such laws every day. At once active and lazy, wanting to accomplish a great deal while hiding its impotence, mediocrity makes new and easy paths around the obstacles it cannot surmount. And what can time not bring to pass in its long and constant course? A moment may arrive—indeed it seems already to have arrived—when, especially in large cities, amusement is a continual need almost as much for those whom indigence seems to have destined for daily toil as for those whose wealth permits them to be idle. Performances then become routine, and with the same spectators returning frequently, plays age rapidly and new ones are greeted more on the basis of need than merit. A hackneyed plot is accepted provided it has some striking incident, and this easy road to success so encourages younger artists that plays which daily grow more extravagant and shoddy, attract even the enlightened public—a public that forgets what used to please it when it

Isabelle van Tuyll de Zuylen de Charrière (1740–1805)

was less hungry and more selective. The theater is no longer a great pleasure, but it is needed for filling time. It does not confer great renown on any actor, but many young people, by causing some tears to fall or by making a few jokes with multiple meanings, enjoy the honor of not being entirely unknown. The esteem they enjoy within their own family and circle leads others to envy and emulate them, and if these rivals cannot aspire to dramatic glory, they compensate for it by taking smaller honors and by writing all those verse plays we see hatching every day. Let us not disturb the happiness of any one of them or deprive the public of any innocent pleasure; I want simply to express the desire to see some other name given to productions so different from those that have, for centuries, been admired under the name of comedy or tragedy.* Let us call them dramatic tableaux, pathetic or gay dramas, farcical or serious melodramas and refrain from announcing a new comedy or tragedy unless their authors know the rules and wish to follow them, know the difficulties involved and are able to handle them. Then there may arise, from the hope of success and fear of failure, the kind of unrest that inspires genius and calls forth ardent and assiduous effort.

Frenchmen, you love the theater so much that you will, I hope, excuse me for seeming to think only of the rules and the genius that preside over it.

But will not emulation, respect for rules, and scrupulous obedience to them pass from the theater to all branches of poetry, to courtroom eloquence, even to the eloquence of the pulpit and to the labors of the muse of history? Will not all that is slipshod be swept out of language? Will not style be kept safe from useless turgidity, from the excessive effort that often mars it, from those jumbled and incoherent images that authors allow themselves in the name of boldness, but that readers, unable to settle their minds on something solid, find impossible to understand?

Since time is running out, let us cast another glance at the arts with which we began. Painting needs no additional encouragement in France; never has it or its sister, sculpture, or music, that most consoling friend of men, shone more brightly there; but isn't architecture often degraded by parasitical ornaments that overwhelm the available space? Don't we often see that in some buildings materials are far too thin or too stingily applied? Their audacious fragility is frightening, whereas the excessive, useless, and expensive solidity of other buildings is no less disagreeable. Architecture, first of the fine arts and alone among them in bestowing pleasure instead of selling it—for the penniless Citizen walking over our bridges or wan-

---

*Corneille sometimes did in fact change scenes, and I recall that in the *Suite du menteur* one sees Dorante in prison, but I do not think that Molière, outside of *Le Médecin malgré lui*, ever took the same license.[14]

dering near our churches or palaces admires and enjoys them—architecture, today you are worthy of all kinds of gratitude. You will one day supply to the crippled and suffering poor, locked in wretched asylums, all the relief that comes from your attentions: why should these monuments of charity not have a noble and imposing appearance that gratitude may take pleasure in contemplating? You artists charged with planning these interesting buildings, imagine that when we stop at their entrances, we are forced to think of the suffering of our fellow men and of the vicissitudes of fate. The rich who are moved to pity, the poor who are visited, assisted, and consoled, how much they will owe you! Ah! if you would like to produce these touching effects, study the models and the rules; keep from believing that you can violate them. Experience brought about their discovery in the very nature of man and things; experience also attests to the necessity of obeying them.

And you, enlightened and learned societies, protectors and guardians of the arts, I pray that you will continue to exercise the useful discipline of restraining and restoring taste. The century of Louis XIV has so often been compared to the age of Augustus, and our century to the age of decadence following that brilliant time, that we are almost accustomed to the idea of decline. But this judgment is no less sad for having been so long proclaimed, and it is the sorrow of witnessing its enactment in almost all branches of literature that made me so zealously raise a voice that is all too feeble and too little exercised. May the moment when this Academy called for a discussion of the rights of genius and the basis for artistic rules also be the moment for a happy revolution in our conception of both. May a troop of stalwarts arise and follow our great masters, guides, and respected banners and raise again the hopes of those who have longed for pleasure and glory in the perfection of the arts!

Translated by Susan S. Lanser and Jack Undank

Camilla, or, The New Novel (1796)

Virtue alone assures constancy in love.

—Crébillon

Preface

My plan in writing this little work has been to change what novels always do, which is to make the heroine beautiful as the day: here I will make her ugly as the night. It is on behalf of this difference from other novels that I beg the indulgence of those who are going to read this work.

Translated by Susan S. Lanser

Notes

1. The poet Thespis is credited with introducing the speaking actor into Greek tragedy around 535–533 B.C.E. Before this time, Greek tragedy was entirely choral; the single speaker invented by Thespis allegedly delivered prologues and entered into conversation with the chorus-leader.

2. Aeschylus (c. 525–456 B.C.E.) is the first of the three major Greek tragic dramatists. He is thought to have given Greek drama its traditional character by increasing the number of actors to two, diminishing the role of the chorus, giving pre-eminence to dialogue, and introducing certain aspects of costume and decor. His successors Sophocles (c. 496–406 B.C.E.) and Euripides (c. 480–406 B.C.E.) further expanded the dramatic aspects of tragedy and formalized the unities of time, place, and action later observed by French classical playwrights such as Jean Racine (see n. 6).

3. The Goths were a Germanic people who lived in the region of the Elbe; Charrière is referring here to the architectural style known as Gothic, which dominated Western Europe from the twelfth through the fifteenth centuries and which was characterized by slender vertical constructions supporting converging weights, buttresses, and pointed arches.

4. The *Persae* and the *Oresteia* trilogy (comprising the *Agamemnon*, *Choephoroe*, and *Eumenides*) are major works of Aeschylus.

5. The Greek philosopher Aristotle (384–322 B.C.E.), the Latin poet Horace (65–8 B.C.E.), and the French critic Boileau (1636–1711) all sought to establish or refine the principles of poetry. Charrière's point is that she is speaking to the English not of these "foreign" upholders of classical convention but of their own Shakespeare.

6. Jean Racine (1639–1699) and Pierre Corneille (1606–1684) are considered the greatest creators of classical French tragedy.

7. Melusina and Merlin are characters in medieval romance; the wizard Merlin is best known through the Arthurian legends. Admetus received from Apollo the gift of immortality, but his wife, Alceste, had to lay down her life for him. Hercules then brought Alceste back from Hell in gratitude for Admetus's kindnesses to him.

8. François-Marie Arouet (1694–1778), known by the pseudonym Voltaire, was one of the major architects of Enlightenment thought. A philosopher, poet, novelist, critic, and dramatist, he argued in both his "Discours sur la tragédie" (1731) and his "Dissertation sur la tragédie" (1748) that seating should be removed from the stage area because theater needs a sense of vastness like that of the Greek stage.

9. Corneille's *Cinna* was written in 1640–1641, Racine's *Brittanicus* in 1669.

10. Molière was the pseudonym of Jean-Baptiste Poquelin (1622–1673), considered the greatest French writer of comedy. Like his contemporaries Racine and Corneille, he follows classical conventions.

11. In Greek mythology Icarus was the son of the inventor Daedalus. When the two were imprisoned by Minos, Daedalus fashioned wings of waxed feathers as a means of escape. Daedalus's escape succeeded, but Icarus's wings melted when he flew too close to the sun, and he fell into the sea. Phaeton (or Phaethon), son of Helios, persuaded his father to let him drive the chariot of the sun for a day. He lost control of the horses, which rushed too near the earth, burning the area that is now the Sahara Desert. Zeus subsequently struck Phaeton with a thunderbolt so that he could do no more damage to the earth.

12. According to legend, the Curiaces (or Curiati) were triplet brothers of seventh-century B.C.E. Rome who were defeated in combat by another set of triplets named the Horaces (or Horatii). Of the six men, only one Horace survived to claim victory. Returning from conquest, he encountered his sister, who was in mourning for the one of the Curiati to whom she had been betrothed; angered that his sister was grieving over the death of an enemy, he slew his sister. This story is the subject of Corneille's tragedy *Horace* (1640).

13. The Manlius to whom Charrière refers is probably the son of Manlius Torquatus, who supposedly put his son to death, although he had won an honorable victory, because he had engaged in combat without his father's consent.

14. Corneille's highly acclaimed comedy *Le Menteur* was presented in 1643, followed by his last comedy, *La Suite du menteur*, in 1644.

MARY ALCOCK (c. 1742–1798)

MARY ALCOCK was the daughter of Joanna Bentley and Denison Cumberland, granddaughter of the scholar Richard Bentley, and sister of the dramatist Richard Cumberland. She moved with her parents to Ireland in 1763 when her father, Master of Trinity College, Cambridge, became Bishop of Clonfert. Married and widowed in Ireland, Alcock settled in Bath after her husband's death. There she contributed to Lady Miller's poetry contests in 1781. She published *The Air-Balloon; or, The Flying Mortal* (1784), on the contemporary interest in aeronautics, and *The Confined Debtor. A Fragment from A Prison,* which solicited charitable contributions for the release of debtors in Ilchester. Alcock's collected poems were published in 1799, a year after her death, edited with a memoir by Joanna Hughes. Hughes describes Alcock as memorable for her good deeds and claims that the poet "never held herself up as a writer" and kept her poems private. Among some six hundred subscribers for this edition of *Poems* were Elizabeth Carter, William Cowper, and Hannah More.

As a critic, Alcock addressed her remarks to the novel. Her two notable pieces of criticism are her prose commentary "The Scribbler" and her poem "A Receipt for Writing A Novel," both included in her collection of poems. In "The Scribbler," Alcock complains that novels are "such an inundation of hobgoblin nonsense" and warns of "the dangerous tendency of such studies to young and unformed minds." Like many of her contemporaries, she was particularly concerned with the effects of novels on young women. This prose piece ends with an explanation of why Alcock wrote "A Receipt." Finding that the novel had become a system in which authors were "distressing and terrifying on one side" and readers "distressed and terrified on the other," she explained, "I bethought that a written prescription for the advantage of young beginners might not be unacceptable." Her poem shows the skill with which she is able to ridicule the absurdities of the contemporary sentimental novel, especially its all too predictable reliance on convoluted plots that end inevitably in marriage after recounting thwarted love, tormenting passions, madness, and hysteria.

Poems (London: C. Dilly, 1799).

A Receipt for Writing a Novel (1799)

WOULD you a fav'rite novel make,
Try hard your reader's heart to break,
For who is pleas'd, if not tormented?
(Novels for that were first invented).
'Gainst nature, reason, sense, combine
To carry on your bold design,
And those ingredients I shall mention,
Compounded with your own invention,
I'm sure will answer my intention.
Of love take first a due proportion—   10
It serves to keep the heart in motion:
Of jealousy a powerful zest,
Of all tormenting passions best;
Of horror mix a copious share,
And duels you must never spare;
Hysteric fits at least a score,
Or, if you find occasion, more;
But fainting fits you need not measure,
The fair ones have them at their pleasure;
Of sighs and groans take no account,   20
But throw them in to vast amount;
A frantic fever you may add,
Most authors make their lovers mad;
Rack well your hero's nerves and heart,
And let your heroine take her part;
Her fine blue eyes were made to weep,
Nor should she ever taste of sleep;
Ply her with terrors day or night,
And keep her always in a fright,
But in a carriage when you get her,   30
Be sure you fairly overset her;
If she will break her bones—why let her:
Again, if e'er she walks abroad,
Of course you bring some wicked lord,
Who with three ruffians snaps his prey,
And to a castle speeds away;
There, close confin'd in haunted tower,
You leave your captive in his power,
Till dead with horror and dismay,
She scales the walls and flies away.   40

Mary Alcock (c. 1742–1798)

Now you contrive the lovers meeting,
To set your reader's heart abeating,
But ere they've had a moment's leisure,
Be sure to interrupt their pleasure;
Provide yourself with fresh alarms
To tear 'em from each other's arms;
No matter by what fate they're parted,
So that you keep them broken-hearted.

A cruel father some prepare
To drag her by her flaxen hair;   50
Some raise a storm, and some a ghost,
Take either, which may please you most.
But this you must with care observe,
That when you've wound up every nerve
With expectation, hope and fear,
Hero and heroine must disappear.
Some fill one book, some two without 'em,
And ne'er concern their heads about 'em,
This greatly rests the writer's brain,
For any story, that gives pain,   60
You now throw in—no matter what,
However foreign to the plot,
So it but serves to swell the book,
You foist it in with desperate hook
A masquerade, a murder'd peer,
His throat just cut from ear to ear—
A rake turn'd hermit—a fond maid
Run mad, by some false loon betray'd—
These stores supply the female pen,
Which writes them o'er and o'er again,   70
And readers likewise may be found
To circulate them round and round.

Now at your fable's close devise
Some grand event to give surprize—
Suppose your hero knows no mother—
Suppose he proves the heroine's brother—
This at one stroke dissolves each tie,
Far as from east to west they fly:
At length when every woe's expended,
And your last volume's nearly ended,   80
Clear the mistake, and introduce
Some tatt'ling nurse to cut the noose,

The spell is broke—again they meet
Expiring at each other's feet;
Their friends lie breathless on the floor—
You drop your pen; you can no more—
And ere your reader can recover,
They're married—and your history's over.

ANNA SEWARD (1742-1809)

ANNA SEWARD's father reportedly had her reading Milton at age two. When the family moved to Lichfield in 1754 they entered a thriving intellectual society that boasted the occasional presence of Samuel Johnson, Thomas Day, and Richard Lovell Edgeworth. Known as the "Swan of Lichfield," Seward lived out her life in the cathedral town, seldom venturing far from home. She refused all offers of marriage. She is known to have had passionate attachments to women and perhaps also to men. She was an intimate friend of Sarah Butler and Eleanor Ponsonby, the renowned "Ladies of Llangollen." Late in life she took a keen interest in the young Walter Scott and bequeathed her literary manuscripts to him with the request that he edit them, which he did in 1810. A six-volume selection of her letters written between 1784 and 1807 was published in 1811, though many more, along with criticism, journals, and sermons, remain unpublished.

Seward was an admired poet and intellectual in her time, so admired in fact that when her best-known poem, "Monody on the Death of Major André," reproached George Washington for his part in the trial of Major André, Washington sent a personal envoy to Seward with proof of his innocence.

Seward's letters are more lively than her poems. Directed to a host of literary figures, including Helen Maria Williams, Hester Thrale Piozzi, and the Edgeworths, they are often biting observations on a variety of topics. Many were published in the *Gentleman's Magazine*, in which she carried on several critical debates, including one with Boswell on Johnson (whom she disliked), one on the relative merits of Pope and Dryden, and the one included here with Clara Reeve. Seward took strenuous objection to Reeve's preference, stated in *The Progress of Romance*, for *Pamela* over *Clarissa*. Though in the Boswell exchange Seward had claimed to be shocked that anyone would attack a defenseless woman in print, she was far from defenseless herself and not above literary sniping if the occasion called for it.

Gentleman's Magazine (London: David Henry, January–April 1786).

Correspondence between Anna Seward and Clara Reeve
from the *Gentleman's Magazine* (1786)

Dec. 12

Mr Urban,

In the line of Criticism, till one false prophet arose amongst us, who, like Mahomet, by his great ability, and by the destroying edge of that broad sword sophistical wit, taught dazzled multitudes to think his devastations holy, and to bear, without general indignation, the demolition of their poetic shrines; till he waved the heretical banner, ignorance and envy were seldom bold enough to publish decisions that arrogantly controverted universal opinion; they were awed into silence by the splendor of established fame. But now, beneath the shield of the late arch-infidel to the scriptures of Apollo, no absurdity is thought too flagrant to be foisted upon the attention of the public, and the press teems with the monsters of unfeeling criticism.

I saw an extract lately, in one of the periodical publications, from Clara Reeves's[1] *Progress of Romance*, in which she is ridiculous enough to place Richardson's two immortal works, *Grandison*, and *Clarissa*, below his perishable *Pamela*, whose rememberance is only kept alive by the illustrious name of its parent; a withering branch on a tree of amaranth.

The yet unsated pleasure which I had received from repeated perusals of the ENGLISH BARON, excited an affectionate regard for its author, and solicitude for her fame; therefore did the absurdity of asserting, that *Pamela* is the *chef d'oeuvre* of Richardson, *pain* as well as *disgust* me; and without any personal knowledge of this lady, excite those unpleasant sensations which we feel from contemplating folly in our friends, which we know must injure them.

There is but one way of accounting for a decision so senseless. The *English Baron*, charming as it is, can stand on no line of equality with *Grandison*, and the yet greater *Clarissa*; which the late Dr. Johnson, amidst his too frequent injustice to authors, and general parsimony of praise, uniformly asserted to be not only the first novel, but that perhaps it was the first work in the English language. The *English Baron*, its author well knows, is better written than *Pamela*, that dim dawn of an illustrious genius; and the heart of Clara Reeves, less candid and sincere than her imagination is happy, with the co-operation of that eternal misleader self-conceit, suggested this too common practice of disingenuous spirits, to attempt the degradation of a superior writer, by extolling a work of his, which they know they can *themselves* excel, *above* those *higher* efforts of his genius, which they feel unattainable.

Let the ingenuous reader always recollect, that there is a great deal of this finesse practised by authors whose abilities ought to set them above it. The consciousness of this truth may preserve young minds from too implicit a faith in the decisions of even the greatest writers upon the compositions of their brethren.

Mr. Hayley[2] thus beautifully addresses rising genius on that subject in his *Essay on Epic Poetry*; and the passage applies equally to ingenious readers as to those who write:

> The inborn vigour of your souls defend,
> Nor lean too fondly on the firmest friend;
> Genius may sink on Criticism's breast
> By weak dependence on her truth opprest;
> Sleep on her lap, and stretch his lifeless length,
> Shorn by her soothing hand of all his strength.

But, to return from general ideas on critical decision to the strange assertion of Clara Reeves. No person endowed with any refinement of perception, any accuracy of judgement, can think *Pamela* superior to *Grandison*, and *Clarissa*.

No mind, defective in those powers, could have dictated the *English Baron*. Either then that work was not written by Clara Reeves, or she is convicted of a design to mislead the taste of the public. She had not been more absurd, had she asserted that *Titus Andronicus* is the most sublime, and *Love's Labour Lost* the most interesting of Shakespeare's plays. Verily we have seen decisions from a greater pen than Clara Reeves no whit less extraordinary. Witness that which pronounces Dryden's bombast poem on the death of Anne Killigrew to be the noblest ode in the English language!

The observations on Rousseau's *Eloisa*,[3] quoted from the PROGRESS OF ROMANCE, are just, but they are not new; they are not Clara Reeves's. The author himself insinuates his reasons for the composition of this work in the preface, given under the form of a dialogue, full of pretended reproach for that unfashionable philosophy, which ventures to excuse the indiscretion of a single woman, and treats the gallantries of the married ones with such unbounded severity. These reasons are also covertly given in a letter of St. Preux to Eloisa from Paris, in which he declaims upon the innocence of their attachment, yet unstain'd by infidelity, compared with the inconstant libertinism of the Parisian married ladies.

In those passages, Rousseau covertly suggests his own apology for the most faulty part of Eloisa. There is, therefore, no new light thrown upon that work by Miss Reeves.

To what heights of arrogance is public criticism arrived, when one Mr. Heron,[4] of "unbashful forehead," denies poetic sublimity to the language of the SCRIPTURES; and, in a style deformed by perpetual vulgarisms, decides upon the style of others, and gives the lie to the admiring fiat of ages; who denies to Virgil and to Pope a grain of original genius; pronounces the first of all professedly descriptive poems, *Thomson's Seasons*, a nauseous work, and sentences it to oblivion! And do we not see Mr. Hoole exhibiting the poetaster Scott[5] in the act of impotently attempting to new-model the poetic matter of our greatest masters; mistaking for weeds some of their richest flowers, and, like the owl, finding darkness in excessive light!

Yours, &c. A. S.

Ipswich, Feb. 10.

Mr. Urban,

I find myself called to the disagreeable task of speaking publicly in my own defence, in answer to a very extraordinary letter that appeared in your magazine of last month, p. 16, in which I am treated very cavalierly, and in a way that is perfectly new to me.

Had the writer of that letter only imputed to me an error in judgement, I might have sat down in silence under the charge, which has been extended to many writers of abilities infinitely superior to mine, and is indeed common to human nature. But this unmerciful critic charges me with disingenuousness, and a design to mislead the judgement of others; a fault of a much higher nature, which I shall not take to myself while I have power to prove myself innocent of it. He says, "that I have, against my own judgement, praised Mr. Richardson's first and lowest work, and deprecated his superior ones, in order to injure his reputation as a writer." I trust that the manner in which he has treated me will, in some degree, defeat his intention; for his malevolence is but too apparent, notwithstanding his panygeric on the "English Baron," which he uses as a shield, behind which he may, with surer aim, direct his arrows of censure and calumny. It is better to crr in judgement than to have a bad heart. I could forgive and pass by any injustice to my abilities as a writer, but I must feel an attack upon my moral character; though it is not uncommon for any author, who has been favoured by the public, to meet with many false and illiberal attacks upon both. After having thrown out his reflections in a general way, he draws his argument to a point, that clearly shews his injurious intention in one or both the alternatives he gives me. "No person (says he) of any perception or judgement could think 'Pamela' superior to 'Grandison' or 'Clarissa.' No person defective in these points could have written the 'English Baron;' either then that work is not written by Clara Reeves, or else she is convicted of a design to mislead the public." I am well aware of the oblique insinuation, as well as the direct attack; but I trust that I cannot be hurt by either, because I have means in my own hands by which I can easily disprove them both. I shall offer one proof only of my integrity and veracity; but it shall be plain and simple, and it shall carry conviction with it.

"Now mark how plain a tale shall put you down." SHAKESPEARE[6]

I have lived many years in intimate friendship with a daughter of Mr. Richardson, the only one now living, a lady of superior understanding, sound judgement, great reading, and uncommon modesty and humility. Through her I am known to many others of that respected family. I would not lift up the veil of retirement that conceals her from impertinent and obtrusive observers, but to bear witness to the truth of what I shall communicate to you, Sir. I have shewed most of my writings to this dear lady; I have asked her opinion of them, and often, very often, have preferred her judgement to my own. She saw the "English Baron" in every stage of it, from first to last. She saw likewise every sheet of the "Progress of Romance" before it went to press. I asked her opinion of the whole but particularly that part which speaks of her revered father. "Are you satisfied with what I have written (said I); is there any thing you would wish to have altered?" She answered, No, she had no objection to make; that some others thought as I did; and that I had a right to speak my true opinion. Is it likely that the daughter and descendent of Mr. Richardson should be less jealous of his reputation than a stranger, who takes, uncalled upon, the liberty to defend what has never been called in question? Of this any impartial person may be convinced who will refer to the "Progress of Romance," where he will find the text very different from the commentary, where every token of respect, even to veneration, is shewn to Mr. Richardson; and what I have given as my own opinion (which I do not retract) is with all deference and liberality to that of others. I shall only recite the concluding sentence, which will properly finish the subject.

"That all Richardson's works are of capital merit is indisputable; but it seems to me that 'Pamela' has the most originality; 'Grandison' the greatest regularity and equality; 'Clarissa' the highest graces and the most defects."

I shall need say but little on the other subject, viz. the remarks upon Rousseau's "Eloisa." A good-natured critic would have observed, that they proceed from the mouth of Hortensius; into whose character I have thrown all such observations as are not properly my own, and for which I am obliged to my friends. I hope, in repelling this illiberal attack, I have kept in view that temper and candour which no injury should make any person lose sight of. I should be ashamed to use such language as I have received: *ridiculous*, *absurd*, *senseless*, are the epithets which my polite critic has thrown at me. While he is shooting his arrows at me and others, let him take heed that none of them recoil upon himself, who has indeed, with "unbashful forehead," censured the writings of others in a more unjust and uncandid manner than that he condemns. I had rather have been excused this appeal to my friends; but, thus called upon, I dare affirm that I am above the base motive imputed to me, and also equally above the meanness of malice or revenge.

> You may think
> I who command myself have brib'd a fool
> To be my herald;—yet a modest mind,
> T'oppose the darts of calumny, may wear
> Its innocence in sight; a safer shield
> Than adamant or gold.
>
> FENTON'S Mariamne.[7]

You will please to observe, Sir, that I have addressed my reply as to a man; for I cannot conceive it possible that so much malevolence, with so little delicacy, could proceed from the pen of one of my own sex.

CLARA REEVE.

March 12, 1786

Mr. Urban,

Whatever interpretation *Miss Reeve* may chuse to put upon the spirited censure of her *decree*, respecting Mr. Richardson's works, no discerning mind, that is unprejudiced, can mistake it for a sally of dark-spirited malice.

Had Miss Reeve apologized to the world for her strange dissent from the universal voice on that subject—had she only said that Pamela was more to her taste than Clarissa, or Sir Charles Grandison, that taste had perhaps been pitied in silence; but the cool arrogance of an absolute decision, that Pamela is the *chef d'oeuvre* of Richardson, must prove a daring contradiction of the general opinion, which deserved the pointed reprehension it has met.

In her letter of *self*-defence, this lady shews a consciousness of something wrong, since, referring to the censured passages in her own work, she suppresses the *offensive diction*, which produced the comments so *displeasing* to *her*. Had she said no more on the subject than she has there instanced, *viz.* that Pamela seemed to her to have the most originality, the unmeaning stricture had only excited observations to the following purpose;

An interesting story, carried on through many volumes, in a series of familiar letters, was a new mode of novel-writing, struck out by Mr. Richardson.—Pamela was the first attempt. It was naturally written, and sometimes pathetic; but tedious, and destitute of the higher graces of composition. The Author afterwards established those beautiful and perfect works, Clarissa and Grandison, upon the same epistolary plan. Are they less original for being *infinitely* more various, more abundantly rich in contrasted characters; in wit, in humour, of which there are scarce any gleams in Pamela; more polished; more pathetic; and beyond all bounds of comparison more *sublime*? Surely, therefore, the observation, that the latter works of Mr. Richardson are less *original* than his first, is highly irrational. Can an author, thus improving upon his *own* plan, be deemed, either directly, or indirectly, a *Copyist*? What former writings of any *other* author do the Clarissa and the Grandison resemble? They have every possible claim to be considered as great and *perfect* originals.

Our incensed Critic will allow no merit to her Hypercritic, for the generous testimony borne to the merit of her ENGLISH BARON. It is very *fair* to deny the possibility of ingenuousness to a positive preference, so inconsistent with the marked ability of *that* work.

Let the Public judge who is the malicious and unjust accuser!—the person who avows the apprehended impossibility, that a woman of *genius* can think Pamela is the chef d'oeuvre of Richardson, or Miss Reeve, who asserts, that "this person has censured the writings of *others* in a more unjust and uncandid manner, than that he condemns;" because his letter not only disallows the decree of Miss Reeve, in question, but bears honest testimony against the critical decisions of a yet greater writer, where they attempt to tear the wreaths from the shrines of departed Genius; also against the effrontery of Mr. Heron, who denies poetic sublimity to the scriptures; and to Virgil and Pope an *atom* of real genius; and who sentences Thomson to speedy oblivion, and against the posthumous dogmas of Mr. Scott, who attempts to prune, mutilate and arange afresh the ideas and language of

Thomson, Goldsmith and Gray, without ever having possessed a tenth part of either their genius or judgement.

It is the *duty* of all people, who are themselves candidates for the palm of Fame, to guard with active zeal those she has already conferred upon their illustrious predecessors, when either able, or impotent defamers, directly or indirectly, seek to blight, or eclipse them.

Surely Mr. Richardson's daughter ill deserves the honour of her birth, if she could approve the injustice of Miss Reeve to the later works of her glorious father.—But I correct myself—genius, or accurate literary taste, are not always hereditary. Mr. Richardson's daughter may be of that order of beings, who, with plain sense, and a thousand amiable qualities, might possibily *think* Pamela a more perfect compostion than Clarissa and Grandison.

> "Peace to all such!—but should there one, whose fires
> "Invention kindles, and fair fame inspires;"
> A charming Novelist!—should she appear
> With aim, degrading, as the critic sneer;
> Which Atticus, endeavouring to promote,
> Deserv'd the just reproach Musaeus wrote;[8]
> Should she, perversely throwing into shade
> The fairest products Fancy e'er display'd;
> Since, on our Shakespear's page, the Goddess threw
> Her fruits, and florets of immortal hue;
> Should such a one, as Richardson's lov's name
> She breathes, and seems to analyze his claim,
> Should she, insidious to the trail bring
> The pale crude berries of his earthly Spring,
> And swear their flavour has the fruits outdone
> His genius ripen'd in its Summer fun!
> "Shall we not laugh if such a judge there be?
> "Shall we not rave if ★★★★★ ★★★★★ is she?"

A CONSTANT READER

Notes

1. In her first letter, Seward consistently misspells Reeve's name.

2. William Hayley (1745–1820), a prolific and popular poet, was offered the laureateship in 1790. He refused.

3. *Eloisa* is *La Nouvelle Héloïse* (1761), the extremely popular novel by Jean-Jacques Rousseau. Reeve defends it in *Progress of Romance*, Vol. II, pp. 13–19.

4. Mr. Heron is a pseudonym for John Pinkerton, whose *Letters on Literature* appeared in 1785. Among other unpopular opinions, he deprecates the classical authors, particularly Virgil, for lacking originality.

5. John Scott, a minor poet, whose *Critical Essays* were published in 1785, two years after his death.

6. *I King Henry IV*, Act II, iv. Prince Hal says this to Falstaff after catching him out in a lie.

7. Elijah Fenton, poet, playwright, and translator. His tragedy *Mariamne*, about the virtuous wife of Herod the Great who, though innocent, was put to death because of his jealousy, was first acted in 1723. It remained popular throughout the century.

8. "Atticus" refers to Thomas Cooke (1703–1756), who wrote letters under this name to the *London Journal* in 1729–1730. In these letters and in his earlier poem "The Battle of the Poets" (1725), Cooke was highly critical of Pope, Swift, and their literary friends. Pope, styled "Musaeus" in a poem by William Mason written on Pope's death, retaliated against Cooke in the *Dunciad* and "Epistle to Dr. Arbuthnot." Thus Seward is casting Reeve in the role of literary leveler and herself as defender of the faith. Seward parodies Pope's famous satiric portrait of Addison under the name of Atticus in his "Epistle."

ANNA LAETITIA AIKEN BARBAULD
(1743–1825)

ANNA LAETITIA AIKEN was the daughter of a distinguished Dissenting minister who educated her in classical and English literatures. As a youth, she benefited from the stimulating intellectual atmosphere at the Dissenting academy at Warrington, where her father was a teacher. She was encouraged by her brother to publish a volume of her poems and collaborated with him on *Miscellaneous Pieces in Prose* (both 1773), which established her as a respected writer. She became a friend of Samuel Johnson, Hannah More, Elizabeth Montagu, and, later, Joanna Baillie and Maria Edgeworth. After she married Rochemont Barbauld in 1774, she devoted herself to helping to manage his boarding school, teaching little boys, and publishing books for small children.

Subsequent political events stimulated Barbauld to write brilliant, stinging attacks on the government for reaffirming the laws that limited the civil rights of Dissenters (*An Address to the Opposers of the Repeal of the Corporation and Test Acts*, 1790), for rejecting the bill to abolish the slave trade (*An Epistle to William Wilberforce*, 1791), and for declaring war on the new French Republic (*Sins of Government, Sins of the Nation*, 1793). Meanwhile her marriage deteriorated; Rochemont Barbauld became insane and threatened her life on two occasions. She separated from him but was deeply distressed by his eventual suicide.

Anna Barbauld's career as a critic began when she edited the letters of Samuel Richardson (1804), followed by selections from the *Tatler* and *Spectator* (1804), the poems of William Collins and Mark Akenside, and a fifty-volume set, *The British Novelists* (1810), all with long biographical-critical prefaces. Barbauld's wide learning, substantial reasoning, and systematic approach mark her as a thorough professional, and her work on the novel is groundbreaking.

The British Novelists; with an Essay, and Prefaces Biographical and Critical (London: F. C. and J. Rivington et al., 1820).

Anna Laetitia Aiken Barbauld (1743–1825)

From "On the Origin and Progress of Novel-Writing" (1810)

A Collection of Novels has a better chance of giving pleasure than of commanding respect. Books of this description are condemned by the grave,
and despised by the fastidious; but their leaves are seldom found unopened,
and they occupy the parlour and the dressing-room while productions of
higher name are often gathering dust upon the shelf. It might not perhaps
be difficult to show that this species of composition is entitled to a higher
rank than has been generally assigned it. Fictitious adventures, in one form
or other, have made a part of the polite literature of every age and nation.
These have been grafted upon the actions of their heroes; they have been
interwoven with their mythology; they have been moulded upon the manners of the age,—and, in return, have influenced the manners of the succeeding generation by the sentiments they have infused and the sensibilities
they have excited.

Adorned with the embellishments of Poetry, they produce the epic;
more concentrated in the story, and exchanging narrative for action, they
become dramatic. When allied with some great moral end, as in the *Tele-
maque* of Fenelon, and Marmontel's *Belisaire*, they may be termed didactic.
They are often made the vehicles of satire, as in Swift's *Gulliver's Travels*, and
the *Candide* and *Babone* of Voltaire. They take a tincture from the learning
and politics of the times, and are made use of successfully to attack or recommend the prevailing systems of the day. When the range of this king of
writing is so extensive, and its effect so great, it seems evident that it ought
to hold a respectable place among the productions of genius; nor is it easy
to say, why the poet, who deals in one kind of fiction, should have so high
a place allotted him in the temple of fame; and the romance-writer so low
a one as in the general estimation he is confined to. To measure the dignity
of a writer by the pleasure he affords his readers is not perhaps using an
accurate criterion; but the invention of a story, the choice of proper incidents, the ordonnance of the plan, occasional beauties of description, and
above all, the power exercised over the reader's heart by filling it with the
successive emotions of love, pity, joy, anguish, transport, or indignation, together with the grave impressive moral resulting from the whole, imply
talents of the highest order, and ought to be appreciated accordingly. A good
novel is an epic in prose, with more of character and less (indeed in modern
novels nothing) of the supernatural machinery.

If we look for the origin of fictitious tales and adventures, we shall be obliged to go to the earliest accounts of the literature of every age and country. The Eastern nations have always been fond of this species of mental gratification. . . .

Romance writing was destined to revive with greater splendour under the Gothic powers, and it sprung out of the histories of the times, enlarged and exaggerated into fable. Indeed all fictions have probably grown out of real adventures. The actions of heroes would be the most natural subject for recital in a warlike age; a little flattery and a little love of the marvellous would overstep the modesty of truth in the narration. A champion of extraordinary size would be easily magnified into a giant. Tales of magic and enchantment probably took their rise from the awe and wonder with which the vulgar looked upon any instance of superior skill in mechanics or medicine, or acquaintance with any of the hidden properties of nature. The Arabian tales, so well known and so delightful, bear testimony to this. At a fair in Tartary a magician appears, who brings various curiosities, the idea of which was probably suggested by inventions they had heard of, which to people totally ignorant of the mechanical powers would appear the effect of enchantment. How easily might the exhibition at Merlin's, or the tricks of Jonas, be made to pass for magic in New Holland or Otaheite![1] Letters and figures were easily turned into talismans by illiterate men, who saw that a great deal was effected by them, and intelligence conveyed from place to place in a manner they could not account for. . . .

The first Gothic romances appeared under the venerable guise of history. Arthur and the knights of the round table, Charlemagne and his peers, were their favourite heroes. The extended empire of Charlemagne and his conquests naturally offered themselves as subjects for recital; but it seems extraordinary that Arthur, a British prince, the scene of whose exploits was in Wales, a country little known to the rest of Europe, and who was continually struggling against ill-fortune, should have been so great a favourite upon the continent. Perhaps, however, the comparative obscurity of his situation might favour the genius of the composition, and the intercourse between Wales and Brittany would contribute to diffuse and exaggerate the stories of his exploits. . . .

Of these heroic romances, the Troubadours were in France the chief composers: they began to flourish about the end of the tenth century. They by degrees mingled a taste for gallantry and romantic love with the adventures of heroes, and they gave to that passion an importance and a refinement which it had never possessed among the ancients. It was a compound of devotion, metaphysics, Platonism, and chivalry, making altogether such a mixture as the world had never seen before. There is something extremely mysterious in the manner in which ladies of rank allowed themselves to be addressed by these poetical lovers; sometimes no doubt a real passion was produced, and some instances there are of its having had tragical consequences: but in general it may be suspected that the addresses of the Troubadours and other poets were rather a tribute paid to rank than to beauty; and that it was customary for young men of parts, who had their fortune to make, to attach themselves to a patroness, of whom they made a kind of idol, sometimes in the hopes of rising by her means, sometimes merely as a subject for their wit. . . .

In the mean time Europe settled into a state of comparative tranquillity: castles and knights and adventures of distressed damsels ceased to be the topics of the day, and romances founded upon them had begun to be insipid when the immortal satire of Cervantes drove them off the field, and they have never since been able to rally their forces. . . .

Marivaux excelled in a different style. His *Marianne* and *Paisan Parvenu* give a picture of French manners with all their refinement and delicacy of sentiment. He lays open the heart, particularly the female heart, in its inmost folds and recesses: its little vanities and affectations as well as its finer feelings. He abounds in wit, but it is of a refined kind, and requires thought in the reader to enter into it. He has also much humour, and describes comic scenes and characters amongst the lower and middle ranks with a great deal of the comic effect, but without the coarseness, of Fielding. He eluded the difficulty of winding up a story by leaving both his pieces unfinished. Marivaux was contemporary with our Richardson: his style is found fault with by some French critics. From his time, novels of all kinds have made a large and attractive portion of French literature.

At the head of writers of this class stands the seductive, the passionate Rousseau,—the most eloquent writer in the most eloquent modern language: whether his glowing pencil paints the strong emotions of passion, or the enchanting scenery of nature in his own romantic country, or his peculiar cast of moral sentiment,—a charm is spread over every part of the work, which scarcely leaves the judgement free to condemn what in it is dangerous or reprehensible. His are truly the "Thoughts that breathe and words that burn."[2] He has hardly any thing of story; he has but few figures upon his canvass; he wants them not; his characters are drawn more from a creative imagination than from real life, and we wonder that what has so little to do with nature should have so much to do with the heart. Our censure of the tendency of this work will be softened, if we reflect that Rousseau's aim, as far as he had a moral aim, seems to have been to give a striking example of fidelity in the *married* state, which, it is well known, is little thought of by the French; though they would judge with the greatest severity the more pardonable failure of an unmarried woman. But Rousseau has not reflected that Julie ought to have considered herself as indissolubly united to St. Preux; her marriage with another was the infidelity.[3] . . .

In England, most of the earlier romances, from the days of Chaucer to James the First, were translations from the Spanish or French. One of the most celebrated of our own growth is Sir Philip Sidney's *Arcadia*, dedicated to his sister the Countess of Pembroke. It is a kind of pastoral romance, mingled with adventures of the heroic and chivalrous kind. It has great beauties, particularly in poetic imagery. It is a book which all have heard of, which some few possess, but which nobody reads. The taste of the times seems to have been for ponderous performances. The Duchess of Newcastle was an indefatigable writer in this way. . . .

The first author amongst us who distinguished himself by natural painting, was that truly original genius De Foe. His *Robinson Crusoe* is to this day an *unique* in its kind, and he has made it very interesting without applying to the common resource of love. At length, in the reign of George the Second, Richardson, Fielding, and Smollet, appeared in quick succession; and their success raised such a demand for this kind of entertainment, that it has ever since been furnished from the press, rather as a regular and necessary supply, than as an occasional gratification. Novels have indeed been numerous "as leaves in Vallombrosa."[4] . . .

About fifty years ago a very singular work appeared, somewhat in the guise of a novel, which gave a new impulse to writings of this stamp; namely, *The Life and Opinions of Tristam Shandy*, followed by *The Sentimental Journey*, by the Rev. Mr. Sterne, a clergyman of York. They exhibit much originality, wit, and beautiful strokes of pathos, but a total want of plan or adventure, being made up of conversations and detached incidents. It is the peculiar characteristic of this writer, that he affects the heart, not by long drawn tales of distress, but by light electric touches which thrill the nerves of the reader who possesses a correspondent sensibility of frame. His characters, in like manner, are struck out by a few masterly touches. He resembles those painters who can give expression to a figure by two or three strokes of bold outline, leaving the imagination to fill up the sketch; the feelings are awakened as really by the story of La Fevre, as by the narrative of *Clarissa*. The indelicacies of these volumes are very reprehensible, and indeed in a clergyman scandalous, particularly in the first publication, which however has the richest vein of humour. The two Shandys, Trim, Dr. Slop, are all drawn with a masterly hand. It is one of the merits of Sterne that he has awakened the attention of his readers to the wrongs of the poor negroes, and certainly a great spirit of tenderness and humanity breathes throughout the work. It is rather mortifying to reflect how little the power of expressing these feelings is connected with moral worth; for Sterne was a man by no means attentive to the happiness of those connected with him; and we are forced to confess that an author may conceive the idea of "brushing away flies without killing them," and yet behave ill in every relation of life.[5]

It has lately been said that Sterne has been indebted for much of his wit to Burton's *Anatomy of Melancholy*. He certainly exhibits a good deal of reading in that and many other books out of the common way, but the wit is in the application, and that is his own. . . .

Many tears have been shed by the young and tender-hearted over *Sidney Biddulph*, the production of Mrs. Sheridan, the wife of Mr. Thomas Sheridan the lecturer, an ingenious and amiable woman: the sentiments of this work are pure and virtuous, but the author seems to have taken pleasure in heaping distress upon virtue and innocence, merely to prove, what no one will deny, that the best dispositions are not always sufficient to ward off the evils of life.[6] Why is it that women when they write are apt to give a melancholy tinge to their compositions? Is it that they suffer more, and have fewer resources against melancholy? Is it that men, mixing at large in society, have a brisker flow of ideas, and, seeing a greater variety of characters, introduce more of the business and pleasures of life into their productions? Is it that humour is a scarcer product of the mind than sentiment, and more congenial to the stronger powers of man? Is it that women nurse those feelings in secrecy and silence, and diversify the expression of them with endless shades of sentiment, which are more transiently felt, and with fewer modifications of delicacy, by the other sex? The remark, if true, has no doubt many exceptions; but the productions of several ladies, both French and English, seem to countenance it. . . .

If the end and object of this species of writing be asked, many no doubt will be ready to tell us that its object is,—to call in fancy to the aid of reason, to deceive the mind into embracing truth under the guise of fiction . . . with such-like reasons equally grave and dignified. For my own part, I scruple not to confess that, when I take up a novel, my end and object is entertainment; and as I suspect that to be the case with most readers, I hesitate not to say that entertainment is their legitimate end and object. To read the productions of wit and genius is a very high pleasure to all persons of taste, and the avidity with which they are read by all such shows sufficiently

that they are calculated to answer this end. Reading is the cheapest of pleasures: it is a domestic pleasure. Dramatic exhibitions give a more poignant
delight, but they are seldom enjoyed in perfection, and never without ex-
pense and trouble. Poetry requires in the reader a certain elevation of mind
and a practised ear. It is seldom relished unless a taste be formed for it pretty
early. But the humble novel is always ready to enliven the gloom of solitude,
to soothe the languor of debility and disease, to win the attention from
pain or vexatious occurrences, to take man from himself, (at many seasons
the worst company he can be in,) and, while the moving picture of life
passes before him, to make him forget the subject of his own complaints.
It is pleasant to the mind to sport in the boundless regions of possibility;
to find relief from the sameness of every-day occurrences by expatiating
amidst brighter skies and fairer fields; to exhibit love that is always happy,
valour that is always successful; to feed the appetite for wonder by a quick
succession of marvellous events; and to distribute, like a ruling providence,
rewards and punishments which fall just where they ought to fall.

It is sufficient therefore as an end, that these writings add to the innocent pleasures of life; and if they do no harm, the entertainment they give
is a sufficient good. We cut down the tree that bears no fruit, but we ask
nothing of a flower beyond its scent and its colour. The unpardonable sin
in a novel is dullness: however grave or wise it may be, if its author possesses
no powers of amusing, he has no business to write novels; he should employ
his pen in some more serious part of literature.

But it is not necessary to rest the credit of these works on amusement
alone, since it is certain they have had a very strong effect in infusing principles and moral feelings. It is impossible to deny that the most glowing and
impressive sentiments of virtue are to be found in many of these compositions, and have been deeply imbibed by their youthful readers. They
awaken a sense of finer feelings than the commerce of ordinary life inspires.
Many a young woman has caught from such works as *Clarissa* or *Cecilia*,
ideas of delicacy and refinement which were not, perhaps, to be gained in
any society she could have access to. Many a maxim of prudence is laid up
in the memory from these stores, ready to operate when occasion offers.

The passion of love, the most seductive of all the passions, they certainly
paint too high, and represent its influence beyond what it will be found to
be in real life; but if they soften the heart they also refine it. They mix with
the natural passions of our nature all that is tender in virtuous affection; all
that is estimable in high principle and unshaken constancy; all that grace,
delicacy, and sentiment can bestow of touching and attractive. Benevolence

and sensibility to distress are almost always insisted on in modern works of this kind; and perhaps it is not too much to say, that much of the softness of our present manners, much of that tincture of humanity so conspicuous amidst all our vices, is owing to the bias given by our dramatic writings and fictitious stories. A high regard to female honour, generosity, and a spirit of self-sacrifice, are strongly inculcated. It costs nothing, it is true, to an author to make his hero generous, and very often he is extravagantly so; still, sentiments of this kind serve in some measure to counteract the spirit of the world, where selfish considerations have always more than their due weight. In what discourse from the pulpit are religious feelings more strongly raised than in the prison sermon of *The Vicar of Wakefield*, or some parts of *The Fool of Quality*?[7]

But not only those splendid sentiments with which, when properly presented, our feelings readily take part, and kindle as we read; the more severe and homely virtues of prudence and œconomy have been enforced in the writings of a Burney and an Edgeworth. Writers of their good sense have observed, that while these compositions cherished even a romantic degree of sensibility, the duties that have less brilliancy to recommend them were neglected. Where can be found a more striking lesson against unfeeling dissipation than the story of the Harrels? Where have order, neatness, industry, sobriety, been recommended with more strength than in the agreeable tales of Miss Edgeworth? If a parent wishes his child to avoid caprice, irregularities of temper, procrastination, coquetry, affectation,—all those faults and blemishes which undermine family happiness, and destroy the every-day comforts of common life,—whence can he derive more impressive morality than from the same source?[8] When works of fancy are thus made subservient to the improvement of the rising generation, they certainly stand on a higher ground than mere entertainment, and we revere while we admire.

Some knowledge of the world is also gained by these writings, imperfect indeed, but attained with more ease, and attended with less danger, than by mixing in real life. If the stage is a mirror of life, so is the novel, and perhaps a more accurate one, as less is sacrificed to effect and representation. There are many descriptions of characters in the busy world, which a young woman in the retired scenes of life hardly meets with at all, and many whom it is safer to read of than to meet; and to either sex it must be desirable that the first impressions of fraud, selfishness, profligacy and perfidy should be connected, as in good novels they always will be, with infamy and ruin. At any rate, it is safer to meet with a bad character in the pages of a fictitious story, than in the polluted walks of life; but an author solicitous for the morals of his readers will be sparing in the introduction of such characters.—It is an aphorism of Pope,

> "Vice is a monster of such frightful mien
> As to be hated, needs but to be seen."

But he adds,

> "But seen too oft, familiar with her face,
> We first endure, then pity, then embrace."[9]

Indeed the former assertion is not true without considerable modifications. If presented in its naked deformity, vice will indeed give disgust; but it may be so surrounded with splendid and engaging qualities, that the disgust is lost in admiration. Besides, though the selfish and mean propensities are radically unlovely, it is not the same with those passions which all have felt, and few are even desirous to resist. To present these to the young mind in the glowing colours of a Rousseau or a Madame de Stael is to awaken and increase sensibilities, which it is the office of wise restraint to calm and to moderate.[10] Humour covers the disgust which the grosser vices would occasion; passion veils the danger of the more seducing ones.

After all, the effect of novel-reading must depend, as in every other kind of reading, on the choice which is made. If the looser compositions of this sort are excluded, and the sentimental ones chiefly perused, perhaps the danger lies more in fixing the standard of virtue and delicacy too high for real use, than in debasing it. Generosity is carried to such excess as would soon dissipate even a princely fortune; a weak compassion often allows vice to escape with impunity; an over-strained delicacy, or regard to a rash vow, is allowed to mar all the prospects of a long life: dangers are despised, and self is annihilated, to a degree that prudence does not warrant, and virtue is far from requiring. The most generous man living, the most affectionate friend, the most dutiful child, would find his character fall far short of the perfections exhibited in a highly-wrought novel.

Love is a passion particularly exaggerated in novels. It forms the chief interest of, by far, the greater part of them. In order to increase this interest, a false idea is given of the importance of the passion. It occupies the serious hours of life; events all hinge upon it; every thing gives way to its influence, and no length of time wears it out. When a young lady, having imbibed these notions, comes into the world, she finds that this formidable passion acts a very subordinate part on the great theatre of the world; that its vivid

Anna Laetitia Aiken Barbauld (1743–1825)

sensations are mostly limited to a very early period and that it is by no means, as the poet sings,

"All the colour of remaining life."

She will find but few minds susceptible of its more delicate influences. Where it is really felt, she will see it continually overcome by duty, by prudence, or merely by a regard for the show and splendour of life; and that in fact it has a very small share in the transactions of the busy world, and is often little consulted even in choosing a partner for life. In civilized life both men and women acquire so early a command over their passions, that the strongest of them are taught to give way to circumstances, and a moderate liking will appear apathy itself, to one accustomed to see the passion painted in its most glowing colours. Least of all will a course of novels prepare a young lady for the neglect and tedium of life which she is perhaps doomed to encounter. If the novels she reads are virtuous, she has learned how to arm herself with proper reserve against the ardour of her lover; she has been instructed how to behave with the utmost propriety when run away with, like Miss Byron, or locked up by a cruel parent, like Clarissa;[11] but she is not prepared for indifference and neglect. Though young and beautiful, she may see her youth and beauty pass away without conquests, and the monotony of her life will be apt to appear more insipid when contrasted with scenes of perpetual courtship and passion.

It may be added with regard to the knowledge of the world, which, it is allowed, these writings are calculated in some degree to give, that, let them be as well written and with as much attention to real life and manners as they can possibly be, they will in some respects give false ideas, from the very nature of fictitious writing. Every such work is a *whole*, in which the fates and fortunes of the personages are brought to a conclusion, agreeably to the author's own preconceived idea. Every incident in a well written composition is introduced for a certain purpose, and made to forward a certain plan. A sagacious reader is never disappointed in his forebodings. If a prominent circumstance is presented to him, he lays hold on it, and may be very sure it will introduce some striking event; and if a character has strongly engaged his affections, he need not fear being obliged to withdraw them: the personages never turn out differently from what their first appearance gave him a right to expect; they gradually open, indeed; they may surprise, but they never disappoint him. Even from the elegance of a name he may give a guess at the amenity of the character. But real life is a kind of chance-medley,[12] consisting of many unconnected scenes. The great author of the drama of life has not finished his piece; but the author must finish his; and vice must be punished and virtue rewarded in the compass of a few volumes; and it is a fault in *his* composition if every circumstance does not answer the reasonable expectations of the reader. But in real life our reasonable expectations are often disappointed; many incidents occur which are like "passages that lead to nothing," and characters occasionally turn out quite different from what our fond expectations have led us to expect.

In short, the reader of a novel forms his expectations from what he supposes passes in the mind of the author, and guesses rightly at his intentions, but would often guess wrong if he were considering the real course of nature. It was very probable, at some periods of his history, that Gil Blas, if a real character, would come to be hanged; but the practised novel-reader knows well that no such event can await the hero of the tale. Let us suppose a person speculating on the character of Tom Jones as the production of an author, whose business it is pleasingly to interest his readers. He has no doubt but that, in spite of his irregularities and distresses, his history will come to an agreeable termination. He has no doubt but that his parents will be discovered in due time; he has no doubt but that his love for Sophia will be rewarded sooner or later with her hand; he has no doubt of the constancy of that young lady, or of their entire happiness after marriage. And why does he foresee all this? Not from the real tendencies of things, but from what he has dicovered of the author's intentions. But what would have been the probability in real life? Why, that the parents would either never have been found, or have proved to be persons of no consequence—that Jones would pass from one vicious indulgence to another, till his natural good disposition was quite smothered under his irregularities—that Sophia would either have married her lover clandestinely, and have been poor and unhappy, or she would have conquered her passion and married some country gentleman with whom she would have lived in moderate happiness, according to the usual routine of married life. But the author would have done very ill so to have constructed this story. If Booth had been a real character, it is probable his Amelia and her family would not only have been brought to poverty, but left in it; but to the reader it is much more probable that by some means or other they will be rescued from it, and left in possession of all the comforts of life. It is *probable* in *Zeluco* that the detestable husband will some way or other be got rid of; but woe to the young lady, who, when married, should be led, by contemplating the possibility of such an event, to cherish a passion which ought to be entirely relinquished![13]

Though a great deal of trash is every season poured out upon the public from the English presses, yet in general our novels are not vicious; the food has neither flavour nor nourishment, but at least it is not poisoned. Our national taste and habits are still turned towards domestic life and matrimonial happiness, and the chief harm done by a circulating library is occasioned by the frivolity of its furniture, and the loss of time incurred. Now and then a girl perhaps may be led by them to elope with a coxcomb; or, if she is handsome, to expect the homage of a Sir Harry or My lord, instead of the plain tradesman suitable to her situation in life; but she will not have her mind contaminated with such scenes and ideas as Crebillon, Louvet, and others of that class have published in France.

And indeed, notwithstanding the many paltry books of this kind published in the course of every year, it may safely be affirmed that we have more good writers in this walk living at the present time, than at any period since the days of Richardson and Fielding. A very great proportion of these are ladies: and surely it will not be said that either taste or morals have been losers by their taking the pen in hand. The names of D'Arblay, Edgeworth, Inchbald, Radcliffe, and a number more, will vindicate this assertion.[14]

No small proportion of modern novels have been devoted to recommend, or to mark with reprobation, those systems of philosophy or politics which have raised so much ferment of late years. Mr. Holcroft's *Anna St. Ives* is of this number: its beauties, and beauties it certainly has, do not make amends for its absurdities. What can be more absurd than to represent a young lady gravely considering, in the disposal of her hand, how she shall promote the greatest possible good of the system? Mr. Holcroft was a man of strong powers, and his novels are by no means without merit, but his satire is often partial, and his representations of life unfair. On the other side may be reckoned *The modern Philosophers*, and the novels of Mrs. West.[15] In the war of systems these light skirmishing troops have been often employed with great effect; and, so long as they are content with fair, general warfare, without taking aim at individuals, are perfectly allowable. We have lately seen the gravest theological discussions presented to the world under the attractive form of a novel, and with a success which seems to show that the interest, even of the generality of readers, is most strongly excited when some serious end is kept in view.

It is not the intention in these slight remarks to enumerate those of the present day who have successfully entertained the public; otherwise Mr. Cumberland might be mentioned, that veteran in every field of literature; otherwise a tribute ought to be paid to the peculiarly pathetic powers of Mrs. Opie; nor would it be possible to forget the very striking and original novel of *Caleb Williams*, in which the author, without the assistance of any of the common events of feelings on which these stories generally turn, has kept up the curiosity and interest of the reader in the most lively manner; nor his *St. Leon*, the ingenious speculation of a philosophical mind, which is also much out of the common track. It will bear an advantageous comparison with Swift's picture of the Strulbrugs in his Voyage to Laputa, the tendency of which seems to be to repress the wish of never-ending life in this world: but in fact it does not bear at all upon the question, for no one ever did wish for immortal life without immortal youth to accompany it, the one wish being as easily formed as the other; but *St. Leon* shows, from a variety of striking circumstances, that both together would pall, and that an immortal *human* creature would grow an insulated unhappy being.[16] . . . Some perhaps may think that too much importance has been already given to a subject so frivolous, but a discriminating taste is no where more called for than with regard to a species of books which every body reads. It was said by Fletcher of Saltoun, "Let me make the ballads of a nation, and I care not who makes the laws."[17] Might it not be said with as much propriety, Let me make the novels of a country, and let who will make the systems?

From Preface to Richardson, in *The British Novelists* (1810)

. . . The production upon which the fame of Richardson is principally founded, that which will transmit his name to posterity as one of the first geniuses of the age in which he lived, is undoubtedly his *Clarissa*. Nothing can be more simple than the story:—A young lady, pressed by her parents to marry a man every way disagreeable to her, and placed under the most cruel restraint, leaves her father's house, and throws herself upon the protection of her lover, a man of sense and spirit, but a libertine. When he finds her in his power, he artfully declines marriage, and conveys her to a house kept for the worst of purposes. There, after many fruitless attempts to ensnare her virtue, he at length violates her person. She escapes from further outrage: he finds her out in her retreat; offers her marriage, which she rejects. Her friends are obdurate. She retires to solitary lodgings; grief and shame overwhelm her, and she dies broken-hearted. Her friends lament their severity when too late. Her violator is transiently stung with remorse, but not reformed; he leaves the kingdom in order to dissipate his chagrin, and is killed in a duel by a relation of the lady's.

On this slight foundation, and on a story not very agreeable or promising in its rude outline, has our author founded a most pathetic tale, and raised a noble temple to female virtue. The first volumes are somewhat tedious, from the prolixity incident to letter-writing, and require a persevering reader to get through them: but the circumstantial manner of writing which Richardson practised, has the advantage of making the reader thoroughly acquainted with those in whose fate he is to be interested. In consequence of this, our feelings are not transient, elicited here and there by a pathetic stroke; but we regard his characters as real personages, whom we know and converse with, and whose fate remains to be decided in the course of events. The characters, much more numerous than in *Pamela*, are all distinctly drawn and well preserved, and there is a proper contrast and variety in the casting of the parts. The plot, as we have seen, is simple, and no under-plots interfere with the main design. No digressions, no episodes. It is wonderful that without these helps of common writers, he could support a work of such length. With Clarissa it begins,—with Clarissa it ends. We do not come upon unexpected adventures and wonderful recognitions, by quick turns and surprises: we see her fate from afar, as it were through a long avenue, the gradual approach to which, without ever losing sight of the object, has more of simplicity and grandeur than the most cunning labyrinth that can be contrived by art. In the approach to the modern country-seat, we are made to catch transiently a side-view of it through an opening of the trees, or to burst upon it from a sudden turning in the road; but the old mansion stood full in the eye of the traveller, as he drew near it, contemplating its turrets, which grew larger and more distinct every step that he advanced, and leisurely filling his eye and his imagination with still increasing ideas of its magnificence.—As the work advances, the character rises; the distress is deepened; our hearts are torn with pity and indignation; bursts of grief succeed one another, till at length the mind is composed and harmonized with emotions of milder sorrow; we are calmed into resignation, elevated with pious hope, and dismissed glowing with the conscious triumphs of virtue.

The first group which presents itself is that of the Harlowe family. They are sufficiently discriminated, yet preserve a family likeness. The stern father, the passionate and dark-souled brother, the envious and ill-natured sister, the money-loving uncles, the gentle but weak-spirited mother, are all assimilated by that stiffness, love of parade, and solemnity, which is thrown over the whole, and by the interested family views in which they all concur. . . . The character of Clarissa herself is very highly wrought: she has all the grace, and dignity, and delicacy, of a finished model of female excellence. Her duty to her parents is implicit, except in the article of sacrificing herself to a man utterly disgustful to her; and she bears with the greatest meekness the ill usage she receives from the other branches of the family. Duty, indeed, is the great principle of her conduct. Her affections are always completely under command; and her going off with Lovelace appears a step she was betrayed, not persuaded, into. His persuasions she had withstood; and it was fear, not love, that at last precipitated her into his protection. If, therefore, the author meant to represent her subsequent misfortunes as a punishment, he has scarcely made her faulty enough. That a young lady had eloped from her father's house with a libertine, sounds, indeed, like a grave offence; but the fault, when it is examined into, is softened and shaded off by such a variety of circumstances, that it becomes almost evanescent. Who that reads the treatment she experienced, does not wonder at her long-suffering? After Clarissa finds herself, against her will and intention, in the power of her lover, the story becomes, for a while, a game at chess, in which both parties exert great skill and presence of mind, and quick observation of each other's motions. Not a moment of weakness does Clarissa betray; and she only loses the game because she plays fairly and with integrity, while he is guilty of the basest frauds.

During this part of the story, the generality of readers are perhaps inclined to wish that Lovelace should give up his wicked intentions, reform, and make Clarissa happy in the marriage state. This was the conclusion which Lady Bradshaigh so vehemently and passionately urged the author to adopt. But when the unfeeling character of Lovelace proceeds to deeper and darker wickedness; when his unrelenting cruelty meditates, and actually perpetrates, the last unmanly outrage upon unprotected innocence and virtue,—the heart surely cannot have right feelings that does not cordially detest so black a villain, notwithstanding the agreeable qualities which are thrown into his character; and that woman must have little delicacy, who does not feel that his crime has raised an eternal wall of separation between him and the victim of his treachery, whatever affection she might have previously entertained for him. Yet it is said by some, that the author has made Lovelace too agreeable, and his character has been much the object of criticism. But a little reflection will show us, that the author had a more difficult part to manage, in drawing his character, than that of any other in the work, and that he could not well have made him different from what he is. If he had drawn a mean-spirited dark villain, without any specious qualities, his Clarissa would have been degraded. Lovelace, as he is to win the affections of the heroine, is necessarily, in some sort, the hero of the piece, and no one in it must be permitted to outshine him. The author, therefore, gives him wit and spirit, and courage, and generosity, and manly genteel address, and also transient gleams of feeling, and transient stings of remorse; so that we are often led to hope he may follow his better angel, and give up his atrocious designs. This the author has done, and less he could not do, for the man whom Clarissa was inclined to favour. Besides, if it was part of his intention to warn young women against placing their affections upon libertines, it was certainly only against the agreeable ones of that class that he had any occasion to warn them. He tells us in one of his letters, that finding he had made him too much a favourite, he had thrown in some darker shades to obviate the objection; and surely the shades are dark enough. In one particular, however, the author might perhaps have improved the moral effect of the work; he might have given more of horror to the last scene of Lovelace's life. When Clarissa and he were finally separated, there was no occasion to keep measures with him; and why should Belton die a death of so much horror, and Lovelace of calm composure and self-possession? . . .

But if the author might have improved in this respect the character of Lovelace, that of Clarissa comes up to all the ideas we can form of female loveliness and dignified suffering. The first scenes with her hard-hearted family show the severe struggles she had with herself, before she could withdraw her obedience from her parents. The measure of that obedience in Richardson's mind was very high; and therefore Clarissa seems all along, rather to lament the cruelty, than to resent the injustice, of imposing a husband upon her without her own consent. It is easy to see she would have thought it her duty to comply, if he had not been quite so disagreeable. The mother is a very mean character; she gives a tacit permission to Clarissa to correspond with Lovelace to prevent mischief, and yet consents to be the tool of the family in persecuting her innocent and generous daughter;—but this was her duty to her husband!—Yet, distressing as Clarissa's situation is in her father's house, the author has had the address to make the reader feel, the moment she has got out of it, that he would give the world to have her safe back again. Nothing takes place of that pleasure and endearment which might naturally be expected on the meeting of two lovers: we feel that she has been hunted into the toils, and that every avenue is closed against her escape. No young person, on reading *Clarissa*, even at this period of the story, can think of putting herself into the power of a lover, without annexing to it the strongest sense of degradation and anxiety. A great deal of contrivance is expended by the author, in the various plots set on foot by Lovelace, to keep his victim tolerably easy in her ambiguous situation; and though some of these are tedious, it was necessary, for Clarissa's honour, to make the reader sensible that she had an inextricable net wound around her, and that it was not owing to her want of prudence or vigilance that she did not escape. In the mean time the wit of Lovelace and the sprightliness of Miss Howe prevent monotony. In one instance, however, Clarissa certainly sins against the delicacy of her character, that is, in allowing herself to be made a show of to the loose companions of Lovelace:—But, how does her character rise, when we come to the more distressful scenes; the view of her horror, when, deluded by the pretended relations, she reenters the fatal house; her temporary insanity after the outrage, in which she so affectingly holds up to Lovelace the license he had procured; and her dignified behaviour when she first sees her ravisher, after the perpetration of his crime. What finer subject could be presented to the painter, than that in which Clarissa grasps the penknife in her hand, "her eyes lifted up to heaven, the whites of them only visible," ready to plunge it in her breast, to preserve herself from further outrage; Lovelace, aghast with terror, and speechless, thrown back to the further end of the room!—or the prison scene, where she is represented kneeling amidst the gloom and horror of the dismal abode; illuminating, as it were, the dark chamber; her face reclining on her crossed arms, her white garments floating round her in the negligence of woe; Belford contemplating her with respectful commiseration:—or the scene of calmer but heart-piercing sorrow, in the interview Colonel Morden has with her in her dying moments: She is represented "fallen into a slumber in her elbow-chair, leaning on the widow Lovick, whose left arm is around her neck; one faded cheek resting on the good woman's bosom, the kindly warmth of which had overspread it with a faintish flush, the other pale and hollow, as if already iced over by death; her hand, the blueness of the veins contrasting their whiteness, hanging lifelessly before her, the widow's tears dropping unfelt upon her face—Colonel Morden, with his arms folded, gazing on her in silence, her coffin just appearing behind a screen." What admiration, what reverence does the author inspire us with for the innocent sufferer,—the sufferings too of such a peculiar nature!

There is something in virgin purity, to which the imagination willingly pays homage. In all ages, something saintly has been attached to the idea of unblemished chastity. . . .

It was reserved for Richardson to overcome all circumstances of dishonour and disgrace, and to throw a splendour round the *violated virgin*, more radiant than she possessed in her first bloom. He has made the flower, which grew

"—— sweet to sense, and lovely to the eye,"

throw out a richer fragrance *after* "the cruel spoiler has *cropped the fair rose and rifled its sweetness*." He has drawn the triumph of mental chastity; he has drawn it uncontaminated, untarnished, and incapable of mingling with pollution.—The scenes which follow the death of the heroine, exhibit grief in an affecting variety of forms, as it is modified by the characters of different survivors. They run into considerable length; but we have been so deeply interested, that we feel it a relief to have our grief drawn off, as it were, by a variety of sluices, and we are glad not to be dismissed till we have shed tears, even to satiety. We enjoy, besides, the punishment of the Harlowes, in the contemplation of their merited anguish. Sentiments of piety pervade the whole work; but the deathbed of Clarissa, her Christian forgiveness, and her meek resignation, are particularly edifying. . . .

That *Clarissa* is a highly moral work, has been always allowed;—but what is the moral?—Is it that a young lady who places her affections upon a libertine, will be deceived and ruined? Though the author no doubt intended this as one of the conclusions to be drawn, such a maxim has not dignity or force enough in it to be the chief moral of this interesting tale. And it has been already mentioned that Clarissa can hardly stand as an example of such a choice, as she never fairly made the choice. On the contrary, she is always ready, both before her elopement and after it, to resign the moderate, the almost insensible predilection she feels for Lovelace, to the will of her parents, if she might only be permitted to refuse the object of her aversion. Is she, then, exhibited as a rare pattern of chastity? Surely this is an idea very degrading to the sex. Lovelace, indeed, who has a very bad opinion of women, and thinks that hardly any woman can resist him, talks of trying her virtue, and speaks as if he expected her to fail in the trial. But surely the virtue of Clarissa could never have been in the smallest danger. The virtue of Pamela was tried, because the pecuniary offers were a temptation which many in her station of life would have yielded to; and because their different situations in life opposed a bar to their legitimate union, which she might well believe would be insuperable. The virtue of Werter's Charlotte was tried, and the virtue of the wife of Zeluco was tried, because the previous marriage of one of the parties made a virtuous union impossible.[1]—But Clarissa! a young lady of birth and fortune, marriage completely in her lover's power—she could have felt nothing but indignation at the first idea which entered her mind that he meant to degrade her into a mistress. Was it likely that she, who had shown that her affections were so much under her command while the object of his addresses appeared to be honourable marriage, should not guard against every freedom with the most cautious vigilance, as soon as she experienced a behaviour in him which must at once destroy her esteem for him, and be offensive to her just pride, as well as to her modesty? It is absurd therefore in Lovelace to speak of trying her chastity; and the author is not free from blame in favouring the idea that such resistance had any thing in it uncommon, or peculiarly meritorious. But the real moral of *Clarissa* is, that virtue is triumphant in every situation; that in circumstances the most painful and degrading,—in a prison, in a brothel, in grief, in distraction, in despair,—it is still lovely, still commanding, still the object of our veneration, of our fondest affections: that if it is seated on the ground, it can still say with Constance,

"Here is my throne; kings, come and bow to it!"[2]

The novelist that has produced this effect has performed his office well, and it is immaterial what particular maxim is selected under the name of a moral, while such are the reader's feelings. If our feelings are in favour of virtue, the novel is virtuous; if of vice, the novel is vicious. The greatness of Clarissa is shown by her separating herself from her lover as soon as she perceives his dishonourable views; her choosing death rather than a repetition of the outrage; in her rejection of those overtures of marriage, which a common mind might have accepted of, as a refuge against worldly dishonour; in her firm indignant carriage, mixed with calm patience and Christian resignation; and in the greatness of mind with which she views and enjoys the approaches of death, and her meek forgiveness of her unfeeling relations. . . .

There is an improbability which the author could not well avoid, as it resulted from his plan of carrying on the narrative by letters; and that is, the tame acquiescence of Belford in a villainy which he all along so strongly disapproves.[3] It is true, as a man of honour, he might think himself obliged not to betray his friend's secrets; but his disapprobation would certainly have prevented his friend from communicating those secrets. Belford is, in fact, reformed, from the time we first hear of him; and therefore those intimate communications could not any longer have subsisted. But Belford is a being created in order to carry on the story, and must not be made too strictly the object of criticism. A novel-writer must violate probability somewhere, and a reader ought to make all handsome and generous allowances for it. We should open a book as we enter into a company, well persuaded that we must not expect perfection. In Belford, too, we have a reformed libertine, one whom the reader regards with esteem and affection. . . .

The author of *Sir Charles*[4] often mentions in his letters, that he was importuned by many of his friends to give them another volume; and the Gottenburg translators sent for the rest of the work, supposing it incomplete: he ought to have received it as a proof that it was too long, and not too

short. He had already continued it a whole volume beyond the proper termination—the marriage of his hero; and having done so, he might, without
more impropriety, have gone on to the next point of view, and the next, till
he had given the history of two or three generations. *Clarissa*, perhaps, runs
out into too great a length, but bold were the hand that should attempt to
shorten it. *Sir Charles*, on the contrary, would be improved by merely striking out the last volume, and, indeed, a good part of the sixth, where descriptions of dress, and parade, and furniture, after the interest is completely
over, like the gaudy colouring of a western sky, give symptoms of a setting
sun. But it is ungrateful to dwell on the faults of genius. . . .

From Preface to Fielding, in *The British Novelists* (1810)

[*Tom Jones*] contains a story involving a number of adventures, and a variety
of characters, all of which are strictly connected with the main design, and
tend to the development of the plot; which yet is so artfully concealed, that
it may be doubted whether it was ever anticipated by the most practised
and suspicious reader. The story contains all that we require in a regular
epopea or drama; strict unity of design, a change of fortune, a discovery,
punishment and reward distributed according to poetical or rather moral
justice. The clearing up the character of Jones to Alworthy, the discovery
of his relationship to him, and his union with Sophia, are all brought about
at the end of the piece, and all obscurities satisfactorily cleared up; so that
the reader can never doubt, as in some novels he may, whether the work
should have ended a volume before, or have been carried on a volume after,
the author's conclusion. The peculiar beauty of the plot consists in this; that
though the author's secret is impenetrable, the discovery is artfully prepared
by a number of circumstances, not attended to at the time, and by obscure
hints thrown out, which, when the reader looks back upon them, are found
to agree exactly with the concealed event. Of this nature is the cool un-
abashed behaviour of Jenny, the supposed delinquent, when she acknowledges herself the mother of the child; the flitting appearance from time to
time of the attorney Dowling; and especially the behaviour of Mrs. Blifil
to her son, which is wonderfully well managed in this respect. She appears
at first to notice him only in compliance, and an ungracious compliance
too, with her brother's request; yet many touches of the mother are recollected when the secret is known; and the more open affection she shows
him afterwards, when a youth of eighteen, has a turn given it which effectually misleads the reader. If he is very sagacious, he may perhaps suspect
some mystery from the frequent appearance of Dowling; but he has no clue

to find out what the mystery is, nor can he anticipate the very moment of discovery.

But intricacy of plot, admirable as this is, is still of secondary merit compared with the exhibition of character, of which there is in this work a rich variety. Of the humorous ones Squire Western and his sister are the most prominent. They are admirably contrasted. . . . Jones is a youth of true feeling, honour, and generosity; open and affectionate in his disposition, but very accessible to the temptations of pleasure. Blifil, with great apparent sobriety and decorum of manners, is a mean selfish hypocrite, possessing a mind of thorough baseness and depravity. In characters so contrasted, it is not doubtful to which of them the reader will, or ought to give the preference. To the faults of Blifil the reader has no inclination to be partial. They revolt the mind, particularly the minds of youth. The case is not the same with those more pardonable deviations from morals which are incident to youths of a warm temperament and an impressible heart: these are contagious in their very nature, and therefore the objections which have been made to the moral tendency of this novel are no doubt in some measure just. It is said to have been forbidden in France on its first publication. The faults of Jones are less than those of almost every other person who is brought upon the stage; yet they are of more dangerous example, because they are mixed with so many qualities which excite our affections. Still, his character is of a totally different stamp from the heroes of Smollet's novels. He has an excellent heart and a refined sensibility, though he has also passions of a lower order. In every instance where he transgresses the rules of virtue, he is the seduced, and not the seducer; his youth, his constitution, his unprotected situation after he left Alworthy's, palliate his faults, and in honourable love he is tender and constant. His refusal of the young widow who makes him an offer of her hand does him honour. In one instance only is he *degraded*,—his affair with Lady Bellaston.[1]

The character of Sophia was probably formed according to the author's ideas of female perfection: she is very beautiful, very sweet-tempered, very fond and constant to her lover; but her behaviour will scarcely satisfy one who has conceived high ideas of the delicacy of the female character. A young woman just come from reading *Clarissa* must be strangely shocked at seeing the heroine of the tale riding about the country on post-horses after her lover; and the incidents at Upton are highly indelicate. It is observable that Fielding uniformly keeps down the characters of his women, as much as Richardson elevates his. A yielding easiness of disposition is what he seems to lay the greatest stress upon. Alworthy is made to tell Sophia, that what had chiefly charmed him in her behaviour was the great deference he had observed in her for the opinions of men. Yet Sophia, methinks, had not been extraordinarily well situated for imbibing such reverence. Any portion of learning in women is constantly united in this author with something disagreeable. It is given to Jenny, the supposed mother of Jones. It is given in a higher degree to that very disgusting character Mrs. Bennet in *Amelia*; Mrs. Western, too, is a woman of reading. A man of licentious manners, and such was Fielding, seldom respects the sex. . . . The character of Alworthy is not a shining one; he is imposed upon by every body: this may be consistent with goodness, but it is not consistent with that dignity in which an eminently virtuous character, meant to be exhibited as a pattern of excellence, ought to appear. But Fielding could not draw such a character. Traits of humanity and kindness he is able to give in all their beauty; but a religious and strictly moral character was probably connected in his mind with a want of sagacity, which those who have been conversant with the vicious part of the world are very apt to imagine must be the consequence of keeping aloof from it. Besides, it was necessary for the plot that Alworthy should be imposed upon. . . .

Upon the whole, *Tom Jones* is certainly for humour, wit, character, and plot, one of the most entertaining and perfect novels we possess. With regard to its moral tendency we must content ourselves with more qualified praise. A young man may imbibe from it sentiments of humanity, generosity, and all the more amiable virtues; a detestation of meanness, hypocrisy, and treachery: but he is not likely to gain from it firmness to resist temptation, or to have his ideas of moral purity heightened or refined by the perusal. More men would be apt to imitate Jones than would copy Lovelace; and it is to be feared there are few women who would not like him better than Sir Charles Grandison. The greater refinement also and delicacy of the present age, a sure test of national civilization, though a very equivocal one of national virtue, has almost proscribed much of that broad humour which appears in the works of Fielding's times, and we should scarcely bear, in a new novel, the indelicate pictures which are occasionally presented to the imagination. The scenes at inns also are coarse, and too often repeated. The introductory chapters ought not to be passed over; they have much wit and grave Cervantic humour, and occasionally display the author's familiarity with the classics.

Fielding's vein was not yet exhausted; he produced a third novel called *Amelia*. If this has less of the author's characteristic humour, it has more scenes of domestic tenderness. Contrary to the usual practice of novel-writers, the story begins after the marriage of the principal personages. The hero, Mr. Booth, is introduced to us in a prison; the distresses of the piece arise from the vicious indulgencies of the husband, combined with unfortunate circumstances; and in the character of Booth, Fielding is generally supposed to have delineated his own. Amelia is such a wife as most men of that stamp would deem the model of female perfection, such a one as a man, conscious of a good many frailties and vices, usually wishes for. Faithful, fond, and indulgent, the prospect of immediate ruin cannot draw from her one murmur against her husband, and she willingly sacrifices to him her jewels and every article in her possession. Booth is represented as good-natured, thoughtless, and extravagant; passionately fond of his wife, notwithstanding occasional breaches of fidelity to her; and very ready to receive the sacrifices she makes, even to the pawning of her clothes and moveables, for the discharge of his gaming debts. Amelia, indeed, is a heroine of affection and obedience, and the impression upon the reader is certainly that of her being a very amiable and interesting[2] woman; but her character exhibits a great degree of weakness, particularly in her behaviour to the nobleman who is endeavouring to seduce her. What woman of any sense could suppose, that a gay nobleman would frequent her house for the sake of amusing himself with her little ones?

Notes

"On the Origin and Progress of Novel-Writing"

1. Merlin and Jonas were apparently professional magicians. Western Australia and Tahiti were formerly named New Holland and Otaheite.

2. Thomas Gray, "The Progress of Poesy" (1757), III.3.4.

3. Jean-Jacques Rousseau's *Julie, or the New Heloise* (1761) was much admired for its glowing but idealized representation of erotic passion in an idyllic natural setting in Switzerland. Julie and her tutor Saint-Preux fall in love and have an affair, but her father forces her to marry a middle-aged nobleman; although Julie and Saint-Preux live in the same house and continue to love each other, Julie maintains strict fidelity to her husband.

4. John Milton, *Paradise Lost* (1667), III, 302–303 (slightly inaccurate).

5. Barbauld accurately describes the appeal of Laurence Sterne's *Tristram Shandy* (1760–1767). The deathbed of the officer Le Fevre is lightly sketched (VI, chaps. 6–10), while Clarissa's sufferings are developed at length. The eccentric brothers Walter and Toby Shandy, Toby's servant Trim, and the "man-midwife" Dr. Slop are major comic characters. Toby and Trim deplore cruelty to black slaves in IX, chap. 6. In II, chap. 12, Toby tenderly catches and releases out the window a fly that had buzzed around his

nose all through dinner. Much of Sterne's humor comes from creative borrowing from books such as Robert Burton's *Anatomy of Melancholy* (1621).

6. Frances Sheridan's *Memoirs of Miss Sidney Bidulph* (1761) details at length the afflictions of an impeccably virtuous heroine.

7. In Oliver Goldsmith's *Vicar of Wakefield* (1766), virtuous Dr. Primrose, imprisoned for debt, reforms his fellow prisoners by his wise preaching (II, chaps. 7 and 8). The kind and generous hero of Henry Brooke's *Fool of Quality* (1766–1772) constantly relieves unfortunate people.

8. The fashionable Harrels in Frances Burney's *Cecilia* (1782) ruin themselves by irresponsible extravagance. Maria Edgeworth's fictions for adolescents, such as *Moral Tales for Young People* (1801), engage interest by their understanding of children and teach lessons of prudence, consideration for others, freedom from affectation, etc.

9. Alexander Pope, *An Essay on Man* (1732–1734), II, ll. 217–220 (slightly inaccurate).

10. Germaine de Staël's heroines Delphine (1802) and Corinne (1807) are highly attractive and amiable, like Rousseau's lovers; their intense passions flout contemporary standards of feminine propriety.

11. Samuel Richardson's Miss Byron (in *The History of Sir Charles Grandison*, 1753–1754) is abducted by a rake; his Clarissa (1747–1748) is locked up by her family for refusing to marry the man of their choice.

12. Haphazard action.

13. Gil Blas, hero of Alain-René Lesage's picaresque tale (1715–1735), is a rogue who escapes punishment for his misdeeds. Henry Fielding's Tom Jones (1749), a foundling whose imprudence constantly gets him into trouble, is discovered to be well-born, marries Sophia, and lives happily ever after. Booth (in Fielding's *Amelia*, 1751) cannot support his family, but they are made prosperous by the discovery of a concealed will. The amiable heroine of John Moore's *Zeluco* (1786) is released from her marriage to the anti-hero when he is stabbed by his mistress's lover.

14. Frances Burney d'Arblay (*Evelina*, 1778, *Cecilia*, 1782, etc.), Maria Edgeworth (*Castle Rackrent*, 1800, *Belinda*, 1801, etc.), Elizabeth Inchbald (*A Simple Story*, 1791), Ann Radcliffe (*The Mysteries of Udolpho*, 1794, *The Italian*, 1797, etc.).

15. Thomas Holcroft's *Anna St. Ives* (1792) preaches politically radical virtue; its heroine intends to reject the man she loves in favor of a dissolute aristocrat whom she can marry and reform. Elizabeth Hamilton's *Memoirs of Modern Philosophers* (1800) satirizes the radicalism of Holcroft and William Godwin, and Jane West's novels (*A Tale of the Times*, 1799, etc.) are extremely conservative.

16. Richard Cumberland, primarily a playwright, wrote two novels, *Arundel* (1789) and *Henry* (1795). Amelia Opie's *Adeline Mowbray* (1804) and other novels make effective use of pathos. Godwin's *Caleb Williams* (1794) is a tale of guilt, persecution, and class oppression. The hero of his *St. Leon* (1799) is immortal; Jonathan Swift's Struldbruggs (in Book III of *Gulliver's Travels*, 1726) grow old but never die.

17. Andrew Fletcher of Saltoun, *Conversation concerning a Right Regulation of Government* (1703) (slightly inaccurate).

Preface to Richardson

1. Richardson's *Pamela* (1740) is a servant aggressively courted by her employer; Goethe's Charlotte (in *The Sorrows of Young Werther*, 1774) loves Werther but is married

to another man; Zeluco's wife remains faithful to the villain who ill-treats her, even though she loves a worthy man who loves her.

2. William Shakespeare, *King John* (1590s), III.i.74 (slightly inaccurate). Queen Constance's son, the rightful heir to the English throne, has just been defrauded of his inheritance.

3. *Clarissa* is narrated through the correspondences of Clarissa with Anna Howe and Lovelace with Belford.

4. *The History of Sir Charles Grandison* extends to seven volumes in the standard edition of Richardson's works; *Clarissa*, to eight.

Preface to Fielding

1. Tobias Smollett's heroes, such as Roderick Random (1748) and Peregrine Pickle (1751), are as conspicuously virile as Tom Jones but lack his sympathy and tenderness. Tom refuses an advantageous proposal from a widow, even though Sophia seems lost to him, because he does not love her (Book XV, chap. 11). He does, however, allow himself to be kept by the dissolute Lady Bellaston.

2. Touching.

HANNAH PARKHOUSE COWLEY
(1743-1809)

Hannah Parkhouse was born into a literary family; her father, Philip Parkhouse, was a bookseller in Tiverton, Devonshire. At the age of twenty-five, she married Thomas Cowley, a government clerk and writer who became a captain in the East India Company. Hannah Cowley's literary career began early in 1776 when, attending a play with her husband, she declared, "Why, I could write as well." Within two weeks she composed her first play, *The Runaway,* which was successfully produced at Drury Lane. Over the next nineteen years she wrote twelve more plays, mostly comedies but also several tragedies and a farce. By far her best-known play is the comedy *The Belle's Stratagem* (1782).

Cowley was something of an iconoclast, frequently at odds with England's literary and political establishment. *The Runaway* mocked the literary accomplishments of the Bluestockings, and she later became embroiled in a newspaper war with Hannah More, whom she accused of plagiarism. In the preface to her last play, *The Town Before You* (1795), Cowley blasts the corrupt taste of London and promises never to write again for the stage—a promise she kept.

In her address to readers of *A School for Greybeards*, Cowley responds to charges of impropriety leveled against the play after its first performance at Drury Lane on November 25, 1786; she forcefully argues for the right of playwrights, including women playwrights, to present realistic character, speech, and action. Cowley's plot closely follows its acknowledged source, Aphra Behn's *Lucky Chance* (1686). In Behn's play, Bellmour is in love with Leticia but must hide to avoid arrest for his participation in a duel. Leticia in the meantime agrees to marry the elderly alderman Sir Feeble Fainwood after he convinces her that Bellmour is dead. After returning to London in disguise and discovering that Leticia still loves him despite her engagement to Fainwood, Bellmour appears as the ghost of himself and scares Fainwood out of the marriage. In *A School for Greybeards*, set in Portugal, Antonia, Henry, and Gasper take the places of Leticia, Bellmour, and Fainwood. The charges of impropriety were leveled against the play even though Cowley had toned down considerably the bawdiness of Behn's original.

A School for Greybeards; or, The Morning Bride (London: G. G. J. and J. Robinson, 1786)

"An Address" from *A School for Greybeards* (1786)

I offer the following Comedy to the public, under a circumstance which has given my mind the most exquisite uneasiness. On the morning after the first representation, it was observed by the papers that there had been persons present at the Theatre the preceding evening, who went there *determined* to disapprove at all events. From such a determination it is hard indeed to escape! And the opposition intended, was justified it seems, by the indecency of some of the expressions.—From such a charge I feel it impossible to defend myself; for against an imputation like this, even *vindication* becomes disgraceful!

As I was not at the Theatre, I should have had some difficulty in understanding at what passages the objections were levelled, had not one of the papers recorded them, with many cruel remarks. The particulars which were thus pointed out, will, I trust be a sufficient apology for themselves. In the following pages they are *all* restored; that the public AT LARGE may have the power to adjudge me, as well as that small part of it, confined within the walls of a Theatre.

These passages have not been restored from any pertinacious opinion of their beauty—for other expressions might have conveyed my intention as well; but had I allowed one line to stand as altered for the stage, what might not that reprobated line have been supposed to express? I shrink from the idea! And therefore most solemnly aver, that the Comedy, as now printed, contains EVERY WORD which was opposed the first night, from the suspicion of indelicacy; hoping their *obvious* meaning only will be attended to, without the coarse ingenuity of strained explanations; which have been made, by persons who seem desirous to surround my task of dramatic writing, with as many difficulties as possible.

A celebrated Critic, more attended to for the discrimination and learning which appear in his strictures, than for their *lenity*; in his observations on the Greybeards, has the following.

Hannah Parkhouse Cowley (1743–1809)

When Mrs. Cowley gets possession of the spirit and turn of a character, she speaks the language of *that* character better than *any* of her dramatic contemporaries.

This, I confess, I hold to be very high praise; and it is to this very praise, which my contemporaries resolve I shall have no claim. They will allow me, indeed, to draw strong character, but it must be without speaking its language. I may give vulgar or low bred persons, but they must converse in a stile of elegance. I may design the coarsest manners, or the most disgusting folly, but its expressions must not deviate from the line of politeness. Surely it would be as just to exact from the Artists who are painting the Gallery of Shakespeare, that they should compleat their designs without the use of light and shade.

It cannot be the *Poet's* mind, which the public desire to trace, in dramatic representations; but the mind of the *characters*, and the truth of their colouring. Yet in my case it seems resolved that the point to be considered, is not whether that *dotard*, or that *pretender*, or that *coquet*, would so have given their feelings, but whether Mrs. Cowley ought so to have expressed herself.

This is a criterion which happily no author is subjected to, but those of the drama. The Novelist may use the boldest tints;—seizing Nature for her guide, she may dart through every rank of society, drag forth not only the accomplished, but the ignorant, the coarse, and the vulgar-rich; display them in their strongest colours, and snatch immortality both for them, and for herself! I, on the contrary, feel encompassed with chains when I write, which check me in my happiest flights, and force me continually to reflect, not, whether *this is just?* but, whether *this is safe?*

These are vain regrets, which I hope my readers will pardon me, for having a moment indulged. I now hasten to that part of the Comedy which will be found in the following sheets, as *altered* for the second representation.

The idea of the business which concerns Antonia, Henry, and Gasper was presented to me in an obsolete comedy; the work of a poet of the drama, once highly celebrated.[1] I say the *idea*, for when it is known that in the original the scene lay amongst traders in the city of London—and those traders of the lowest and most detestable manners, it will be conceived at once, that in removing it to Portugal, and fixing the characters amongst the nobility, it was hardly possible to carry with me *more* than the idea. The circumstance which most particularly interested me, and fixed itself in my mind, was that of snatching a young woman from a hateful marriage, the moment before that marriage became valid—that is to say, after the ceremony. This very circumstance to which the Comedy owes its existence, was that, which some of the audience found discordant to their feelings. An event which had in the last century been stampt with the highest applause, (tho' surrounded by many repulsive circumstances) was found in this, to be ill-conceived. I did not, however, dispute the decision of my Critics,—and the marriage has been in course dissolved.

The manner in which the Comedy has since been received, gives room to suppose that the alteration is approved. It has struggled with many oppressive circumstances: the chasm in the performance, occasioned by the repeated illness of Mr. Parsons,[2] was sufficient to have sunk it;—but neither that, nor the sterile month of December, always *against* the Theatres, has prevented its being distinguished by many brilliant and crouded nights. I now resign it to the closet, where without the aid of fine acting, or the fascinations of beauty, and deriving all its little force from the pen which composed it, it hopes still to amuse;—the innocent flame of Seraphina's coquetry may still shed rays of delight on her readers, and the affecting situation of Antonia interest them.

Notes

1. Aphra Behn's *Lucky Chance* (1687).
2. William Parsons, member of the Drury Lane Company, acted in many of Cowley's plays. In *A School for Greybeards* he played Don Gasper, the elderly fiancé of Antonia.

HANNAH MORE (1745–1833)

HANNAH MORE was the fourth of the daughters of a village schoolmaster who taught her Latin and mathematics but dropped the latter when she became uncomfortably proficient for a woman. The oldest daughter established a school in Bristol, where she was joined by her sisters, first as students and then as teachers. The school became extremely successful. More began making annual visits to London, where she met Samuel Johnson and his friends and became a member of the Bluestocking circle. Always strictly pious, as she grew older she devoted herself increasingly to religious and humanitarian causes. She actively campaigned for the abolition of the slave trade, organized a system of Sunday schools in areas where no education of any kind had been available to the poor, and produced a long series of *Cheap Repository Tracts* (1795–1798), intended to appeal to working-class readers and to counteract the influence of obscene or politically inflammatory pamphlets.

Everything More wrote was phenomenally successful, from her early tragedy *Percy* (1777) to her moralistic novel *Coelebs in Search of a Wife* (1809) to her lengthy treatises on morals and education. *Strictures on the Modern System of Female Education* (1799) argues that girls should be given an intellectually substantial education as well as a moral one. With as much fervor as Mary Wollstonecraft, she denounces contemporary practices that encouraged girls to be frivolous and trained them to be sexual objects. In the passage from the *Strictures* excerpted here, however, More reacts against the radical and sentimental tendency to set good feeling above moral law. Novels encourage this dangerous tendency by their sympathetic representation of warm feelings, including illicit passions; moreover, at the end of the eighteenth century, radical writers like William Godwin were using novels to spread revolutionary politics and religious infidelity. Many conservatives of More's time shared her apprehensions about the effects of novels on injudicious minds.

Strictures on the Modern System of Female Education (1799; rpt New York: Garland, 1974).

From *Strictures on the Modern System of Female Education* (1799)

. . . Novels, which used chiefly to be dangerous in one respect, are now
become mischievous in a thousand. They are continually shifting their
ground, and enlarging their sphere, and are daily becoming vehicles of wider
mischief. Sometimes they concentrate their force, and are at once employed
to diffuse destructive politics, deplorable profligacy, and impudent infidelity.
Rousseau was the first popular dispenser of this complicated drug, in which
the deleterious infusion was strong, and the effect proportionably fatal. For
he does not attempt to seduce the affections but through the medium of
the principles. He does not paint an innocent woman, ruined, repenting,
and restored; but with a far more mischievous refinement, he annihilates
the value of chastity, and with pernicious subtlety attempts to make his
heroine appear almost more amiable without it. He exhibits a virtuous
woman, the victim not of temptation but of reason, not of vice but of
sentiment, not of passion but of conviction; and strikes at the very root of
honour by elevating a crime into a principle. With a metaphysical sophistry
the most plausible, he debauches the heart of woman, by cherishing her
vanity in the erection of a system of male virtues, to which, with a lofty
dereliction of those that are her more peculiar and characteristic praise, he
tempts her to aspire; powerfully insinuating, that to this splendid system
chastity does not necessarily belong: thus corrupting the judgment and be-
wildering the understanding, as the most effectual way to inflame the imagination and deprave the heart.[1]

The rare mischief of this author consists in his power of seducing by
falsehood those who love truth, but whose minds are still wavering, and
whose principles are not yet formed. He allures the warm-hearted to embrace vice, not because they prefer vice, but because he gives to vice so
natural an air of virtue: and ardent and enthusiastic youth, too confidently
trusting in their integrity and in their teacher, will be undone, while they
fancy they are indulging in the noblest feelings of their nature. Many
authors will more infallibly complete the ruin of the loose and ill-disposed;
but perhaps (if I may change the figure) there never was a net of such
exquisite art and inextricable workmanship, spread to entangle innocence
and ensnare inexperience, as the writings of Rousseau: and unhappily, the
victim does not even struggle in the toils, because part of the delusion consists in imagining that he is set at liberty.

Some of our recent popular publications have adopted all the mischiefs of this school, and the principal evil arising from them is, that the virtues they exhibit are almost more dangerous than the vices. The chief materials out of which these delusive systems are framed, are characters who practice superfluous acts of generosity, while they are trampling on obvious and commanded duties; who combine sentiments of honour with actions the most flagitious: a high-tone of self-confidence, with a perpetual breach of self-denial: pathetic apostrophes to the passions, but no attempt to resist them. They teach that no duty exists which is not prompted by feeling: that impulse is the main spring of virtuous actions, while laws and principles are only unjust restraints; the former imposed by arbitrary men, the latter by the absurd prejudices of timorous and unenlightened conscience. In some of the most splendid of these characters, compassion is erected into the throne of justice, and justice is degraded into the rank of plebeian virtues. Creditors are defrauded, while the money due to them is lavished in dazzling acts of charity to some object that affected their senses; which fits of charity are made the sponge of every sin, and the substitute of every virtue: the whole indirectly tending to intimate how very *benevolent people are who are not Christians*. From many of these compositions, indeed, Christianity is systematically, and always virtually excluded; for the law and the prophets and the gospel *can* make no part of a scheme in which this world is looked upon as all in all; in which poverty and misery are considered as evils arising solely from human governments, and not from the dispensations of God. this poverty is represented as the greatest of evils, and the restraints which tend to keep the poor honest, as the most flagrant injustice. The gospel can have nothing to do with a system in which sin is reduced to a little human imperfection, and Old Bailey crimes are softened down into a few engaging weaknesses; and in which the turpitude of all the vices a man himself consists, is done away by his *candour* in tolerating all the vices committed by others.

But the most fatal part of the system to that class whom I am addressing is, that even in those works which do not go all the lengths of treating marriage as an unjust infringement on liberty, and a tyrannical deduction from general happiness; yet it commonly happens that the hero or heroine, who has practically violated the letter of the seventh commandment,[2] and continues to live in the allowed violation of its spirit, is painted as so amiable and so benevolent, so tender or so brave; and the temptation is represented as so *irresistible*, (for all these philosophers are fatalists,) the predominant and cherished sin is so filtered and purged of its pollutions, and is so sheltered and surrounded, and relieved with shining qualities, that the innocent and impressible young reader is brought to lose all horror of the awful crime in question, in the complacency she feels for the engaging virtues of the criminal. . . .

Notes

1. Jean-Jacques Rousseau's Julie, in *La Nouvelle Héloïse* (*The New Heloise*, 1761), is represented as highly amiable and virtuous, even though she has a premarital affair and continues to love her lover after her marriage to another man (to whom, however, she remains strictly faithful).

2. "Thou shalt not commit adultery" (Exodus 20:14).

STÉPHANIE-FÉLICITÉ DUCREST, COMTESSE DE GENLIS (1746–1830)

Born into a family of the French provincial nobility, Stéphanie-Félicité Ducrest received an indifferent education but nevertheless stood out for her intellect, her liveliness, and her capacity to work extremely hard. This last served her well during those periods when she was obliged to support herself by writing. Over the course of a long career, she produced more than one hundred works, many of them successful novels, plays, and religious and pedagogic texts used in her work as a teacher of royal children.

At seventeen, she married the Comte Charles-Alexis de Genlis, a naval officer and heir to a considerable fortune. She lived happily for a time in Paris with her husband and three children, but at twenty-two she met Philippe, Duc de Chartres, son of the Duc d'Orléans, with whom she fell much in love. Eventually Philippe appointed Félicité governess to his children—the boys as well as the girls. She even insisted upon becoming their tutor in matters of religion, and it was she rather than any cleric who prepared them for their first communion. Her interest in religion led her to oppose the *philosophes* for their anti-clerical views, though she shared many of their ideas about the need for political reform. At one point, she was offered a seat in the Académie Française—the first for a woman—if she would agree not to write against *philosophes*. This she refused. She was also a lifelong royalist, though she did advocate the establishment of a constitutional monarchy before the Revolution. After the Revolution began, she lived nine years in exile and poverty, during which time both her husband and Philippe, by then Duc d'Orléans, were put to death in Paris. Upon her return to France, she was able to establish good relations with Napoleon, who gave her lodgings at the Arsenal library and a small income in exchange for biweekly letters to him on politics, finance, literature, or morality. On the eve of her death in 1830, her pupil Louis-Philippe d'Orléans became King of France.

The present texts are drawn from her *Influence of Women on French Literature* (1811), in which she describes and defends the contributions of women authors and *salonières* over the whole course of French literary history, and from *La Feuille des gens du monde, ou Le Journal imaginaire* (1813), in which she evaluates many authors of her own era; the excerpt on comedies of character explores the tensions between comic conventions and modern verisimilitude.

De L'Influence des femmes sur la littérature française (Paris: Maradan 1811); *La Feuille des gens du monde, ou Le Journal imaginaire* (Paris, 1813).

From "Preliminary Reflections" to
The Influence of Women on French Literature (1811)

Men of letters have over women authors a superiority of achievement that, assuredly, one cannot fail to recognize or contest. All of the works of women taken together are not worth a few choice pages from Bossuet or Pascal, or a few scenes from Corneille, Racine, or Molière.[1] But it is not necessary to infer from this that women's natural ability is inferior to that of men. Genius composes itself out of all those qualities which we know that women possess, often to the highest degree: imagination, sensibility, and elevation of spirit. Lack of study and education having in all ages cut off women from a literary vocation, they have displayed their grandeur of spirit not through tracing historic deeds, nor in presenting ingenious fictions, but rather through genuine, material actions. They have done more than write: they have often, by their conduct, furnished models of sublime heroism. It may be true that not one woman has, in her writing, painted the great spirit of Cornelia, but what does this matter, seeing that Cornelia herself is not an imaginary being?[2] And have we not seen, in our days, during the revolutionary tempests, some women equal the male heroes by the vigor of their courage and grandeur of their spirit? "Great thoughts come from the heart,"* and similar effects should spring (when nothing is there to obstruct them) from the same source.

In order to establish woman's inferiority, men repeat that not one woman has penned good tragedy or epic poetry. An innumerable multitude of men of letters have written tragedies, yet when we count only four great French tragic poems, it is thought a great number, considering that no other nation can count as many. On the other hand, we have just one French epic poem, and we must admit that it is extremely inferior to *Paradise Lost* or

*Vauvenarques.[3]

Jerusalem Delivered.[4] Only five women among us have tried their hand at tragedy. Not only were none of these women exposed, as some authors are, to the vexation of shameful failure, but all of their tragedies experienced great success on opening night.★

Young men at college, nourished by reading Greek and Latin, are almost all poets. If they have a little talent, they form the ambitious desire of working for the theatre. We ought to acknowledge that this idea does not naturally occur to a convent student or a young woman who has just entered the world. Can we say that none of our kings, great captains, or men of state have possessed genius, merely because not one of them has written a tragedy, even though several have been poets? Can we say of the Swiss, the Danes, the Russians, the Poles, and the Dutch—people so lively and so civilized—that their mental capacity is inferior to that of the French, the English, the Italians, the Spanish, and the Germans just because they have not produced great dramatic poetry? We can only excel in a particular art when that art is generally cultivated in our nation, and by the class into which we are born. The Romans, the most celebrated people in history, did not have good tragic poets. Millions of street porters, thousands of nuns or mothers—any of these people could have, with a different education and in different circumstances, composed excellent tragedies. The ability to feel and admire that which is good and which is beautiful, and the power to love, are the same for men and women. Therefore, they are morally equal.

But if too few women (for want of study and sheer audacity) have written tragedies in order to prove that they could equal men in this regard, they have often surpassed men in another genre. Not a single man has left behind a collection of personal letters which can hold a candle to the letters of Madame de Sévigné or Madame de Maintenon.[5] *La Princesse de Clèves*, the *Lettres Péruviennes*, the letters of Madame Riccoboni, and the two most recent novels of Madame Cotin are infinitely superior to the entire output of the male romancers.[6] I am not excepting the works of Marivaux from this evaluation or worse still, the boring and voluminous works of l'Abbé Prevot.[7] And *Gilblas* is another sort of work; it is a picture of vice, of the ridiculous products of ambition, vanity and cupidity, and not the development of the natural sentiments of the heart—love, friendship, jealousy, filial piety, and so on.[8] The author, spirited and often quite profound in his wit-

---

★*Arrie et Petus*, by Mademoiselle Barbier, was performed sixteen times. *Laodamie*, by Mademoiselle Bernard, was performed twenty times, and her *Brutus* received twenty-five showings. *Les Amazons*, by Madame du Bocage, was also performed many times. Her epic poem, the *Colombiade*, was a great success and was translated into several languages.

ticisms, had only studied subaltern intrigues and the absurdities of pride. When he lays down his satiric pencil, he becomes common; all the episodes of *Gilblas* intended to be interesting and touching are instead poorly written and dull.

Madame Deshoulières had no equal for the genre of poetry in which she left such charming models.[9] The men who assign ranks in literature—dispensing honors and distributing places to authors, always excluding women—often give celebrity to talents which are quite mediocre. For example, if d'Alembert[10] were neither a geometrician, nor a member of the French Academy—despite his relentless hatred of religion and his contempt for France and her king—his writing, so cold, so devoid of substance, grace and naturalness, would be forgotten already. A woman, if she had the unhappiness of having composed the majority of his academic eulogies, would be dismissed by the public as a *"précieuse ridicule."*[11] And yet the Academy received d'Alembert as a most distinguished writer. The author of *Ariane* and *Comte d'Essex*,[12] brother to the creator of French tragedy and comedy, was elected only after the death of the great Corneille; the marquis of Saint-Aulaire, however, was welcomed for a madrigal.[13] The son of the great Racine, himself author of a beautiful poem, was never admitted![14] This same Academy issued a most unjust critique of *The Cid*,[15] the first masterpiece to grace the French stage, yet went into mourning for the death of Voiture![16] . . . If there existed an academy of women, one ventures to guess that it could, without trouble, better conduct itself and judge more sanely.

It is difficult to reconcile the various judgments made of women; they are either contradictory or devoid of sense. Women are said to possess an extreme sensibility, beyond that of men, and a lack of energy. But what is an extreme sensibility without energy? It is a sensibility incapable of making all the sacrifices of a great devotion. And what is energy, or else this strength of spirit, this power of the will which, well or poorly employed, provides unshakable constancy in order to arrive at its mark and braves everything—all obstacles, peril and death—for the object of a dominant passion? Women's tenacity of will for all that they ardently desire has passed into proverb. Therefore, one does not contest that they possess the type of energy which requires an extreme perseverance. Who could not fail to recognize in women the energy which an heroic courage demands? Does she lack it, that unfortunate princess who has just hurled herself into flames to find her daughter? And among so many noble victims of the faith, so many martyrs who persisted in their belief with an energy so sublime, and despite the horror of shocking torments, do you not count as many women as men?

Stéphanie-Félicité Ducrest, Comtesse de Genlis (1746–1830)

We maintain that women are endowed with a delicacy that men can not possess. This favorable judgment does not appear to me better founded than all of the others which are to the disadvantage of women. Several works by men of letters prove that this quality is by no means an exclusively female trait, but it is true that it is one of the distinctive characteristics of almost all their works.

That must be because education and propriety impose upon them the law of restraint—of concentrating almost all of their feelings, of always softening their expressions by delicate turns of phrase. This delicacy tries to convey what they cannot venture to explain. This is not dissimulation; this art, in general, is not hiding what one feels. Its perfection, to the contrary, is making known without explaining, without using the words that one could cite as a positive confession. Love especially renders this delicacy ingenious. In such a case, it grants women a touching and mysterious language that, because it is made only for the heart and the imagination, has something heavenly in it. Spoken words are nothing; the secret sense is all, and is fully understood only by the lover to whom it is addressed.

Apart from all the principles which render modesty and discretion so indispensable in a woman, what contrasts are provided by timidity on the one hand and audacity and ardor on the other! Grace exists in a young woman when she is that which she must be: all of her is in accord: the delicacy of her traits and of her discourse, the modesty of her bearing, of her long garments, and the sweetness of her voice and character. She does not disguise herself, but she always conceals herself. Her expressions of affection are all the more touching because she does not exaggerate; rather she must understate her feeling. Her sensibility is more profound than that of men because she is more constrained. She discloses herself, but not completely. In order to know and understand her, it is necessary to conjecture about her. She appeals as much by the attraction of piqued curiosity as by genuine charms. What poor taste it is to unveil all of this mystery, to destroy all these graces, by presenting the heroine of a novel or play without modesty, and having her express the most impetuous outbursts of love! Yet this is what we have seen for some years now. In thus transforming women, we believed we were giving them energy, but we deceived ourselves. Not only were we unable to strip them of their natural graces without removing all their dignity, but this vehement and passionate language strips them also of all they might possess of what is truly stirring and moving.

Translated by Matthew Bray and Amy Simowitz

Reflections on Comedies of Character (1813)*

Before actually writing a comedy of character, the playwright, it seems to me, must first examine which type of play would be appropriate and create the best moral results for the specific character he has in mind: a comedy in the burlesque manner, a noble comedy, or, finally, a pathetic drama. The character of the miser, for example, furnishes much more comic scenes than does the misanthrope.[1] Since it is necessary to place the character one wishes to depict in situations that will make him stand out, the *colérique* is not suited for comedy: this character belongs strictly in tragedies. He was portrayed in *Vinceslas*, in *Le duc de Foix*, etc.[2] *Le Joueur anglais* and *l'Imitation*, by Saurin, are both mediocre works, but they were good and moral in presenting the deadly consequences of the *colérique*.[3] It was necessary to treat him in this genre, not so that the gambler was made to amuse the spectators, but rather so that he made them tremble. The character of the *Méchant* especially demanded a profoundly constructed intrigue; and it is this which was needed in a piece otherwise so charming.[4] Congreve portrayed the *méchant* with much more genius in the *Double Dealer*. The intrigue in this work is masterly.†[5]

All lower characters have come to be banished from the serious genres, where they could not fail to appear insipid and disgusting. The character of the hypocrite cannot, with much success, be placed in any but a comic piece. Voltaire made ambition the dominant trait of Mahomet—hypocrisy was only his medium—and he could have called his play *l'Ambitieux*.[6] The *glorieux* (braggart, vainglorious) should produce a comedy in a noble genre. It would be necessary to represent an insolent and contemptuous Lord, whose pride was, however, necessarily tempered by living at court according to the ways of the world—as Alceste's misanthropy is constrained by the same decorum.[7] One could not make the *glorieux* ridiculous in a gross and unsubtle manner. It would be necessary to be more refined and profound. Destouches is not able to do this; his *Glorieux* resembles no one.[8]

---

*The author wrote these reflections for publication in a journal some years ago, but they are further developed here.

†The dénouement in this play is worthless, and the license of this piece is extreme. But with some changes, it would be easy to enrich our theatre by conserving the superior beauties of this comedy. It is astonishing that our critics, when speaking of Congreve, never mention this work, which is his masterpiece.

Stéphanie-Félicité Ducrest, Comtesse de Genlis (1746–1830)

This work, in fact, offers the singular example of an interesting play, replete with merit, in which, nevertheless, the principal character is poorly realized.

After deciding in which manner one should offer the character—that is to say, whether this manner will be comic or serious—one ought to be interested in placing him in an embarrassing situation that, while fully developing his character, will cause him all the discomfort he can suffer. For this, it is always necessary to contrast the situation with the character. It is thus that Molière places his miser in the position of having to spend great sums of money to give a feast; it is thus that he represents the misanthrope as passionately in love with a coquette who only loves dissipation and worldly things. There are some characters who demand an intrigue, such as the *méchant*, the *jaloux*, and the *ambitieux*. An English woman, who possessed much talent as well as a singular name (Suzanne Cent Livres),* wrote a charming comedy of character and intrigue, *The Busy Body*, a name that one cannot express in French except as *Affairé*.[9] But in order properly to express the sense of this English work, one must say *l'Affairé, Officieux et Brouillon*.

Great characters, that is to say those which are dominated by a vice or a conspicuous flaw, are not only used up in literature, but no longer exist in society. The latest stage of civilization has mitigated and concealed them, without destroying them. The social graces, become ordinary, soften these traits. Self-love adds other flaws, resulting in composite characters. They are no longer theatrical—the fundamental vice is the same, but ridicule is no longer possible. Our good, present-day painters of manners are able, more than ever, to show finesse and penetration, but they cannot make comedy, cannot create laughter. One cannot find in all of Paris a single Harpagon.[10] Since our present-day Harpagons all possess good manners and reasonable language, we can only portray them by their actions—and nothing could be less pleasing or amusing. Formerly, there were many misers as frank as that of Molière; this character was all the more comic for spectators because the love of money was not at all a general vice then. We are, therefore, mistaken to reproach our dramatic authors for only knowing how to cheer us up with their buffooneries and caricatures. That which can furnish good comic material can no longer be found in society. There are no more originals, no more ridiculous figures. We frankly admit that in making this remark, we have no intention of praising the present times.

Translated by Amy Simowitz

---

*Her husband, a Frenchman, was named Cent Livres.

Notes

"Preliminary Reflections"

1. Jacques-Bénigne Bossuet (1627–1704) was a theologian, moralist, and orator famed for his sermons and funeral orations as well as for the educational works he used in his role as tutor to the Dauphin, eldest son of Louis XIV. The mathematician and philosopher Blaise Pascal (1623–1662) is best known for his *Pensées*. Jean Racine (1639–1699) and Pierre Corneille (1606–1684) are considered the greatest French writers of classical tragedy, and Molière (1694–1778) holds the same status in French comedy.

2. Cornelia lived in the second century B.C.E. and was considered an ideal mother. Her two sons, Tiberius and Caius Gracchus, were both orators and important men of state.

3. Luc de Clapiers, Marquis de Vauvenarques (1715–1747) was a moralist known for his *Introduction à la connaissance de l'esprit humain, suivie de réflexions et maximes* (1746).

4. John Milton, *Paradise Lost* (1667); Tasso, *Jerusalem Delivered* (1581).

5. Madame de Sévigné (1626–1696) wrote the famous *Lettres* over a period of thirty years; Madame de Maintenon (1635–1719), tutor to the children of Louis XIV and Madame de Montespan, married the king in 1683.

6. *La Princesse de Clèves* (1678) by Madame de La Fayette; *Lettres péruviennes* (1747) by Madame de Graffigny; *Lettres de Mistress Fanny Butler* (1757) by Madame de Riccoboni; the two novels of Madame de Cottin are probably *Mathilde* (1805), a tale of the Crusades so successful that it influenced women's fashions, and *Elisabeth, ou les Exilés de Sibérie* (1806).

7. Marivaux, author of *Marianne* (1731–1741) and *Le Paysan parvenu* (1735); l'Abbé Prévost (1697–1763). His best-known novel is *Manon Lescaut* (1731).

8. *Gil Blas:* full title *Histoire de Gil Blas de Santillane* (1715–1735), by Lesage.

9. Madame Deshoulières (1637–1694), author of pastoral poetry.

10. Jean LeRond D'Alembert (1717–1783), an outstanding scientist and *philosophe*, edited the great *Encyclopédie* with Denis Diderot and wrote the *Discours préliminaire de l'Encyclopédie* (1751).

11. Molière's *Les Précieuses ridicules* (1659) mocks intellectual women.

12. Thomas Corneille, author of *Ariane* (1672) and *Le Comte d'Essex* (1678).

13. Marquis de Saint Aulaire (1643–1742); at sixty, he began publishing light verse.

14. Louis Racine (1692–1763) wrote the poem *La Religion*, which was inspired by Jansenism.

15. *Le Cid* (1636–1637) by Pierre Corneille.

16. Vincent Voiture (1597–1648), a poet in the school of *préciosité*.

Reflections on Comedies of Character

1. This refers to two plays of Molière, *L'Avare* (*The Miser*, 1668) and *Le Misanthrope* (1666). Alceste, hero of *The Misanthrope*, is an exaggerated idealist, while Harpagon, the Miser, is a comic butt.

2. *Vinceslas* (1752) and *Le Duc de Foix* (1752) are both by Voltaire.

3. *Le Joueur anglais;* probably the play *Béverlei* (1768) by Bernard-Joseph Saurin.

Béverlei is a *tragédie bourgeoise* in free verse about the career of a gambler, based on Edward Moore's *Gamester* (1753).

4. *Le Méchant* (1747) by Jean Baptiste Louis Gresset. This play portrays an evil man, Cléon, against the background of a society so corrupt that it cannot see that he is wicked.

5. *The Double Dealer* (1694) by William Congreve.

6. *Mahomet* (1742) by Voltaire; *L'Ambitieux* (1737) by Philippe Destouches.

7. See n. 1.

8. *Le Glorieux* (1732), Destouches's best-known play.

9. *The Busy Body* (1709) by Susanna Centlivre.

10. See n. 1.

CHARLOTTE TURNER SMITH
(1749–1806)

CHARLOTTE SMITH was the eldest daughter of Nicholas Turner, a landed gentleman, and his first wife, Anna Towers, who died when Charlotte was three years old. After her father became engaged to remarry in 1764, Smith's life took a radical turn for the worse. To avoid potential conflict between Charlotte and her stepmother, her aunt arranged for her marriage, at age fifteen, to Benjamin Smith, son of a wealthy merchant. Between 1766 and 1785 she bore twelve children. Having suffered constant physical and emotional abuse from her husband, in 1787 she took the unusual step of separating from him. Her father-in-law, cognizant of his son's irresponsibility, left a generous inheritance for Charlotte and her children when he died in 1776. However, because this inheritance remained tied up in legal disputes, Smith had to rely upon her writing to support her family.

Between 1784 and 1806, Smith wrote three volumes of poetry, ten novels including *Emmeline* (1788) and *The Old Manor House* (1793), two translations of French works, and six books for children. All her novels treat the oppressive condition of British women's lives. In the passage from *Marchmont* (1796) presented here, Smith protests against the conventions limiting the depiction of the heroine in women's novels, although she never succeeded in surmounting them herself.

Desmond was the most controversial of her novels: its hero expresses the revolutionary ideas of Thomas Paine and is idealistically but ardently in love with an unhappily married woman. In her preface to *Desmond*, Smith anticipates objections to the novel's strong political content and to its depiction of Lionel Desmond's love for Geraldine Verney. She carefully lays out the reasons why women should be allowed to write about political matters, while appealing to realism to justify her apparently one-sided representation of the French Revolution debate. Contemporary reviewers generally accepted Smith's argument in defense of women writing about politics, while faulting what the *Monthly Review* termed Lionel's "criminal *amour*" with Geraldine Verney.

Desmond. A Novel (London:. G. G. J. and J. Robinson, 1792); *Marchmont: A Novel*, Vol. I (London: Sampson Low, 1796).

Preface to *Desmond* (1792)

In sending into the world a work so unlike those of my former writings, which have been honored by its approbation, I feel some degree of apprehension which an Author is sensible of on a first publication.[1]

This arises partly from my doubts of succeeding so well in letters as in narrative; and partly from a supposition, that there are Readers, to whom the fictitious occurrences, and others to whom the political remarks in these volumes may be displeasing.

To the first I beg leave to suggest, that in representing a young man, nourishing an ardent but concealed passion for a married woman; I certainly do not mean to encourage or justify such attachments; but no delineation of character appears to me more interesting, than that of a man capable of such a passion so generous and disinterested as to seek only the good of its object; nor any story more moral, than one that represents the existence of an affection so regulated.

As to the political passages dispersed through the work, they are for the most part, drawn from conversations to which I have been a witness, in England, and France, during the last twelve months.[2] In carrying on my story in those countries, and at a period when their political situation (but particularly that of the latter) is the general topic of discourse in both; I have given to my imaginary characters the arguments I have heard on both sides; and if those in favor of one party have evidently the advantage, it is not owing to my partial representation, but to the power of truth and reason, which can neither be altered nor concealed.

But women it is said have no business with politics—Why not?—Have they no interest in the scenes that are acting around them, in which they have fathers, brothers, husbands, sons, or friends engaged?—Even in the commonest course of female education, they are expected to acquire some knowledge of history; and yet, if they are to have no opinion of what *is* passing, it avails little that they should be informed of what *has passed*, in a world where they are subject to such mental degradation; where they are censured as affecting masculine knowledge if they happen to have any understanding; or despised as insignificant triflers if they have none.

Knowledge, which qualifies women to speak or to write on any other than the most common and trivial subjects, is supposed to be of so difficult attainment, that it cannot be acquired but by the sacrifice of domestic virtues or the neglect of domestic duties.—*I* however may safely say, that it was in the *observance*, not in the *breach* of duty, *I* became an Author; and it has happened, that the circumstances which have compelled me to write, have introduced me to those scenes of life, and those varieties of character which I should otherwise have never seen;[3] Tho' alas! it is from thence, that I am too well enabled to describe from *immediate* observation,

> "The proud man's contumely, th'oppressors wrong;
> The laws delay, the insolence of office."[4]

But, while in consequence of the affairs of my family, being most unhappily in the power of men who *seem to exercise all these with impunity*, I am become an *Author by profession*, and feel every year more acutely, "*that hope delayed maketh the heart sick*."[5] I am sensible also (to use another quotation) that

> ———"Adversity———
> Tho' like a toad ugly and venemous,
> Wears yet a precious jewel in its head."[6]

For it is to my involuntary appearance in that character, that I am indebted, for all that makes my continuance in the world desirable; all that softens the rigor of my destiny and enables me to sustain it: I mean friends among those, who, while their talents are the boast of their country, are yet more respectable for the goodness and integrity of their hearts.

Among these I include a female friend, to whom I owe the beautiful little Ode in the last volume; who having written it for this work, allows me thus publicly to boast of friendship, which is the pride and pleasure of my life.[7]

If I may be indulged a moment longer in my egotism, it shall be only while I apologize for the typographical errors of the work, which may have been in some measure occasioned by the detached and hurried way, in which the sheets were sometimes sent to the press when I was at a distance from it; and when my attention was distracted by the troubles, which it seems to be the particular delight of the persons who are concerned in the management of my childrens affairs, to inflict upon me. With all this the Public have nothing to do: but were it proper to relate all the disadvantages from anxiety of mind and local circumstances, under which these volumes have been composed, such a detail might be admitted as an excuse for more material errors.

For that asperity of remark, which will arise on the part of those whose political tenets I may offend, I am prepared; those who object to the matter, will probably arraign the manner, and exclaim against the impropriety of making a book of entertainment the vehicle of political discussion. I am however conscious that in making these slight sketches, of manners and opinions, as they fluctuated around me; I have not sacrificed truth to any party—Nothing appears to me more respectable than national pride; nothing so absurd as national prejudice—And in the faithful representation of the manners of other countries, surely Englishmen may find abundant reason to indulge the one, while they conquer the other. To those however who still cherish the idea of our having a *natural* enemy in the French nation; and that they are still more *naturally* our foes, because they have dared to be freemen, I can only say, that against the phalanx of prejudice kept in constant pay, and under strict discipline by interest, the slight skirmishing of a novel writer can have no effect: we see it remains hitherto unbroken against the powerful efforts of learning and genius—though united in that cause which *must* finally triumph—the cause of truth, reason, and humanity.

From *Marchmont* (1796)

The Characters of women in general have been said to be nothing—'Matter too soft a lasting form to bear.'[1] Perhaps very young women have no striking traits of character to distinguish them, till some circumstance in their lives either calls forth their understanding, or decides that they have none.—What appears discriminating, like the colours of cultivated flowers, is often an accidental variety; the shades and tints are different, the species remains the same. It has been said that Shakespeare, the great delineator of human character, has failed in distinguishing his principal women—and that such as he meant to be amiable are all equally gentle and good. How difficult then is it for a novelist to give to one of his heroines any very marked feature which shall not disfigure her! Too much reason and self-command destroy the interest we take in her distresses. It has been observed, that Clarissa is so equal to every trial as to diminish our pity. Other virtues than gentleness, pity, filial obedience, or faithful attachment, hardly belong to the sex, and are certainly called forth only by unusual circumstances. Such undoubtedly was the lot of Althea, and they formed her character; for in the hard school of adversity she acquired that fortitude and strength of mind which gave an energy to an understanding, naturally of the first class.

Notes

Preface to *Desmond*

1. Smith is referring to both *Desmond*'s epistolary form and its strong political content.

2. Smith was very well known in British and French radical circles. This statement provides the only evidence for Smith's being in France any time after she and her husband fled to Normandy in the winter of 1784–1785 to avoid debtors' prison.

3. Smith published *Elegiac Sonnets* to rescue her family from desperate financial straits. After separating from her husband in 1787, she began to write novels to support herself and her children. She refers here to her husband's abuse and to the lawyers who endlessly deferred the settlement of her father-in-law's will, which would have given her financial independence.

4. *Hamlet* III.i.70–72 (slightly misquoted).

5. Proverbs 13:12 (slightly misquoted).

6. *As You Like It* II.i.12–14 (slightly misquoted).

7. "Ode to the Poppy," by the Irish poet Henrietta O'Neill, appears in Volume III of *Desmond*.

Marchmont

1. Alexander Pope, *An Epistle to a Lady* (1735), line 3.

JUDITH SARGENT MURRAY
(1751–1820)

J∪DITH SARGENT MURRAY was born in Gloucester, Massachusetts, and was educated with her brother as he prepared for Harvard. She was married twice, in 1769 and 1786, the second time to the controversial minister John Murray. She wrote essays and poetry, publishing a number of them in the *Massachusetts Magazine*. The early "Essay on the Equality of the Sexes" (1779) reveals her feminist leanings. The series of essays entitled "The Gleaner," for which she is now best known, appeared in the *Massachusetts Magazine* between February 1792 and August 1794. During these years the Murrays moved to Boston, where the author wrote two plays, *The Medium, or A Happy Tea-Party* (published as *The Medium, or Virtue Triumphant*) (1795) and *The Traveller Returned* (1796). "The Gleaner" essays were published in book form by subscription in 1798. Afterward Murray continued to publish poetry; she devoted her final efforts as a writer to editing her husband's letters and sermons (1812–1813) and completing his autobiography (1816). In that year she moved to Natchez, Mississippi, where she spent her remaining years with her daughter.

Addressing a wide variety of topics, Murray's periodical writings are perhaps most notable for their commentary on American culture and character. *The Gleaner* was dedicated to John Adams, and chief among the subscribers was George Washington. Though the essays were initially published under a male pseudonym, Murray exposed herself as "Constantia" in this 1798 volume, lamenting the "indifferences, not to say contempt, with which female productions are regarded."

Murray's writings on literature often reflect a distinctly national perspective, as in her comments on the American theater reprinted here from *The Gleaner* number 24. By the time Murray's own plays appeared (1795 and 1796), professional theater in colonial New England was established and plays were regularly performed. Yet New England's long hostility to the theater was widespread, especially during the seventeenth century. Various forms of official and social censorship derived from both religious opposition to the claimed immorality of plays and a more general sense that drama was frivolous. Only after the mid-eighteenth century did this situation begin to change.

Like many of her contemporaries in England and North America, Murray also addressed herself to the effects of the novel on young women. In her remarks in *The Gleaner* number 40, she defends the novel as a positive influence, holding up Richardson's *Clarissa* as a model of pleasurable and instructive reading. Murray is notable both for her defense of literature in "this new world" and for directly addressing some of her literary criticism to women readers.

The Gleaner. A Miscellaneous Production (Boston: I. Thomas and E. T. Andrews, 1798), nos. 24 and 40.

From *The Gleaner* (1798)

Leaning on morals when the Drama moves,
Friendly to virtue when the vision proves—
Lessons adopting form'd to mend the heart,
Truths meliorated, potent to impart;
Her splendid fictions wisdom will embrace,
And all her scenic paths enraptur'd trace.

The various parterres, now putting forth their promising buds, in many sections, in this our country, looks with a very favourable aspect upon a man of my profession; and I cannot but hope, that in the occupation of a Gleaner, I shall be able to cull many a fragrant flower, wherewith to compose a bouquet, that may throw an agreeable perfume over the leisure hours of the sentimental speculator.

To *express myself less technically.* The progress of the Drama, in this new world, must assuredly interest the feelings of every observer; and, being under the pleasing necessity, in the routine of my excursions, of visiting many parts of the United States, and thus, having frequent opportunities of presenting myself in our several theatres, from the elegant house in Philadelphia to the temporary resorts of itinerant companies, in those little country towns, which will invariably copy the examples they receive from the metropolis, I naturally, in the course of my perambulations, pick up many observations, that may possibly serve for the amusement of my readers.

The great question which does, and *ought* to occupy the mind of every patriotic moralist, is the *utility* of licensed stage-playing. Perhaps I may as well withdraw the word *licensed*; for, in the present enlightened era and administration of liberty, the citizen would hardly consent to an abridgment of those amusements, the evil tendency of which could not be unequivocally demonstrated to his understanding; and the late struggle in the State of Massachusetts, evinces the futility of erecting barriers, not substantiated by reason.

The law in that State was outraged in its very face: the flimsy subterfuge of *moral lectures* deceived no one; and though, as I am informed, the theatrical prohibition is but *partially repealed respecting the Bostonians, and remains in full force upon the rest of the State*, yet it is notorious, that itinerant players are constantly marching and counter-marching from town to town, to the no small diversion of the good people of this very respectable member of the Union. But, without presuming to intermeddle with the policy of the legislature, my design is, to hazard a few remarks upon the subject in general.

As I abhor the domination of prejudice, and, upon the strongest conviction, regard it as a tyrant, that if once brought to the guillotine, would (*provided it is not of the Hydra kind*) leave an opening for the introduction of an era far more friendly to the progress of *genuine* and *corrected* liberty, than the murder of all the *humane, virtuous,* and *religious princes in the universe*; so I most sincerely deprecate its despotism; and whenever I seat myself, with the pen of inquiry, I am solicitous to raise a rebellion against encroachments, that, however sanctioned by time cannot, in my opinion, be considered in a court of equity, as legal or natural. The objections to theatrical amusements are many and plausible. I pretend not to decide for others; I would only investigate.

If I mistake not—*Waste of time—Imprudent expenditures—Encouragement of idleness*—and, *Relaxation of morals*, stand foremost in the catalogue of objections.

Prodigality of time, is indeed an irremediable evil; and if it can be proved, that an hour devoted to the theatre would certainly have been appropriated to any beneficial employment, for which no moment of leisure will in future present, I, for one, shall be impelled to allow the validity of the allegation; and, I do hereby invest such plea with full authority to detain every such person from all dramatical representations whatever: But, with the same breath I contend, that those evenings which are immolated at the shrine of Bacchus, which are loitered in a tavern, in unnecessary gossiping, cards, scandal, and the numerous vagaries of fashion, will be *comparatively redeemed*, if marked by an entertainment so incontrovertibly rational.

The complaint of exorbitant expenditures, is of a similar description. A friend of mine, who resided for sometime abroad, once informed me, that he had frequently been stopped, when in full career to the playhouse, by a consideration that the indulgence he was about to procure himself, would supply some tearful sufferer with bread, for at least one whole week. Now, all such persons, provided they can make it appear, they are not in the use of any as *expensive and more superfluous gratification*, shall be released, upon their parole: given, that they will absolutely and *bona fide* employ their six shillings to the aforesaid purpose.

To the third objection I cannot allow the smallest weight: *Who, I would ask, are the Idlers?* Perhaps there is no mode of life which requires more assiduous and laborious application, than that of a *good* and *consistent* actor. School exercises are certainly not the most *pleasurable* employments of adolescence; and every adult can tell, how much more easily he could imprint the memory of his early years, than that retention which is the accompaniment of his matured life. But the *ambitious* and *principled* actor hath past the age of flexibility, and still his days are, almost unceasingly, devoted to study: By frequent repetitions, such is the constitution of the mind, the finest sentiments too often pall; and the well informed, ingenious and meritorious performer is in danger of losing his taste for the highest mental enjoyments; while the entertainment which he produces for others, is the result of unremitted and painful labour to himself.

Why then, permit me to ask, if he is solicitous to blend, with our amusements, the highest possible improvement; if he professedly pursues the means of living; if his manners and his morals are unblemished; and if, by becoming stationary, he in effect takes rank with our citizens—why, I ask, is he *so lightly esteemed?* Surely, if, under the influence of reason, of gratitude and impartiality, I must unhesitatingly acknowledge, persons ardently engaged in procuring for us a *rational entertainment*, are entitled to a *degree of genuine respect*, to encouragement, and even to patronage.

It is asserted, and the assertion does not appear unfounded, that a *virtuous theatre* is highly influential in regulating the opinions, manners, and morals of the populace.

Here we are naturally led to the fourth and last division of our subject.

Relaxation of morals.—And I ask, Doth not a *virtuous theatre* exemplify the lessons which the ethic preacher labours to inculcate? I take it for granted, that none but a *virtuous and well regulated theatre* will be tolerated. In the southern and middle States, Philadelphia particularly, no performance can make its appearance upon the stage, without passing under the previous examination of the governor and two other respectable magistrates, who, by their avowed approbation, become responsible to the public for the merit of the piece. Similar restrictions will, perhaps, be adopted, wherever the Drama shall progress; and my confidence in the trustees of the Boston theatre, represents to my view every apprehension, not only as superfluous, but absolutely injurious.

Virtue then will be adorned with all her native loveliness, and vice exhibited, deformed and mishapen, as that detested hag, which Milton's energetic pen hath so hideously pourtrayed. Is there a bosom that will not hasten to embrace the one? Is there a mind that will not shrink with horror from the other? The man of firmness, of principle, and of worth innate; the mild, the consistent, the regular, the maternal fair one; these shall be rewarded with bursts of heart-felt applause; while the imbecile or irresolute votary of error, the unprincipled betrayer, the fraudulent villain, the licentious, perverse and abandoned female; these *characters* shall be stigmatized with reproach, exhibited in their native atrocity, and set up as beacons to deter our young people from pursuing a path, which will render them odious to every person possessed of sentiment and virtue.

Socrates, Cicero, and even Cato, have mingled with the audience in a theatre; and as it is presumed that the buffoonery of an Aristophanes will not be tolerated upon an American stage, it is pleasingly believed, that the dignity of years, of wisdom, and of virtue, will, in no instance, be outraged by the children of the Drama.

The Pompeys of our day, it is to be hoped, will learn many a useful lesson; they will commence students in the school of the *rights of man*; and, becoming proficients in the laws of equity and of nature, like the Roman general, they will retire from the theatre, converts to the virtuous and impartial designations of equality.

Religious worship, it is said, gave birth to the Drama; and under proper regulations, it may still conduce to acts of devotional piety. To Athens and to Rome, the theatre became a source of information, refined perception, and genuine morality; and we have only to avoid the causes which finally produced its degeneracy in the elder world, to continue it among us, in these States, an excellent exemplar and preservative of rectitude. The theatre opens a wide field for literary exertions; and we anticipate a rich harvest of intellectual pleasure and improvement. The sons and daughters of fancy, the sentimentalist, and the moralist; these will engage in the interesting competition. They will consider that their productions are not intended barely for the amusement of a solitary hour; that the Drama, pointing every excellence, will imprint upon the heart the sentiment of worth; that it may be in their power to fashion, and to lead, a *national taste*; that by *exalting virtue, and adorning religion, rendering vice disgusting, and stigmatizing infidelity*, they will most effectually second the endeavours of that revered body, professedly engaged to beautify morality, and elevate religion.

We trust that a spirit of *laudable emulation* will be excited; and while the summit of fame, in brightening perspective, uprears its wreath-crowned head, writers will be animated to the splendid career, and with glowing ardour they will hasten forward to the desired goal. How delightful the employ! the mind, while engaged in painting the native charms of genuine and philanthropic religion, catching the fervour of divine inspiration, will necessarily become rectified and ameliorated by the delineation. Rectitude, adorned by her sister graces, heaven-born contentment, consequent felicity, and ever blooming joy—these will captivate every beholder. Economy, attired by her handmaid competence, with serene tranquillity, presenting to view the peace reflecting mirror, will not fail of reclaiming from the paths of profligacy the most dissipated wanderer; and frugality and equity will remain prevalent in the mind. Nor will the exhibition of vice be unattended with its salutary effects. Conviction will be pointed to the bosom of the aggressor; the deformity of atrocious offences, striking by illustrating examples, will present the disgusting figure, which the conscious culprit will assuredly recognize, and the probability is, that abhorrence and reformation will ensue.

Shakespeare, that penetrating observer, skilful investigator, and indisputable judge of the human heart, makes his Hamlet say, *"I've heard, that guilty creatures, at a play, have, by the very cunning of the scene, been struck so to the soul, that presently they have proclaimed their malefactions. I'll have these players play something like the murder of my father, before my uncle."* And again; *"The play's the thing, wherein I'll catch the conscience of the king."*

If it may be presumed, that the stated objections, thus considered, are obviated, I conceive it will not be denied that, from a *chaste and discreetly regulated* theatre, many attendant advantages will indisputably result. Young persons will acquire a refinement of taste and manners; they will learn to think, speak, and act, with propriety; a thirst for knowledge will be originated; and from attentions, at first, perhaps, constituting only the amusement of the hour, they will gradually proceed to more important inquiries.

Yes, indeed, I do conceive that the hand of skilful cultivation may implant an ardent thirst for knowledge; or, in other words, a love of reading in that mind of which it was not the original growth; nay, further, I affirm, upon the authority of experience, that the useful and fertile exotic will take as deep root, flourish as luxuriantly, and produce as plentiful a harvest, as in its native soil; and perhaps the conformation of this artificial taste, is one of the *most eligible uses which can be made of novel reading.* Curiosity in the minds of young people is generally if not always upon the wing; and I have regarded curiosity, combined with necessity, as the grand stamina of almost every improvement. Narrative, unencumbered with dry reflections, and adorned with all the flowers of fiction, possesses for the new plumed fancy a most fascinating charm; attention is arrested, every faculty of the soul is engaged, and the pages of the interesting and entertaining novelist are almost devoured. Thus an attachment to reading is formed, and this primary object once obtained, in that paucity of those kind of writings, *which the watchful parent will know how to create*, the entertaining biographer will become an acceptable substitute; the transition to history will be in course; geography constitutes an essential part of history; and the annals of the heavenly bodies will ultimately be studied with avidity. Pope's Homer[1] may originate a taste for poetry, even in the very soul of frigidity; and a perusal of the beautifully diversified and richly ornamented numbers of the Adventurer,[2] induces a perigrination through every essay which has been written, from the days of their great primogenitures, Steele and Addison,[3] down to the simple numbers of the humble Gleaner. In this view, novels may be considered as rendering an important service to society; and I question whether there is not less risk in placing volumes of this kind in the hands of girls of *ten or twelve years of age*, than during that interesting period which revolves from *fifteen to twenty*. The mind is instructed with much more facility, at an early age, than afterwards; and I have thought that many a complete letter writer has been produced from the school of the novelist; and hence, possibly, it is, that females have acquired so palpable a superiority over us, in this elegant and useful art. Novels, I think, may very properly and advantageously constitute the *amusement* of a girl from *eight to fourteen years of age, provided always that she pursues her reading under the judicious direction of her guardian friend*: By the time she hath completed her fourteenth year, (supposing the voice of well-judged and tender premonition has occasionally sounded in her ears) I am mistaken if her understanding will not have made such progress, as to give her to rise from the table with proper ideas of the lightness of the repast; of the frivolity of those scenes to which she hath attended; of their insufficiency, as sources of that kind of information which is the off-spring of truth, and of their inability to bestow *real knowledge*, or those substantial qualities that nerve the mind, and endow it with the fortitude so necessary in the career of life.

Under the requisite guidance, she will learn properly to appreciate the heroes and heroines of the novelist; repetition will create satiety, and she will have risen from the banquet before the consequences of her intoxication can materially injure her future life. She will have drank largely, it is true, but revolving hours will give her to recover from her inebriety, and happily those hours will intervene ere yet she is called to act the part assigned her; and she will have extracted every advantage within the reach of possibility, from this line of reading, while the pernicious effects attributed thereto, can in no respect essentially hurt her.

When a torrent of novels bursts suddenly on a girl, who, bidding adieu to childhood, hath already entered a career, to her of such vast importance, the evils of which they may be productive are indeed incalculable! aided by a glowing imagination, she will take a deep interest in the fascinating enthusiasm they inspire; each gilded illusion will pass for a splendid reality; *she will sigh to become the heroine of the drama; and, selecting her hero, it is possible she may be precipitated into irremediable evil, before she may have learned to make a just estimation of the glittering trifles, by which she is thus captivated.* I say, therefore, I would confine novels to girls from eight to fourteen years of age; and I would then lay them by, for the amusement of those vacant hours, which, in advanced years, are frequently marked by a kind of *ennui*, the result, probably, of a separation from those companions, with whom we have filled the more busy scenes of life.

I grant that novels, under proper direction, might be made much more extensively subservient to the well being of society, than, *with a very few exceptions*, they have ever yet been. Was not *love, unconquerable, unchanging, and omnipotent, their everlasting theme*, they might abound with precepts and examples conducive to the best of purposes. This remark leads to the consideration of the question proposed by my anxious correspondent. *In my toleration of novels, have I not exercised a discriminating power?* Most assuredly I have. There is a class of novels, and of plays, which it appears to me should be burnt by the hands of the common executioner; and were it not that the *good natured world* generally takes part with the sufferer, I could wish to see strong marks of public odium affixed upon the authors of those libidinous productions.

But it is as painful to dwell upon subjects of reprehension as it is pleasurable to hold the pen of panegyric—let me hasten, therefore, to a selection which I have conceived indisputably worthy of preference; and, in the first grade of those writings, that take rank under the general description of novels, and that are entitled to the highest notes of eulogy, I have been accustomed to place the history of Clarissa Harlowe.[4]

In my decided approbation of this admired production, I have the satisfaction to reflect that I am not singular. My paternal grand-father, who was one of the most respectable characters of the era in which he lived, indulged, perhaps to excess, an invincible aversion to novels. Yet, the Holy Bible and Clarissa Harlowe, were the books in which he accustomed his daughters to read alternately, during those hours in which he attended to them himself. The Rev. James Hervey, Rector of Weston Favell, in North-amptonshire in England, celebrated as well for an exemplary life and purity of manners, as for the elegance and piety of his literary compositions, in a treatise written upon the education of daughters, recommends Clarissa, as a suitable present to those young ladies, who are to be trained in the paths of virtue and propriety; and a *late writer*, has asserted, that Clarissa Harlowe is the *first human production now extant*. He hesitates not to place it, for *literary excellence, above the Iliad of Homer, or any other work, ancient or modern, the sacred oracles excepted*.

But without taking it upon me to defend this opinion I will only say, that it appears to me admirably well calculated as a useful companion for a female, from the first dawn of her reason, to the closing scene of life. It has been said that many a Lovelace has availed himself of plots, fabricated and developed in those volumes, which would never else have entered his imagination—be it so, I only contend for the placing them in female hands; and I affirm that they contain the best code of regulations, the best directions in every situation which they exemplify—in one word, the best model for the sex, that I have ever yet seen pourtrayed. The character of Clarissa, it has been asserted, is too highly wrought: but I ask, what perfection did she possess that we should be willing to dispense with, in the female, who we should delineate as an accomplished woman? Was I to advance an objection against a work of such acknowledged merit, I would say that it is the character of Lovelace, and more particularly of the Sinclairs, the Martins, the Hortons, and the Harlowes, of those pages, which are *too highly wrought*. It is surely much more easy to conceive of an amiable woman, acting precisely as did Clarissa, than of that degree of turpitude and inexorable severity, which must have preceded the perpetration of actions so black, and the manifestation of rigour so ill founded and unrelenting.

It has been generally imagined that Clarissa's only deviation from strict propriety, consisted in her flight from the protection of her father; but a moment's reflection will evince the error of this conclusion—*that cannot be a fault to which I am compelled*. Clarissa met her betrayer with a design to remonstrate, and to conciliate, but with a *determined resolution not to abandon the paternal mansion*; it appears that she was precipitated upon that fatal step, and, envisioned by the deep laid machination of the deceiver, her escape would have been miraculous, yet she continued to struggle, and even at the moment she was hurried away, the beauteous sufferer still vehemently protested against accompanying the wretch, who was armed for her destruction. Clarissa's *error (if indeed, all circumstances considered, she was ever in any sort reprehensible)* must be traced further back; it consisted in her *correspondence after the parental prohibition, and in her consenting to meet the treacherous villain.* Yet, when we take a view of the *motives* which stimulated her to those decisive measures, we can scarcely deem her censurable; and she extorts from every bosom that kind of applause, which we spontaneously yield to persecuted merit.

Love, in the bosom of Clarissa, was always subservient to virtue. It would never have taken the lead of duty; and, had she been left to the free exercise of her fine faculties, had she been permitted to call into action those rare abilities of which she was mistress, she would have *completely extricated herself from every embarrassment.* Love, in the bosom of Clarissa, was the *noblest of principles*; it was uniformly solicitous for the *genuine felicity, establishment and election of its object*; but it would never have permitted her to have allied herself to a man, who could *barbarously triumph in the destruction of that sweet peace of mind, which is the bosom friend of the innocent and of the good; who could inhumanly meditate the ruin of those confiding females who were entitled to his pity and his protection.* Liberated from the resentment of her hard hearted relations, and moving in that enlarged and elevated sphere, to which her matchless intellect and uncommon information entitled her, she would doubtless have investigated. The libertine would inevitably have stood confessed, and would as assuredly have been discarded from her favour. In one word, love, in the bosom of Clarissa, was what I wish, from my soul, it may become in the bosom of every female.

The deportment of Clarissa, after Lovelace had so artfully betrayed her into a step which her judgment invariably condemned, has been the subject of much cavilling; she is accused of undue haughtiness; but surely such censurers have not well weighed either her character and situation, or that ambiguous mode of conduct, which the despoiler so early assumed. How often did he *hold her soul in suspense*, and how necessary was it for his nefarious purposes thus to do.

Notes

1. Alexander Pope's translation of the *Iliad*, in six volumes (1715–1719), to which Pope added his preface.
2. John Hawkesworth (1715–1773) published the *Adventurer*, a biweekly periodical that appeared from 1752 to 1754 as the successor to Samuel Johnson's *Rambler*. Johnson himself contributed regularly to the *Adventurer*.
3. Joseph Addison (1672–1719) and Sir Richard Steele (1672–1729), periodical writers and publishers of the *Tatler*, the *Spectator*, and the *Guardian*.
4. Samuel Richardson's *Clarissa* (1747–1748).

FRANCES BURNEY D'ARBLAY
(1752-1840)

Frances Burney, daughter of the music teacher and musicologist Charles Burney, picked up her education from her gifted family and the varied, often brilliant company that frequented her father's house. All her life she was devoted to her father, a charming and exploitative man. He was a member of Samuel Johnson's Literary Club, and she herself was a favorite with Johnson. Frances wrote voluminously from her early teens, producing stories and a diary that evolved into journal-letters that circulated among her appreciative family circle. In these journals she developed her ability to re-create lifelike, self-revealing dialogue and to report vividly on the social scene. She made the most of these skills in her first novel, *Evelina* (1778), which she wrote and sent to a publisher in secret. It proved to be a sensational success, and after her authorship gradually became known, she was welcomed into elite society.

Her second novel, *Cecilia* (1782), was equally successful. But it was not sufficiently profitable to support a still-unmarried woman, and Burney was pressured into accepting an appointment as Second Keeper of the Robes to Queen Charlotte. After five stultifying years she escaped back into private life, fell in love with and married a penniless French émigre, Alexandre d'Arblay, and had a son. The necessity of supporting her family motivated her to drive an advantageous bargain for her third novel, *Camilla* (1796), which brought her two thousand pounds. She wrote most of her last novel, *The Wanderer* (1814), in France, where the family had moved to try to recoup d'Arblay's property and became trapped for ten years while France was at war with England.

Burney's two early journal entries show her interest in fiction that addressed the feelings and concerns of a young woman. They also speak of the ideal that she was to aim at in her own novels, and which she writes about in the preface and dedication given here: a representation that will edify her readers but that is, above all, true to life. The letter is to Samuel "Daddy" Crisp, a family friend and an important mentor of Burney's.

Early Journals and Letters, ed. Lars Troide (Montreal: McGill-Queens University Press, 1988); *Evelina, or The History of a Young Lady's Entrance into the*

World, ed. Annie Raine Ellis (London: George Bell, 1883); *Diary and Letters of Madame d'Arblay*, ed. Charlotte Barrett (London: Macmillan, 1904); *The Wanderer, or Female Difficulties* (London: Longman, Hurst, 1814).

From *Journal* (1768)

I am Reading the 'Letters of Henry & Frances,'[1] & like them prodidgiously. I have Just finish'd Mrs Rowe's Letters from the Dead to the Living—& moral & Entertaining.[2]—I had heard a great deal of them before I saw them, & am sorry to tell you I was much disappointed with them: they are so very enthusiastick, that the religion she preaches rather disgusts & cloys than charms & elevates—& so romantick, that every word betrays improbability, instead of disguising fiction, & displays the Author, instead of human nature. For my own part, I cannot be much pleased without an appearance of truth; at least of possibility—I wish the history to be natural tho' the sentiments are refined; & the Characters to be probable, tho' their behaviour is excelling. . . .

I have this very moment finish'd Reading a Novel call'd the Vicar of Wakefield.[3] It was wrote by Dr Goldsmith, Athour [*sic*] of the Comedy of the Good-natured Man—& several Essays. His style is prudent & I knew it again immediately. This Book is of a very singular kind—I own I began it with distaste & disrelish, having Just Read the elegant Letters of Henry—the beginning of it, even disgusted me—he mentions his wife with such indifference—such contempt—the contrast of Henry's treatment of Frances struck me—the more so, as it is real—while this tale is fictitious—& then the style of the latter is so elegantly natural, so tenderly manly, so unassumingly rational!—I own, I was tempted to thro' the Book aside—but there was something in the situation of his Family, which if it did not interest me, at least drew me on—& as I proceeded, I was better pleased—the description of his rural felicity, his simple, unaffected contentment—& family domestic happiness, gave me much pleasure—but still, I was not *satisfied* as a *something* was wanting to make the Book please me—to make me *feel* for the vicar in every line he writes—nevertheless, before I was half thro' the 1st volume, I was, as I may truly express myself, *surprised into Tears*—& in the 2^d Volume, I really sobb'd. It appears to me, to be impossible any person could Read this Book thro' with a dry Eye & yet, I don't much like it—my sensations on reading it were woful and tender—but it is an inconsistent performance all the same—I was affected without being interested, I was moved without being pleased, . . . He advances many very bold & singular opinions—for example, he avers that murder is the sole Crime for which Death ought to be the punishment—he goes even farther, & ventures to affirm that our laws in regard to penaltys & punishment are *all* too severe. This Doctrine might be contradicted from the very essence of our religion—Scripture— . . . But this Author shews in all his works a love of peculiarity & of making originality of Character in others; & therefore I am not surprised he possesses it himself. This vicar is a very venerable old man—his distresses *must* move you tho' the Tale in itself may fail to please. There is but very little story, the plot is thin, the incidents very rare, the sentiments uncommon, the vicar is contented, humble, pious, virtuous—but upon the whole the Book has not at all satisfied my expectations—how far more was I pleased with the genuine productions of Mr Griffith's pen—for that is the real name of Henry.—I hear that 2 more volumes are lately published—I wish I could get them—I have read but 2—the elegance & delicacy of the manner—expressions—style—of that Book are so superiour!— How much I should like to be Acquainted with the Writers of it!—those Letters are doubly pleasing, charming to me, for being genuine—of which, if their own authors left no record, I have *proof positive* from my Mama, who saw the original Letters, with the post marks on them all, at the Publisher's Shop. That Book has encreased my relish for minute, heartfelt writing, and encouraged me in my attempts to give an opinion of the Books I Read.

Author's Preface to *Evelina* (1778)

IN the republic of letters, there is no member of such inferior rank, or who is so much disdained by his brethren of the quill, as the humble Novelist: nor is his fate less hard in the world at large, since, among the whole class of writers, perhaps not one can be named of which the votaries are more numerous but less respectable.

Yet, while in the annals of those few of our predecessors, to whom this species of writing is indebted for being saved from contempt, and rescued from depravity, we can trace such names as Rousseau, Johnson,[1] Marivaux, Fielding, Richardson, and Smollett, no man need blush at starting from the same post, though many, nay most men, may sigh at finding themselves distanced.

The following letters are presented to the Public—for such by novel writers, novel readers will be called,—with a very singular mixture of timidity and confidence, resulting from the peculiar situation of the editor; who, though trembling for their success from a consciousness of their imperfections, yet fears not being involved in their disgrace, while happily wrapped up in a mantle of impenetrable obscurity.

To draw characters from nature, though not from life, and to mark the manners of the times, is the attempted plan of the following letters. For this purpose, a young female, educated in the most secluded retirement, makes, at the age of seventeen, her first appearance upon the great and busy stage of life; with a virtuous mind, a cultivated understanding, and a feeling heart, her ignorance of the forms, and inexperience in the manners, of the world, occasion all the little incidents which this volume records, and which form the natural progression of the life of a young woman of obscure birth, but conspicuous beauty, for the first six months after her *entrance into the world*.

Perhaps were it possible to effect the total extirpation of novels, our young ladies in general, and boarding-school damsels in particular, might profit by their annihilation; but since the distemper they have spread seems incurable, since their contagion bids defiance to the medicine of advice or reprehension, and since they are found to baffle all the mental art of physic, save what is prescribed by the slow regimen of Time, and bitter diet of Experience, surely all attempts to contribute to the number of those which may be read, if not with advantage, at least without injury, ought rather to be encouraged than contemned.

Let me, therefore, prepare for disappointment those who, in the perusal of these sheets, entertain the gentle expectation of being transported to the fantastic regions of Romance, where Fiction is coloured by all the gay tints of luxurious Imagination, where Reason is an outcast, and where the sublimity of the *Marvellous* rejects all aid from sober Probability. The heroine of these memoirs, young, artless, and inexperienced, is

No faultless Monster, that the world ne'er saw,[2]

but the offspring of Nature, and of Nature in her simplest attire.

In all the Arts, the value of copies can only be proportioned to the scarceness of originals; among sculptors and painters, a fine statue, or a beautiful picture, of some great master, may deservedly employ the imitative talents of younger and inferior artists, that their appropriation to one spot, may not wholly prevent the more general expansion of their excellence; but, among authors, the reverse is the case, since the noblest productions of literature are almost equally attainable with the meanest. In books, therefore, imitation cannot be shunned too sedulously; for the very perfection of a model which is frequently seen, serves but more forcibly to mark the inferiority of a copy.

To avoid what is common, without adopting what is unnatural, must limit the ambition of the vulgar herd of authors; however zealous, therefore, my veneration of the great writers I have mentioned, however I may feel myself enlightened by the knowledge of Johnson, charmed with the eloquence of Rousseau, softened by the pathetic powers of Richardson, and exhilarated by the wit of Fielding, and humour of Smollett; I yet presume not to attempt pursuing the same ground which they have tracked; whence, though they may have cleared the weeds, they have also culled the flowers, and though they have rendered the path plain, they have left it barren.

The candour of my readers, I have not the impertinence to doubt, and to their indulgence, I am sensible I have no claim; I have, therefore, only to entreat, that my own words may not pronounce my condemnation, and that what I have here ventured to say in regard to imitation, may be understood, as it is meant, in a general sense, and not be imputed to an opinion of my own originality, which I have not the vanity, the folly, or the blindness, to entertain.

Whatever may be the fate of these letters, the editor is satisfied they will meet with justice; and commits them to the press, though hopeless of fame, yet not regardless of censure.

Letter to Samuel Crisp (6 April 1782)

. . . With respect, however, to the great point of Cecilia's fortune, I have much to urge in my own defence, only now I can spare no time, and I must frankly confess I shall think I have rather written a farce than a serious history, if the whole is to end, like the hack Italian operas, with a jolly chorus that makes all parties good and all parties happy! The people I have ever met with who have been fond of blood and family, have all scouted *title* when put in any competition with it. How then should those proud Delviles think a new-created peerage any equivalent for calling their sons' sons, for future generations, by the name of Beverley? Besides, I think the book, in its present conclusion, somewhat original, for the hero and heroine are neither plunged in the depths of misery, nor exalted to UN*human* happiness. Is not such a middle state more natural, more according to real life, and less resembling every other book of fiction?[1]

Besides, my own end will be lost if I change the conclusion, which was chiefly to point out the absurdity and shortsightedness of those *name-compelling* wills . . . if I am made to give up this point, my whole plan is rendered abortive, and the last page of any novel in Mr. Noble's circulating library may serve for the last page of mine, since a marriage, a reconciliation, and some sudden expedient for great riches, concludes them all alike.

From Dedication to *The Wanderer* (1814)

. . . Here, they [readers] will simply meet, what the Authour has thrice
sought to present to them already, a composition upon general life, manners,
and characters; without any species of personality, either in the form of
foreign influence, or of national partiality. I have felt, indeed, no disposition,—I ought rather, perhaps, to say talent,—for venturing upon the
stormy sea of politics; whose waves, for ever either receding or encroaching,
with difficulty can be stemmed, and never can be trusted.

Even when I began;—how unconsciously you, dear Sir,[1] well know,—
what I may now, perhaps venture to style my literary career, nothing can
more clearly prove that I turned, instinctively, from the tempestuous course,
than the equal favour with which I was immediately distinguished by those
two celebrated, immortal authors, Dr Johnson and the Right Honourable
Edmund Burke; whose sentiments upon public affairs divided, almost separated them, at that epoch; yet who, then, and to their last hours, I had the
pride, the delight, and the astonishment to find the warmest, as well as the
most eminent supporters of my honoured essays.[2] Latterly, indeed, their political opinions assimilated; but when each, separately, though at the same
time, condescended to stand for the champion of my first small work; ere
ever I had had the happiness of being presented to either; and ere they knew
that I bore, my Father! your honoured name; that small work was nearly the
only subject upon which they met without contestation:—if I except the
equally ingenious and ingenuous friend whom they vied with each other
to praise, to appreciate, and to love; and whose name can never vibrate on
our ears but to bring emotion to our hearts;—Sir Joshua Reynolds.

If, therefore, then,—when every tie, whether public or mental, was single; and every wish had one direction; I held political topics to be without
my sphere, or beyond my skill; who shall wonder that now,—united, alike
by choice and by duty, to a member of a foreign nation, yet adhering, with
primæval enthusiasm, to the country of my birth, I should leave all discussions of national rights, and modes, or acts of government, to those whose
wishes have no opposing calls; whose duties are undivided; and whose opinions are unbiassed by individual bosom feelings; which, where strongly impelled by dependent happiness, insiduously, unconsciously direct our views,
colour our ideas, and entangle our partiality in our interests.

Nevertheless, to avoid disserting upon these topics as matter of speculation, implies not an observance of silence to the events which they pro-

duce, as matter of fact: on the contrary, to attempt to delineate, in whatever form, any picture of actual human life, without reference to the French Revolution, would be as little possible, as to give an idea of the English government, without reference to our own:[3] for not more unavoidably is the last blended with the history of our nation, than the first, with every intellectual survey of the present times.

Anxious, however,—inexpressibly!—to steer clear, alike, of all animadversions that, to my adoptive country, may seem ungrateful, or, to the country of my birth unnatural; I have chosen, with respect to what, in these volumes, has any reference to the French Revolution, a period which, completely past, can excite no rival sentiments, nor awaken any party spirit; yet of which the stupendous iniquity and cruelty, though already historical, have left traces, that, handed down, even but traditionally, will be sought with curiosity, though reverted to with horrour, from generation to generation. . . .

With regard to the very serious subject treated upon, from time to time, in this work,[4] some,—perhaps many,—may ask, Is a Novel the vehicle for such considerations? such discussions?

Permit me to answer; whatever, in illustrating the characters, manners, or opinions of the day, exhibits what is noxious or reprehensible, should scrupulously be accompanied by what is salubrious, or chastening. Not that poison ought to be infused merely to display the virtues of an antidote; but that, where errour and mischief bask in the broad light of day, truth ought not to be suffered to shrink timidly into the shade.

Divest, for a moment, the title of Novel from its stationary standard of insignificance, and say! What is the species of writing that offers fairer opportunities for conveying useful precepts? It is, or it ought to be, a picture of supposed, but natural and probable human existence. It holds, therefore, in its hands our best affections; it exercises our imaginations; it points out the path of honour; and gives to juvenile credulity knowledge of the world, without ruin, or repentance; and the lessons of experience, without its tears.

And is not a Novel, permit me, also, to ask, in common with every other literary work, entitled to receive its stamp as useful, mischievous, or nugatory, from its execution? not necessarily, and in its changeless state, to be branded as a mere vehicle for frivolous, or seductive amusement? If many may turn aside from all but mere entertainment presented under this form, many, also, may, unconsciously, be allured by it into reading the severest truths, who would not even open any work of a graver denomination.

What is it that gives the universally acknowledged superiority to the epic poem? Its historic truth? No; the three poems, which, during so many centuries, and till Milton arose, stood unrivalled in celebrity, are, with respect to fact, of constantly disputed, or, rather, disproved authenticity.[5] Nor is it even the sweet witchery of sound; the ode, the lyric, the elegiac, and other species of poetry, have risen to equal metrical beauty:-

'Tis the grandeur, yet singleness of the plan; the never broken, yet never obvious adherence to its execution; the delineation and support of character; the invention of incident; the contrast of situation; the grace of diction, and the beauty of imagery; joined to a judicious choice of combinations, and a living interest in every partial detail, that give to that sovereign species of the works of fiction, its glorious pre-eminence.

Will my dear Father smile at this seeming approximation of the compositions which stand foremost, with those which are sunk lowest in literary estimation? No; he will feel that it is not the futile presumption of a comparison that would be preposterous; but a fond desire to separate,—with a high hand!—falsehood, that would deceive to evil, from fiction, that would attract another way;—and to rescue from ill opinion the sort of production, call it by what name we may, that his daughter ventures to lay at his feet, through the alluring, but awful tribunal of the public.

He will recollect, also, how often their so mutually honoured Dr Johnson has said to her, 'Always aim at the eagle!—even though you expect but to reach a sparrow!'

The power of prejudice annexed to nomenclature is universal: the same being who, unnamed, passes unnoticed, if preceded by the title of a hero, or a potentate, catches every eye, and is pursued with clamorous praise, or,—its common reverberatory!—abuse: but in nothing is the force of denomination more striking than in the term Novel; a species of writing which, though never mentioned, even by its supporter, but with a look that fears contempt, is not more rigidly excommunicated, from its appellation, in theory, than sought and fostered, from its attractions, in practice.

So early was I impressed myself with ideas that fastened degradation to this class of composition, that at the age of adolescence, I struggled against the propensity which, even in childhood, even from the moment I could hold a pen, had impelled me into its toils; and on my fifteenth birth-day, I made so resolute a conquest over an inclination at which I blushed, and that I had always kept secret, that I committed to the flames whatever, up to that moment, I had committed to paper. And so enormous was the pile, that I thought it prudent to consume it in the garden.

You, dear Sir, knew nothing of its extinction, for you had never known of its existence. Our darling Susanna, to whom alone I had ever ventured to read its contents, alone witnessed the conflagration; and—well I remember!—and wept, with tender partiality, over the imaginary ashes of Caroline Evelyn, the mother of Evelina.[6]

The passion, however, though resisted, was not annihilated: my bureau was cleared; but my head was not emptied; and, in defiance of every self-effort, Evelina struggled herself into life.

If then, even in the season of youth, I felt ashamed of appearing to be a votary to a species of writing that by you, Sir, liberal as I knew you to be, I thought condemned; since your large library, of which I was then the principal librarian, contained only one work of that class; how much deeper must now be my blush,—now, when that spring of existence has so long taken its flight,—transferring, I must hope, its genial vigour upon your grandson!—if the work which I here present to you, may not shew, in the observations which it contains upon various characters, ways, or excentricities of human life, that an exteriour the most frivolous may enwrap illustrations of conduct, that the most rigid preceptor need not deem dangerous to entrust to his pupils; for, if what is inculcated is right, it will not, I trust, be cast aside, merely because so conveyed as not to be received as a task. On the contrary, to make pleasant the path of propriety, is snatching from evil its most alluring mode of ascendancy. And your fortunate daughter, though past the period of chusing to write, or desiring to read, a merely romantic love-tale, or a story of improbable wonders, may still hope to retain,—if she has ever possessed it,—the power of interesting the affections, while still awake to them herself, through the many much loved agents of sensibility, that still hold in their pristine energy her conjugal, maternal, fraternal, friendly, and,—dearest Sir!—her filial feelings. . . .

Notes

Journal

1. Richard and Elizabeth Griffith published their correspondence during courtship and marriage as *A Series of Genuine Letters between Henry and Frances*, in five volumes (1757, 1767, 1770). The letters are tender, refined, and sentimental.

2. Elizabeth Rowe's *Friendship in Death, or Letters from the Dead to the Living* (1728) and *Letters Moral and Entertaining* (1728–1732) are elevated religious fictions that make little attempt at realism.

3. Oliver Goldsmith's *Vicar of Wakefield* (1766) relates the humorous and pathetic

adventures of a country vicar's family. The vicar belittles his foolish wife, whom he regards as a helpmate rather than a tender friend.

Author's Preface to *Evelina*

1. "However superior the capacities in which these great writers deserve to be considered, they must pardon me that, for the dignity of my subject, I have to rank the authors of *Rasselas* and *Eloise* as Novelists" (Burney's note). Jean-Jacques Rousseau, author of *Julie, or the New Heloise* (1761), and Samuel Johnson, author of *Rasselas* (1759), were not primarily novelists, as were the other authors she lists. Marivaux wrote *The Life of Marianne* (1731–1741), etc.; Henry Fielding, *Tom Jones* (1749), etc.; Samuel Richardson, *Clarissa* (1747–1748), etc.; Tobias Smollett, *Roderick Random* (1748), etc.

2. John Sheffield, Duke of Buckingham, *An Essay on Poetry* (1682), l. 235 (slightly inaccurate).

Letter to Samuel Crisp

1. Under her uncle's will, the heiress Cecilia Beverley will lose her fortune unless the man she marries agrees to take her surname. Delvile, the aristocratic (but not titled) man she loves, refuses to make this sacrifice, so her money is lost when they marry. Despite this happy marriage, the ending of *Cecilia* emphasizes loss and limitation.

Dedication to *The Wanderer*

1. Her father, Charles Burney, to whom she dedicated *The Wanderer*.

2. Samuel Johnson and Edmund Burke, two of the most distinguished intellectuals in the Literary Club, strongly disagreed about the American Revolution, which Johnson condemned and Burke supported.

3. As the Glorious Revolution of 1688–1689 settled the form of English constitutional government, the French Revolution profoundly influenced life and thought in Europe from 1789 into the nineteenth century.

4. The morality of suicide, debated by Harleigh, the hero, and Elinor, the anti-heroine, in chap. 85.

5. Homer's *Iliad* and *Odyssey* and Virgil's *Aeneid* present mythical stories.

6. Susanna was Frances's dearest sister and confidante. The destroyed novel told the sad story of Caroline Evelyn, summarized in *Evelina*.

PHILLIS WHEATLEY (1753?–1784)

Pʜɪʟʟɪꜱ Wʜᴇᴀᴛʟᴇʏ was born in West Africa and brought to the United States on a slave ship in 1761. She was educated by Susannah Wheatley, wife of the Boston tailor who purchased the child slave. Immersed in the culture of eighteenth-century New England, Wheatley became a member of the Old South Church of Boston and studied classical myth and history, Latin, and English literature. She began writing poetry when she was very young, publishing her first poem in 1770. Three years later, to improve her poor health, she was taken to England, where her collection, *Poems on Various Subjects, Religious and Moral,* appeared in 1773. Shortly after she returned to the United States, both of her owners died and Wheatley was left to support herself. In 1778 she married John Peters, also a "free Negro." Although she published a few more poems and planned another volume, illness and poverty consumed her final years. All three of her children died in infancy, and Wheatley herself died alone in 1784.

Long recognized for her poetry, Wheatley was also concerned with aesthetic matters that became increasingly important in nineteenth-century criticism. Her reflections on the poetic power of recollection and imagination, in particular, take their place in the history of critical writings devoted to poetic inspiration and, as John Shields argues, anticipate ideas of Kant and Coleridge. Wheatley's poem "To S. M. a young *African* Painter, on seeing his Works" was a tribute to the slave artist Scipio Moorhead. Directly addressing an African subject, this poem helps locate Wheatley's aesthetic concerns more fully in the context of her race and offers a rare early view of the implications of slavery and oppression for art.

Poems on Various Subjects, Religious and Moral (London: A. Bell, 1773).

On Recollection (1773)

Mneme[1] begin. Inspire, ye sacred nine,
Your vent'rous *Afric* in her great design.
Mneme, immortal pow'r, I trace thy spring:
Assist my strains, while I thy glories sing:
The acts of long departed years, by thee   5
Recover'd, in due order rang'd we see:

Thy pow'r the long-forgotten calls from night,
That sweetly plays before the *fancy's* sight.

    Mneme in our nocturnal visions pours
The ample treasure of her secret stores;   10
Swift from above she wings her silent flight
Through Phœbe's realms, fair regent of the night;
And, in her pomp of images display'd,
To the high-raptur'd poet gives her aid,
Through the unbounded regions of the mind,   15
Diffusing light celestial and refin'd.
The heav'nly *phantom* paints the actions done
By ev'ry tribe beneath the rolling sun.

    Mneme, enthron'd within the human breast,
Has vice condemn'd, and ev'ry virtue blest.   20
How sweet the sound when we her plaudit hear?
Sweeter than music to the ravish'd ear,
Sweeter than Maro's[2] entertaining strains
Resounding through the groves, and hills, and plains.
But how is Mneme dreaded by the race,   25
Who scorn her warnings, and despise her grace?
By her unveil'd each horrid crime appears,
Her awful hand a cup of wormwood bears.
Days, years mispent, O what a hell of woe!
Hers the worst tortures that our souls can know.   30

    Now eighteen years their destin'd course have run,
In fast succession round the central sun.
How did the follies of that period pass
Unnotic'd, but behold them writ in brass!
In Recollection see them fresh return,   35
And sure 'tis mine to be asham'd, and mourn.

    O *Virtue*, smiling in immortal green,
Do thou exert thy pow'r, and change the scene;
Be thine employ to guide my future days,
And mine to pay the tribute of my praise.   40

    Of *Recollection* such the pow'r enthron'd
In ev'ry breast, and thus her pow'r is own'd.
The wretch, who dar'd the vengeance of the skies,
At last awakes in horror and surprize,
By her alarm'd, he sees impending fate,   45
He howls in anguish and repents too late.

Phillis Wheatley (1753?–1784)

But O! what peace, what joys are hers t' impart
To ev'ry holy, ev'ry upright heart!
Thrice blest the man, who, in her sacred shrine,
Feels himself shelter'd from the wrath divine!   50

On Imagination (1773)

Thy various works, imperial queen, we see,
How bright their forms! how deck'd with pomp by thee!
Thy wond'rous acts in beauteous order stand,
And all attest how potent is thine hand.

   From Helicon's refulgent heights attend,   5
Ye sacred choir, and my attempts befriend:
To tell her glories with a faithful tongue,
Ye blooming graces, triumph in my song.

   Now here, now there, the roving *Fancy* flies,
Till some lov'd object strikes her wand'ring eyes   10
Whose silken fetters all the senses bind,
And soft captivity involves the mind.

   Imagination! who can sing thy force?
Or who describe the swiftness of thy course?
Soaring through air to find the bright abode,   15
Th' empyreal palace of the thund'ring God,
We on thy pinions can surpass the wind,
And leave the rolling universe behind:
From star to star the mental optics rove,
Measure the skies, and range the realms above.   20
There in one view we grasp the mighty whole,
Or with new worlds amaze th' unbounded soul.

   Though *Winter* frowns to *Fancy's* raptur'd eyes
The fields may flourish, and gay scenes arise;
The frozen deeps may break their iron bands,   25
And bid their waters murmur o'er the sands.
Fair Flora may resume her fragrant reign,
And with her flow'ry riches deck the plain;
Sylvanus may diffuse his honours round,
And all the forest may with leaves be crown'd: 30
Show'rs may descend, and dews their gems disclose,
And nectar sparkle on the blooming rose.

Such is thy pow'r, nor are thine orders vain,
O thou the leader of the mental train:
In full perfection all thy works are wrought,   35
And thine the sceptre o'er the realms of thought.
Before thy throne the subject-passions bow,
Of subject-passions sov'reign ruler Thou;
At thy command joy rushes on the heart,
And through the glowing veins the spirits dart.   40

Fancy might now her silken pinions try
To rise from earth, and sweep th' expanse on high;
From Tithon's bed now might Aurora rise,
Her cheeks all glowing with celestial dies,
While a pure stream of light o'erflows the skies.   45
The monarch of the day I might behold,
And all the mountains tipt with radiant gold,
But I reluctant leave the pleasing views,
Which *Fancy* dresses to delight the *Muse*;
Winter austere forbids me to aspire,   50
And northern tempests damp the rising fire;
They chill the tides of *Fancy's* flowing sea,
Cease then, my song, cease the unequal lay.

To S. M. a young *African* Painter, on seeing his Works (1773)

To show the lab'ring bosom's deep intent,
And thought in living characters to paint,
When first thy pencil did those beauties give,
And breathing figures learnt from thee to live,
How did those prospects give my soul delight,   5
A new creation rushing on my sight?[1]
Still, wond'rous youth! each noble path pursue,
On deathless glories fix thine ardent view:
Still may the painter's and the poet's fire
To aid thy pencil, and thy verse conspire!   10
And may the charms of each seraphic theme
Conduct thy footsteps to immortal fame!
High to the blissful wonders of the skies
Elate thy soul, and raise thy wishful eyes.
Thrice happy, when exalted to survey   15
That splendid city, crown'd with endless day,
Whose twice six gates on radiant hinges ring:
Celestial Salem blooms in endless spring.

Phillis Wheatley (1753?–1784)

Calm and serene thy moments glide along,
And may the muse inspire each future song!   20
Still, with the sweets of contemplation bless'd,
May peace with balmy wings your soul invest!
But when these shades of time are chas'd away,
And darkness ends in everlasting day,
On what seraphic pinions shall we move,   25
And view the landscapes in the realms above?
There shall thy tongue in heav'nly murmurs flow,
And there my muse with heav'nly transport glow:
No more to tell of Damon's tender sighs,
Or rising radiance of Aurora's eyes,   30
For nobler themes demand a nobler strain,
And purer language on th' ethereal plain.
Cease, gentle muse! the solemn gloom of night
Now seals the fair creation from my sight.

Notes

On Recollection

 1. Mnemosyne, one of the Titans of early Greek mythology, represents memory.
 2. Maro refers to Virgil.

To S. M. a young *African* Painter, on seeing his Works

 1. The poem is addressed to Scipio Moorhead, the slave artist who may have executed the engraving of Wheatley's portrait for the 1773 *Poems* frontispiece.

ELIZABETH SIMPSON INCHBALD
(1753-1821)

ELIZABETH INCHBALD was the daughter of Catholics John and Mary Simpson. In 1772 she left home determined to carve out a career as an actress, aided by beauty but impeded by a stammer. After her marriage to Joseph Inchbald in 1772, she spent several years on provincial stages, becoming intimate with Sarah Siddons and John Philip Kemble. After her husband's death, she finally appeared on the London stage, in 1780. In spite of several roles at Covent Garden, she was never popular and she eventually retired from acting in 1789. Her writing career was far more successful: by the time she died in August 1821, she had accumulated an estate of six thousand pounds, had been painted by Sir Thomas Lawrence, and had been published in the prestigious *Edinburgh Review.*

Inchbald's dramatic output was enormous: she wrote original comedies, adapted French and German plays, and edited three collections of drama, including the twenty-five-volume *British Theatre* (1806–1809). Her first novel, *A Simple Story* (1791), was highly esteemed in her own time and is now firmly in the canon of eighteenth-century fiction.

In translating, evaluating, and altering the work of others, Inchbald drew upon not only her experience as an actress but also her critical judgment about the kind of language, moral stance, and historical accuracy necessary in dramatic presentation. In her prefatory remarks to plays anthologized in *The British Theatre*, she confidently critiques weak or inappropriate dramaturgy, at the same time acknowledging the difficulties inherent in writing for the stage. Indeed, the remarks clearly reflect her own experience: they often emphasize the actor's role in the success of a play; they raise questions about the relative poverty of playwrights; and they reflect Inchbald's social and political concerns.

The British Theatre; or, A Collection of Plays, which are acted at the Theatres Royal, Drury Lane, Covent Garden, and Haymarket (London: Longman, Hurst, Rees, and Orme, 1808).

Elizabeth Simpson Inchbald (1753–1821)

Selected *Remarks* from *The British Theatre* (1808)

The fable of this admired tragedy [*Romeo and Juliet*], however romantic it may appear, is founded on real events, which took place in Verona, at the beginning of the fourteenth century.

Mr. Malone[1] says, that "Breval, in his travels, on a strict inquiry into the histories of Verona, found, that Shakspeare had varied very little from the truth, either in the names, characters, or circumstances of this play."

Such an extraordinary and affecting story as that of Romeo and Juliet soon became the subject of poems, novels, and other literary works, all over Italy, and from thence found its way into other countries.

A poem, from this little Italian history, by Mr. Arthur Brooke[2] is supposed to have been the production from whence Shakspeare formed the present drama.

The following title, according to the fashion of those distant days, was affixed to that poem:—

"The tragical History of Romeus and Julict, containing a rare Example of true Constancie: with the subtill Counsels and Practices of an old Fryer, and their ill Event."

Shakspeare has produced, from the "Tragical History," one of his most admirable plays: Yet, had the subject fallen to Otway's pen, though he would have treated it less excellently, he would have rendered it more affecting.

"Romeo and Juliet" is called a pathetic tragedy, but it is not so in reality. It charms the understanding, and delights the imagination, without melting, though it touches, the heart.

The reason that an auditor or reader cannot feel a powerful sympathy in the sorrows of these fervent lovers, is, because they have witnessed the growth of their passion from its birth to its maturity, and do not honour it with that warmth of sentiment as if they had conceived it to have been of longer duration; fixed by time, and rendered more tender by familiarity.

The ardour of the youthful pair, like the fervency of children, gives high amusement, without much anxiety that their wishes should be accomplished—they have been so suddenly enamoured of each other, that it seems matter of doubt whether they would not as quickly have fallen in love a second time, or as soon have become languid through satiety, if all obstacles to their bliss had been removed. Shakspeare has shown himself versed in the passion of love beyond other dramatists, by giving it this wild, vehement, yet childish tendency.

The illustrious author of this drama well knew, that the passion of love, in the young, is seldom constant, as poets describe it, but fickle as violent. In his just knowledge of the human heart, then, he has given, in the original play, a less stable character to this soft passion, that is even here described; for, in the original, Romeo commences the tragedy with sighing for Rosaline, and ends it by dying for Juliet. Such was Shakspeare's respect for the consistency of a lover.

The play is certainly made much more interesting by the alteration, which omits all mention of the beloved, and then forsaken, Rosaline; yet surely, by the exclusion of that circumstance, an incident but too natural, is lost.[3]

As Shakspeare found those hasty, inconsiderate, lovers, unable in themselves to protect his drama, he provided ample means of support in the additional characters. In these he has combined the most varied excellence;—the mirthful elegance of Mercutio, the comic humour of the Nurse, the sage reasoning of the Friar, together with a whole group of no less natural, though less prominent, persons.

The events which he caused to arise from his plot, the numerous and important occurrences that are perpetually diversifying the scene, and aiding the effect of the characters and fable, united with them, have drawn from his great commentator the declaration, that "this play is one of the most pleasing of our author's performances."[4]

But, with all the genuine merit of this play, it seldom attracts an elegant audience. The company, that frequent the side-boxes, will not come to a tragedy, unless to weep in torrents—and "Romeo and Juliet" will not draw even a copious shower of tears.

Garrick altered the play to its present state, and himself performed Romeo, but with no impressive talents. Mrs. Cibber's Juliet was held superior. Love, in Garrick's description, never seemed more than a fabulous sensation.[5]

It is said, in the "Roscius Anglicanus," that James Howard, Esq. made alterations in this drama previous to Garrick's;[6] and that, being of a compassionate disposition, he preserved the lives of both Romeo and Juliet, and ended the play happily. It is also added, that when Sir William Davenant[7] was manager of the theatre, he had the original and the altered play alternately performed for several nights together; thus consulting the different tastes of the auditors for joy or for sorrow.

The Italian author, who first related the sad story on which this drama has been founded, gives the following account of the punishment inflicted on those persons, who acted as accomplices in the unfortunate death of these lovers.

"Juliet's female attendant (Shakspear's Nurse) was banished for conceal-ing the marriage.

"The apothecary, for selling the poison, was tortured, condemned, and hanged.

"Friar Lawrence was permitted to retire to a hermitage, near Verona, where he ended his days in penitence; while Romeo's servant was set at liberty, because he had only acted in obedience to his master's orders."

It is no slight honour to this play [*All for Love*, by John Dryden], that it was written by the illustrious author of the "Ode on St. Cecilia's Day." The play, in return, confers but little honour upon Dryden.

The burning bosom, throbbing heart, the enchanting sensations, which the author, in his odes and poems, inspires, are rarely excited by his dramatic works. The stage, which exalts the muse of many an author, humbles that of the present great poet; and he ranks as a dramatist beneath those rivals who can move the passions by a more judicious adherence to nature and simplicity.

"All for Love" was the author's favourite drama;—he said, he wrote it solely to please himself, and had succeeded in his design. Yet, were it not for the interest which attaches to the names of his hero and heroine, their characters are too feebly drawn to produce those emotions which an audi-ence at a tragedy come prepared to feel.

Who can be inattentive to the loves of Marc Antony and Cleopatra? Yet, thus described, their fate in presentation seldom draws a tear, or gives rise to the transport of passion in the breast of the most deserving auditor. The work is, nevertheless, highly valuable. It is one of the most interesting parts of Roman and Egyptian history; and the historian—Dryden.

There is certainly in this short history, compared with more copious ones, a diminution of Cleopatra's faults: yet her character is by no means so graced with virtues, and dignified by heroism in this drama as in the tragedy of Pompée, by the great Corneille.[8]

The wife of Antony, in the present composition is, unexpectedly, the most affecting personage in the whole piece: and the comic sentences of Ventidius the sole support of those scenes, where the tragic parts, more par-ticularly, decline into languor.

The author was an advocate for tragi-comedy, and held, that all theat-rical productions required alternate scenes of grief and joy, to render the whole a more perfect picture of nature, than could be given by one con-tinued view of either. Some of his biographers have said, that, in his latter days, Dryden altered this opinion, and was convinced, that tragedy and comedy should never unite. It is probable he recanted; and it is consolatory to reflect, that this great man was as apt perhaps to change his mind upon all other subjects, as upon that in which his political interest was concerned.

In politics, the author of this tragedy was so inconstant, that he wrote funeral lamentations on the death of Oliver Cromwell, and hymns of joy on the restoration of King Charles.

He wrote "The Spanish Friar,"[9] to vilify the Roman Catholic religion, whilst that religion was persecuted and translated an ancient Father, to prove it the true faith, when the King on the throne professed himself one of its members.

This extraordinary man was a grandson of Sir Erasmus Dryden, of Northamptonshire, and born near Oundle, in that county. His hereditary income seems to have been extremely confined, yet he was educated for no profession; whilst the emoluments of a poet, like those of a soldier, scarcely ever supply the various necessities of the gentleman.

He married Lady C. Howard, sister to the Earl of Berkshire; but this union could not give much aid to his finances, as it is testified, that the world has been indebted for his works to his poverty. His pen was not more pre-eminent than reluctant.

Dryden's manners were meek and modest in the same remarkable degree as his satire on his enemies was bold and revengeful; for, like other able writers of his time, his days were embittered by the envy and malignity of rivals.

But with all their slander, and all his own in return, he was not so worn by evil passions as to die much before the age of seventy. He departed this life in the year 1701, at his house in Gerrard Street, professing the faith of the Church of Rome.

So distinguished a believer might have done honour to that Church—but Dryden believed also in astrology.

The valuable half of this drama [*Oroonoko*, by Thomas Southerne], which is the tragic part, is founded neither upon fictitious characters nor events. Such an African prince, as Oroonoko, stolen from his native kingdom of Angola, was actually brought to an English settlement in the West Indies, and sold for a slave.

This pitiable occurrence took place in the reign of Charles II. at the time that Mrs. Behn, the well-known dramatic writer, whom Pope has honoured by a satire, resided at Surinam with her family; her father having been appointed lieutenant general of that settlement, and of thirty neighbouring islands.[10]

It was at Surinam, that Mrs. Behn, not only saw, but became intimately acquainted with the unfortunate, but still proud and dignified, Oroonoko. She was witness to his bravery and skill in arms, upon the occasion of some danger threatening the island: and she beheld his humility and moderation, when all his martial feats were performed, and tranquillity restored. She knew his Imoinda, and saw with delight their rapturous affection for each other.

On the return of Mrs. Behn to England, she published the memoirs of those ill-fated lovers; from which publication, Southern has selected materials for this pathetic tragedy.

Whether the comic characters are taken from persons in real life, or from the poet's fancy, is not known: nor is it of much consequence from whence they came, as they can do no great degree of honour to their birthplace.

The repulsive qualities of some of those characters, joined to the little which has been allotted for the heroine to perform, have been obstacles to the attraction of this drama, and it is seldom acted. Yet, some years past, Mr. Pope,[11] in his very first appearance upon any stage, encountered, and triumphantly overcame, all impediments to the favourable reception of Oroonoko; and made the play so impressive, by his talents in the representation of that character, that for many nights it drew to the theatre a crowded audience. His acting was remarkably fine in the last scene; whilst his youth, person, deportment, and even features, gave an accurate portraiture of one of Africa's princely sons.

But could the ancient Roscius[12] ascend from his grave to personate the hero of this piece, there is a great mercantile town in England, whose opulent inhabitants would not permit the play to appear in their magnificent theatre. The tragedy of "Oroonoko" is never acted in Liverpool, for the very reason why it ought to be acted there oftener that at any other place—The merchants of that great city acquire their riches by the slave trade.[13]

If any defect can be attributed to Southern in the tragic fable, either of this play or of "Isabella," it is, that in the one, his first male character wants importance, and in the other, his principal female.[14] Still, in both plays, he makes his tale, a tale of woe, though only a single personage becomes the object of deep concern.

That the poet Gray was an admirer of this tragedy, is seen in a letter of his to Horace Walpole, dated, Burnham in Buckinghamshire, 1737; wherein he says, "We have old Mr. Southern, at a gentleman's house a little way off, who often comes to see us. He is now seventy years old, and has almost wholly lost his memory; but is as agreeable an old man as can be; at least, I persuade myself so, when I look at him, and think of Isabella and Oroonoko★."

Southern is an exception from most poets, in having been wealthy; but he procured some of his wealth by a means, which all poets should rather submit to poverty than employ: he printed tickets on his benefit nights as an author, and even urged their sale among his noble and distinguished friends. Thus, vilely reducing himself to dependence, in order to become rich; in lieu of honourably seeking riches, that he might become independent.

This play [*The Careless Husband*, by Colley Cibber] will ever be a memorial of the injustice of Pope.

It was Colley Cibber, the author of this excellent, this moral, comedy, whom Pope made the hero of his "Dunciad."[16]

Pope, it is said, was an unsuccessful dramatist, and ever after hated both plays and players. This hatred was the genuine product of a disappointed artist, for he hated only the skilful ones. A man of less talent than Cibber, and less favoured by the town, had been too mean for the great poet's vengeance—the man, who was already ridiculous, it had been loss of time to ridicule—Pope chose the very person, on whom his shafts could make the deepest wound: One, who like Cibber, wrote so much, that he sometimes failed of writing well; and yet who, at times, wrote so excellently, that reputation was dear to him. As a proof that it was, he did not even affect to disguise the impression which this wanton attack made upon him; and in a letter to the author of "The Dunciad," complaining on the subject, he asserts, that his enemy can give no proof, but that the object of his satire had ever been his ardent admirer. Then, alluding to the miserable excuse given by Pope for this outrage—"The dulness of him he assailed"—Cibber thus reasonably and feelingly proceeds.

"Dulness can be no vice or crime; or is, at worst, but a misfortune, and you ought no more to censure or revile a man for it, than for his being blind or lame. But, if you please, I will wave this part of my argument, and, for once, take no advantage of it, but will suppose dulness to be actually

★See Mason's Life of Gray.[15]

criminal, and then will leave it to your own conscience to declare, whether you really think I am so guilty of it as to deserve the name of the dull fellow you make me? Now, if I am called upon to speak from my own conscience on the question, I do, from my heart, solemnly declare, that I don't believe you do think so of me. This, I grant, may be vanity in me to say; but, if what I believe is true, what a slovenly conscience do you show your face with!"

It is for the reader of "The Careless Husband" to decide at once, whether its author was, or was not, a dunce. In a production, where less weight of argument would be given on the side of the author, it might be deemed impertinent to anticipate the reader's pleasure of judging for himself; but the high character of this play, joined to that which it will instantly say in its own defence, banishes all doubt upon the subject. The author must be acquitted by the reader of his accuser's charge—and the accuser must be condemned.

"The Careless Husband" is, as originally written, very long—it contains more pages than most plays—but, containing more matter too, it seems short in the perusal.

The dialogue is so brilliant, at the same time, so very natural, that its force will admit of no augmentation, even from the delivery of the best actors: nor is this admirable work, according to the present demand for perpetual incident, so well calculated to please on the stage, as in the closet.

The occurrences, which take place in this drama, are of that delicate, as well as probable kind, that their effect is not sufficiently powerful in the representation—whereas, in reading, they come to the heart with infinitely more force, for want of that extravagance, which public exhibition requires. The smaller avenues to the mind and bosom are often the surest passages to convey sensations of pain or delight; and the connoisseur in all the little touches of refined nature, may here indulge his taste, whilst, as an auditor, he might possibly be deprived of his enjoyment, by the vain endeavour of performers, to display, by imitation, that, which only real life can show, or imagination pourtray.

Here are no violent passions, such as are usually depicted on a stage; but merely such as commonly govern mankind.

Sir Charles's tenderness for his wife is so unforced, and his contempt for his mistresses so undesignedly cool, that an actor must possess the most consummate talents, in the minutiæ of his art, before he can affect an audience by the one, or edify them by the other—yet, the first is extremely moving, and the last, highly instructive.[7]

Nor is there an actress who could utter the common-place reproaches of Lady Graveairs, most pleasantly unconnected with sense, half so well as the reader's fancy can hear them.

Characteristic traits, such as these, too diminutive indeed for the tongue to reveal, or the ear to catch, in a theatre, abound throughout this whole comedy; and seem to have been produced by a judgment somewhat too nice, considering they were meant for dramatic action.

It is not the fault of Cibber, if the virtues of Lady Easy appear old to the reader—the plagiarism of subsequent authors, can alone take from the just appearance of their originality.

Although every character of this drama (now a hundred years old) is a person of fashion—and fashion changes perpetually,—still every one, here described, is, at this very time, perfectly fashionable. They talk, they think, they act, they love, and hate like people of rank to this very day. Change but their dinner hour, from four to seven, and blot out the line where a lady says, "she is going to church," and every article, in the whole composition, will be perfectly modern.

Cibber's grand foe, even Pope, was compelled to own the merit of this play; but, then he alleged, it must be written by mere accident. Pope's party went farther, and said, that Cibber claimed that which was not his but was assuredly written by another.

Cibber's person was insignificant, and his mind addicted to vanity—misfortunes which mostly combine. He was, nevertheless, goodnatured and forgiving—but he was honoured with the patronage and friendship of the great; and this, in his occupation of a player, was an unpardonable failing in the eye of his enemy.

That admirable poet should have considered, that, of all artists, the actor is most an object of curiosity and incitement to personal acquaintance. The purchaser of a picture, or a book, makes the genius of the painter, or the author, who have produced these works, as it were, of his household, and he requires no farther intimacy—But the actor must come himself to his admirer, as the only means of yielding, to his domestic pleasures, even the shadow of his art.

The author of this popular tragedy [*Venice Preserved*, by Thomas Otway] died in the reign of Charles the second. He was the son of a clergyman, and was born at Trotting, in Sussex, where his father resided, in 1651.

Otway received his early education at a school near Winchester, and then became a commoner of Christ Church, Oxford. Soon after his return from the university, his passionate admiration of dramatic amusements, induced him to venture his abilities on the stage, as an actor: In this attempt he wholly mistook the department of the theatre, which his talents were calculated to grace: but not till he had changed the profession of a comedian for that of a soldier, and had served in Flanders as a cornet of horse, did he try the force of his genius in the art, by which he has procured his renown.

"Venice Preserved" is the favourite work of Otway. It is played repeatedly every year; except when an order from the Lord Chamberlain forbids its representation, lest some of the speeches of Pierre should be applied, by the ignorant part of the audience, to certain men, or assemblies, in the English state.[18]

The story of this play is taken from St. Real's Conspiracy of the Marquis de Bedamar, and the Duke d'Ossuna, against the republic of Venice:[19] and amongst a great deal of political declamation, anger, and fury, is interwoven the tenderest, and most pathetic distress. It is Otway's highest praise, that he moves his audience to pity, more than any other dramatic writer.

The passion of love, finely portrayed on the stage, is supposed to engage every heart, because it is supposed, that every heart has already been softened by its power.—But, although an audience be chiefly composed of the unmarried part of society, still conjugal love has a deeper interest in the bosom of every auditor, than any other affection. The connubial state of Jaffier and Belvidera causes that sympathy in their grief from beholders, which neither the harmonious numbers of the poet, nor the exquisite acting of the performers, could awaken, merely on the part of two lovers. Some passages of this tragedy have, however, been attributed to the sentiments which the author's own sufferings inspired, rather than to the fictitious woes of those, his creatures of imagination.—

Though the poverty of authors be proverbial, Otway appears to have been among the poorest, and most destitute of all the class. The following lines, spoken by Jaffier, were, probably, written with the exact feelings, which his own distresses had aroused.

> "There's not a wretch, that lives on common charity,
> "But's happier than me: for I have known
> "The luscious sweets of plenty," &c.

And farther,

> "Tell me why, good Heaven,
> "Thou mad'st me what I am, with all the spirit,

"Aspiring thoughts, and elegant desires,
"That fill the happiest man?——
"Why have I sense to know the curse that's on me?

It is reported, that the author of "Venice Preserved" perished for want of food: and, whatsoever well-disposed person shall read his Dedication of this very tragedy to the Duchess of Portsmouth (one of King Charles's mistresses), wherein he calls her—"The pious mother of a prince, whose blooming virtues declare the mighty stock he comes from"—such reader will own, that, if he *were* starved to death, the event at least, did some honour to his patroness;—as it showed her proper contempt for his base flattery.

This tragedy [*Mahomet*, by Voltaire] is a translation from the French, by the Rev. James Miller, who possessed the living of Upcerne, in Dorsetshire. He was a very extraordinary man—a political writer, who refused a large bribe, to abandon his opinions, and favour ministers of state.

A second instance of political firmness is connected with this drama. On its first representation, on the Dublin stage, a few sentences in the part of Alcanor, had such accidental allusion to some great men, or man, then in power in that nation, that the audience, enraptured upon the utterance, and willing to show their own implication, encored those lines with such unanimous vehemence, that the performer thought it his duty to repeat them, in compliance with their desire.

The late Mr. Sheridan, father of the author of "The School for Scandal," was, at that time, manager of the theatre of Dublin, in which adventure, all his property, all his hopes, were embarked;[20] yet, he boldly censured the actor, who had yielded to the command of the audience, and forbade a repetition of any speech in the part of Alcanor, however loudly it might be called for, on the following night.

Mr. Sheridan knew the predicament in which he was placed; he knew the fury of an exasperated audience in Ireland—he knew their power over all his possessions; yet, firm in his politics, he beheld, on the next evening, his theatre totally demolished, and his own life in danger, without revoking the peremptory order he had issued.

But upon higher ground is this tragedy worthy of note: it is, in the original, the production of Voltaire—[21] has deep interest—and some of the happiest thoughts of that celebrated writer are here delivered by the renowned, or affecting personages introduced; whilst tumultuous passions, of various tendency, give energy to every sentence.

The action of this drama commences just a few years after the foundation of the Mahometan empire; and, as there are many allusions in the course of the work to the preceding part of the Impostor's life, a short detail from history, of previous events, may enliven the reader's memory, and increase his attention to the scenes which follow.

Mahomet, the founder of a religion, which soon became, and still continues to be, the prevailing religion of the East, was born in 570, at Mecca, a city of Arabia. His parents were poor, and, having both died in his early age, the guardianship of their orphan devolved on an uncle, who employed him to go with his caravans, from Mecca to Damascus.

In this employment of camel-driver, Mahomet continued till he was twenty-eight years of age, when he married a rich widow. Whether riches first inspired him with ambition, or ambition had induced him to marry for wealth, has not been determined; but, no sooner did he find himself elevated above his original rank in society, than he formed the mighty plan of subjugating the whole Eastern world to his dominion.

Mahomet, perhaps, falsely conceived, that imposition was the basis, on which all governments were built; and that, instead of being singular in his conduct, he merely followed the examples of other law-givers, when he became sanctified in appearance, and when he boldly spoke of prodigies, by which he was invested with sovereign power from Heaven, both as a king and prophet.

Whatever were his notions of past events, he formed an accurate judgment of the future—he foresaw that an impostor might be obeyed—adored;—and that no extravagance of mystery or miracle, was too wonderful, or too ridiculous, for a people's belief.

Though Mahomet was too illiterate to write his own sacred laws in his divine book, the Koran, he possessed the knowledge to tell a surprising tale of its being entrusted to his hands by an Angel from heaven;—which incredible occurrence had more power in gaining him proselytes, than all the moral precepts gathered from the jewish and christian scriptures, with which the learned men whose services he purchased, had adorned this work.

No sooner was the supposed prophet followed, and his creed accepted by the poor and ignorant, than, like, most innovators, he was accused of profanation, by the rich and the wise.—To escape the punishment of the enraged senate at Mecca, he took refuge in Medina; there, first established his temporal, as well as his spiritual power, and taught, that his doctrines were to be enforced by the sword.

Mecca, and all the jewish Arabs, were the first who experienced the cruel progress of the Impostor's faith. In vanquishing all Arabia, twice he

besieged the city of his birth-place, some years elapsing between the attacks.—On his second assault upon Mecca it is, that this tragedy opens,
with one of its first citizens and senators—Alcanor.

This is a tragedy [*The Mourning Bride*, by William Congreve], which
engages the attention, pleases the ear, and charms the eye, but never touches
the heart.

Love is a fervid passion to feel, but an insipid one to see. Imagination,
fancy, whim, a kind of enchanting influence, presides over this tender emotion of the mind; but persons, on whom its magic has no immediate power,
look coldly upon those ideal joys and sorrows, which the lover considers as
realities.

Love, in this play, is, however, substantiated by wedlock, which is no
chimera:—still the marriage of Alphonso and Almeria is merely bridal; neither cemented by long friendship, offspring, or any of those positive ties of
affection, which would infallibly win the audience to sympathize in their
mutual fondness.[22]

"The Mourning Bride" is fortunate in an attractive title, and more fortunate in the name of its author.

A tragedy from the pen of the first comic writer of the age was, at the
time it was announced (1691), a subject of respect and curiosity. The learned
and critical part of the town crowded the theatre on the first night, and had,
at least, some of their senses charmed, for the play had an unequivocal good
reception. The great Dryden was present, and is said to have been enraptured. But it is with poets as with politicians; few persons are sufficiently
independent of fortune or affections, to speak exactly what they think on
public topics; and where it is held prudent to disguise thoughts, it is surely
discreet to pay little regard to words.

Churchill[23] calls "The Mourning Bride" a pantomime. Dr. Johnson
gives it the extreme praise of containing, in the following speech of Almeria
(when she visits the vaulted aisle, to behold the tomb of Anselmo), an image
the most poetical of any in the English language[24]:

"How rev'rend is the face of this tall pile,
"Whose ancient pillars rear their marble heads,
"To bear aloft its arch'd and pond'rous roof,
"By its own weight made stedfast and immoveable,
"Looking tranquillity!—It strikes an awe
"And terror on my aching sight.—The tombs

Elizabeth Simpson Inchbald (1753–1821)

"And monumental caves of death look cold,
"And shoot a chillness to my trembling heart!"

Whatever merit this tragedy possesses, it is certain that its being placed upon the list of acting plays at present, is wholly to be ascribed to the magnificent representation of Zara by Mrs. Siddons.[25]

Mrs. H. Siddons has every grace and sensibility requisite for the part of Almeria.

There is but one male character in this play worthy the talents of a superior actor; nor will some actors allow that one: Osmyn (or Alphonso) is not a favourite with any performer. Garrick had great spirit and fire in every scene of the part—but not the fire of love. Kemble has not even the sparks. Yet Kemble looks nobly, majestically, in Osmyn; and reminds the audience of the lines just quoted.

—"Tall pillar rears its marble head,
"Looking tranquillity.—
"And shoots a chillness to the trembling heart!"

When a zealous christian* writes in favour of a jew, it is a proof of the truest christianity.

The author of this play [*The Jew,* by Richard Cumberland] has done more than befriend one unfortunate descendant of Abraham; he has taken the twelve tribes of Israel under his protection.

The bravery of this enterprise was equal to its charity—the execution has been masterly—and complete success the reward of that compassion, which incited him to his labour.

This is one of the very few dramas, on a simple construction, which have been eminently successful upon the English stage. The play, in its formation, is adverse to the public taste, and in its sentiments contrary to public prejudice; still the public were charmed with it. Nor is its power of giving delight confined to the circle of a theatre; it has nearly the same influence in the closet.[27]

One character alone supports this comedy; for those persons introduced exclusive of the Jew, are insignificant, or merely foils to him—but he is of himself so potent, that one other prominent character would have been

---

*Mr. Cumberland has written a reply to some of Gibbon's doubts, respecting the miracles contained in the New Testament.—Also a poem, entitled "Calvary" and other works in honour of his religion.[26]

superfluous; and would have perhaps weakened, by dividing, that interest, which he, by dint of moral principles, sound understanding, eloquent sentences, and a tender nature, creates.

So pointed are some of Sheva's replies, that they might justly receive the denomination of wit. Yet, with all his most excellent conversation, his most admirable observations, and keen retorts, his discourse is so natural, that it is never once elevated above the plainest familiarity.

Though Sheva has infinitely more of the force of novelty, by his professing the jewish faith, still his character would be new to the stage, common as it is in real life, were he the follower of any other doctrine.—A virtuous miser is as much a wonder in the production of a dramatist, as a virtuous jew; and Mr. Cumberland has in one single part, rescued two unpopular characters from the stigma under which they both innocently suffered.[28]

Poets, whose poverty is in general the consequence of their extravagance, condemn the miser's wealth and independence; whilst, with the same pen, they lament their own indigence and slavery. They should reflect, that it is wise in the hoarder of money to prevent in himself the sin of peevish discontent, malice, and all the temptations consequent to dependence which assail the bosom of the prodigal. They should reflect too, that the accumulator of riches *may* be a good man, whilst the profuse can never be such. The spendthrift's means are lavished on himself, or upon the instruments of his luxurious pleasures; and yet his reputation stands fairer with the inconsiderate multitude, than his, who neglects even the nourishment of his own body, to preserve a sane and purified mind.

Burnet[29] has said, in the cause of morality and religion—"Economy is the greatest security of principles." And Johnson has said, in the cause of self-interest—"A man who keeps his money, has more use from it than he can have by spending it."

Notwithstanding the testimonies of those great men, indiscriminate profusion has been the dramatic hero's virtue in every comedy, till Cumberland showed to the long blinded world, that—the less a man gives to himself, the more, it is probable, he bestows upon his neighbour. This conclusion is derived from the certainty that—the less a man loves himself, the more he is affectionate to others.

In the representation of this part of miser, jew and philanthropist, Mr. Bannister[30] did the highest honour to his art, in combining the three characters so excellently, that they seemed all to be united with strict adherence to nature. On the first night of performing this play, when the last character of a benevolent man burst forth from the other two degraded names, the audience, as taken by surprise, seemed suddenly to recollect the following lines of the Prologue, and gave token of their admiration by enthusiastic applause.

"———To your candour we appeal this night,
"For a poor client, for a luckless wight,
"Whom bard ne'er favour'd; whose sad fate has been,
· "Never to share in one applauding scene.
"In souls like yours, there should be found a place
"For ev'ry victim of unjust disgrace."

Plays, founded on German dramas, have long been a subject both of ridicule and of serious animadversion. Ridicule is a jocund slanderer; and who does not love to be merry? but the detraction, that is dull, is inexcusable calumny.

The grand moral of this play [*Lovers' Vows*, by Elizabeth Inchbald][31] is—to set forth the miserable consequences which arise from the neglect, and to enforce the watchful care, of illegitimate offspring; and surely, as the pulpit has not had eloquence to eradicate the crime of seduction, the stage may be allowed an humble endeavour to prevent its most fatal effects.

But there are some pious declaimers against theatrical exhibitions, so zealous to do good,—they grudge the poor dramatist his share in the virtuous concern.

Not furnished with one plea throughout four acts of "Lovers' Vows" for accusation, those critics arraign its catastrophe, and say,—"the wicked should be punished."—They forget there is a punishment called *conscience*, which, though it seldom troubles the defamer's peace, may weigh heavy on the fallen female and her libertine seducer.

But as a probationary prelude to the supposed happiness of the frail personages of this drama, the author has plunged the offender, Agatha, in bitterest poverty and woe; which she receives as a contrite penitent, atoning for her sins. The Baron Wildenhaim, living in power and splendour, is still more rigorously visited by remorse: and, in the reproaches uttered by his outcast son, (become, by the father's criminal disregard of his necessities, a culprit subject to death by the law,) the Baron's guilt has sure exemplary chastisement. But yet, after all the varied anguish of his mind, should tranquillity promise, at length, to crown his future days, where is the immorality? If holy books teach, that the wicked too often prosper, why are plays to be withheld from inculcating the self-same doctrine? Not that a worldly man would class it amongst the prosperous events of life, to be (like the Baron) compelled to marry his cast-off mistress, after twenty years absence.

It may not here be wholly useless to observe—that, in the scene in the fourth act, just mentioned, between the Baron and his son—the actor, who plays Frederick, too frequently forms his notion of the passion he is to pourtray, through the interview, from the following lines, at the end of one of his speeches:

"And, when he dies, a funeral sermon will praise his great benevolence, his christian charities."

The sarcasm here to be expressed, should be evinced in no one sentence else. Where, in a preceding speech, he says, the Baron is—"a man, kind, generous, beloved by his tenants:"—he certainly means *this* to be his character. Frederick is not ironical, except by accident. Irony and sarcasm do not appertain to youth: open, plain, downright habits, are the endearing qualities of the young. Moreover, a son, urged by cruel injuries, may upbraid his father even to rage, and the audience will yet feel interest for them both; but if he contemn or deride him, all respect is lost, both for the one and the other.

The passions which take possession of this young soldier's heart, when admitted to the presence of the Baron, knowing him to be his father, are various; but scorn is not amongst the number. Awe gives the first sensation, and is subdued by pride: filial tenderness would next force its way, and is overwhelmed by anger. These passions strive in his breast, till grief for his mother's wrongs, and his own ignominious state, burst all restraint—and as fury drives him to the point of distraction, he changes his accents to a tone of irony, in the lines just quoted.

"Oh! there be actors I have seen, and heard others praise, who, (not to speak it profanely,) have"—scornfully sneered at their father through this whole scene and yet, been highly applauded.

While it is the fashion to see German plays, both the German and the English author will patiently bear the displeasure of a small party of critics, as the absolute conditions on which they enjoy popularity. Nor, till the historian is forbid to tell, how tyrants have success in vanquishing nations; or the artist be compelled to paint the beauteous courtezan with hideous features, as the emblem of her mind, shall the free dramatist be untrue to his science; which, like theirs, is to follow nature through all her rightful course. Deception, beyond the result of genuine imitative art, he will disclaim, and say with Shakspeare to the self-approving zealot:

Elizabeth Simpson Inchbald (1753–1821)

"Virtue itself turns vice, being misapplied,
And vice sometime's by action dignified."

Letter to George Colman, the Younger (1818)

MY DEAR SIR,[1]

As I have offended you, I take it kind that you have publicly told me so, because it gives me an opportunity thus openly to avow my regret, and, at the same time, to offer you all the atonement which is now in my power.

In one of those unfortunate moments, which leaves us years of repentance, I accepted an overture, to write from two to four pages, in the manner of preface, to be introduced before a certain number of plays, for the perusal, or information, of such persons as have not access to any diffuse compositions, either in biography or criticism, but who are yet very liberal contributors to the treasury of a theatre.—Even for so humble a task I did not conceive myself competent, till I submitted my own opinion to that of the proprietors of the plays in question. . . .

The judgement on which I placed my reliance on this occasion was— that many readers might be amused and informed, whilst no one dramatist could possibly be offended, by the cursory remarks of a female observer, upon works which had gone through various editions, had received the unanimous applause of every British theatre, and the final approbation or censure of all our learned Reviews;—and that, any injudicious critique of such a female might involve her own reputation, (as far as a woman's reputation depends on being a critic,) but could not depreciate the worth of the writings upon which she gave her brief intelligence, and random comments. . . .

Humility, and not vanity, I know to be the cause of that sensation which my slight animadversions have excited: but this is cherishing a degree of self-contempt, which I may be pardoned for never having supposed, that any one of my "manly contemporaries in the drama" could have indulged.

Of your respected father,[2] I have said nothing that he would not approve were he living. He had too high an opinion of his own talents, to have repined under criticisms such as mine; and too much respect for other pursuits, to have blushed at being cloyed with the drama:—Yet you did me justice, when you imagined that the mere supposition of my ingratitude to him would give me pain. This was the design meditated in your accusation; for, had I either wronged or slighted his memory, you would have spared your reproach, and not have aimed it at a heart too callous to have received the impression.—But, in thus acknowledging my obligations to Mr. Colman, the elder, let it be understood, that they amounted to no more than those usual attentions which every manager of a theatre is supposed to confer, when he first selects a novice in dramatic writing, as worthy of being introduced, on his stage, to the public. . . .

Permit me, not withstanding this acquiescence in your contempt for my literary acquirements, to apprize you—that, in comparing me, as a critic, with Madame Dacier,[3] you have, inadvertently, placed yourself, as an author, in the rank with Homer. I might as well aspire to write remarks on "The Iliad," as Dacier condescend to comments on "The Mountaineers."[4] Be that as it may, I willingly subscribe myself an unlettered woman; and as willingly yield to you, all those scholastic honours, which you have so excellently described in the following play.

> I am,
> Dear Sir,
> (With too much pride at having
> been admitted a dramatist along
> with the Colmans, father and son,
> to wish to diminish the
> reputation of either,)
> Yours,
> Most truly and sincerely
> ELIZABETH INCHBALD

Notes

Selected Remarks

1. Edmond Malone (1741–1812), a noted Shakespearean scholar.

2. Arthur Brooke (d. 1562), *Tragicall Historye of Romeus and Juliet* (1562).

3. David Garrick (1717–1779), reacting to audience feeling that Romeo's sudden change in affections was "a blemish on his character," eliminated the character of Rosaline.

4. Samuel Johnson, in his edition of Shakespeare (1765).

5. Susannah Maria Cibber (1714–1766) was a leading tragic actress.

6. James Howard (fl. 1674), playwright, best known for *All Mistaken; or The Mad Couple* (1665).

7. Sir William Davenant (1606–1668), granted a patent for the Duke's Company in 1660.

8. Pierre Corneille's *La Mort de Pompée* was first performed in 1643 at Théâtre

Elizabeth Simpson Inchbald (1753–1821)

du Marais in Paris. Dryden's Cleopatra is more refined and more devoted to Antony than is Shakespeare's in *Antony and Cleopatra*. Dryden also greatly expanded the characters of Octavia, Antony's wife, and Ventidius, his loyal general.

9. Dryden's *Spanish Fryar* (1680) features a greedy, unscrupulous friar.

10. Aphra Behn (1640–1689) claimed in her popular novella *Oroonoko* (1688) that she lived in Surinam and knew her characters. The claim may be partly true but cannot be taken at face value. Pope satirized Behn for lewd writing in *Imitations of Horace*, Ep.II.i.290–291. Oroonoko is a heroic African king, kidnapped into slavery, who leads a revolt and is defeated and executed. Imoinda is his wife.

11. The actor Alexander Pope (1763–1835) specialized in tragic and sentimental roles.

12. Roscius, a Roman, is the prototypical great actor.

13. Liverpool was the center of the British slave trade, conducting 70–85 percent of it.

14. *Isabella, or The Fatal Marriage* (1694) was Thomas Southerne's other well-known tragedy.

15. William Mason (1725–1797), Gray's literary executor, published his *Life and Letters of Gray* in 1774.

16. Cibber replaced Lewis Theobald as the target in Pope's 1742 version of *The Dunciad*. Cibber, a favorite target of satirists, had particularly offended Pope by publicly mocking his unsuccessful farce *Three Hours after Marriage* (1717).

17. Sir Charles Easy, the hero, conducts adulterous affairs with his wife's maid and with Lady Graveairs; but he is reformed by his virtuous wife's forgiveness.

18. Pierre, the hero's friend, enlists him in a conspiracy to overthrow the corrupt, unjust government.

19. Otway based his play on *La Conjuration des Espagnols contre la République de Venise* (1674), which was translated into English in 1675.

20. Thomas Sheridan (1719–1788), Irish actor and manager, father of Richard Brinsley Sheridan (1751–1816).

21. Voltaire's *Mahomet, ou le Fanatisme* (1742).

22. Almeria, daughter of the King of Granada, has secretly married Alphonso, prince of an enemy state. Alphonso is captured by her father and condemned to death.

23. Charles Churchill (1731–1764), poet and satirist of theater—*The Rosciad* (1761).

24. Johnson, "Life of Congreve," in *Lives of the English Poets* (1779–1781).

25. Mrs. Sarah Siddons first acted Zara, the passionate villainess of *The Mourning Bride*, in 1776. Mrs. H. Siddons, her daughter-in-law Harriet (1783–1844), played virtuous Almeria.

26. The atheism of Edward Gibbon (1737–1794) was notorious in his own time and beyond.

27. Small private room.

28. Sheva, a comically thrifty Jew, proves to be benevolent and generous to others.

29. Bishop Gilbert Burnet (1643–1715).

30. John Bannister (1760–1836).

31. Inchbald's adaptation of August Friedrich Ferdinand von Kotzebue's *Das Kind der Liebe*, first performed in October 1798 at Covent Garden. Agatha, who has been seduced in youth by Baron Wildenhaim, is living in bitter poverty with their son,

Frederick. To relieve her distress, he attempts to rob a man who, unknown to him, is his father; and Frederick is condemned to death. They discover each other's identities, and Frederick persuades the baron to marry Agatha. *Lovers' Vows* is the play that causes so much trouble among the Bertrams in Austen's *Mansfield Park*.

Letter to George Colman the Younger

1. This "letter" is from Inchbald's edition of George Colman the Younger's *Heir at Law* (1797), in vol. 21 of *British Theatre*.

2. George Colman the Elder (1732–1794), playwright and manager of Covent Garden, who had accepted her first plays for production.

3. Madame Anne Lefèvre Dacier (1654–1720), classicist and critic, translator of Homer.

4. *The Mountaineers* was a play by Colman that Inchbald had highly criticized in an earlier volume. She refers in her last sentence to Dr. Pangloss, a ridiculous pedant in *The Heir at Law.*

MARY ROBINSON (1758–1800)

THE FACTS of Mary Robinson's life demonstrate both the social constraints placed on female behavior at the end of the eighteenth century and the ways in which a resourceful woman could maneuver within them. Disappointed first by her father and then by a gambling and womanizing husband, Robinson embarked on a successful stage career with the assistance of David Garrick. Performing the role of Perdita in *The Winter's Tale*, she caught the eye of the adolescent Prince of Wales, who promised her £20,000 upon his coming of age, but who, after ending their relationship, had to be blackmailed into honoring a much smaller version of his financial promise. Subjected to public derision and tabloid lampooning as a result of this liaison, Robinson set about recreating herself as a literary figure. Writing under a series of pseudonyms, she rode the wave of public enthusiasm for ornate Della Cruscan verse at the end of the 1780s and sustained a more enduring popularity than that enjoyed by the other participants in this literary fad.

Robinson published a juvenile volume of poems in 1775 in an effort to get her husband out of debt, but the decade of the 1790s saw her chief literary flowering. She then published novels and volumes of poetry at a prodigious rate and served as the poetry editor of the *Morning Post* in the last years of that decade. Her novels include *Vancenza, or, The Dangers of Credulity* (1792), *Walsingham, or, The Pupil of Nature* (1797), and *The Natural Daughter* (1799). Her last and most interesting volume of poetry, the *Lyrical Tales* (1800), responds to Wordsworth's *Lyrical Ballads* (1798). A three-volume *Poetical Works* (1806) appeared after her death.

Since Robinson was called "the English Sappho" by the British press, her adoption of the persona of the erotic Greek poet in *Sappho and Phaon* drew attention to her own history. In her preface, Robinson presents an excursus on the history of the sonnet and proclaims herself the standard-bearer of British prosody. In defending her own "legitimate" sonnets, she adds her voice to a debate over sonnet form carried on in the wake of a rebirth that was due in no small measure to the success of Charlotte Smith's *Elegiac Sonnets* (1784 and subsequent editions).

Sappho and Phaon. In a Series of Legitimate Sonnets, with Thoughts on Poetical Subjects, and Anecdotes of the Grecian Poetess (London: Hookham and Carpenter, 1796).

Preface to *Sappho and Phaon* (1796)

It must strike every admirer of poetical compositions, that the modern sonnet, concluding with two lines, winding up the sentiment of the whole,
confines the poet's fancy, and frequently occasions an abrupt termination
of a beautiful and interesting picture; and that the ancient, or what is generally denominated, the LEGITIMATE SONNET, may be carried on in a series
of sketches, composing, in parts, one historical or imaginary subject, and
forming in the whole a complete and connected story.

With this idea, I have ventured to compose the following collection;
not presuming to offer them as imitations of PETRARCH, but as specimens
of that species of sonnet writing, so seldom attempted in the English language; though adopted by that sublime Bard, whose Muse produced the
grand epic of Paradise Lost, and the humbler effusion, which I produce as
an example of the measure to which I allude, and which is termed by the
most classical writers, the *legitimate sonnet.*

> O Nightingale, that on yon bloomy spray
>   Warblest at eve, when all the woods are still,
>   Thou with fresh hope the lover's heart dost fill,
> While the jolly hours lead on propitious May.
> Thy liquid notes that close the eye of day
>   First heard before the shallow cuccoo's bill,
>   Portend success in love; O if Jove's will
> Have link'd that amorous power to thy soft lay,
>   Now timely sing, ere the rude bird of hate
> Foretel my hopeless doom in some grove nigh,
>   As thou from year to year hast sung too late
> For my relief, yet hadst no reason why:
>   Whether the Muse, or Love call thee his mate,
> Both them I serve, and of their train am I.[1]

To enumerate the variety of authors who have written sonnets of all
descriptions, would be endless; indeed few of them deserve notice: and
where, among the heterogeneous mass of insipid and laboured efforts, sometimes a bright gem sheds lustre on the page of poesy, it scarcely excites
attention, owing to the disrepute into which sonnets are fallen. So little is
rule attended to by many, who profess the art of poetry, that I have seen a
composition of more than thirty lines, ushered into the world under the
name of Sonnet, and that, from the pen of a writer, whose classical taste
ought to have avoided such a misnomer.

Mary Robinson (1758–1800)

Doctor Johnson describes a Sonnet, as "a short poem, consisting of four-teen lines, of which the rhymes are adjusted by a particular rule." He further adds, "It has not been used by any man of eminence since MILTON."★ [2]

Sensible of the extreme difficulty I shall have to encounter, in offering to the world a little wreath, gathered in that path, which, even the best poets have thought it dangerous to tread; and knowing that the English language is, of all others, the least congenial to such an undertaking, (for, I believe, that the construction of this kind of sonnet was originally in the Italian, where the vowels are used almost every other letter,) I only point out the track where more able pens may follow with success; and where the most classical beauties may be adopted, and drawn forth with peculiar advantage.

Sophisticated sonnets are so common, for every rhapsody of rhyme, from six lines to sixty comes under that denomination, that the eye fre-quently turns from this species of poem with disgust. Every school-boy, every romantic scribbler, thinks a sonnet a task of little difficulty. From this ignorance in some, and vanity in others, we see the monthly and diurnal publications abounding with ballads, odes, elegies, epitaphs, and allegories, the non-descript ephemera from the heated brains of self-important poet-asters, all ushered into notice under the appellation of SONNET!

I confess myself such an enthusiastic votary of the Muse, that any in-novation which seems to threaten even the least of her established rights,

★Since the death of Doctor Johnson a few ingenious and elegant writers have composed sonnets, according to the rules described by him: of their merits the public will judge, and the *literati* decide. The following quotations are given as the opinions of living authors, respecting the legitimate sonnet.

"The little poems which are here called Sonnets, have, I believe, no very just claim to that title: but they consist of fourteen lines, and appear to me no improper vehicle for a single sentiment. I am told, and I read it as the opinion of very good judges, that the legitimate sonnet is ill calculated for our language. The specimens Mr. Hayley has given, though they form a strong exception, prove no more, than that the difficulties of the attempt vanish before uncommon powers." *Mrs. C. Smith's Preface to her Elegiac Sonnets.* [3]

Likewise in the preface to a volume of very charming poems, (among which are many *legitimate sonnets*) by Mr. William Kendall, of Exeter, the following opinion is given of the Italian rythm, which constitutes the legitimate sonnet: he describes it as—

"A chaste and elegant model, which the most enlightened poet of our own country disdained not to contemplate. Amidst the degeneracy of modern taste, if the studies of a Milton have lost their attraction, legitimate sonnets, enriched by varying pauses, and an elaborate recurrence of rhyme, still assert their superiority over those tasteless and inartificial productions, which assume the name, without evincing a single characteristic of distinguishing modulation." [4]

makes me tremble, lest that chaos of dissipated pursuits which has too long been growing like an overwhelming shadow, and menacing the lustre of intellectual light, should, aided by the idleness of some, and the profligacy of others, at last obscure the finer mental powers, and reduce the dignity of talents to the lowest degradation.

As poetry has the power to raise, so has it also the magic to refine. The ancients considered the art of such importance, that before they led forth their heroes to the most glorious enterprizes, they animated them by the recital of grand and harmonious compositions. The wisest scrupled not to reverence the invocations of minds, graced with the charm of numbers:[5] so mystically fraught are powers said to be, which look beyond the surface of events, that an admired and classical writer,* describing the inspirations of the MUSE, thus expresses his opinion:

> So when remote futurity is brought
> Before the keen inquiry of her thought,
> A terrible sagacity informs
> The Poet's heart, he looks to distant storms,
> He hears the thunder ere the tempest low'rs,
> And, arm'd with strength surpassing human pow'rs,
> Seizes events as yet unknown to man,
> And darts his soul into the dawning plan.
> Hence in a Roman mouth the graceful name
> Of Prophet and of Poet was the same,
> Hence British poets too the priesthood shar'd,
> And ev'ry hallow'd druid—was a bard.

That poetry ought to be cherished as a national ornament, cannot be more strongly exemplified than in the simple fact, that, in those centuries when the poets' laurels have been most generously fostered in Britain, the minds and manners of the natives have been most polished and enlightened. Even the language of a country refines into purity by the elegance of numbers: the strains of WALLER have done more to effect that, than all the labours of monkish pedantry, since the days of druidical mystery and superstition.

Though different minds are variously affected by the infinite diversity of harmonious effusions, there are, I believe, very few that are wholly insensible to the powers of poetic compositions. Cold must that bosom be, which can resist the magical versification of Eloisa to Abelard;[6] and torpid to all the more exalted sensations of the soul is that being, whose ear is not

*Cowper.

delighted by the grand and sublime effusions of the divine Milton! The romantic chivalry of Spencer vivifies the imagination; while the plaintive sweetness of Collins soothes and penetrates the heart.[7] How much would Britain have been deficient in a comparison with other countries on the scale of intellectual grace, had these poets never existed! yet it is a melancholy truth, that here, where the attributes of genius have been diffused by the liberal hand of nature, almost to prodigality, there has not been, during a long series of years, the smallest mark of public distinction bestowed on literary talents. Many individuals, whose works are held in the highest estimation, now that their ashes sleep in the sepulchre, were, when living, suffered to languish, and even to perish, in obscure poverty: as if it were the peculiar fate of genius, to be neglected while existing, and only honoured when the consciousness of inspiration is vanished for ever.

The ingenious mechanic has the gratification of seeing his labours patronized, and is rewarded for his invention while he has the powers of enjoying its produce. But the Poet's life is one perpetual scene of warfare: he is assailed by envy, stung by malice, and wounded by the fastidious comments of concealed assassins. The more eminently beautiful his compositions are, the larger is the phalanx he has to encounter; for the enemies of genius are multitudinous.

It is the interest of the ignorant and powerful, to suppress the effusions of enlightened minds: when only monks could write, and nobles read, authority rose triumphant over right; and the slave, spell-bound in ignorance, hugged his fetters without repining. It was then that the best powers of reason lay buried like the gem in the dark mine; by a slow and tedious progress they have been drawn forth, and must, ere long, diffuse an universal lustre: for that era is rapidly advancing, when talents will tower like an unperishable column, while the globe will be strewed with the wrecks of superstition.

As it was the opinion of the ancients, that poets possessed the powers of prophecy, the name was consequently held in the most unbounded veneration. In less remote periods the bard has been publicly distinguished; princes and priests have bowed before the majesty of genius: Petrarch was crowned with laurels, the noblest diadem, in the Capitol of Rome: his admirers were liberal; his contemporaries were just; and his name will stand upon record, with the united and honourable testimony of his own talents, and the generosity of his country.

It is at once a melancholy truth, and a national disgrace, that this Island, so profusely favoured by nature, should be marked, of all enlightened countries, as the most neglectful of literary merit! and I will venture to believe, that there are both POETS and PHILOSOPHERS, now living in Britain, who, had they been born in any *other* clime, would have been honoured with the proudest distinctions, and immortalized to the latest posterity.

I cannot conclude these opinions without paying tribute to the talents of my illustrious country-women; who, unpatronized by courts, and unprotected by the powerful, persevere in the paths of literature, and ennoble themselves by the unperishable lustre of MENTAL PRE-EMINENCE!

Notes

1. John Milton, Sonnet I, "O Nightingale!" (1630).
2. Samuel Johnson, *A Dictionary of the English Language* (1755).
3. Charlotte Smith's *Elegiac Sonnets* appeared in 1784 and by 1796 had reached its seventh edition. William Hayley (1745–1820) was a poet and patron of Smith, William Cowper, and William Blake.
4. *Poems by William Kendall, Exeter* (1793).
5. "Numbers" here refers to measured rhythm in verse.
6. *Eloisa to Abelard*, Alexander Pope's 1717 version of the tragic love story of Heloise and Abelard, was extremely popular.
7. Edmund Spenser (1552?–1599); William Collins (1721–1759).

ELIZABETH HAMILTON
(1758-1816)

ELIZABETH HAMILTON was born in Belfast of a Scottish father and an Irish mother, both of whom died by the time she was nine years old. She was raised by a paternal aunt and attended a mixed school until she was thirteen. She was further educated through correspondence with her brother Charles, who carried out military duty in India and translated one of the chief commentaries on Muslim law. Hamilton moved to London to be with her brother in 1790 and wrote her first novel, *Letters of a Hindoo Rajah* (1796), which in its advocacy of female competency introduces a feminist strain that runs through nearly all her published works. Hamilton was active in philanthropy, most notably in the establishment of a female house of industry in Edinburgh, where she moved in 1804. She was held in high esteem by her contemporaries and counted among her female friends Joanna Baillie and Maria Edgeworth. Plagued for years with gout, she was eventually further disabled by an eye disease.

Perhaps Hamilton's most interesting literary work was her *Memoirs of Modern Philosophers* (1800), which caricatures the Godwin circle (with the exception of Mary Wollstonecraft) and Godwinian ideas. In addition to three novels, Hamilton published the influential *Letters on Education* (1801), which argued that mothers should raise boys and girls equally, and *Letters Addressed to the Daughter of a Nobleman on the Formation of the Religious and the Moral Principle* (1806), based on her experience as a tutor in an aristocrat's household.

According to Elizabeth Benger's *Memoirs of the Late Mrs. Elizabeth Hamilton* (1818), Hamilton's essay series *The Breakfast Table* was composed for a periodical paper which she and several of her literary friends hoped to establish; this scheme was eventually abandoned. In these essays Hamilton adopts the persona of a country gentleman. The excerpt included here, number 2, contrasts the characters and literary talents of Samuel Johnson

273

and Joseph Addison, arguing that moral character and literary brilliance do not necessarily coincide.

"The Breakfast Table," No. 2, from Elizabeth Benger, *Memoirs of the late Mrs. Elizabeth Hamilton* (London: Longman, Hurst, Rees, 1818).

From "The Breakfast Table" (1818)

The title GREAT MORALIST has been long and universally applied to Johnson; but, however highly we may estimate his merit, and however useful we may, on the whole, deem his writings, the epithet Great may, perhaps justly, be objected to.

To be *great* implies more of eminent superiority than can often be claimed. The man who is a great, must be an almost perfect moralist; but in Johnson, if there is much to be applauded, there is much also which may mislead. He viewed life with a keen and scrutinizing eye; but his imagination, morbid and irritable, distorted every object from its true place, and expanded his own gloom over the whole surface of creation. We should scarcely select him as the guide of our journey, who thought only of hurricanes and of quicksands—who saw in every shadow an assassin, in every passing cloud an overwhelming torrent, in every quiet stream an unfathomable abyss.

Among the striking features of Johnson's page, none are more obvious than a propensity to aggravate the ills of life—a fixed habit of depreciating all human excellence. If Johnson is to be credited, we shall no longer retain a friend than whilst self has neither claims nor wishes with which friendship can interfere. If we rise in the world, what was once affection is now envy; if we fall, it is contempt. The fidelity of a mistress may be expected till some more splendid admirer shall approach; and that son is gifted with no common portion of filial regard, who shall fail to number the wrinkles on his father's brow. The poor man pants for riches, whilst the rich man, in the vain hope to purchase happiness, squanders his wealth around. He who is idle sinks into joyless languor; and he who is busy feels each hour a torment, till he shall again be at rest.

Such are the views of life with which Johnson so often presents us—views, at once contrary to truth and to religion. He who sees nothing in the being with which he is endowed but the unnumbered modifications which wretchedness may assume, will be inclined little to value the gift itself, and not much to regard the hand which gave.

As a moralist, the character of Addison is far more unexceptionable. He contemplated the scenes of life without prejudice, and described them with fidelity. He laughed at the follies of mankind, and rebuked their vices; but their virtues he described with ardour, and threw every colour around them which could either attract or delight.

Few persons have read the *Spectator* without improvement, both in virtue and in wisdom; but how many have laid down the *Rambler*, disgusted with the state of existence in which they were placed; more indifferent than before to the well-being of their species; more cold, more hardened than ever to all the charities of life.[1]

It is not my present intention to discuss the general principles of Addison and of Johnson, I mean to view them as authors rather than as moralists; and to compare them as to style, rather than as to matter. I have yet thought proper to prefix these few observations, lest it should be supposed, that in admiring the writer I preferred the man.

The subject of my discussion is not new, unless that may be considered new which has been laid aside till it is forgotten. It is, however, worthy of revival; the writers of the present day having agreed to call feebleness nature, and to stigmatise strength of language with the charge of turgidity. That there is policy in this conduct is not to be denied; for every man can be feeble; but to combine elegance with force is the lot of those alone who, to natural vigour, have added the labour of cultivation.

Whatever may be said of his imitators, the characteristic of Addison himself is not feebleness, but want of positive energy. He has not the prowess of a giant, yet he is no dwarf. At the same time, a careful examination of his style will produce little else than a string of negatives. He is not coarse; he is not harsh; he is not vapid; but expression eminently beautiful, language modulated to positive harmony, thoughts pointed and energetic, have seldom proceeded from his pen. The merit of Johnson, on the other hand, is far beyond negative: his conceptions are forcible, his numbers varied and sonorous, and his phraseology has a fertility and precision, which have rarely been equalled, and never excelled.[2]

These two writers shall speak for themselves. For a moment let me compare them with their contemporaries and their imitators. Addison's papers, in the Spectator, are readily distinguished from those of his associates; but it is rather from the assiduousness of care, than from pre-excellence of manner. Steele is, in general, vulgar, loose, and slovenly, perpetually offending against decency, good manners, and good sense: but where he does take the trouble to think, and attends to the expression of his thought, he is scarcely to be distinguished from his more celebrated coadjutor. Addison's papers★ are not known from one or two sentences, or from particular beauty of parts; but from the correctness of the whole. His mind was elegant, his observation acute, and his ear rejected whatever was harsh in composition; yet he rarely attained to positive excellence of manner. He had nothing which was peculiarly his own—nothing which others laboured for without attaining. The case of Johnson is widely different: it is allowed by all, by adversaries as well as admirers, that his style is marked and peculiar: the number of his imitators is almost countless; yet, perhaps, not one of them ever put three sentences together, without laying himself open to detection. Hawkesworth, in the *Adventurer*, approaches nearer to the manner of Johnson than any other man has done; but, though nearest, he is yet far distant.[3] If Hawkesworth wrote the first *Adventurer*, he has a claim to be excepted from the above assertion; for it is throughout Johnsonian; but that he wrote this number may well be doubted. Johnson's contributions to the work were numerous; and though he ordinarily assumes the signature *T*, all the papers marked *T* are not his; and others, which have no distinguishing mark, proceeded from his pen. Independent of internal evidence, there is a probability that this paper was Johnson's. His regard for Hawkesworth is well known; and the solicitude he at various times expressed for the success of the *Adventurer* was great. The composition of Prefaces, Dedications, and Introductory Essays, was Johnson's peculiar forte. Is it, then, unlikely he should give assistance to a friend in the most difficult part of his labour—in the production of an impressive Exordium?

Whatever may be the case with respect to this individual paper, if Hawkesworth, for a moment, wound up his strength to the pitch of his great master, his nerves became again speedily relaxed. Allowing him a general resemblance to Johnson, it is that resemblance which the miniature bears to the man: the features may be similar, but the size and dignity of the figure are lost.

If Hawkesworth followed Johnson with a feeble pace, perhaps it cannot be said of any other man, that he even entered on his path. To him who possesses a dictionary of the English language, the selection of rumbling polysyllables is a task of little labour; and to pile up loads of cumbrous epithet is not less easy. This has frequently been done; and this has been called an imitation of Johnson: but the occasional use of uncouth words is

---

★It must be remembered, that the humour of Addison is not meant to be depreciated: in that he is unrivalled.

Johnson's vice, and not his excellence; and never did any writer use epithets with an appropriation so exact and forcible.

Addison was well acquainted with polite literature; his judgment was sound and his taste correct; but for the characteristic of energy his writings will be examined in vain. His perceptions were distinct; his language flowing and easy; but with that glowing ardour, that towering and animated spirit, which distinguish Johnson, his mind was unimpressed. Though admirably delicate in passages of humour, his stores of imagination were not great or varied: neatness of elucidation, rather than splendour of ornament, was what he aimed at, and what he attained. His style may be called truly Attic, if, according to some, clearness of expression, and a careful selection of words, were the sole characteristics of the Attic style. We may say of Addison, as was said of Demosthenes by Cicero, that he was one *"quo ne Athenas ipsas quidem magis credo fuisse Atticas."*[4]

Far different from these are the characteristics of Johnson. He conceived with ardour, and never failed to infuse his feelings into those whom he addressed. To excel was his passion; and, from the earliest period of his life, he was, on all occasions, determined "to do his best." Whatever was his subject—a taylor's thimble, or a butcher's block, he clothed it with dignity and importance; and he could detail the composition of a pudding with more force than another could picture the horrors of a battle. His reading was miscellaneous and extensive; his memory, in a high degree, tenacious, and his efforts to improve incessant. If he read much, he reflected more; and his mind became a store of imagery, of language, and of observation.

It is most clear that Johnson's energy never sunk into the languid tone of ordinary existence. He was at all times himself; and hence, though never little on great occasions, on little occasions he might be sometimes too great. If Addison, on the contrary, was thinking better than other men, he was feeling as they felt. Johnson's feelings were as peculiar and as elevated as his thoughts.

What is eloquence but "the effusion of an animated mind?" The elaborate efforts of cold industry may construct an harmonious sentence, or carefully select a well-adapted epithet; but the vigour which is not felt can never be inspired. The style of a calm and equable temper is naturally contracted: when once the thought is expressed, the desired object is complete, and the author proceeds in his course. Eloquence, on the contrary, is expansive. We unwillingly relinquish that by which we are interested and occupied. Simply to express the idea is not enough; we dwell on it, repeat it under varied forms, and scarce pause till the powers of diction are exhausted.

Notes

1. The *Spectator* was a daily periodical produced jointly by Richard Steele and Joseph Addison in 1711–1712. It was resumed briefly by Addison in 1714. Samuel Johnson published the *Rambler*, a series of periodical essays, from 1750 to 1752.

2. "Numbers" here refers to measured rhythm in verse.

3. *The Adventurer*, by John Hawkesworth (1753).

4. I.e., I believe that not even Athens itself was more Attic [than Demosthenes] in his style.

HANNAH WEBSTER FOSTER
(1758–1840)

Hannah Webster Foster's novel *The Coquette* (1797) was one of the two best-selling American works of the 1790s. Born on September 10, 1758, Hannah was sent to boarding school at age four, after the death of her mother. In 1785 she married the Reverend John Foster, with whom she had six children. She published only one other book, *The Boarding School* (1798), but encouraged the writing careers of two of her daughters, Eliza Lanesford Cushing and Harriet Vaughan Cheney.

A set of didactic essays cast as a novel, *The Boarding School* brings to the forefront what seems to be one of the most important critical issues for Foster. She sees women's writing as a tool for the creation in the new republic of female communities impervious to the necessary separations that the duties of marriage and family entail. The first part of *The Boarding School* presents the academic and social precepts of Mrs. Williams, who runs a small school for girls. The second part comprises letters that pass among the girls after they leave their school. The mere fact that they keep in touch becomes almost as important as the content of their letters, which ranges from literary criticism of Pope, Richardson, Hester Chapone, and Madame de Sévigné to thoughts on marriage and the joys of solitude. Indeed, in *The Coquette*, the heroine Eliza's failure to write, which leads to her losing touch with the women who are trying to save her from the worthless Sanford, is depicted as both a reason for and a marker of her downfall. Given Foster's attitude toward women's writing, it becomes all the more poignant that she herself was silent after *The Boarding School*.

The Boarding School; or, Lessons of a Preceptress to her Pupils (Boston: I. Thomas and E. T. Andrews, 1798).

From *The Boarding School* (1798)

Being assembled, this afternoon, Mrs. Williams thus resumed her discourse.

"Reading is so common a part of education, that the value of it is not duly estimated, nor the manner of performing it, sufficiently attended to.

It is not the mere propriety of pronunciation, accent, and cadence, which constitutes good reading. You must enter into the spirit of the subject, and feel interested in the matter, before you can profit by the exercise.

"But you are so well acquainted with the manner of reading, that the quality of books most worthy of your perusal is the only point on which I need to enlarge.

"Romances, the taste of former times, are now so far out of vogue, that it is hardly necessary to warn you against them. They exhibit the spirit of chivalry, knight-errantry, and extravagant folly, which prevailed in the age they depict. But they are not interesting; nor can they be pleasing to the correct taste and refined delicacy of the present day.

"Novels are the favourite, and the most dangerous kind of reading, now adopted by the generality of young ladies. I say dangerous, because the influence, which, with very few exceptions, they must have upon the passions of youth, bears an unfavourable aspect on their purity and virtue. The style in which they are written is commonly captivating; and the luxuriance of the descriptions with which they abound, extremely agreeable to the sprightly fancy, and high expectations of the inexperienced and unreflecting. Their romantic pictures of love, beauty, and magnificence, fill the imagination with ideas which lead to impure desires, a vanity of exterior charms, and a fondness for show and dissipation, by no means consistent with that simplicity, modesty, and chastity, which should be the constant inmates of the female breast. They often pervert the judgment, mislead the affections, and blind the understanding.

[This point is illustrated with the cautionary tale of Juliana, whose reading of novels misleads her into rejecting a worthy man for a worthless officer who courts her with romantic extravagance.]

"But I would not be understood to condemn all novels indiscriminately; though great prudence is necessary to make a useful selection. Some of them are fraught with sentiment; convey lessons for moral improvement; and exhibit striking pictures of virtue rewarded; and of vice, folly, and indiscretion punished; which may prove encouragements to imitate, or warnings to avoid similar practices. I shall not descend to particulars. Those, which are sanctioned by the general voice of delicacy and refinement, may be allowed a reading; yet none should engross your minds, to the neglect of more important objects; nor be suffered to monopolize too large a portion of your time.

"Novels are a kind of light reading, on which the imagination feasts, while the more substantial food which is requisite to the nourishment of the understanding, is either untasted or undigested. Imagination is a sportive faculty, which should be curbed by the reins of prudence and judgment. Its sallies are delightful in youth, provided they be not too excursive . . .

"But among your hours devoted to reading, history must not be without a place. Here an extensive field of ages and generations, which have gone before you, is opened to your view. Here your curiosity may be gratified by a retrospection of events, which, by conducting your thoughts to remotest climes and periods, interests and enlarges the mind. Here the various revolutions, the rise, fall, and dismemberment of ancient kingdoms and states may be traced to the different springs of action, in which they originated. Hence you may gain a competent acquaintance with human nature in all its modifications, from the most rude and barbarous, to the most civilized and polished stages of society. This is a species of knowledge, which will not only be of constant use to you, in the government of your own temper and manners, but highly ornamental in your intercourse with the polite and learned world . . .

"When you read for mere amusement, (which should seldom happen) be careful not to corrupt and vitiate your taste by frothy and illiberal performances, which will degrade the dignity and sully the purity of your minds. That time is very greatly mispent, which is bestowed in reading what can yield no instruction. Not a moment's attention should be given to books which afford not some degree of improvement. Always have an eye, therefore, to profit, as well as to pleasure. Remember that youth is the seed-time of life. You are now to cultivate that knowledge, which future years must ripen. Free from those domestic cares, which will engross and occupy your minds, when placed at the head of families, a most inestimable price is now put into your hands to get wisdom. Now you may learn; then you must practice.

"Now, therefore, lay up in store some provision for every exigence, some embellishment for every station . . .

"Writing is productive both of pleasure and improvement. It is a source of entertainment which enlarges the mental powers more, perhaps, than any other. The mind is obliged to exertion for materials to supply the pen. Hence it collects new stores of knowledge, and is enriched by its own labours. It imperceptibly treasures up the ideas, which the hand impresses. An opportunity is furnished of reviewing our sentiments before they are exposed; and we have the privilege of correcting or expunging such as are erroneous. For this purpose, you will find it a good method to collect and write your thoughts upon any subject that occurs; for by repeatedly arranging and revising your expressions and opinions, you may daily improve them, and learn to think and reason properly on every occasion. By this mean you may likewise provide yourselves with a fund of matter for future use, which, without this assistance, the memory would not retain. It will be of great service to note down in your common-place book such particulars as you may judge worth remembering, with your own observations upon them. This will be a kind of amusement which will exercise your thinking powers at the time, and, by recurring to it afterwards, it may afford you many useful hints.

"The frequent use of the pen is calculated to refine and enlarge your understandings. Have you any talent at composition? it will be increased by cultivation.

"Neglect no opportunity, therefore, which your leisure affords, of delighting your friends, and accomplishing yourselves by the exercise of your genius in this way.

"Thrice blessed are we, the happy daughters of this land of liberty, where the female mind is unshackled by the restraints of tyrannical custom, which in many other regions confines the exertions of genius to the usurped powers of lordly man! Here virtue, merit, and abilities are properly estimated under whatever form they appear. Here the widely extended fields of literature court attention; and the American fair are invited to cull the flowers, and cultivate the expanding laurel.

"But the species of writing, which is open to every capacity, and ornamental to every station, is the epistolary. This, between particular friends, is highly agreeable and interesting. It is a method of interchanging sentiments, and of enjoying intercourse with those from whom you are far removed, which is a happy substitute for personal conversation. In a correspondence of this sort, all affectation, formality, and bombast should be laid aside.

"Ease, frankness, simplicity, and sincerity should be its leading traits. Yet let not your letters be composed of mere sounding terms, and verbose egotism; but intermix sentiment with expression, in such a manner as may be improving as well as pleasing. Letters of friendship should conduce no less to the advantage than entertainment of the person addressed; and mere cursory letters, of general acquaintance, must, at least, be written with propriety and accuracy. The formation of the characters, the spelling, the punctuation, as well as the style and sense, must be attended to.

"Never omit noticing the receipt of letters, unless you mean to affront the writers. Not to answer a letter, without being able to assign some special reason for the neglect, is equally unpardonable as to keep silence when conversation is addressed to you in person.

"By habituating yourselves to writing, what may, at first, appear a task, will become extremely pleasant. Refuse not, then, to improve this part of your education, especially by your frequent and dutifully affectionate epistles to your parents, when absent from them. Express your gratitude for their care, and convince them it has not been lost upon you.

"Always employ your pens upon something useful and refined. Let no light or loose compositions occupy your time and thoughts; but remember that what you utter in this way is in some measure the picture of your hearts. Virtue forbid, that this favourite employment should be disgraced by impurity, indelicacy, or the communication of vicious and ignoble sentiments.

"One of the sages of antiquity being asked why he was so long in writing his opinion, replied, "I am writing for futurity."

"Your characters during life, and even when you shall sleep in the dust, may rest on the efforts of your pens. Beware then how you employ them. Let not the merit of your attainments in this noble art be degraded by improper subjects for its exercise. Suffer not the expectation of secrecy to induce you to indulge your pens upon subjects, which you would blush to have exposed. In this way your characters may be injured, and your happiness destroyed."

MARY WOLLSTONECRAFT
(1759–1797)

HAVING EXPERIENCED poverty and the abuse of an alcoholic father, Mary Wollstonecraft at nineteen set out to earn her own livelihood—first as companion, then as teacher in a school she organized with her sisters. This experience stimulated her first book, *Thoughts on the Education of Daughters* (1787), which she sold for ten guineas. While serving as a governess in Ireland, Wollstonecraft wrote her first novel, *Mary, A Fiction* (1788), based in part on the life of her friend Fanny Blood, who had died in childbirth. In pursuit of a literary career, Wollstonecraft took a position in London as editorial assistant to Joseph Johnson, publisher of the *Analytical Review*, for which she wrote articles such as the reviews included here. In this period she also published two books for children, *Original Stories from Real Life* (1788) and *The Female Reader* (1789), and two translations.

Excited by political conversations in the group around Johnson, Wollstonecraft wrote *A Vindication of the Rights of Men* (1790), a response to Edmund Burke's conservative *Reflections on the Revolution in France* (1790), and her most famous work, *A Vindication of the Rights of Woman* (1792). Unhappy when the married painter Henry Fuseli rebuffed her, she went to Paris to study the Revolution, recording her views in *An Historical and Moral View of the Origin and Progress of the French Revolution* (1794). There she fell in love with the American Gilbert Imlay, who fathered her daughter Fanny. To get rid of her, Imlay sent Mary to Scandinavia on a business trip, about which she published an account in *Letters Written during a Short Residence in Sweden, Norway, and Denmark* (1796). Twice she attempted suicide over Imlay's rejection.

Later she married William Godwin, father of her daughter Mary, who as Mary Shelley would become famous herself as an author. During this pregnancy Wollstonecraft started a second novel, *The Wrongs of Woman: or, Maria*, left unfinished at her death from childbirth and published by Godwin in 1798. After her death Godwin also published a memoir of his wife, as well as her letters to Imlay and to himself.

Mary, a Fiction (London: J. Johnson, 1788); *The Analytical Review* (1789–1790); "On Poetry and Our Relish for the Beauties of Nature," *Monthly*

Magazine (April 1797); *The Wrongs of Woman: or, Maria* in *The Posthumous Works of Mary Wollstonecraft*, 4 vols., ed. William Godwin (London: J. Johnson, 1798); *The Collected Letters of Mary Wollstonecraft*, ed. Ralph M. Wardle (Ithaca: Cornell University Press, 1979).

Advertisement to *Mary, a Fiction* (1788)

In delineating the Heroine of this Fiction, the Author attempts to develop a character different from those generally portrayed. This woman is neither a Clarissa, a Lady G—, nor a Sophie.[1]—It would be vain to mention the various modifications of these models, as it would to remark, how widely artists wander from nature, when they copy the originals of great masters. They catch the gross parts; but the subtile spirit evaporates; and not having the just ties, affectation disgusts, when grace was expected to charm.

Those compositions only have power to delight, and carry us willing captives, where the soul of the author is exhibited, and animates the hidden springs. Lost in a pleasing enthusiasm, they live in the scenes they represent; and do not measure their steps in a beaten track, solicitous to gather expected flowers, and bind them in a wreath, according to the prescribed rules of art.

These chosen few, wish to speak for themselves, and not to be an echo—even of the sweetest sounds—or the reflector of the most sublime beams. The* paradise they ramble in, must be of their own creating—or the prospect soon grows insipid, and not varied by a vivifying principle, fades and dies.

In an artless tale, without episodes, the mind of a woman, who has thinking powers is displayed. The female organs have been thought too weak for this arduous employment; and experience seems to justify the assertion. Without arguing physically about *possibilities*—in a fiction, such a being may be allowed to exist; whose grandeur is derived from the operations of its own faculties, not subjugated to opinion; but drawn by the individual from the original source.

Selected Reviews from *The Analytical Review* (1790)

ART. XLIII. *Euphemia.* By Mrs. Charlotte Lennox. In Four Volumes 12mo. 957 p. Pr. 12s. sewed. Cadell. 1790.

---

*1 here give the Reviewers an opportunity of being very witty about the Paradise of Fools, &c.

As a great number of pernicious and frivolous novels are daily pub-lished, which only serve to heat and corrupt the minds of young women, and plunge them (by co-operating with their amusements) into that con-tinual dissipation of thought which renders all serious employment irksome, we open a novel with a certain degree of pleasure, when a respectable name appears in the title-page. This was the case with the present work; but as we advanced, so many cold romantic flights struck us in the main story, and still more in the episodes, that we could not avoid ranking it with those novels, which, perhaps, tend to lead the female mind further astray from nature and common sense, than even the tales of chivalry to which Mrs. L. has allowed no quarter.[1] Her notions of female delicacy and reserve are carried as far as any sentimental French writer ever pushed them; and though this prudery might arise from a different cause, yet it may be equally baneful in its effects, and banish true frankness and delicacy of mind, to make room for that false enervating refinement, which eradicates not only simplicity, but all dignity of character. We will appeal to any of our readers whether they would not think that woman very affected, or *ridiculously* squeamish, who could promise to give her hand to her lover one moment, and the next scruple to admit him to a tête-à-tête breakfast. But if the ladies are to be cold and *indisposed to the marriage state*, the gentlemen are sufficiently ardent; weep, kneel and faint in the most impassioned manner. With respect to Mr. Harley, who is termed a hero for acting as any man would have done, that had the least spark of honour in his soul, to say noth-ing of religion, we think no knight of ancient days ever cherished a more *refined* passion, or more accidentally gained his bride. If the ladies, for such artificial beings must not be familiarly called women, are something like the cherubim under the organ-loft, soft, simple, and good, the gentlemen, and more particularly the poor husbands, are painted in stronger colours, and several of them appear to be drawn from the life by a faithful feminine pencil: the maternal affection and solicitude, which takes place of every other, is much of the same cast, blind and weak; but the virtue of Mrs. Freeman towers above her sex—Lucretia[2] was a washerwoman to her!

In speaking thus of Mrs. L.'s production, which we were sorry to find so much on a par with the general run of novels, we do not mean to in-sinuate that it has not sufficient merit to come forward in the second class; nay, we wish to add, that the information it contains respecting America is both curious and entertaining. . . . [3]

ART. XVII. *The Life of Daniel De Foe.* By George Chalmers, Esq. Royal 8vo.
86 p. Price 3s. 6d. sewed. Stockdale. 1790.

The life of such an amusing writer as De Foe naturally excites curiosity,
and becomes an interesting subject of literary enquiry; especially, when a
list of his works, set in battle-array, show the vigour of his understanding,
and the versatility of his talents. But his sensible biographer appears to have
had a nobler end in view than to gratify harmless curiosity or rational enquiry, for he industriously endeavours, by substantiating facts, and by pertinent illustrative reflections, to wipe off some ignominious spots which
have sullied the memory of the author of Robinson Crusoe. Amongst other
aspersions, it has long been a prevailing opinion, that the papers, which were
supposed to form the ground-work of this very entertaining novel, had been
surreptitiously obtained of Alexander Selkirk. . . . [4]

De Foe has also been called a foreigner, by common fame; and this
rumour he may have countenanced; or, at least, not contradicted; for few
men who have raised themselves to eminence have had sufficient strength
of mind to advert to the obscurity which clouded their birth, though their
mounting above it, is, perhaps, the strongest proof of intellectual power and
decided superiority. The thick atmosphere of prejudice, which surrounds us
all, gives its colour even to the most original thoughts and characters; and
when Shakespear and Milton, in their daring flights, could not always soar
into purer air, we should make some allowance for Swift and De Foe, though
the former condescended to prevarication to avoid the name of an *Irishman*;
and the latter to alter his name, lest his origin should be traced to the sham-
bles; for it is at length known, with sufficient certainty, that he was the son
of James Foe, of the parish of St. Giles, Cripplegate, citizen and *butcher.*

To attempt to give an abridged account of De Foe's life, without alluding to his multifarious productions, would be an arduous task; for, as is
usually the case in the literary world, the accidents which attended and
followed their publication, produced the most important events, which the
biographer could collect, to characterize the man. But, as merely the enu-
meration of them would carry us far beyond our limits, and still not be
very satisfactory to our readers, we must refer them to the work itself for
information and entertainment, and they will soon discover that it is written with considerable judgment and taste.

Upon the whole, it appears that De Foe, through a long tumultuous life,
exercised his uncommon talents to supply his necessities, without stooping

to meanness; but, as he often wrote on the spur of the occasion, many of his popular works died with him; and those that survived the author a little while, were kept alive by the merit of his other productions, raised on a more solid foundation. It is to be lamented, that many original as well as useful thoughts, interspersed in polemic and political writings, thrown out with spirit, and characteristic of that sharp shrewdness, which argumentative warmth naturally produces, should be lost; but the minutiae of quarrels, which set whole nations in a blaze, becoming as tedious as a thrice-told joke, when clashing interests no longer feed the flame, who will wade through the mouldering rubbish in search of a few scattered diamonds, though of the purest water?

De Foe is described 'as a middle-sized spare man, of a brown complexion, and dark brown hair, having a hook'd nose, a sharp chin, grey eyes, and a large mole near his mouth.' And, of his mind, a contemporary seems to have a just idea. P. 64. 'John Dunton, who personally knew our author, describes him, in 1705, as a man of good parts and clear sense; of a conversation, ingenious and brisk; of a spirit, enterprising and bold, but of little prudence, with good nature and real honesty.'[5] His works still more forcibly paint his character. In them he appears to be a man of quick feelings and strong discernment, who knew the human heart, and did not always view its frailties with a serious or patient countenance. Every where glows that energy of mind, which leads us to expect rather comprehension of thought, and simple force of diction, than those studied graces, which may please the fastidious ear; but seldom reach the heart or inform the understanding. De Foe, probably, had not time or taste sufficient to polish the firm texture of his thoughts; or to soften his satires, which were sometimes as coarse as they were forcible; but it may be made a question whether delicacy of taste and vigour of conception are not incompatible; or, at least, that when a man is eager to convince or instruct, he may be allowed to consider *the graces* as subordinate, without deserving censure for not uniting what has seldom been united. With respect to narration, the criterion is, the interest excited; and to this test we resign De Foe, for his tale comes home to every bosom, and his book is closed with regret by both young and old. A book, Dr. Johnson would say, that is generally read, must have merit: and who has not heard of Robinson Crusoe? Some people, that delight in paradoxes, have asserted, that the man who only writes from his head, may reach our hearts; but we must be allowed to doubt the fact, and to respect the heart which dictates sentiments simple, because they are true, and consistent, because they are unforced.

ART. XXII. *The Sorrows of Werter, a Poem.* By Amelia Pickering. 4to. 69 p. Price 5s. sewed. Cadell.

The mind is so framed that it is seldom affected by the same pathetic tale in different forms. If the original has warmly interested us, we reluctantly enter again into what bears every mark of fiction:—instead of feeling, we are comparing; the shifting of the scene rouses reason, and we are no longer lost in a waking dream: this remark extends to the poem we are reviewing; we wish the Lady had chosen a less hackneyed subject.

To pity Werter we must read the original:[6] in it we find an energy and beauty of language, a uniformity in the extravagancies of passion that arrests our attention, and gives such reality to his misery, that we are affected by his sorrows, even while we lament the wanderings of his distempered mind, the sad perversion of those talents which might have rendered him a useful and respectable being. His ungoverned sensibility would have been, in every situation, hostile to his peace, finding some unattainable object to pine after. Characters of this kind, like a view of a wild uncultivated country, raise lively emotions in the mind; yet who would wish to fix their constant residence on the most picturesque rock or romantic mountain? The sensations of the moment are confounded with the convictions of reason; and the distinction is only perceived by the consequences.

The energy, so conspicuous in the original, is lost in this smooth, and even faithful, imitation; and some natural touches, that play on the heart-strings, were too fine for a copyist to catch.—Werter is dead from the beginning; we hear his very words; but the spirit which animated them is fled:—we do not perceive the gradations in his disorder, the mortal sadness that precedes death, and prepares us for the catastrophe.

The additional letter written by Charlotte, after the death of Werter, is injudicious.—What should we say of the copyist who would unveil the countenance the ingenious painter threw into a shade, unable to depict the anguish it should express? Besides, a dry moral, was not sufficiently powerful to expel the insinuated poison.

From Letter to Mary Hays (1792)

London Nov[r] 12th 92

Dear Madam.—[1]

. . . I am going to treat you with still greater frankness—I do not approve of your preface—and I will tell you why. If your work should deserve attention it is a blur on the very face of it.—Disadvantages of education &c ought, in my opinion, never to be pleaded (with the public) in excuse for defects of any importance, because if the writer has not sufficient strength of mind to overcome the common difficulties which lie in his way, nature seems to command him, with a very audible voice, to leave the task of instructing others to those who can. This kind of vain humility has ever disgusted me—and I should say to an author, who humbly sued for forbearance, 'if you have not a tolerably good opinion of your own production, why intrude it on the public? we have plenty of bad books already, that have just gasped for breath and died.'

The last paragraph I particularly object to, it is so full of vanity. Your male friends will still treat you like a woman—and many a man, for instance D[r] Johnson, Lord Littelton, and even D[r] Priestley,[2] have insensibly been led to utter warm elogiums in private that they would be sorry openly to avow without some cooling explanatory ifs. An author, especially a woman, should be cautious lest she too hastily swallows the crude praises which partial friend and polite acquaintance bestow thoughtlessly when the supplicating eye looks for them. In short, it requires great resolution to try rather to be useful than to please. With this remark in your head I must beg you to pardon any freedom whilst you consider the purport of what I am going to add.—Rest, on yourself—if your essays have merit they will stand alone, if not the *shouldering up* of D[r] this or that will not long keep them from falling to the ground. . . .

On Poetry and our Relish for the Beauties of Nature (1797)

A taste for rural scenes, in the present state of society, appears to be very often an artificial sentiment, rather inspired by poetry and romances, than a real perception of the beauties of nature.[1] But, as it is reckoned a proof of refined taste to praise the calm pleasures which the country affords, the theme is never exhausted. Yet it may be made a question, whether this romantic kind of declamation, has much effect on the conduct of those, who leave, for a season, the crowded cities in which they were bred.

I have been led to these reflections, by observing, when I have resided for any length of time in the country, how few people seem to contemplate nature with their own eyes. I have "brushed the dew away" in the morning; but, pacing over the printless grass, I have wondered that, in such delightful situations, the sun was allowed to rise in solitary majesty, whilst my eyes alone hailed its beautifying beams. The webs of the evening have still been spread across the hedged path, unless some labouring man, trudging to work,

Mary Wollstonecraft (1759–1797)

disturbed the fairy structure; yet, in spite of this supineness, when I joined the social circle, every tongue rang changes on the pleasures of the country.

Having frequently had occasion to make the same observation, I was led to endeavour, in one of my solitary rambles, to trace the cause, and likewise to enquire why the poetry written in the infancy of society, is most natural: which, strictly speaking (for *natural* is a very indefinite expression) is merely to say, that it is the transcript of immediate sensations, in all their native wildness and simplicity, when fancy, awakened by the sight of interesting objects, was most actively at work. At such moments, sensibility quickly furnishes similes, and the sublimated spirits combine images, which rising spontaneously, it is not necessary coldly to ransack the understanding or memory, till the laborious efforts of judgment exclude present sensations, and damp the fire of enthusiasm. . . .

The poet, the man of strong feelings, gives us only an image of his mind, when he was actually alone, conversing with himself, and marking the impression which nature had made on his own heart.—If, at this sacred moment, the idea of some departed friend, some tender recollection when the soul was most alive to tenderness, intruded unawares into his thoughts, the sorrow which it produced is artlessly, yet poetically expressed—and who can avoid sympathizing?

Love to man leads to devotion—grand and sublime images strike the imagination—God is seen in every floating cloud, and comes from the misty mountain to receive the noblest homage of an intelligent creature— praise. How solemn is the moment, when all affections and remembrances fade before the sublime admiration which the wisdom and goodness of God inspires, when he is worshipped in a *temple not made with hands,*[2] and the world seems to contain only the mind that formed, and the mind that contemplates it! These are not the weak responses of ceremonial devotion; nor, to express them, would the poet need another poet's aid: his heart burns within him, and he speaks the language of truth and nature with resistless energy.

Inequalities, of course, are observable in his effusions; and a less vigorous fancy, with more taste, would have produced more elegance and uniformity; but, as passages are softened or expunged during the cooler moments of reflection, the understanding is gratified at the expence of those involuntary sensations, which, like the beauteous tints of an evening sky, are so evanescent, that they melt into new forms before they can be analyzed. For however eloquently we may boast of our reason, man must often be delighted he cannot tell why, or his blunt feelings are not made to relish the beauties which nature, poetry, or any of the imitative arts, afford.

The imagery of the ancients seems naturally to have been borrowed from surrounding objects and their mythology. When a hero is to be transported from one place to another, across pathless wastes, is any vehicle so natural, as one of the fleecy clouds on which the poet has often gazed, scarcely conscious that he wished to make it his chariot? Again, when nature seems to present obstacles to his progress at almost every step, when the tangled forest and steep mountain stand as barriers, to pass over which the mind longs for supernatural aid; an interposing deity, who walks on the waves, and rules the storm, severely felt in the first attempts to cultivate a country, will receive from the impassioned fancy "a local habitation and a name."[3]

It would be a philosophical enquiry, and throw some light on the history of the human mind, to trace, as far as our information will allow us to trace, the spontaneous feelings and ideas which have produced the images that now frequently appear unnatural, because they are remote; and disgusting, because they have been servilely copied by poets, whose habits of thinking, and views of nature must have been different; for, though the understanding seldom disturbs the current of our present feelings, without dissipating the gay clouds which fancy has been embracing, yet it silently gives the colour to the whole tenour of them, and the dream is over, when truth is grossly violated, or images introduced, selected from books, and not from local manners or popular prejudices.

In a more advanced state of civilization, a poet is rather the creature of art, than of nature. The books that he reads in his youth, become a hotbed in which artificial fruits are produced, beautiful to the common eye, though they want the true hue and flavour. His images do not arise from sensations; they are copies; and, like the works of the painters who copy ancient statues when they draw men and women of their own times, we acknowledge that the features are fine, and the proportions just; yet they are men of stone; insipid figures, that never convey to the mind the idea of a portrait taken from life, where the soul gives spirit and homogeneity to the whole. The silken wings of fancy are shrivelled by rules; and a desire of attaining elegance of diction, occasions an attention to words, incompatible with sublime, impassioned thoughts.

A boy of abilities, who has been taught the structure of verse at school, and been roused by emulation to compose rhymes whilst he was reading works of genius, may, by practice, produce pretty verses, and even become what is often termed an elegant poet: yet his readers, without knowing what to find fault with, do not find themselves warmly interested. In the works of the poets who fasten on their affections, they see grosser faults,

Mary Wollstonecraft (1759–1797)

and the very images which shock their taste in the modern; still they do not appear as puerile or extrinsic in one as the other.—Why?—because they did not appear so to the author.

It may sound paradoxical, after observing that those productions want vigour, that are merely the work of imitation, in which the understanding has violently directed, if not extinguished, the blaze of fancy, to assert, that, though genius be only another word for exquisite sensibility, the first observers of nature, the true poets, exercised their understanding much more than their imitators. But they exercised it to discriminate things, whilst their followers were busy to borrow sentiments and arrange words.

Boys who have received a classical education, load their memory with words, and the correspondent ideas are perhaps never distinctly comprehended. As a proof of this assertion, I must observe, that I have known many young people who could write tolerably smooth verses, and string epithets prettily together, when their prose themes showed the barrenness of their minds, and how superficial the cultivation must have been, which their understanding had received. . . .

But, though it should be allowed that books may produce some poets, I fear they will never be the poets who charm our cares to sleep, or extort admiration. They may diffuse taste, and polish the language; but I am inclined to conclude that they will seldom rouse the passions, or amend the heart. . . .

Preface to *The Wrongs of Woman: or, Maria* (1798)

The Wrongs of Woman, like the wrongs of the oppressed part of mankind, may be deemed necessary by their oppressors: but surely there are a few, who will dare to advance before the improvement of the age, and grant that my sketches are not the abortion of a distempered fancy, or the strong delineations of a wounded heart.

In writing this novel, I have rather endeavoured to pourtray passions than manners.

In many instances I could have made the incidents more dramatic, would I have sacrificed my main object, the desire of exhibiting the misery and oppression, peculiar to women, that arise out of the partial laws and customs of society.

In the invention of the story, this view restrained my fancy; and the history ought rather to be considered, as of woman, than of an individual.

The sentiments I have embodied.

In many works of this species, the hero is allowed to be mortal, and to become wise and virtuous as well as happy, by a train of events and circumstances. The heroines, on the contrary, are to be born immaculate; and to act like goddesses of wisdom, just come forth highly finished Minervas from the head of Jove.

Notes

Mary, a Fiction

1. Clarissa is the heroine of Samuel Richardson's novel *Clarissa* (1747), Lady G—— is a character in Richardson's *Sir Charles Grandison* (1753–1754), and Sophie appears in Jean-Jacques Rousseau's novel *Emile* (1762).

Selected Reviews

1. An allusion to Charlotte Lennox's best-selling novel *The Female Quixote*, a parody of earlier French romantic novels.

2. Lucretia, the legendary Roman matron who killed herself to remove the blemish of her dishonor after being raped by Tarquin.

3. *Euphemia*, written when Lennox was an old woman, drew, like her first novel, on her experiences as a child at the fur-trading fort at Albany, New York. Curiously, Wollstonecraft does not comment on the novel's negative depiction of marriage, a view she would have shared. Her review concludes with a long excerpt from the novel in which Lennox discusses the relationship of the Mohawk Indians and Europeans near the fort at Albany.

4. Selkirk, a Scottish sailor, was marooned for four years on an island. An account of his experiences had been published in 1712. Wollstonecraft quotes Chalmers that all the episodes and details of Defoe's work were original.

5. Dunton was a publisher of the *Athenian Mercury*, for which Defoe was a contributor.

6. The original, *Die Leiden des jungen Werther* (1774), was a powerful first novel by the German poet Johann Wolfgang von Goethe (1749–1832) that became an immediate worldwide sensation.

Letter to Mary Hays

1. Hays had submitted an original composition for publication by Joseph Johnson, for whom Wollstonecraft worked as an editorial assistant.

2. Dr. Samuel Johnson; George, First Baron Lyttleton (1709–1773), a minor poet; and Joseph Priestley (1733–1804), discoverer of oxygen and a member of an intellectual circle, including Wollstonecraft, that gathered at Joseph Johnson's home.

On Poetry

1. "On Poetry and our Relish for the Beauties of Nature" first appeared in the *Monthly Magazine* (April 1797). It was reprinted in *Posthumous Works of the Author of a Vindication of the Rights of Woman*, vol. 4 (London: Printed for J. Johnson, 1798).

2. The New Jerusalem, the city of God, described in Revelations 21.
3. See Shakespeare's *Midsummer Night's Dream*, V.i:

The poet's eye, in a fine frenzy rolling,
Doth glance from heaven to earth, from earth to heaven;
And, as imagination bodies forth
The form of things unknown, the poet's pen
Turns them to shapes, and gives to airy nothing
A local habitation and a name.

MARY HAYS (1760–1843)

THE DAUGHTER of Rational Dissenters, Mary Hays acquired her education through a variety of means. She attended lectures at the Dissenting Academy in Hackney, studied French, mathematics, and religious literature on her own, and carried out an intellectual correspondence with her first love, John Eccles. Eccles died before they could be married, and though Hays had a later, unrequited attachment to William Frend, her most sustained passion was reserved for ideas, especially Dissenting and feminist beliefs. She met Mary Wollstonecraft in 1792 and mentions her in the preface to the *Letters and Essays, Moral, and Miscellaneous* as "the sensible vindicator of female rights." Along with Eliza Fenwick, she attended Wollstonecraft on her deathbed. She corresponded with William Godwin while writing the *Memoirs of Emma Courtney* (1796), a novel which responds to the rationalist project of Godwin's *Political Justice*. At the end of her life, possibly as a result of the prevailing backlash against feminist ideas, Hays toned down her radicalism, publishing moral works for the poor.

Hays's reputation was sullied by being publicly identified with her most famous fictional character, Emma Courtney, who pursues the man she loves and offers to live with him outside marriage. Hays argued for the potential of female intellect in the *Monthly Magazine* and championed vocational training for women in her anonymously published *Appeal to the Men of Great Britain in Behalf of Women* (1798). Her six-volume *Female Biography* (1803) includes the lives of nearly three hundred distinguished women.

In letter number 7 of *Letters and Essays, Moral and Miscellaneous*, excerpted here, Hays provides a defense of novel reading by young women. She reads *Clarissa* as a morality lesson, registering her own entry in the ongoing debate over female education and countering the prevailing view of the novel as a dangerous influence on young women.

Letters and Essays, Moral, and Miscellaneous (London: T. Knott, 1793).

Mary Hays (1760–1843)

From *Letters and Essays, Moral, and Miscellaneous* (1793)

To Mrs. ——

Be not too much alarmed, my friend, at your daughter's predilection for novels and romances; nor think of restraining her by authority from this her favourite pursuit; as by so doing, you would probably lose her confidence, without correcting her taste; in which case the mischief might indeed become serious. . . .

I have scarce ever known an amiable young mind that has not been a little tinctured, with what "the sons of interest" deem "romance." If the first steps into life are marked by coldness, and caution, such a character will never possess any other than negative virtues, though it may incur few hazards.

"Youth's the lovely source of generous foibles."

Where nothing is risqued, nothing can be gained. We shall certainly be subjected to disappointment, by forming flushed and ardent expectations; and find perhaps a brake of thorns, where we expected a parterre of flowers. Yet, "the exertion of our own faculties (says a sensible writer) will be the blessed fruit of disappointed hope." . . .

But the age of chivalry (as a certain rhetoritician laments) is no more! The present race of young people are too vapid, and too dissipated to be captivated by sublime descriptions of heroic virtue; and too much engrossed by the important pursuit, of varying their outward appearance with the constant fluctuation of mode, to have leisure to attend to the dangerous refinements of sentiment. Yet do not mistake me, nor suppose that I mean to recommend the indiscriminate perusal of romances and novels; on the contrary, I think with you, that the generality of works of this kind are frivolous, if not pernicious; though there are undoubtedly, many exceptions. But the love of the marvellous, or of extraordinary, and unexpected coincidences, is natural to young minds, that have any degree of energy and fancy. I would only wish them to be fond of books, and I should have no doubt of being able to lead their taste, from the pursuit of mere amusement, to solid improvement. Awaken but the desire of information, and the gradation from pursuing "the mazes of some wondrous tale," up to the highest degree of interesting and useful knowledge, is easy and natural. Accustom your daughters by a cheerful and amiable frankness, to do nothing without consulting you; let them read with you, and let the choice of their books be free. Converse with them on the merits of the various authors, and accustom them to critical, and literary discussions. They will soon be emulous of gaining your approbation by entering into your ideas, and will be ashamed of being pleased with what you ridicule as absurd, and out of nature, or disapprove, as having an improper and immoral tendency. You have only to persuade them that you have a confidence in their principles, and good sense, and they will be eager to justify your favourable opinion. The human heart in early life, before the world, the mean, unfeeling, selfish world, breaks in upon its gay mistakes, is naturally grateful, and susceptible of lively impressions from kind and generous treatment. This sensibility properly cherished, and cultivated, may be made to produce the noblest fruits. . . .

Your Elizabeth, you tell me, is reading the Sorrows of Werter (notwithstanding your remonstrances) and seems much affected by it: at which I am not surprised.[1] The flowery, and enthusiastic style, in which it is written, is calculated to catch the imagination, and move the passions; but when this tumult of the senses subsides, and we calmly reflect on the events, by which we have suffered ourselves to be agitated, we blush to find we have been sympathising with the extravagant, and fastidious distresses of a madman, made up of pride, caprice, and passion; full of erroneous sentiments, sophistical notions, and real vices; slightly varnished over by superficial, and fanciful perfections; indulging without restraint, an impetuous and criminal attachment, from which he makes no efforts to free himself; consuming the season for active life in enervating indolence; justifying, and allowing himself in flights of vehement and extravagant passions, by which he is ever on the brink of the most fatal, and cruel outrages. Yet this man so weak, so wicked! dignifies his excesses by the names of sentiment, delicacy, and tenderness; and deliberately talks of entering with a pure heart, into the presence of his Creator, while arraigning his dispensations, and contemning his power, by resolving to terminate his own existence, and impiously—"To pluck from God's right hand, his instruments of death."

You ask, if I would advise you to put Richardson's Clarissa into the hands of your daughters, which they seem very desirous of perusing? If we may judge of the merit of a work by the effects which it produces on the mind, I confess, this is a book, which I would recommend to the attention of any young persons under my care. I read it repeatedly in very early life, and ever found my mind more pure, more chastened, more elevated after the perusal of it. The extreme youth and beauty, fine talents, and exalted piety of the heroine, render her character, I allow, something like the fine ideal beauty of the ancients. Yet in contemplating the perfect model, the imagination is raised, and the soul affected; we perceive the pencil of genius, and while we admire, catch the glorious enthusiasm. The characters are well preserved, and the epistolary style of the several writers marked with peculiar distinction. It is generally (and perhaps not without reason) thought too prolix, but I own, I ever felt myself more interested from this minuteness, and perceived, in the nicer shades and touches, the hand of a master. The closing scenes of the lives of Clarissa, Belton, Sinclair, and Lovelace, afford an affecting and admirable lesson. The vivacity of Miss Howe, the virtue and piety of Clarissa, the brilliant wit of Lovelace, and the manly integrity and good sense of the reformed Belford, enliven the narrative with a beautiful variety, and keep up the attention. Rousseau's Heloise seems written on the plan of Clarissa; but Rousseau is not a writer equally pure.[2] Of his works I would never pretend to give a cool judgment; for such are the graces of his style, that it is scarcely possible to read them dispassionately. The man of feeling, by the author of the Mirrour, is an elegant and picturesque little performance;[3] it has all the pathos of Sterne, without any of his faults. Would it not be easy to lead young persons from these works to the periodical Essays, which are continually interspersed with lively, and entertaining narrations, and where instruction comes in the dress of amusement. From thence, the transition to biography would not be difficult; the Life of Petrarch, as translated by Mrs. Dobson, is an interesting and charming work, that cannot fail to engage a youthful and sensible heart.[4] Voltaire's History of Charles the Twelfth of Sweden, and Peter the Great, and Rollins's Account of Cyrus and Alexander, are highly calculated to gratify a love of the marvellous, by the uncommon and striking incidents with which they abound.[5] Sully's Memoirs of Henry the Fourth of France, and Stuart's History of the unfortunate Mary, Queen of Scots, at once excite our sympathy, engage our affections, and awaken our curiosity.[6] Wraxhall's Memoirs of the Kings of France, and Voltaire's Account of the Reign of Louis the Fourteenth, are also composed in a manner to amuse and instruct, and to generate a taste for historical reading:[7] when the mind expanded, and liberalized by tracing the fate of nations, and the rise and fall of empires, will proceed to studies still more interesting; to philosophical, political, moral, and religious truth. The love of information will by innumerable associations, become at length almost disinterested, and every interval from active employment will be devoted to mental improvement. . . .

Notes

1. Johann Wolfgang von Goethe's *The Sorrows of Young Werther* (1774) achieved cult status with young men across Europe almost at once.

2. Jean-Jacques Rousseau, *Julie, or the New Heloise* (1761). The fact that Julie has a sexual liaison with her tutor is perhaps the impetus behind Hays's unfavorable comparison of Rousseau to Richardson.

3. Henry Mackenzie, *The Man of Feeling* (1771).

4. *The Life of Petrarch*, translated by Susanna Dobson (1775).

5. Voltaire, *The History of Charles XII, King of Sweden* (English edition, 1732), and *The History of the Russian Empire under Peter the Great* (English edition, 1761); Charles Rollin, *The History of Cyrus translated from the French* (1740) and *The Life of Alexander the Great* (2d ed., 1770).

6. *Memoirs of Maximilian de Bethune, Duke of Sully, Prime Minister of Henry the Great* (English ed., 1751); Gilbert Stuart, *The History of Scotland, from the establishment of the Reformation, till the death of Queen Mary* (1782).

7. Sir Nathaniel William Wraxall, *Memoirs of the Kings of France of the Race of Valois* (1777); Voltaire, *The Age of Louis XV* (English ed., 1739).

JOANNA BAILLIE (1762–1851)

BORN AND educated in Scotland, Joanna Baillie exhibited an early interest in the stage; while at boarding school she wrote plays, designed costumes, and distinguished herself by her acting skill. She moved to London in 1783 with her mother, brother, and sister, and published a collection of poems before beginning the plays that make up her most famous work, *A Series of Plays: In Which it is Attempted to delineate the Stronger Passions of the Mind, Each passion being the subject of a tragedy and a comedy* (1798–1836). She settled in Hampstead with her mother and sister and became part of a distinguished circle of literary neighbors. Anna Barbauld lived nearby, Sir Walter Scott visited frequently, and Byron and Wordsworth were among her acquaintances. In her eighties Baillie grew increasingly interested in religion and philanthropic activity, but she continued to add to her dramatic and poetic oeuvre.

Baillie's *Series of Plays*, also known as *Plays on the Passions*, attracted the interest of the foremost theater people of the era. In 1798 John Kemble produced *De Monfort*, dedicated to the passion of hate, at Drury Lane with himself and Sarah Siddons in the main roles. Baillie's 1810 historical tragedy, *The Family Legend*, was produced at the Edinburgh theater with Scott's support and with an epilogue by Henry Mackenzie. Among her more interesting experiments in verse is the 1821 *Metrical Legends of Exalted Character*, which included a poem on Baillie's ancestor, Lady Griselda Baillie, presented as a female ideal.

In Baillie's address "To the Reader" (1812) that precedes the third series of her *Plays on the Passions*, she examines the effects of the new, larger theaters on the acting and staging of plays. The "Introductory Discourse" (1798) to the first series of the same collection presents the rationale for her ambition to write a tragedy and a comedy devoted to each passion of the human mind, and, in so doing, sets forth a manifesto for Romantic drama. Her theory of dramatic art is predicated upon the concept of sympathetic curiosity; a spectator's strong emotional response to the passions presented in her plays will, she believes, contribute to heightening his or her sense of moral responsibility.

"Introductory Discourse," *Plays on the Passions*, vol. 1 (London: T. Cadell, 1798); *A Series of Plays: In Which it is Attempted to delineate the Stronger Passions of the Mind*, vol. 3 (London: Longman, Hurst, Rees, Orme, and Brown, 1812).

From "Introductory Discourse," *Plays on the Passions* (1798)

Our desire to know what men are in the closet as well as the field, by the blazing hearth, and at the social board, as well as in the council and the throne, is very imperfectly gratified by real history; romance writers, therefore, stepped boldly forth to supply the deficiency; and tale writers, and novel writers, of many descriptions, followed after. If they have not been very skilful in their delineations of nature; if they have represented men and women speaking and acting as men and women never did speak or act; if they have caricatured both our virtues and our vices; if they have given us such pure and unmixed, or such heterogeneous combinations of character as real life never presented, and yet have pleased and interested us, let it not be imputed to the dulness of man in discerning what is genuinely natural in himself. There are many inclinations belonging to us, besides this great master-propensity of which I am treating. Our love of the grand, the beautiful, the novel, and above all of the marvellous, is very strong; and if we are richly fed with what we have a good relish for, we may be weaned to forget our native and favourite aliment. Yet we can never so far forget it, but that we will cling to, and acknowledge it again, whenever it is presented before us. In a work abounding with the marvellous and unnatural, if the author has any how stumbled upon an unsophisticated genuine stroke of nature, we will immediately perceive and be delighted with it, though we are foolish enough to admire at the same time, all the nonsense with which it is surrounded. After all the wonderful incidents, dark mysteries, and secrets revealed, which eventful novel so liberally presents to us; after the beautiful fairy ground, and even the grand and sublime scenes of nature with which descriptive novel so often enchants us; those works which most strongly characterize human nature in the middling and lower classes of society, where it is to be discovered by stronger and more unequivocal marks, will ever be the most popular. For though great pains have been taken in our higher sentimental novels to interest us in the delicacies, embarrassments, and artificial distresses of the more refined part of society, they have never been able to cope in the publick opinion with these. The one is a dressed and beautiful pleasure-ground, in which we are enchanted for a while, amongst the delicate and unknown plants of artful cultivation; the other is a rough forest of our native land; the oak, the elm, the hazle, and the bramble are there; and amidst the endless varieties of its paths we can wander for ever. Into whatever scenes the novelist may conduct us, what objects soever he may present to our view, still is our attention most sensibly awake to every touch faithful to nature; still are we upon the watch for every thing that speaks to us of ourselves.

The fair field of what is properly called poetry, is enriched with so many beauties, that in it we are often tempted to forget what we really are, and what kind of beings we belong to. Who in the enchanted regions of simile, metaphor, allegory and description, can remember the plain order of things in this every-day world? From heroes whose majestick forms rise like a lofty tower, whose eyes are lightening, whose arms are irresistible, whose course is like the storms of heaven, bold and exalted sentiments we will readily receive; and will not examine them very accurately by that rule of nature which our own breast prescribes to us. A shepherd whose sheep, with fleeces of the purest snow, browze the flowery herbage of the most beautiful vallies; whose flute is ever melodious, and whose shepherdess is ever crowned with roses; whose every care is love, will not be called very strictly to account for the loftiness and refinement of his thoughts. The fair Nymph, who sighs out her sorrows to the conscious and compassionate wilds; whose eyes gleam like the bright drops of heaven; whose loose tresses stream to the breeze, may say what she pleases with impunity. I will venture, however, to say, that amidst all this decoration and ornament, all this loftiness and refinement, let one simple trait of the human heart, one expression of passion genuine and true to nature, be introduced, and it will stand forth alone in the boldness of reality, whilst the false and unnatural around it, fades away upon every side, like the rising exhalations of the morning. With admiration, and often with enthusiasm we proceed on our way through the grand and the beautiful images, raised to our imagination by the lofty Epic muse; but what even here are those things that strike upon the heart; that we feel and remember? Neither the descriptions of war, the sound of the trumpet, the clanging of arms, the combat of heroes, nor the death of the mighty, will interest our minds like the fall of the feeble stranger, who simply expresses the anguish of his soul, at the thoughts of that far-distant home which he must never return to again, and closes his eyes amongst the ignoble and forgotten; like the timid stripling goaded by the shame of reproach, who urges his trembling steps to the fight, and falls like a tender flower before the first blast of winter. How often will some simple picture of this kind be all that remains upon our minds of the terrifick and magnificent battle, whose description we have read with admiration! How comes it that we relish so much the episodes of an heroick poem? It cannot merely be that we are pleased with a resting-place, where we enjoy the variety of contrast; for were the poem of the simple and familiar kind, and an episode after the heroick style introduced into it, ninety readers out of an hundred would pass over it altogether. Is it not that we meet such a story, so situated, with a kind of sympathetick good will, as in passing through a country of castles and of palaces, we should pop unawares upon some humble cottage, resembling the dwellings of our own native land, and gaze upon it with affection. The highest pleasures we receive from poetry, as well as from the real objects which surround us in the world, are derived from the sympathetick interest we all take in beings like ourselves; and I will even venture to say, that were the grandest scenes which can enter into the imagination of man, presented to our view, and all reference to man completely shut out from our thoughts, the objects that composed it would convey to our minds little better than dry ideas of magnitude, colour, and form; and the remembrance of them would rest upon our minds like the measurement and distances of the planets.

If the study of human nature then, is so useful to the poet, the novelist, the historian, and the philosopher, of how much greater importance must it be to the dramatick writer? To them it is a powerful auxiliary, to him it is the centre and strength of the battle. If characteristick views of human nature enliven not their pages, there are many excellencies with which they can, in some degree, make up for the deficiency, it is what we receive from them with pleasure rather than demand. But in his works no richness of invention, harmony of language, nor grandeur of sentiment will supply the place of faithfully delineated nature. The poet and the novelist may represent to you their great characters from the cradle to the tomb. They may represent them in any mood or temper, and under the influence of any passion which they see proper, without being obliged to put words into their mouths, those great betrayers of the feigned and adopted. They may relate every circumstance however trifling and minute, that serves to develope their tempers and dispositions. They tell us what kind of people they intend their men and women to be, and as such we receive them. If they are to move us with any scene of distress, every circumstance regarding the parties concerned in it, how they looked, how they moved, how they sighed, how the tears gushed from their eyes, how the very light and shadow fell upon them, is carefully described, and the few things that are given them to say along with all this assistance, must be very unnatural indeed if we refuse to sympathize with them. But the characters of the drama must speak directly for themselves. Under the influence of every passion, humour, and impression; in the artificial veilings of hypocrisy and ceremony, in the openness of freedom and confidence, and in the lonely hour of meditation they speak. He who made us hath placed within our breast a judge that judges instantaneously of every thing they say. We expect to find them creatures like ourselves; and if they are untrue to nature, we feel that we are imposed upon; as though the poet had introduced to us for brethren, creatures of a different race, beings of another world.

As in other works deficiency in characteristick truth may be compensated by excellencies of a different kind, in the drama characteristick truth will compensate every other defect. Nay, it will do what appears a contradiction; one strong genuine stroke of nature will cover a multitude of sins even against nature herself. When we meet in some scene of a good play a very fine stroke of this kind, we are apt to become so intoxicated with it, and so perfectly convinced of the author's great knowledge of the human heart, that we are unwilling to suppose that the whole of it has not been suggested by the same penetrating spirit. Many well-meaning enthusiastick criticks have given themselves a great deal of trouble in this way; and have shut their eyes most ingeniously against the fair light of nature for the very love of it. They have converted, in their great zeal, sentiments palpably false, both in regard to the character and situation of the persons who utter them, sentiments which a child or a clown would detect, into the most skilful depictments of the heart. I can think of no stronger instance to shew how powerfully this love of nature dwells within us.*

Formed as we are with these sympathetick propensities in regard to our own species, it is not at all wonderful that theatrical exhibition has become the grand and favourite amusement of every nation into which it has been introduced. Savages will, in the wild contortions of a dance, shape out some rude story expressive of character or passion, and such a dance will give more delight to his companions than the most artful exertions of agility. Children in their gambols will make out a mimick representation of the

---

*It appears to me a very strong testimony of the excellence of our great national Dramatist, that so many people have been employed in finding out obscure and refined beauties, in what appear to ordinary observation his very defects. Men, it may be said, do so merely to shew their own superior penetration and ingenuity. But granting this; what could make other men listen to them, and listen so greedily too, if it were not that they have received from the works of Shakspeare, pleasure far beyond what the most perfect poetical compositions of a different character can afford.

manners, characters, and passions of grown men and women, and such a pastime will animate and delight them much more than a treat of the dain- tiest sweetmeats, or the handling of the gaudiest toys. Eagerly as it is enjoyed by the rude and the young, to the polished and the ripe in years it is still the most interesting amusement. Our taste for it is durable as it is universal. Independently of those circumstances which first introduced it, the world would not have long been without it. The progress of society would soon have brought it forth; and men in the whimsical decorations of fancy would have displayed the characters and actions of their heroes, the folly and ab- surdity of their fellow-citizens, had no Priests of Bacchus ever existed.★[1]

In whatever age or country the Drama might have taken its rise, tragedy would have been the first-born of its children. For every nation has its great men, and its great events upon record; and to represent their own forefathers struggling with those difficulties, and braving those dangers, of which they

---

★Though the progress of society would have given us the Drama, independently of the particular cause of its first commencement, the peculiar circumstances connected with its origin, have had considerable influence upon its character and style, in the ages through which it has passed even to our days, and still will continue to affect it. Homer had long preceded the dramatick poets of Greece; poetry was in a high state of cultivation when they began to write; and their style, the construction of their pieces, and the characters of their heroes were different from what they would have been, had theatrical exhibitions been the invention of an earlier age or a ruder people. Their works were represented to an audience, already accustomed to hear long poems rehearsed at their publick games, and the feasts of their gods. A play, with the principal characters of which they were previously acquainted; in which their great men and heroes, in the most beautiful language, complained of their rigorous fate, but piously submitted to the will of the Gods; in which sympathy was chiefly excited by tender and affecting sentiments; in which strong bursts of passion were few; and in which whole scenes frequently passed, without giving the actors any thing to do but to speak, was not too insipid for them. Had the Drama been the invention of a less cultivated nation, more of action and of passion would have been introduced into it. It would have been more irregular, more imperfect, more varied, more interesting. From poor beginnings it would have advanced in a progressive state; and succeeding poets, not having those polished and admired originals to look back upon, would have presented their respective contemporaries with the produce of a free and unbridled imagination. A different class of poets would most likely have been called into existence. The latent powers of men are called forth by contemplating those works in which they find any thing congenial to their own peculiar talents; and if the field, wherein they could have worked, is already enriched with a produce unsuited to their cultivation, they think not of entering it at all. Men, therefore, whose natural turn of mind led them to labour, to reason, to refine and exalt, have caught their animation from the beauties of the Grecian Drama, and they who, perhaps, ought only to have been our Criticks have become our Poets. I mean not, however, in any degree to depreciate the works of the ancients; a great deal we have gained by those beautiful compositions; and what we have lost by them it is impossible to compute. Very strong genius will sometimes break through every disadvantage of circumstances: Shakspeare has arisen in this country, and we ought not to complain.

have heard with admiration, and the effects of which they still, perhaps, experience, would certainly have been the most animating subject for the poet, and the most interesting for his audience, even independently of the natural inclination we all so universally shew for scenes of horrour and distress, of passion and heroick exertion. Tragedy would have been the first child of the Drama, for the same reasons that have made heroick ballad, with all its battles, murders, and disasters, the earliest poetical compositions of every country.

We behold heroes and great men at a distance, unmarked by those small but distinguishing features of the mind, which give a certain individuality to such an infinite variety of similar beings, in the near and familiar inter-course of life. They appear to us from this view like distant mountains, whose dark outlines we trace in the clear horizon, but the varieties of whose roughened sides, shaded with heath and brushwood, and seamed with many a cleft, we perceive not. When accidental anecdote reveals to us any weak-ness or peculiarity belonging to them, we start upon it like a discovery. They are made known to us in history only, by the great events they are connected with, and the part they have taken in extraordinary or important transactions. Even in poetry and romance, with the exception of some love story interwoven with the main events of their lives, they are seldom more intimately made known to us. To Tragedy it belongs to lead them forward to our nearer regard, in all the distinguishing varieties which nearer inspec-tion discovers; with the passions, the humours, the weaknesses, the prejudices of men. It is for her to present to us the great and magnanimous hero, who appears to our distant view as a superior being, as a God, softened down with those smaller frailties and imperfections which enable us to glory in, and claim kindred to his virtues. It is for her to exhibit to us the daring and ambitious man, planning his dark designs, and executing his bloody purposes, mark'd with those appropriate characteristicks, which distinguish him as an individual of that class; and agitated with those varied passions, which disturb the mind of man when he is engaged in the commission of such deeds. It is for her to point out to us the brave and impetuous warrior struck with those visitations of nature, which, in certain situations, will unnerve the strongest arm, and make the boldest heart tremble. It is for her to shew the tender, gentle, and unassuming mind animated with that fire which, by the provocation of circumstances, will give to the kindest heart the ferocity and keenness of a tiger. It is for her to present to us the great and striking characters that are to be found amongst men, in a way which the poet, the novelist, and the historian can but imperfectly attempt. But above all, to her, and to her only it belongs to unveil to us the human mind under the dominion of those strong and fixed passions, which, seemingly unprovoked by outward circumstances, will from small beginnings brood within the breast, till all the better dispositions, all the fair gifts of nature are borne down before them. Those passions which conceal themselves from the observation of men; which cannot unbosom themselves even to the dearest friend; and can, often times, only give their fulness vent in the lonely desert, or in the darkness of midnight. For who hath followed the great man into his secret closet, or stood by the side of his nightly couch, and heard those exclamations of the soul which heaven alone may hear, that the historian should be able to inform us? and what form of story, what mode of rehearsed speech will communicate to us those feelings, whose irregular bursts, abrupt transitions, sudden pauses, and half-uttered suggestions, scorn all harmony of measured verse, all method and order of relation?

On the first part of this task her Bards have eagerly exerted their abilities: and some amongst them, taught by strong original genius to deal immediately with human nature and their own hearts, have laboured in it successfully. But in presenting to us those views of great characters, and of the human mind in difficult and trying situations which peculiarly belong to Tragedy, the far greater proportion, even of those who may be considered as respectable dramatick poets, have very much failed. From the beauty of those original dramas to which they have ever looked back with admiration, they have been tempted to prefer the embellishments of poetry to faithfully delineated nature. They have been more occupied in considering the works of the great Dramatists who have gone before them, and the effects produced by their writings, than the varieties of human character which first furnished materials for those works, or those principles in the mind of man by means of which such effects were produced. Neglecting the boundless variety of nature, certain strong outlines of character, certain bold features of passion, certain grand vicissitudes, and striking dramatick situations have been repeated from one generation to another; whilst a pompous and solemn gravity, which they have supposed to be necessary for the dignity of tragedy, has excluded almost entirely from their works those smaller touches of nature, which so well develope the mind; and by showing men in their hours of state and exertion only, they have consequently shewn them imperfectly. Thus, great and magnanimous heroes, who bear with majestick equanimity every vicissitude of fortune; who in every temptation and trial stand forth in unshaken virtue, like a rock buffeted by the waves; who encompast with the most terrible evils, in calm possession of their souls, reason upon the difficulties of their state; and, even upon the brink of destruction, pronounce long eulogiums on virtue, in the most eloquent and beautiful language, have been held forth to our view as objects of imitation and interest; as though they had entirely forgotten that it is only from creatures like ourselves that we feel, and therefore, only from creatures like ourselves that we receive the instruction of example.* Thus, passionate and impetuous warriors, who are proud, irritable, and vindictive, but generous, daring, and disinterested; setting their lives at a pin's fee for the good of others, but incapable of curbing their own humour of a moment to gain the whole world for themselves; who will pluck the orbs of heaven from their places, and crush the whole universe in one grasp, are called forth to kindle in our souls the generous contempt of every thing abject and base; but with an effect proportionably feeble, as the hero is made to exceed in courage and fire what the standard of humanity will agree to.† Thus, tender and pathetick lovers, full of the most gentle affections, the most amiable disposi-

---

*To a being perfectly free from all human infirmity our sympathy refuses to extend. Our Saviour himself, whose character is so beautiful, and so harmoniously consistent; in whom, with outward proofs of his mission less strong than those that are offered to us, I should still be compelled to believe, from being utterly unable to conceive how the idea of such a character could enter into the imagination of man, never touches the heart more nearly than when he says, "Father, let this cup pass from me."[2] Had he been represented to us in all the unshaken strength of these tragick heroes, his disciples would have made fewer converts, and his precepts would have been listened to coldly. Plays in which heroes of this kind are held forth, and whose aim is, indeed, honourable and praise-worthy, have been admired by the cultivated and refined, but the tears of the simple, the applauses of the young and untaught have been wanting.

†In all burlesque imitations of tragedy, those plays in which this hero is pre-eminent, are always exposed to bear the great brunt of the ridicule; which proves how popular they have been, and how many poets, and good ones too, have been employed upon them. That they have been so popular, however, is not owing to the intrinsick merit of the characters they represent, but their opposition to those mean and contemptible qualities belonging to human nature, of which we are most ashamed. Besides, there is something in the human mind, independently of its love of applause, which inclines it to boast. This is ever the attendant of that elasticity of soul, which makes us bound up from the touch of oppression; and if there is nothing in the accompanying circumstances to create disgust, or suggest suspicions of their sincerity, (as in real life is commonly the case,) we are very apt to be carried along with the boasting of others. Let us in good earnest believe that a man is capable of achieving all that human courage can achieve, and we will suffer him to talk of impossibilities. Amidst all their pomp of words, therefore, our admiration of such heroes is readily excited, (for the understanding is more easily deceived than the heart,) but how stands our sympathy affected? As no caution nor foresight, on their own account, is ever suffered to occupy the thoughts of such bold disinterested beings, we are the more inclined to care for them, and take an interest in their fortune through the course of the play: yet, as their souls are unappalled by any thing; as pain and death are not at all regarded by them; and as we have seen them very ready to plunge their own swords into their own bosoms, on no very weighty occasion, perhaps, their death distresses us but little, and they commonly fall unwept.

tions, and the most exquisite feelings; who present their defenceless bosoms to the storms of this rude world in all the graceful weakness of sensibility, are made to sigh out their sorrows in one unvaried strain of studied pathos, whilst this constant demand upon our feelings makes us absolutely incapable of answering it.★ Thus, also, tyrants are represented as monsters of cruelty, unmixed with any feelings of humanity; and villains as delighting in all manner of treachery and deceit, and acting upon many occasions for the very love of villainy itself; though the perfectly wicked are as ill fitted for the purposes of warning, as the perfectly virtuous are for those of example.† This spirit of imitation, and attention to effect, has likewise confined them very much in their choice of situations and events to bring their great characters into action; rebellions, conspiracies, contentions for empire, and rivalships in love have alone been thought worthy of trying those heroes; and palaces and dungeons the only places magnificent or solemn enough for them to appear in.

They have, indeed, from this regard to the works of preceding authors, and great attention to the beauties of composition, and to dignity of design, enriched their plays with much striking, and sometimes sublime imagery, lofty thoughts, and virtuous sentiments; but in striving so eagerly to excell in those things that belong to tragedy in common with many other compositions, they have very much neglected those that are peculiarly her own. As far as they have been led aside from the first labours of a tragick poet by a desire to communicate more perfect moral instruction, their motive

---

★Were it not, that in tragedies where these heroes preside, the same soft tones of sorrow are so often repeated in our ears, till we are perfectly tired of it, they are more fitted to interest us than any other: both because in seeing them, we own the ties of kindred between ourselves and the frail mortals we lament; and sympathize with the weakness of mortality unmixed with any thing to degrade or disgust; and also, because the misfortunes, which form the story of the play, are frequently of the more familiar and domestick kind. A king driven from his throne, will not move our sympathy so strongly, as a private man torn from the bosom of his family.

†I have said nothing here in regard to female character, though in many tragedies it is brought forward as the principal one of the piece, because what I have said of the above characters is likewise applicable to it. I believe there is no man that ever lived, who has behaved in a certain manner, on a certain occasion, who has not had amongst women some corresponding spirit, who on the like occasion, and every way similarly circumstanced, would have behaved in the like manner. With some degree of softening and refinement, each class of the tragick heroes I have mentioned has its corresponding one amongst the heroines. The tender and pathetick no doubt has the most numerous, but the great and magnanimous is not without it, and the passionate and impetuous boasts of one by no means inconsiderable in numbers, and drawn sometimes to the full as passionate and impetuous as itself.

has been respectable, and they merit our esteem. But this praise-worthy end has been injured instead of promoted by their mode of pursuing it. Every species of moral writing has its own way of conveying instruction, which it can never, but with disadvantage, exchange for any other. The Drama improves us by the knowledge we acquire of our own minds, from the natural desire we have to look into the thoughts, and observe the behaviour of others. Tragedy brings to our view men placed in those elevated situations, exposed to those great trials, and engaged in those extraordinary transactions, in which few of us are called upon to act. As examples applicable to ourselves, therefore, they can but feebly effect us; it is only from the enlargement of our ideas in regard to human nature, from that admiration of virtue, and abhorrence of vice which they excite, that we can expect to be improved by them. But if they are not represented to us as real and natural characters, the lessons we are taught from their conduct and their sentiments will be no more to us than those which we receive from the pages of the poet or the moralist.

But the last part of the task which I have mentioned as peculiarly belonging to tragedy, unveiling the human mind under the dominion of those strong and fixed passions, which seemingly unprovoked by outward circumstances, will from small beginning brood within the breast, till all the better dispositions, all the fair gifts of nature are borne down before them, her poets in general have entirely neglected, and even her first and greatest have but imperfectly attempted. They have made use of the passions to mark their several characters, and animate their scenes, rather than to open to our view the nature and portraitures of those great disturbers of the human breast, with whom we are all, more or less, called upon to contend. With their strong and obvious features, therefore, they have been presented to us, stripped almost entirely of those less obtrusive, but not less discriminating traits, which mark them in their actual operation. To trace them in their rise and progress in the heart, seems but rarely to have been the object of any dramatist. We commonly find the characters of a tragedy affected by the passions in a transient, loose, unconnected manner; or if they are represented as under the permanent influence of the more powerful ones, they are generally introduced to our notice in the very height of their fury, when all that timidity, irresolution, distrust, and a thousand delicate traits, which make the infancy of every great passion more interesting, perhaps, than its full-blown strength, are fled. The impassioned character is generally brought into view under those irresistible attacks of their power, which it is impossible to repell; whilst those gradual steps that led him into this state, in some of which a stand might have been made against the foe, are left entirely in the shade. These passions that may be suddenly excited, and are of short duration, as anger, fear, and oftentimes jealousy, may in this manner be fully represented; but those great masters of the soul, ambition, hatred, love, every passion that is permanent in its nature, and varied in progress, if represented to us but in one stage of its course, is represented imperfectly. It is a characteristick of the more powerful passions that they will encrease and nourish themselves on very slender aliment; it is from within that they are chiefly supplied with what they feed on; and it is in contending with opposite passions and affections of the mind that we least discover their strength, not with events. But in tragedy it is events more frequently than opposite affections which are opposed to them; and those often of such force and magnitude that the passions themselves are almost obscured by the splendour and importance of the transactions to which they are attached. But besides being thus confined and mutilated, the passions have been, in the greater part of our tragedies, deprived of the very power of making themselves known. Bold and figurative language belongs peculiarly to them. Poets, admiring those bold expressions which a mind, labouring with ideas too strong to be conveyed in the ordinary forms of speech, wildly throws out, taking earth, sea, and sky, every thing great and terrible in nature to image forth the violence of its feelings, borrowed them gladly, to adorn the calm sentiments of their premeditated song. It has therefore been thought that the less animated parts of tragedy might be so embellished and enriched. In doing this, however, the passions have been robbed of their native prerogative; and in adorning with their strong figures and lofty expressions the calm speeches of the unruffled, it is found that, when they are called upon to raise their voice, the power of distinguishing themselves has been taken away. This is an injury by no means compensated, but very greatly aggravated by embellishing, in return, the speeches of passion with the ingenious conceits, and compleat similies of premeditated thought.★ There are many other things regarding the manner in which dramatick poets have generally brought forward the passions in tragedy, to the great prejudice of that effect they are naturally fitted to produce upon the mind, which I forbear to mention, lest they should too much increase the length of this discourse; and leave an impression on the mind of my reader, that I write more on

---

★This, perhaps, more than any thing else has injured the higher scenes of tragedy. For having made such free use of bold hyperbolical language in the inferior parts, the poet when he arrives at the highly impassioned sinks into total inability: or if he will force himself to rise still higher on the wing, he flies beyond nature altogether, into the regions of bombast and nonsense.

Joanna Baillie (1762–1851)

the spirit of criticism, than becomes one who is about to bring before the publick a work, with, doubtless, many faults and imperfections on its head.

From this general view, which I have endeavoured to communicate to my reader, of tragedy, and those principles in the human mind upon which the success of her efforts depends, I have been led to believe, that an attempt to write a series of tragedies, of simpler construction, less embellished with poetical decorations, less constrained by that lofty seriousness which has so generally been considered as necessary for the support of tragick dignity, and in which the chief object should be to delineate the progress of the higher passions in the human breast, each play exhibiting a particular passion, might not be unacceptable to the publick. And I have been the more readily induced to act upon this idea, because I am confident, that tragedy, written upon this plan, is fitted to produce stronger moral effect than upon any other. I have said that tragedy in representing to us great characters struggling with difficulties, and placed in situations of eminence and danger, in which few of us have any chance of being called upon to act, conveys its moral efficacy to our minds by the enlarged views which it gives to us of human nature, by the admiration of virtue, and execration of vice which it excites, and not by the examples it holds up for our immediate application. But in opening to us the heart of man under the influence of those passions to which all are liable, this is not the case. Those strong passions that, with small assistance from outward circumstances, work their way in the heart, till they become the tyrannical masters of it, carry on a similar operation in the breast of the Monarch, and the man of low degree. It exhibits to us the mind of man in that state when we are most curious to look into it, and is equally interesting to all. Discrimination of character is a turn of mind, tho' more common than we are aware of, which every body does not possess; but to the expressions of passion, particularly strong passion, the dullest mind is awake; and its true unsophisticated language the dullest understanding will not misinterpret. To hold up for our example those peculiarities in disposition, and modes of thinking which nature has fixed upon us, or which long and early habit has incorporated with our original selves, is almost desiring us to remove the everlasting mountains, to take away the native land-marks of the soul; but representing the passions brings before us the operation of a tempest that rages out its time and passes away. We cannot, it is true, amidst its wild uproar, listen to the voice of reason, and save ourselves from destruction; but we can foresee its coming, we can mark its rising signs, we can know the situations that will most expose us to its rage, and we can shelter our heads from the coming blast. To change a certain disposition of mind which makes us view objects in a particular light, and thereby, oftentimes, unknown to ourselves, influences our conduct and manners, is almost impossible; but in checking and subduing those visitations of the soul, whose causes and effects we are aware of, every one may make considerable progress, if he proves not entirely successful. Above all, looking back to the first rise, and tracing the progress of passion, points out to us those stages in the approach of the enemy, when he might have been combated most successfully; and where the suffering him to pass may be considered as occasioning all the misery that ensues.

Comedy presents to us men as we find them in the ordinary intercourse of the world, with all the weaknesses, follies, caprice, prejudices, and absurdities which a near and familiar view of them discovers. It is her task to exhibit them engaged in the busy turmoil of ordinary life, harassing and perplexing themselves with the endless pursuits of avarice, vanity, and pleasure; and engaged with those smaller trials of the mind, by which men are most apt to be overcome, and from which he, who could have supported with honour the attack of greater occasions, will oftentimes come off most shamefully foiled. It belongs to her to shew the varied fashions and manners of the world, as, from the spirit of vanity, caprice, and imitation, they go on in swift and endless succession; and those disagreeable or absurd peculiarities attached to particular classes and conditions in society. It is for her also to represent men under the influence of the stronger passions; and to trace the rise and progress of them in the heart, in such situations, and attended with such circumstances as take off their sublimity, and the interest we naturally take in a perturbed mind. It is hers to exhibit those terrible tyrants of the soul, whose ungovernable rage has struck us so often with dismay, like wild beasts tied to a post, who growl and paw before us, for our derision and sport. In pourtraying the characters of men she has this advantage over tragedy, that the smallest traits of nature, with the smallest circumstances which serve to bring them forth, may by her be displayed, however ludicrous and trivial in themselves, without any ceremony. And in developing the passions she enjoys a similar advantage; for they often most strongly betray themselves when touched by those small and familiar occurrences which cannot, consistently with the effect it is intended to produce, be admitted into tragedy.

As tragedy has been very much cramped in her endeavours to exalt and improve the mind, by that spirit of imitation and confinement in her successive writers, which the beauty of her earliest poets first gave rise to, so comedy has been led aside from her best purposes by a different temptation. Those endless changes in fashions and in manners, which offer such obvious and ever-new subjects of ridicule; that infinite variety of tricks and manœuvres by which the ludicrous may be produced, and curiosity and laughter excited: the admiration we so generally bestow upon satirical remark, pointed repartee, and whimsical combinations of ideas, have too often led her to forget the warmer interest we feel, and the more profitable lessons we receive from genuine representations of nature. The most interesting and instructive class of comedy, therefore, the real characteristick, has been very much neglected, whilst satirical, witty, sentimental, and, above all, busy or circumstantial comedy have usurped the exertions of the far greater proportion of Dramatick Writers.

In Satirical Comedy, sarcastick and severe reflections on the actions and manners of men, introduced with neatness, force, and poignancy of expression into a lively and well supported dialogue, of whose gay surface they are the embossed ornaments, make the most important and studied part of the work: Character is a thing talked of rather than shewn. The persons of the drama are indebted for the discovery of their peculiarities to what is said to them, rather than to any thing they are made to say or do for themselves. Much incident being unfavourable for studied and elegant dialogue, the plot is commonly simple, and the few events that compose it neither interesting nor striking. It only affords us that kind of moral instruction which an essay or a poem could as well have conveyed, and, though amusing in the closet, is but feebly attractive in the Theatre.★

In what I have termed Witty Comedy, every thing is light, playful, and easy. Strong decided condemnation of vice is too weighty and material to dance upon the surface of that stream, whose shallow currents sparkle in perpetual sun-beams, and cast up their bubbles to the light. Two or three persons of quick thought, and whimsical fancy, who perceive instantaneously the various connections of every passing idea, and the significations, natural or artificial, which single expressions, or particular forms of speech can possibly convey, take the lead thro' the whole, and seem to communicate their own peculiar talent to every creature in the play. The plot is most commonly feeble rather than simple, the incidents being numerous enough, but seldom striking or varied. To amuse, and only to amuse, is its aim: it pretends not to interest nor instruct. It pleases when we read, more than when we see it represented; and pleases still more when we take it up by accident, and read but a scene at a time.

★These plays are generally the work of men, whose judgement and acute observation, enable them admirably well to generalize, and apply to classes of men the remarks they have made upon individuals; yet know not how to dress up, with any natural congruity, an imaginary individual in the attributes they have assigned to those classes.

Sentimental Comedy treats of those embarrassments, difficulties, and scruples, which, though sufficiently distressing to the delicate minds who entertain them, are not powerful enough to gratify the sympathetick desire we all feel to look into the heart of man in difficult and trying situations, which is the sound basis of tragedy, and are destitute of that seasoning of the lively and ludicrous, which prevents the ordinary transactions of comedy from becoming insipid. In real life, those who, from the peculiar frame of their minds, feel most of this refined distress, are not generally communicative upon the subject; and those who do feel and talk about it at the same time, if any such there be, seldom find their friends much inclined to listen to them. It is not to be supposed, then, long conversations upon the stage about small sentimental niceties, can be generally interesting. I am afraid plays of this kind, as well as works of a similar nature, in other departments of literature, have only tended to encrease amongst us a set of sentimental hypocrites; who are the same persons of this age that would have been the religious ones of another; and are daily doing morality the same kind of injury, by substituting the particular excellence which they pretend to possess, for plain simple uprightness and rectitude.

In Busy or Circumstantial Comedy, all those ingenious contrivances of lovers, guardians, governantes and chamber-maids; that ambushed bush-fighting amongst closets, screens, chests, easy-chairs, and toilet-tables, form a gay varied game of dexterity and invention; which, to those who have played at hide-and-seek, who have crouched down, with beating heart, in a dark corner, whilst the enemy groped near the spot; who have joined their busy school-mates in many a deep-laid plan to deceive, perplex, and torment the unhappy mortals deputed to have the charge of them, cannot be seen with indifference. Like an old hunter, who pricks up his ears at the sound of the chace, and starts away from the path of his journey, so, leaving all wisdom and criticism behind us, we follow the varied changes of the plot, and stop not for reflection. The studious man who wants a cessation from thought, the indolent man who dislikes it, and all those who, from habit or circumstances, live in a state of divorce from their own minds, are pleased with an amusement in which they have nothing to do but to open their eyes and behold; the moral tendency of it, however, is very faulty. That mockery of age and domestick authority, so constantly held forth, has a very bad effect upon the younger part of an audience; and that continual lying and deceit in the first characters of the piece, which is necessary for conducting the plot, has a most pernicious one.

But Characteristick Comedy, which represents to us this motley world of men and women in which we live, under those circumstances of ordinary and familiar life most favourable for the discovery of the human heart, offers to us a wide field of instruction, adapted to general application. We find in its varied scenes an exercise of the mind analogous to that which we all, less or more, find out for ourselves, amidst the mixed groupes of people whom we meet with in society; and which I have already mentioned as an exercise universally pleasing to man. As the distinctions which it is its highest aim to discriminate, are those of nature and not situation, they are judged of by all ranks of men; for a peasant will very clearly perceive in the character of a peer, those native peculiarities which belong to him as a man, though he is entirely at a loss in all that regards his manners and address as a nobleman. It illustrates to us the general remarks we have made upon men; and in it we behold, spread before us, plans of those original groundworks, upon which the general ideas we have been taught to conceive of mankind, are founded. It stands but little in need of busy plot, extraordinary incidents, witty repartee, or studied sentiments. It naturally produces for itself all that it requires; characters who are to speak for themselves, who are to be known by their own words and actions, not by the accounts that are given of them by others, cannot well be developed without considerable variety of judicious incident; a smile that is raised by some trait of undisguised nature, and a laugh that is provoked by some ludicrous effect of passion, or clashing of opposite characters, will be more pleasing to the generality of men, than either the one or the other when occasioned by a play upon words, or a whimsical combination of ideas; and to behold the operation and effects of the different propensities and weaknesses of men, will naturally call up in the mind of the spectator moral reflections more applicable, and more impressive, than all the high-sounding sentiments, with which the graver scenes of Satirical and Sentimental Comedy are so frequently interlarded. It is much to be regretted, however, that the eternal introduction of love as the grand business of the Drama, and the consequent necessity for making the chief persons in it such, in regard to age, appearance, manners, dispositions, and endowments, as are proper for interesting lovers, has occasioned so much insipid similarity in the higher characters. It is chiefly, therefore, on the second and inferiour characters, that the efforts, even of our best poets, have been exhausted; and thus we are called upon to be interested in the fortune of one man, whilst our chief attention is directed to the character of another, which produces a disunion of ideas in the mind, injurious to the general effect of the whole. From this cause, also, those characteristick varieties have been very much neglected, which men present to us in the middle stages of life; when they are too old for lovers or the confidents of lovers, and too young to be the fathers, uncles, and guardians, who are contrasted with them; but when they are still in full vigour of mind, eagerly engaged with the world, joining the activity of youth to the providence of age, and offer to our attention objects sufficiently interesting and instructive. It is to be regretted that strong contrasts of character are too often attempted, instead of those harmonious shades of it, which nature so beautifully varies, and which we so greatly delight in, whenever we clearly distinguish them. It is to be regretted that in place of those characters, which present themselves to the imagination of a writer from his general observations upon mankind, inferiour poets have so often pourtrayed with senseless minuteness the characters of particular individuals. We are pleased with the eccentricities of individuals in real life, and also in history or biography, but in fictitious writings, we regard them with suspicion; and no representation of nature, that corresponds not with some of our general ideas in regard to it, will either instruct or inform us. When the originals of such characters are known and remembered, the plays in which they are introduced are oftentimes popular; and their temporary success has induced a still inferiour class of poets to believe, that, by making men strange, and unlike the rest of the world, they have made great discoveries, and mightily enlarged the boundaries of dramatick character. They will, therefore, distinguish one man from another by some strange whim or imagination, which is ever uppermost in his thoughts, and influences every action of his life; by some singular opinion, perhaps, about politicks, fashions, or the position of the stars; by some strong unaccountable love for one thing or aversion from another; entirely forgetting, that such singularities, if they are to be found in nature, can no where be sought for, with such probability of success, as in Bedlam. Above all it is to be regretted that those adventitious distinctions amongst men, of age, fortune, rank, profession, and country, are so often brought forward in preference to the great original distinctions of nature; and our scenes so often filled with courtiers, lawyers, citizens, Frenchmen, &c. &c. With all the characteristicks of their respective conditions, such as they have been represented from time immemorial. This has introduced a great sameness into many of our plays, which all the changes of new fashions burlesqued, and new customs turned into ridicule, cannot conceal.

In comedy, the stronger passions, love excepted, are seldom introduced but in a passing way. We have short bursts of anger, fits of jealousy and impatience; violent passion of any continuance we seldom find. When this is attempted, however, forgetting that mode of exposing the weakness of the human mind, which peculiarly belongs to her, it is too frequently done in the serious spirit of tragedy; and this has produced so many of those

serious comick plays, which so much divide and distract our attention.★
Yet we all know from our own experience in real life, that, in certain situations, and under certain circumstances, the stronger passions are fitted to
produce scenes more exquisitely comick than any other; and one well-
wrought scene of this kind, will have a more powerful effect in repressing
similar intemperance in the mind of a spectator, than many moral cautions,
or even, perhaps, than the terrifick examples of tragedy. There are to be
found, no doubt, in the works of our best dramatick writers, comick scenes
descriptive of the stronger passions, but it is generally the inferiour characters of the piece who are made the subjects of them, very rarely those in
whom we are much interested; and consequently the useful effect of such
scenes upon the mind is very much weakened. This general appropriation
of them has tempted our less-skilful Dramatists to exaggerate, and step, in
further quest of the ludicrous, so much beyond the bounds of nature, that
the very effect they are so anxious to produce is thereby destroyed, and all
useful application of it entirely cut off; for we never apply to ourselves a
false representation of nature.

But a complete exhibition of passion, with its varieties and progress in
the breast of man has, I believe, scarcely ever been attempted in comedy.
Even love, though the chief subject of almost every play, has been pourtrayed in a loose, scattered, and imperfect manner. The story of the lovers
is acted over before us, whilst the characteristicks of that passion by which

---

★Such plays, however excellent the parts may be of which they are composed, can never
produce the same strength and unity of effect upon our minds which we receive from plays
of a simpler undivided construction. If the serious and distressing scenes make a deep
impression, we do not find ourselves in a humour for the comick ones that succeed; and if the
comick scenes enliven us greatly, we feel tardy and unalert in bringing back our minds to a
proper tone for the serious. As in tragedy we smile at those native traits of character, or that
occasional sprightliness of dialogue, which are sometimes introduced, to animate her
less-interesting parts, so may we be moved by comedy; but our tears should be called forth by
those gentle strokes of nature, which come at once with kindred kindness on the heart, and
are quickly succeeded by smiles. Like a small summer-cloud, whose rain-drops sparkle in the
sun, and which swiftly passes away, is the genuine pathetick of comedy: the gathering foreseen
storm, that darkens the whole face of the sky, belongs to tragedy alone. It is often observed, I
confess, that we are more apt to be affected by those scenes of distress which we meet with in
comedy, than the high-wrought woes of tragedy; and I believe it is true. But this arises from
the woes of tragedy being so often appropriated to high and mighty personages, and strained
beyond the modesty of nature, in order to suit their great dignity; or from the softened griefs
of more gentle and familiar characters being rendered feeble and tiresome with too much
repetition and whining. It arises from the greater facility with which we enter into the
distresses of people, more upon a level with ourselves; and whose sorrows are expressed in less
studied and unnatural language.

they are actuated, and which is the great master-spring of the whole, are faintly to be discovered. We are generally introduced to a lover after he has long been acquainted with his mistress, and wants but the consent of some stubborn relation, relief from some embarrassment of situation, or the clearing up some mistake or love-quarrel occasioned by malice or accident, to make him completely happy. To overcome these difficulties, he is engaged in a busy train of contrivance and exertion, in which the spirit, activity and ingenuity of the man is held forth to view, whilst the lover, comparatively speaking, is kept out of sight. But even when this is not the case; when the lover is not so busied and involved, this stage of the passion is exactly the one that is least interesting, and least instructive: not to mention as I have done already, that one stage of any passion must shew it imperfectly.

From this view of the Comick Drama I have been induced to believe, that, as companions to the forementioned tragedies, a series of comedies on a similar plan, in which bustle of plot, brilliancy of dialogue, and even the bold and striking in character, should, to the best of the authour's judgment, be kept in due subordination to nature, might likewise be acceptable to the publick. I am confident that comedy upon this plan is capable of being made as interesting, as entertaining, and superiour in moral tendency to any other. For even in ordinary life, with very slight cause to excite them, strong passions will foster themselves within the breast; and what are all the evils which vanity, folly, prejudice, or peculiarity of temper lead to, compared with those which such unquiet inmates produce? Were they confined to the exalted and the mighty, to those engaged in the great events of the world, to the inhabitants of palaces and camps, how happy comparatively would this world be! But many a miserable being, whom firm principle, timidity of character, or the fear of shame keeps back from the actual commission of crimes, is tormented in obscurity, under the dominion of those passions which set the seducer in ambush, rouse the bold spoiler to wrong, and strengthen the arm of the murderer. Though to those with whom such dangerous enemies have long found shelter, exposing them in an absurd and ridiculous light, may be shooting a finely-pointed arrow against the hardened rock; yet to those with whom they are but new, and less assured guests, this may prove a more successful mode of attack than any other.

It was the saying of a sagacious Scotchman, 'let who will make the laws of a nation, if I have the writing of its ballads.' Something similar to this may be said in regard to the Drama. Its lessons reach not, indeed, to the lowest classes of the labouring people, who are the broad foundation of society, which can never be generally moved without endangering every thing that is constructed upon it, and who are our potent and formidable ballad readers; but they reach to the classes next in order to them, and who will always have over them no inconsiderable influence. The impressions made by it are communicated, at the same instant of time, to a greater number of individuals, than those made by any other species of writing; and they are strengthened in every spectator, by observing their effects upon those who surround him. From this observation, the mind of my reader will suggest of itself, what it would be unnecessary, and, perhaps, improper in me here to enlarge upon. The theatre is a school in which much good or evil may be learned. At the beginning of its career the Drama was employed to mislead and excite; and were I not unwilling to refer to transactions of the present times, I might abundantly confirm what I have said by recent examples. The authour, therefore, who aims in any degree to improve the mode of its instruction, and point to more useful lessons than it is generally employed to dispense, is certainly praiseworthy, though want of abilities may unhappily prevent him from being successful in his efforts.

This idea has prompted me to begin a work in which I am aware of many difficulties. In plays of this nature the passions must be depicted not only with their bold and prominent features, but also with those minute and delicate traits which distinguish them in an infant, growing, and repressed state; which are the most difficult of all to counterfeit, and one of which falsely imagined, will destroy the effect of a whole scene. The characters over whom they are made to usurp dominion, must be powerful and interesting, exercising them with their full measure of opposition and struggle; for the chief antagonists they contend with must be the other passions and propensities of the heart, not outward circumstances and events. Though belonging to such characters, they must still be held to view in their most baleful and unseductive light; and those qualities in the impassioned which are necessary to interest us in their fate, must not be allowed, by any lustre borrowed from them, to diminish our abhorrence of guilt. The second and even the inferiour persons of each play, as they must be kept perfectly distinct from the great impassioned one, should generally be represented in a calm unagitated state, and therefore more pains is necessary than in other dramatick works, to mark them by appropriate distinctions of character, lest they should appear altogether insipid and insignificant. As the great object here is to trace passion through all its varieties, and in every stage, many of which are marked by shades so delicate, that in much bustle of events they would be little attended to, or entirely overlooked, simplicity of plot is more necessary, than in those plays where only occasional bursts of passion are introduced, to distinguish a character, or animate a scene. But where simplicity of plot is necessary, there is very great danger of making a piece appear bare and unvaried, and nothing but great force and truth in the delineations of nature will prevent it from being tiresome.★ Soliloquy, or those overflowings of the perturbed soul, in which it unburthens itself of those thoughts which it cannot communicate to others, and which in certain situations is the only mode that a Dramatist can employ to open to us the mind he would display, must necessarily be often, and to considerable length, introduced. Here, indeed, as it naturally belongs to passion, it will not be so offensive as it generally is in other plays, when a calm unagitated person tells over to himself all that has befallen him, and all his future schemes of intrigue or advancement; yet to make speeches of this kind sufficiently natural and impressive, to excite no degree of weariness nor distaste, will be found to be no easy task. There are, besides these, many other difficulties peculiarly belonging to this undertaking, too minute and tedious to mention. If, fully aware of them, I have not shrunk back from the attempt, it is not from any idea that my own powers or discernment will at all times enable me to overcome them; but I am emboldened by the confidence I feel in that candour and indulgence, with which the good and enlightened do ever regard the experimental efforts of those, who wish in any degree to enlarge the sources of pleasure and instruction amongst men. . . .

From "To the Reader," from *A Series of Plays* (1812)

The Series of Plays was originally published in the hope that some of the pieces it contains, although first given to the Public from the press, might in time make their way to the stage, and there be received and supported

---

★To make up for this simplicity of plot, the shew and decorations of the theatre ought to be allowed, to plays written upon this plan, in their full extent. How fastidious soever some poets may be in regard to these matters, it is much better to relieve our tired-out attention with a battle, a banquet, or a procession, than an accumulation of incidents. In the latter case the mind is harassed and confused with those doubts, conjectures, and disappointments which multiplied events occasion, and in a great measure unfitted for attending to the worthier parts of the piece; but in the former it enjoys a rest, a pleasing pause in its more serious occupation, from which it can return again, without any incumberance of foreign intruding ideas. The shew of a splendid procession will afford to a person of the best understanding, a pleasure in kind, though not in degree, with that which a child would receive from it. But when it is past he thinks no more of it; whereas some confusion of circumstances, some half-explained mistake, which gives him no pleasure at all when it takes place, may take off his attention afterwards from the refined beauties of a natural and characteristick dialogue.

with some degree of public favour.[1] But the present situation of dramatic affairs is greatly against every hope of this kind; and should they ever become more favourable, I have now good reason to believe, that the circumstance of these plays having been already published, would operate strongly against their being received upon the stage. I am therefore strongly of opinion that I ought to reserve the remainder of the work in manuscript, if I would not run the risk of entirely frustrating my original design. Did I believe that their having been already published would not afterwards obstruct their way to the stage, the untowardness of present circumstances should not prevent me from continuing to publish.

Having thus given an account of my views and intentions regarding this work, I hope that, should no more of it be published in my lifetime, it will not be supposed I have abandoned or become weary of my occupation; which is in truth as interesting and pleasing to me now as it was at the beginning.

But when I say, present circumstances are unfavourable for the reception of these Plays upon the stage, let it not be supposed that I mean to throw any reflection upon the prevailing taste for dramatic amusements. The Public have now to chuse between what we shall suppose are well-written and well-acted Plays, the words of which are not heard, or heard but imperfectly by two thirds of the audience, while the finer and more pleasing traits of the acting are by a still greater proportion lost altogether, and splendid pantomime, or pieces whose chief object is to produce striking scenic effect, which can be seen and comprehended by the whole. So situated, it would argue, methinks, a very pedantic love indeed, for what is called legitimate Drama, were we to prefer the former. A love for active, varied movement in the objects before us; for striking contrasts of light and shadow; for splendid decorations and magnificent scenery, is as inherent in us as the interest we take in the representation of the natural passions and characters of men: and the most cultivated minds may relish such exhibitions, if they do not, when both are fairly offered to their choice, prefer them. Did our ears and our eyes permit us to hear and see distinctly in a Theatre so large as to admit of chariots and horsemen, and all the "pomp and circumstance of war," I see no reason why we should reject them. They would give variety, and an appearance of truth to the scenes of heroic Tragedy, that would very much heighten its effect. We ought not, then, to find fault with the taste of the Public for preferring an inferior species of entertainment, good of its kind, to a superior one, faintly and imperfectly given.

It has been urged, as a proof of this supposed bad taste in the Public, by one whose judgment on these subjects is and ought to be high authority, that a play, possessing considerable merit, was produced some years ago on Drury-Lane stage, and notwithstanding the great support it received from excellent acting and magnificent decoration, entirely failed. It is very true that, in spite of all this, it failed, during the eight nights it continued to be acted, to produce houses sufficiently good to induce the Managers to revive it afterwards. But it ought to be acknowledged, that that piece had defects in it as an acting Play, which served to counterbalance those advantages; and likewise that, if any supposed merit in the writing ought to have redeemed those defects, in a theatre, so large and so ill calculated to convey sound as the one in which it was performed, it was impossible this could be felt or comprehended by even a third part of the audience.

The size of our theatres, then, is what I chiefly allude to, when I say, present circumstances are unfavourable for the production of these Plays. While they continue to be of this size, it is a vain thing to complain either of want of taste in the Public, or want of inclination in Managers to bring forward new pieces of merit, taking it for granted that there are such to produce. Nothing can be truly relished by the most cultivated audience that is not distinctly heard and seen, and Managers must produce what will be relished. Shakespeare's Plays, and some of our other old Plays, indeed, attract full houses, though they are often repeated, because, being familiar to the audience, they can still understand and follow them pretty closely, though but imperfectly heard; and surely this is no bad sign of our public taste. And besides this advantage, when a piece is familiar to the audience, the expression of the actors' faces is much better understood, though seen imperfectly; for the stronger marked traits of feeling which even in a large theatre may reach the eyes of a great part of the audience, from the recollection of finer and more delicate indications, formerly seen so delightfully mingled with them in the same countenances during the same passages of the Play, will, by association, still convey them to the mind's eye, though it is the mind's eye only which they have reached.

And this thought leads me to another defect in large theatres, that ought to be considered.

Our great tragic actress, Mrs. Siddons,[2] whose matchless powers of expression have so long been the pride of our stage, and the most admired actors of the present time, have been brought up in their youth in small theatres, where they were encouraged to enter thoroughly into the characters they represented; and to express in their faces that variety of fine fleeting emotion which nature, in moments of agitation, assumes, and the imitation of which we are taught by nature to delight in. But succeeding actors will only consider expression of countenance as addressed to an audience removed from them to a greater distance; and will only attempt such strong expression as can be perceived and have effect at a distance. It may easily be imagined what exaggerated expression will then get into use; and I should think, even this strong expression will not only be exaggerated but false. For, as we are enabled to assume the outward signs of passion, not by mimicking what we have beheld in others, but by internally assuming, in some degree, the passion itself; a mere outline of it cannot, I apprehend, be given as an outline of figure frequently is, where all that is delineated is true though the whole is not filled up. Nay, besides having it exaggerated and false, it will perpetually be thrust in where it ought not to be. For real occasions of strong expression not occurring often enough, and weaker being of no avail, to avoid an apparent barrenness of countenance, they will be tempted to introduce it where it is not wanted, and thereby destroy its effect where it is.—I say nothing of expression of voice, to which the above observations obviously apply. This will become equally, if not in a greater degree, false and exaggerated, in actors trained from their youth in a large theatre.

But the department of acting that will suffer most under these circumstances, is that which particularly regards the gradually unfolding of the passions, and has, perhaps, hitherto been less understood than any other part of the art—I mean Soliloquy. What actor in his senses will then think of giving to the solitary musing of a perturbed mind that muttered, imperfect articulation which grows by degrees into words; that heavy, suppressed voice as of one speaking through sleep; that rapid burst of sounds which often succeeds the slow languid tones of distress; those sudden, untuned exclamations which, as if frightened at their own discord, are struck again into silence as sudden and abrupt, with all the corresponding variety of countenance that belongs to it;—what actor, so situated, will attempt to exhibit all this? No; he will be satisfied, after taking a turn or two across the front of the stage, to place himself directly in the middle of it; and there, spreading out his hands as if he were addressing some person whom it behoved him to treat with great ceremony, to tell to himself, in an audible uniform voice, all the secret thoughts of his own heart. When he has done this, he will think, and he will think rightly, that he has done enough.

The only valuable part of acting that will then remain to us, will be expression of gesture, grace and dignity, supposing that these also shall not become affected by being too much attended to and studied.

It may be urged against such apprehensions that, though the theatres of the metropolis should be large, they will be supplied with actors, who have been trained to the stage in small country-theatres. An actor of ambition (and all actors of genius are such) will practise with little heart in the country what he knows will be of no use to him on a London stage; not to mention that the style of acting in London will naturally be the fashionable and prevailing style elsewhere. Acting will become a less respectable profession than it has continued to be from the days of Garrick; and the few actors, who add to the natural advantages requisite to it, the accomplishments of a scholar and a gentleman, will soon be wed away by the hand of time, leaving nothing of the same species behind them to spring from a neglected and sapless root.

All I have said on this subject, may still in a greater degree be applied to actresses; for the features and voice of a woman, being naturally more delicate than those of a man, she must suffer in proportion from the defects of a large theatre.

The great disadvantage of such over-sized buildings to natural and genuine acting, is, I believe, very obvious; but they have other defects which are not so readily noticed, because they, in some degree, run counter to the common opinion of their great superiority in every thing that regards general effect. The diminutive appearance of individual figures, and the straggling poverty of grouping, which unavoidably takes place when a very wide and lofty stage is not filled by a great number of people, is very injurious to general effect. This is particularly felt in Comedy, and all plays on domestic subjects; and in those scenes also of the grand drama, where two or three persons only are produced at a time. To give figures who move upon it proper effect, there must be depth as well as width of stage; and the one must bear some proportion to the other, if we would not make every closer or more confined scene appear like a section of a long passage, in which the actors move before us, apparently in one line, like the figures of a magic lanthorn.

It appears to me, that when a stage is of such a size that as many persons as generally come into action at one time in our grandest and best-peopled plays, can be produced on the front of it in groups, without crowding together more than they would naturally do any where else for the convenience of speaking to one another, all is gained in point of general effect that can well be gained. When modern gentlemen and ladies talk to one another in a spacious saloon, or when ancient warriors and dames conversed together in an old baronial hall, they do not, and did not stand further apart than when conversing in a room of common dimensions; neither ought they to do so on the stage. All width of stage, beyond what is convenient for such natural grouping, is lost; and worse than lost, for it is injurious. It is continually presenting us with something similar to that which always offends us in a picture, where the canvas is too large for the subject; or in a face where the features are too small for the bald margin of cheeks and forehead that surrounds them.

Even in the scenes of professed shew and spectacle, where nothing else is considered, it appears to me that a very large stage is in some degree injurious to general effect. Even when a battle is represented in our theatres, the great width of the stage is a disadvantage; for as it never can nor ought to be represented but partially, and the part which is seen should be crowded and confused, opening a large front betrays your want of numbers; or should you be rich enough in this respect to fill it sufficiently, imposes upon you a difficulty seldom surmounted, viz. putting the whole mass sufficiently in action to sustain the deception.★ When a moderate number of combatants, so as to make one connected groupe, are fighting on the front of a moderately wide stage, which they sufficiently occupy, it is an easy thing, through the confusion of their brandished weapons and waving banners, to give the appearance of a deep active battle beyond them, seen, as it were, through a narrow pass; and beholding all the tumult of battle in the small view opened before us, our imagination supplies what is hid. If we open a wider view, we give the imagination less to do, and supply what it would have done less perfectly. In narrowing our battle, likewise, we could more easily throw smoke or an appearance of dust over the back ground, and procure for our fancy an unlimited space.

In processions, also, the most pleasing effect to our imaginations is, when the marshalled figures are seen in long perspective which requires only depth of stage; and the only advantage a wide stage has on such occasions is containing the assembled mass of figures, when the moving line stops and gathers itself together on the front. The rich confusion of such a crowd is indeed very brilliant and pleasing for a short time, but it is dearly purchased at the price of many sacrifices.

★The objections above do not apply to scenes where sieges are represented; for then the more diminished the actors appear, the greater is the importance and magnitude given to the walls or castle which they attack, while the towers and buttresses, &c, sufficiently occupy the width and heighth of the stage, and conceal the want of numbers and general activity in the combatants. And the managers of our present large theatre have, in my opinion, shewn great judgment in introducing into their mixed pieces of late so many good scenes of this kind, that have, to my fancy at least, afforded a grand and animating shew. Nor do they fairly apply to those combats or battles into which horses are introduced; for a moderate number of those noble animals may be made to occupy and animate, in one connected groupe, the front of the widest stage that we are in danger of having, and to conceal the want of a numerous host and tumultuous battle behind them.

On those occasions too, when many people are assembled on the front of the stage to give splendour and importance to some particular scene, or to the conclusion of a piece, the general effect is often injured by great width of stage. For the crowd is supposed to be attracted to the spot by something which engages their attention; and, as they must not surround this object of attention, (which would be their natural arrangement,) lest they should conceal it from the audience, they are obliged to spread themselves out in a long straight line on each side of it: now the shorter those lines or wings are, spreading out from the centre figures, the less do they offend against natural arrangement, and the less artificial and formal does the whole scene appear.

In short, I scarcely know of any advantage which a large stage possesses over one of a moderate size without great abatements, even in regard to general effect, unless it be when it is empty, and scenery alone engages our attention, or when figures appear at a distance on the back ground only. Something in confirmation of what I have been saying, has, perhaps, been felt by most people on entering a grand cathedral, where, figures moving in the long aisles at a distance, add grandeur to the building by their diminished appearance; but in approaching near enough to become themselves distinct objects of attention, look stunted and mean, without serving to enlarge by comparison its general dimensions.

There is also, I apprehend, greater difficulty, in a very wide and lofty stage, to produce variety of light and shadow; and this often occasions the more solemn scenes of Tragedy to be represented in a full, staring, uniform light that ought to be dimly seen in twilight uncertainty; or to have the objects on them shewn by partial gleams only, while the deepened shade around gives a sombre indistinctness to the other parts of the stage, particularly favourable to solemn or terrific impressions. And it would be more difficult, I imagine, to throw down light upon the objects on such a stage, which I have never indeed seen attempted in any theatre, though it might surely be done in one of moderate dimensions with admirable effect. In short, a great variety of pleasing effects from light and shadow might be more easily produced on a smaller stage, that would give change and even interest to pieces otherwise monotonous and heavy; and would often be very useful in relieving the exhausted strength of the chief actors, while want of skill in the inferior could be craftily concealed. On this part of the subject, however, I speak with great diffidence, not knowing to what perfection machinery for the management of light may be brought in a large theatre. But at the same time, I am certain that, by a judicious use of light and scenery, an artificial magnitude may be given to a stage of a moderate size, that would, to the eye, as far as distance in perspective is concerned, have an effect almost equal to any thing that can be produced on a larger stage: for that apparent magnitude arising from succession of objects, depends upon the depth of the stage, much more than its width and loftiness, which are often detrimental to it; and a small or moderate sized theatre may have, without injury to proportion, a very deep stage.

It would be, I believe, impertinent to pursue this subject any farther; and I beg pardon for having obtruded it so far where it may not appear naturally to be called for. I plead in my excuse an almost irresistible desire to express my thoughts, in some degree, upon what has occupied them considerably; and a strong persuasion that I ought not, how unimportant soever they may be, entirely to conceal them.

Notes

"Introductory Discourse"

1. Baillie refers here to the notion that tragedy originated in ancient Greek rituals aimed at celebrating the yearly death and rebirth of the nature god Dionysius. Aristotle derives tragedy from the dithyramb, a hymn to Dionysius.

2. From the Gospels (Matthew 26:39, Mark 14:36, Luke 22:42).

"To the Reader"

1. Baillie's ambition in *Plays on the Passions* was to write a separate play to illustrate each of the human emotions or passions.

2. Sarah Siddons (1755–1831), most famous tragic actress of her time.

ANN WARD RADCLIFFE
(1764-1823)

Aɴɴ Rᴀᴅᴄʟɪꜰꜰᴇ was the only daughter of prosperous tradespeople William and Ann Ward. Through her uncle Thomas Bentley and his partner, Josiah Wedgewood, she met a circle of literary people in London, including Hester Thrale and Elizabeth Montagu. Her husband, William Radcliffe, edited the *Gazette* and owned the *English Chronicle*. Her novels—*A Sicilian Romance* (1790), *The Romance of the Forest* (1791), *The Mysteries of Udolpho* (1794), and *The Italian* (1797)—earned her large sums of money and favorable notice both critical and popular. Radcliffe retired from professional writing early, living quietly for the last two decades of her life.

In popular consciousness Radcliffe was a mistress of terror: as Austen's Henry Tilney says of *Udolpho*, "I remember finishing it in two days—my hair standing on end the whole time." Such responses tend to obscure the careful crafting of Radcliffe's works as well as their aesthetic purposes. Her novels may be seen to have put into practice the theories of Edmund Burke's *Philosophical Enquiry into the Origin of Our Ideas of the Sublime and the Beautiful*, particularly his notion that "terror is a passion which always produces delight when it does not press too close" and his emphasis on obscurity as a necessity for the sublime. Distinguishing terror from horror, Radcliffe aims at sublimity by representing terror in the minds of her heroines. But she also seems committed to Joshua Reynolds's tenet in *Discourses on Art* that "in the midst of the highest flights of fancy or imagination, reason ought to preside from first to last." As her criticisms of Dryden's alterations of Shakespeare suggest, she rejects exaggeration on the writer's part. At the same time, she is an early practitioner of textual strategies that build emotional rather than episodic suspense.

The posthumously published essay included here illuminates Radcliffe's aesthetic premises and demonstrates that she was a critic and theorist as well as a writer of thrilling fiction. "On the Supernatural in Poetry" was originally designed as part of *Gaston de Blondville, or The Court of Henry III Keeping Festival in Ardenne, A Romance* (1826). But the novel omits it, only alluding to "a conversation on illusions of the imagination and on the various powers of exciting them, shown by English poets, especially by Shakespeare and Milton, which it is unnecessary to repeat in this place." In exploring the production of terror by England's greatest poets, Radcliffe also suggests the value of her own work.

The New Monthly Magazine and Literary Journal 16 (1826): 145–152.

On the Supernatural in Poetry* (1826)

One of our travellers began a grave dissertation on the illusions of the imagination. "And not only on frivolous occasions," said he, "but in the most important pursuits of life, an object often flatters and charms at a distance, which vanishes into nothing as we approach it; and 'tis well if it leave only disappointment in our hearts. Sometimes a severer monitor is left there."

These truisms, delivered with an air of discovery by Mr. S——, who seldom troubled himself to think upon any subject, except that of a good dinner, were lost upon his companion, who, pursuing the airy conjectures which the present scene, however humbled, had called up, was following Shakspeare into unknown regions. "Where is now the undying spirit," said he, "that could so exquisitely perceive and feel?—that could inspire itself with the various characters of this world, and create worlds of its own; to which the grand and the beautiful, the gloomy and the sublime of visible Nature, up-called not only corresponding feelings, but passions; which seemed to perceive a soul in every thing: and thus, in the secret workings of its own characters, and in the combinations of its incidents, kept the elements and local scenery always in unison with them, heightening their effect. So the conspirators at Rome pass under the fiery showers and sheeted lightning of the thunder-storm, to meet, at midnight, in the porch of Pompey's theatre. The streets being then deserted by the affrighted multitude, that place, open as it was, was convenient for their council; and, as to the storm, they felt it not; it was not more terrible to them than their own passions, nor so terrible to others as the dauntless spirit that makes them, almost unconsciously, brave its fury. These appalling circumstances, with

*Having been permitted to extract the above eloquent passages from the manuscripts of the author of the "Mysteries of Udolpho," we have given this title to them, though certainly they were not intended by the writer to be offered as a formal or deliberate essay, under this, or any other denomination. They were, originally, part of an INTRODUCTION to the Romance, or Phantasie, which is about to appear. The discussion is supposed to be carried on by two travellers in Shakspeare's native county, Warwickshire.

others of supernatural import, attended the fall of the conqueror of the world—a man, whose power Cassius represents to be dreadful as this night, when the sheeted dead were seen in the lightning to glide along the streets of Rome.¹ How much does the sublimity of these attendant circumstances heighten our idea of the power of Cæsar, of the terrific grandeur of his character, and prepare and interest us for his fate. The whole soul is roused and fixed, in the full energy of attention, upon the progress of the conspiracy against him; and, had not Shakspeare wisely withdrawn him from our view, there would have been no balance of our passions."—"Cæsar was a tyrant," said Mr. S———. W——— looked at him for a moment, and smiled, and then silently resumed the course of his own thoughts. No master ever knew how to touch the accordant springs of sympathy by small circumstances like our own Shakspeare. In Cymbeline, for instance, how finely such circumstances are made use of, to awaken, at once, solemn expectation and tenderness, and, by recalling the softened remembrance of a sorrow long past, to prepare the mind to melt at one that was approaching, mingling at the same time, by means of a mysterious occurrence, a slight tremour of awe with our pity. Thus, when Belarius and Arviragus return to the cave where they had left the unhappy and worn-out Imogen to repose, while they are yet standing before it, and Arviragus, speaking of her with tenderest pity, as "the poor sick Fidele," goes out to enquire for her,—solemn music is heard from the cave, sounded by that harp of which Guiderius says, "*Since the death of my dearest mother, it did not speak before. All solemn things should answer solemn accidents.*" Immediately Arviragus enters with Fidele senseless in his arms:

> "The bird is dead, that we have made so much of.
> ———How found you him?
> Stark, as you see, thus smiling.
> ———I thought he slept, and put
> My clouted brogues from off my feet, whose rudeness
> Answered my steps too loud."—"Why he but sleeps!"
>   *   *   *   *   *
>   "With fairest flowers
> While summer lasts, AND I LIVE HERE. FIDELE,
> I'll sweeten thy sad grave———."²

Tears alone can speak the touching simplicity of the whole scene. Macbeth shows, by many instances, how much Shakspeare delighted to heighten the effect of his characters and his story by correspondent scenery: there

the desolate heath, the troubled elements, assist the mischief of his malig-
nant beings. But who, after hearing Macbeth's thrilling question—

> ———"What are these,
> So withered and so wild in their attire,
> That look not like the inhabitants o' the earth,
> And yet are on't?"———3

who would have thought of reducing them to mere human beings, by at-
tiring them not only like the inhabitants of the earth, but in the dress of a
particular country, and making them downright Scotch-women? thus not
only contradicting the very words of Macbeth, but withdrawing from these
cruel agents of the passions all that strange and supernatural air which had
made them so affecting to the imagination, and which was entirely suitable
to the solemn and important events they were foretelling and accomplishing. Another *improvement* on Shakspeare is the introducing a crowd of
witches thus arrayed, instead of the three beings "so withered and so wild
in their attire."4

About the latter part of this sentence, W———, as he was apt to do,
thought aloud, and Mr. S——— said, "*I*, now, have sometimes considered,
that it was quite suitable to make Scotch witches on the stage, appear like
Scotch women. You must recollect that, in the superstition concerning
witches, they lived familiarly upon the earth, mortal sorcerers, and were not
always known from mere old women; consequently they must have appeared in the dress of the country where they happened to live, or they
would have been more than suspected of witchcraft, which we find was
not always the case."

"You are speaking of old women, and not of witches," said W———
laughing, "and I must more than suspect you of crediting that obsolete
superstition which destroyed so many wretched, yet guiltless persons, if I
allow your argument to have any force. I am speaking of the only real witch—
the witch of the poet; and all our notions and feelings connected with terror
accord with his. The wild attire, the look *not of this earth*, are essential traits
of supernatural agents, working evil in the darkness of mystery. Whenever
the poet's witch condescends, according to the vulgar notion, to mingle
mere ordinary mischief with her malignity, and to become familiar, she is
ludicrous, and loses her power over the imagination; the illusion vanishes.
So vexatious is the effect of the stage-witches upon my mind, that I should
probably have left the theatre when they appeared, had not the fascination
of Mrs. Siddons's influence so spread itself over the whole play, as to overcome my disgust, and to make me forget even Shakspeare himself; while

all consciousness of fiction was lost, and his thoughts lived and breathed before me in the very form of truth. Mrs. Siddons, like Shakspeare, always disappears in the character she represents, and throws an illusion over the whole scene around her, that conceals many defects in the arrangements of the theatre.[5] I should suppose she would be the finest Hamlet that ever appeared, excelling even her own brother in that character; she would more fully preserve the tender and refined melancholy, the deep sensibility, which are the peculiar charm of Hamlet, and which appear not only in the ardour, but in the occasional irresolution and weakness of his character—the secret spring that reconciles all his inconsistencies. A sensibility so profound can with difficulty be justly imagined, and therefore can very rarely be assumed. Her brother's firmness, incapable of being always subdued, does not so fully enhance, as her tenderness would, this part of the character. The strong light which shows the mountains of a landscape in all their greatness, and with all their rugged sharpnesses, gives them nothing of the interest with which a more gloomy tint would invest their grandeur; dignifying, though it softens, and magnifying, while it obscures."

"I still think," said Mr. S———, without attending to these remarks, "that, in a popular superstition, it is right to go with the popular notions, and dress your witches like the old women of the place where they are supposed to have appeared."

"As far as these notions prepare us for the awe which the poet designs to excite, I agree with you that he is right in availing himself of them; but, for this purpose, every thing familiar and common should be carefully avoided. In nothing has Shakspeare been more successful than in this; and in another case somewhat more difficult—that of selecting circumstances of manners and appearance for his supernatural beings, which, though wild and remote, in the highest degree, from common apprehension, never shock the understanding by incompatibility with themselves—never compel us, for an instant, to recollect that he has a licence for extravagance. Above every ideal being is the ghost of Hamlet, with all its attendant incidents of time and place. [Mr. W——— describes the mysterious solemnity of the scene preceding Hamlet's encounter with the ghost, insisting that whether or not ghosts exist, "probability is enough for the poet's justification."] . . . There is, however, no little vexation in seeing the ghost of Hamlet *played*. The finest imagination is requisite to give the due colouring to such a character on the stage; and yet almost any actor is thought capable of performing it. In the scene where Horatio breaks his secret to Hamlet, Shakspeare, still true to the touch of circumstances, makes the time evening, and marks it by the very words of Hamlet, 'Good even, sir,' which Hanmer and Warburton changed, without any reason, to 'good morning,' thus making Horatio relate his most interesting and solemn story by the clear light of the cheerfullest part of the day; when busy sounds are stirring, and the sun itself seems to contradict every doubtful tale, and lessen every feeling of terror. The discord of this must immediately be understood by those who have bowed the willing soul to the poet."

"How happens it then," said Mr. S———, "that objects of terror sometimes strike us very forcibly, when introduced into scenes of gaiety and splendour, as, for instance, in the Banquet scene in Macbeth?"[6]

"They strike, then, chiefly by the force or contrast," replied W——— "but the effect, though sudden and strong, is also transient; it is the thrill of horror and surprise, which they then communicate, rather than the deep and solemn feelings excited under more accordant circumstances, and left long upon the mind. Who ever suffered for the ghost of Banquo, the gloomy and sublime kind of terror, which that of Hamlet calls forth? though the appearance of Banquo, at the high festival of Macbeth, not only tells us that he is murdered, but recalls to our minds the fate of the gracious Duncan, laid in silence and death by those who, in this very scene, are revelling in his spoils. There, though deep pity mingles with our surprise and horror, we experience a far less degree of interest, and that interest too of an inferior kind. The union of grandeur and obscurity, which Mr. Burke describes as a sort of tranquillity tinged with terror, and which causes the sublime, is to be found only in Hamlet; or in scenes where circumstances of the same kind prevail."

"That may be," said Mr. S———, "and I perceive you are not one of those who contend that obscurity does not make any part of the sublime." "They must be men of very cold imaginations," said W———, "with whom certainty is more terrible than surmise. Terror and horror are so far opposite, that the first expands the soul, and awakens the faculties to a high degree of life; the other contracts, freezes, and nearly annihilates them. I apprehend, that neither Shakspeare nor Milton by their fictions, nor Mr. Burke by his reasoning, anywhere looked to positive horror as a source of the sublime, though they all agree that terror is a very high one; and where lies the great difference between horror and terror, but in the uncertainty and obscurity, that accompany the first, respecting the dreaded evil?"

"But what say you to Milton's image—

"On his brow sat horror plumed."[7]

"As an image, it certainly is sublime; it fills the mind with an idea of power, but it does not follow that Milton intended to declare the feeling of horror to be sublime; and after all, his image imparts more of terror than of horror; for it is not distinctly pictured forth, but is seen in glimpses through obscuring shades, the great outlines only appearing, which excite the imagination to complete the rest; he only says, 'sat horror plumed;' you will observe, that the look of horror and the other characteristics are left to the imagination of the reader; and according to the strength of that, he will feel Milton's image to be either sublime or otherwise. Milton, when he sketched it, probably felt, that not even his art could fill up the outline, and present to other eyes the countenance which his 'mind's eye' gave to him. Now, if obscurity has so much effect on fiction, what must it have in real life, when to ascertain the object of our terror, is frequently to acquire the means of escaping it. You will observe, that this image, though indistinct or obscure, is not confused."

"How can any thing be indistinct and not confused?" said Mr. S——.

"Ay, that question is from the new school," replied W.; "but recollect, that obscurity, or indistinctness, is only a negative, which leaves the imagination to act upon the few hints that truth reveals to it; confusion is a thing as positive as distinctness, though not necessarily so palpable; and it may, by mingling and confounding one image with another, absolutely counteract the imagination, instead of exciting it. Obscurity leaves something for the imagination to exaggerate; confusion, by blurring one image into another, leaves only a chaos in which the mind can find nothing to be magnificent, nothing to nourish its fears or doubts, or to act upon in any way; yet confusion and obscurity are terms used indiscriminately by those, who would prove, that Shakspeare and Milton were wrong when they employed obscurity as a cause of the sublime, that Mr. Burke was equally mistaken in his reasoning upon the subject, and that mankind have been equally in error, as to the nature of their own feelings, when they were acted upon by the illusions of those great masters of the imagination, at whose so potent bidding, the passions have been awakened from their sleep, and by whose magic a crowded Theatre has been changed to a lonely shore, to a witch's cave, to an enchanted island, to a murderer's castle, to the ramparts of an usurper, to the battle, to the midnight carousal of the camp or the tavern, to every various scene of the living world."

"Yet there are poets, and great ones too," said Mr. S——, "whose minds do not appear to have been very susceptible of those circumstances of time and space—of what you, perhaps, would call the picturesque in feeling—which you seem to think so necessary to the attainment of any powerful effect on the imagination. What say you to Dryden?"

"That he had a very strong imagination, a fertile wit, a mind well prepared by education, and great promptness of feeling; but he had not—at least not in good proportion to his other qualifications—that delicacy of feeling, which we call taste; moreover, that his genius was overpowered by the prevailing taste of the court, and by an intercourse with the world, too often humiliating to his morals, and destructive of his sensibility. Milton's better morals protected his genius, and his imagination was not lowered by the world."

"Then you seem to think there may be great poets, without a full perception of the picturesque; I mean by picturesque, the beautiful and grand in nature and in art—and with little susceptibility to what you would call the accordant circumstances, the harmony of which is essential to any powerful effect upon your feelings."

"No; I cannot allow that. Such men may have high talents, wit, genius, judgment, but not the soul of poetry, which is the spirit of all these, and also something wonderfully higher—something too fine for definition. It certainly includes an instantaneous perception, and an exquisite love of whatever is graceful, grand, and sublime, with the power of seizing and combining such circumstances of them, as to strike and interest a reader by the representation, even more than a general view of the real scene itself could do. Whatever this may be called, which crowns the mind of a poet, and distinguishes it from every other mind, our whole heart instantly acknowledges it in Shakspeare, Milton, Gray, Collins, Beattie, and a very few others, not excepting Thomson, to whose powers the sudden tear of delight and admiration bears at once both testimony and tribute.[8] How deficient Dryden was of a poet's feelings in the fine province of the beautiful and the graceful, is apparent from his alteration of the Tempest, by which he has not only lessened the interest by incumbering the plot, but has absolutely disfigured the character of Miranda, whose simplicity, whose tenderness and innocent affections, might, to use Shakspeare's own words in another play, 'be shrined in crystal.'[9] A love of moral beauty is as essential in the mind of a poet, as a love of picturesque beauty. There is as much difference between the tone of Dryden's moral feelings and those of Milton, as there is between their perceptions of the grand and the beautiful in nature. Yet, when I recollect the 'Alexander's Feast,' I am astonished at the powers of Dryden, and at my own daring opinions upon them; and should be ready to unsay much that I have said, did I not consider this particular instance of the power of music upon Dryden's mind, to be as wonderful as any instance he has exhibited of the effect of that enchanting art in his sublime ode. I cannot, however, allow it to be the finest ode in the English language, so long as I remember Gray's Bard, and Collins's Ode on the Passions.—But, to return to Shakspeare, I have sometimes thought, as I walked in the deep shade of the North Terrace of Windsor Castle, when the moon shone on all beyond, that the scene must have been present in Shakspeare's mind, when he drew the night-scenes in Hamlet; and, as I have stood on the platform, which there projects over the precipice, and have heard only the measured step of a sentinel or the clink of his arms, and have seen his shadow passing by moonlight, at the foot of the high Eastern tower, I have almost expected to see the royal shade armed cap-a-pee standing still on the lonely platform before me. The very star—'yon same star that's westward from the pole'—seemed to watch over the Western towers of the Terrace, whose high dark lines marked themselves upon the heavens. All has been so still and shadowy, so great and solemn, that the scene appeared fit for 'no mortal business nor any sounds that the earth owns.' Did you ever observe the fine effect of the Eastern tower, when you stand near the Western end of the North terrace, and its tall profile rears itself upon the sky, from nearly the base to the battled top, the lowness of the parapet permitting this? It is most striking at night, when the stars appear, at different heights, upon its tall dark line, and when the sentinel on watch moves a shadowy figure at its foot."

Notes

1. *Julius Caesar*, I.iii and II.i.
2. *Cymbeline*, IV.ii.166–191.
3. *Macbeth*, I.iii.38–42.
4. Radcliffe could be referring to a number of "improved" versions of *Macbeth*, such as Davenant's operatic version, which had four witches.
5. Sarah Siddons (1755–1831) was the principal tragic actress of her time, and Lady Macbeth was one of her most famous roles. Her brother, John Philip Kemble (1757–1823), was the principal male actor and manager of Drury Lane from 1788 to 1796, best known for his tragic roles, especially Hamlet.
6. *Macbeth*, III.iv.
7. *Paradise Lost*, 4.989, misquoted.
8. Thomas Gray (1716–1771), William Collins (1721–1759), James Beattie (1735–1803), and James Thomson (1700–1748) were all known as poets of sensibility. Radcliffe compares Gray's *Bard* (1757) and Collins's *Passions. An Ode for Music* (1747) to works of John Dryden (1631–1700), whose *Alexander's Feast* (1697) celebrates the power of music.
9. Dryden and Davenant's version of *The Tempest* (1667) introduced new characters and a new subplot, and was popular well into the eighteenth century.

DOROTHEA MENDELSSOHN VEIT SCHLEGEL (1764–1839)

BORN Brendel Mendelssohn, eldest daughter of the renowned German-Jewish philosopher Moses Mendelssohn, Dorothea (as she liked to call herself) entered an arranged marriage at age nineteen to the banker Simon Veit. In 1797, she met the writer and philosopher Friedrich Schlegel in the salon of her friend Henriette Herz. The ensuing liaison precipitated Dorothea's divorce from Veit, and in 1799 she went with Friedrich to join the literary and artistic community at Jena. In 1804 Dorothea was baptized a Protestant and married Friedrich Schlegel; both converted to Catholicism in 1808 and became more conservative in their later years. They lived in Cologne, Vienna, and Frankfurt until Friedrich's death in 1829. Dorothea remained in close association with the two surviving children from her marriage to Veit, sons who became notable painters.

Schlegel's career was always subordinated to that of her husband: most of her writings, including the unfinished novel *Florentin* (1801), appeared anonymously or under Friedrich's name. These works include critical reviews and essays, medieval tales, and numerous translations, most notably the German rendition of Germaine de Staël's novel *Corinne*. Her letters remain a major source of knowledge about the Romantic movement in Germany.

The excerpt from Dorothea Schlegel's "Conversation about the Latest Novels by French Women Writers" takes as its point of departure the merits of Staël's first novel, *Delphine* (1802), an epistolary work set in Revolutionary France which ends in the heroine's suicide. The "Conversation" typifies the spirit of German Romantic criticism, with one important difference: the discussion is carried out primarily by women. Framed as a letter from one woman to another, it explores different positions regarding the nature of the novel. The three women, Constanze, Adelheid, and Felizia, represent respectively Enlightenment, sentimentalist, and Romantic ideologies. In their dialectical conversation, when Constanze and Adelheid are at cross-purposes with respect to the "morality" of *Delphine*, Felizia directs the conversation to philosophical and historical concerns that the Romantics would call poetic. The one man, Albert, plays a strikingly peripheral role. Although

Felizia does eventually evoke the authority of print, the anonymity of her source also contributes to the authorization of the women as expert critics.

"Gespräch über die neusten Romane der Französinnen," *Europa* 1, no. 2 (1803).

From "A Conversation about the Latest Novels by French Women Writers" (1803)

"Granted," said Constanze, "that Madame de Staël is richer in ideas than women usually are, nonetheless these ideas are of no great value in themselves, although they make woman more interesting to us. Or did you really find that any of these ideas were *new*?"

"Don't say another word," said Adelheid, "or you will convince me that I was wrong to let myself be moved and transported by these depictions! I would certainly not wish to be robbed of every illusion by your reasoning."

"Precisely, Adelheid," Albert called out. "Don't let yourself be robbed of anything that pleases you; but Felizia, why do you remain so unmercifully quiet? Shall we hear nothing from you?"

"How can I say anything when I am busy listening? Both of you are arguing very artfully."

"But who is right?" they both called out.

"Both of you are right, and then again not, according to how you take it."

"Oh, don't try to escape; just say it straight out."

"Well, speaking plainly, I'm of the opinion that it's not a question of being right."

"But certainly," Albert interrupted her, "it is a question of discovering the truth. Why do you refuse to give your opinion?"

"Since you take this so seriously," Felizia resumed, "I believe that despite the flaws that Constanze quite correctly enumerated, one should not judge the book so severely because of the higher aspirations which so plainly mark it, and which must be supported, indeed nurtured and cultivated, because they are rare and beautiful."

"How strange," said Constanze, "since I found everything in it to be so un-beautiful."

"I only mean the beauty of effort, not that of success. It is indeed true that even with all the high aspirations that make it one of the most interesting women's novels of our time, it is nonetheless very flawed. Moreover, I can't really say anything about it, since I am not at all fond of this genre."

"What do you mean? Why don't you care for this genre? What should a novel be like, then?"

"A novel should be romantic."

"What?" asked Adelheid. "Isn't *Delphine* filled with the tenderest delicate enthusiasms and romantic situations?"

"You, Albert, have understood me, and approve. That's not what I mean, dear Adelheid. I mean the spirit of poetry which must in a certain sense animate and enliven the depictions of nature, characters, and events, in order to form them into a romantic poem or novel. *Delphine* lacks poetry; that is why everything there remains stond and fragmented.

"But," objected Adelheid again, "what if the intention of this work was not poetry, but rather the characterization of certain people and the depiction of their moral principles, their lives, their various emotions?"

"By and large," replied Felizia, "every aspect of life can be developed in a novel, as long as a poetic spirit grasps it and represents it, and only then can the view of even the most mundane life become harmonious. If it is your wish to turn every subcategory of social life into the subject of a novel, then I don't see why there can't be legal, economic, and political novels just as well as moral, theological, or psychological ones."

"But it seems to me," said Constanze, "that morality in a novel, as in life, is honorable and necessary."

"Of course it is. But a novel must be a work of art, must be poetry; and in this sense we are speaking of nothing other than the higher morality which is also the only true one. The other morality consists of conventional rules of living that have become a necessity and do not belong in a work of art. Poetry is morality in and of itself, for all laws of eternal goodness are inspiration, poetry. I'd like to read you a passage from a manuscript that concerns this very topic." She searched for the page, and read the following:

" 'In our time, the novel has become something different from what it originally was. In the old romantic poems, the heroes remained what they were, while the events around them changed, propelled by the unfriendly force of Fate. Dangers to their life or their virtue were overcome by the assistance of a benevolent magician or directly through divine intervention, which then allowed them to withstand every test with a hero's courage, until in the end virtue was rewarded and vice was punished.

" 'Onto this background, which except for a few variations remained almost always the same, the lovely flowers of imagination were woven and all the magic of poetry was sprinkled. What soul who revelled in these wonderful images and was inwardly moved by sympathy did not in the process become finer, more cultivated, inspired by a higher feeling for the good and the beautiful! How many riddles of the innermost heart are not solved, as if by a music that is felt if not quite understood! How gladly does the stirred soul rest from the pressures of daily life, and feel refreshed by apparitions from a foreign world! For the past way of life, filled with serious tasks and pious reverence, closed in on itself; it was thus both a joy and a necessity for people to be led out of themselves through poems about a foreign life.

" 'Contemporary life, by contrast, consists more in distraction than in occupation or reverence; the interesting new poems, therefore, attempt to call attention in a pleasant way to our purpose in life, and to prompt us to be more reflective. That is why the events in them are kept simple; indeed, one can barely call them events; they are but changes of costume and scenery; the life of each class, with its particular toils and small pleasures, always stamps each of the heroes. It is neither providence nor chance that leads them into trouble; their difficulties arise from changes within themselves, and they have no other battle to fight than with their own desires, advantages, principles, and renunciations, and with the petty confused circumstances of finer society.

" 'Reading novels no longer exposes today's youth to the danger of being carried away by dreams of the imagination, or of searching restlessly for the ideal. Rather, in the novel they find themselves: in every situation, in every class, lifted securely and easily toward one ideal or another. Once upon a time extraordinary beauty, unusual supernatural powers, and courage, strength and grandeur were required in order for the model heroine of a novel to have a special destiny. But nowadays nothing more is needed than a moral domesticity or a respectable poverty in order to flatter people that these virtues, even when displayed very quietly, won't go undiscovered by some secret writer-observer, and will be richly rewarded here on earth. Thus earthly vanity benefits, while heavenly imagination is robbed.' "

Translated by Simon Richter

ANNE-LOUISE GERMAINE NECKER DE STAËL (1766–1817)

GERMAINE DE STAËL was unusual in every respect, especially for her extraordinary success as a creative writer and critic. Her philosophical writings covered a broad range of ideas from political theory to psychological analysis, always returning to literature as a center. She broke new ground in political science and history, especially in her *Considerations on the French Revolution* (1812). This interest in history and politics also influenced her literary criticism, which undertakes a comparative analysis based on the relationship of literature and the arts to social systems (*On Literature Considered in Its Relationship to Social Institutions* [1800], and *On Germany* [1810]). As the sections concerning Shakespeare and French manners excerpted from *On Literature* suggest, Staël was an early proponent of a "materialist" literary analysis; she believed that literary practices were determined by the political, social, and economic structures of nations. In her *Essay on Fictions* of 1795, she strongly defended the modern novel and encouraged its new direction toward greater realism and historical accuracy; her own novel *Corinne* (1807) was an enormous success.

She had been born in Paris to Swiss Protestant parents. Her wealthy father, the banker Jacques Necker, served Louis XVI as minister of finance. She was fortunate to receive a good education under the direction of her mother, who was inspired in the task by Rousseau's *Emile*. Married at twenty to the Baron Eric de Staël-Holstein, she lived with him only briefly. After the death of their child, she embarked upon a romance with Count Louis de Narbonne which resulted in two sons, Auguste and Albert. She later met the author Benjamin Constant, with whom she had a much-beloved daughter, Albertine.

Staël's intrepid character and her unflinchingly libertarian convictions brought her into conflict with Napoleon, who exiled her first from Paris, then from France. She lived mostly at Coppet, her family's home in Geneva. From her later travels, she developed a strong interest in foreign literatures, especially those of Germany and Italy. Toward the end of her life she married a Swiss, John Rocca, and had a son, Alphonse. After ten years outside France, she finally returned to Paris, her true home.

An Extraordinary Woman: Selected Writings of Germaine de Staël, trans. Vivian Folkenflik (New York: Columbia University Press, 1987); *The Influence of Literature on Society* (Boston: W. Wells and T. B. Wait, 1813).

Essay on Fictions (1795)

Introduction

Man's most valuable faculty is his imagination. Human life seems so little designed for happiness that we need the help of a few creations, a few images, a lucky choice of memories to muster some sparse pleasure on this earth and struggle against the pain of all our destinies—not by philosophical force, but by the more efficient force of distraction. The dangers of imagination have been discussed a good deal, but there is no point in looking up what impotent mediocrity and strict reason have said on this topic over and over again. The human race is not about to give up being stimulated, and anyone who has the gift of appealing to people's emotions is even less likely to give up the success promised by such talent. The number of necessary and evident truths is limited; it will never be enough for the human mind or heart. The highest honor may well go to those who discover such truths, but the authors of books producing sweet emotions or illusions have also done useful work for humanity. Metaphysical precision cannot be applied to man's affections and remain compatible with his nature. Beginnings are all we have on this earth—there is no limit. Virtue is actual and real, but happiness floats in space; anyone who tries to examine happiness inappropriately will destroy it, as we dissolve the brilliant images of the mist if we walk straight through them. And yet the advantage of fictions is not the pleasure they bring. If fictions please nothing but the eye, they do nothing but amuse; but if they touch our hearts, they can have a great influence on all our moral ideas. This talent may be the most powerful way there is of controlling behavior and enlightening the mind. Man has only two distinct faculties: reason and imagination. All the others, even feeling, are simply results or combinations of these two. The realm of fiction, like that of imagination, is therefore vast. Fictions do not find obstacles in passions: they make use of them. Philosophy may be the invisible power in control of fictions, but if she is the first to show herself, she will destroy all their magic.

When I talk about fictions, I will therefore be considering them from two perspectives of content and charm: this kind of writing may contain pleasure without useful purpose, but never vice versa. Fictions are meant to attract us; the more moral or philosophical the result one is trying to achieve, the more they have to be decked out with things to move us, leading us to the goal without advance warning. In mythological fictions I will consider only the poet's talent; these fictions could well be examined in the light of their religious influence, but such a point of view is absolutely foreign to my subject. I will be discussing the writings of the ancients according to the impression they create in our times, so my concern must be with their literary talent rather than their religious beliefs.

Fictions can be divided into three groups: (1) marvelous and allegorical fictions, (2) historical fictions, (3) fictions in which everything is both invented and imitated, where nothing is true and everything is likely.

This topic should really be discussed in an extensive treatise including most existing literary works and involving thoughts on almost every topic, since the complete exposition of any one idea is connected to the whole chain of ideas. But I am only trying to prove that the most useful kind of fiction will be novels taking life as it is, with delicacy, eloquence, depth, and morality, and I have excluded everything irrelevant to that goal from this essay.*

I

The fiction of the marvelous gives us a pleasure that wears thin almost immediately. Adults have to make themselves into children to like these supernatural tableaux, and be touched by feelings of terror and curiosity which do not originate in truth. Philosophers have to turn themselves into common people if they want to grasp useful ideas through the veil of allegory. Classical mythology sometimes contains the sort of simple fables transmitted to idolatrous religions by credulity, time, and priests, but mythology may generally be considered as a series of allegories: personifications of passions, talents, and virtues. There is certainly an initial felicity in the choice of these fictions, a burst of imagination that must guarantee their inventors real glory for devising a style and a language which constantly reminds us of ideas exclusively devoted to poetry, thus saving itself from the vulgarity involved in the continual use of worn, habitual expressions;

---

*I have read several chapters of a book called *The Spirit of Religions*, by M. Benjamin Constant, which offers some extremely ingenious insights into this whole question. The world of letters and philosophers ought to insist that the author of so great a work finish it and publish it.[1]

but new works adding to these accepted fictions would be completely point-less. It takes more talent to get great effects from unassisted nature; there are natural phenomena, metamorphoses, and miracles in human passions, and this mythology is inexhaustible, opening heaven and hell for anyone capable of bringing it to life.

The fiction of the marvelous, on the other hand, casts a pall on every feeling associated with it. There are a thousand different ways to give plea-sure if the only goal is a pretty picture. The eyes are always children, the saying goes; this really applies to the imagination. The imagination needs nothing but amusement; its end is contained in its means. Imagination serves to cheat life, steal time, give night's dreams to the daylight. Its lighthearted activity takes the place of repose, suspending at one blow everything that could move or concern us. When we are trying to make the pleasures of this same imagination serve some moral and coherent end, however, we need a simpler, more logical plan.

Even our impression of Virgil's and Homer's poetry is damaged by this alliance of heroes and gods, men's passions and destiny's decrees. The inven-tor is scarcely able to obtain our indulgence for a genre whose chief merit is its inventiveness. When Dido loves Aeneas only because she has held Love in her arms, disguised by Venus as Ascanius, we miss the talent that could have explained the birth of this passion by a simple portrayal of the work-ings of the heart. When the gods command anger, pain, and Achilles' vic-tories, our admiration is focused on neither Jupiter nor the hero; the first is an abstract being, the second destiny's slave.[2] The absolute power of the character escapes through the marvels surrounding him.

Moreover, there is something about this element of the marvelous—predictable one moment and unpredictable the next—that takes away all the pleasures associated with terror or anticipation according to one's own feelings. When Priam is about to ask Achilles for Hector's body, I would like to be afraid of the dangers he braves for love of his son—to tremble as I see him enter the tent of dread Achilles—to hang on every word of this unfortunate father—and to feel at the same time, through his eloquence, the sensation of the emotion that eloquence expresses and a portent of the events it will determine. But I know perfectly well that Mercury is leading Priam across the Greek camp; that Thetis, at Jupiter's command, has ordered his son to return Hector's corpse. I have no doubts as to the outcome of Priam's enterprise, and my mind has stopped paying attention. Without the name of divine Homer I would not read even one speech that followed the event instead of leading up to it.[3]

I said above that there was something unpredictable about marvelous fiction which, by a contrary effect, takes away the pleasure of anticipation. This happens when the gods undo the best-laid plans, giving their favorites invincible support against the most powerful forces and refusing to let events bear any relation to what we can expect of human beings. The gods are only playing the part of fate, of course: this is chance personified. In fiction, however, it is better to avoid the influence of chance. Everything that is invented should be likely. The reader has to be able to explain every shock by a sequence of moral causes. Not only will the work make a more philosophical effect, but it will provide more of a challenge to talent. Situations which can only be resolved through a stroke of fate are always badly planned, whether they are real or imaginary.

In short, I think that it is better to derive the greatest possible effects from man's character when dealing with mankind. Here is the inexhaustible source from which talent should draw deep and terrible emotions. The bloody crimes we have just witnessed make Dante's underworld take second place.[4] The epic poems most remarkable for the marvelous quality in their fictions are really sublime because of a beauty quite independent of it. What we admire in Milton's Satan is a man; what stays with us about Achilles is his character; what we want to forget in the passion of Rinaldo for Armida is the magic mixed with the attractions inspiring it; what strikes us in the *Aeneid* is a range of emotions belonging to all hearts down through the ages.[5] When our tragic poets have taken topics from ancient authors, they have detached them almost completely from the magical machinery we associate with the beauties of the ancient world.

Chivalric romances make us even more sharply aware of the disadvantages of the marvelous, affecting the characters' development and feelings as well as our interest in the events. Heroes are larger than life, passions far beyond truth. This imaginary moral nature has greater disadvantages than the prodigies of mythology and fairyland. Falsehood is more closely intertwined with truth, and the imagination has less to do. It is no longer a question of inventing, but of exaggerating and caricaturing what is beautiful in real life in a way that would make valor and virtue ridiculous if truth could not be set back in its rightful place by historians and moralists.

In judging human things we should avoid absolute statements, and I do admire the creative genius of these poetic fictions which nourished the human spirit for so long, giving us so many successful and brilliant comparisons. Nevertheless, we may well want the talent of the future to follow a different path. I would like to restrain—or rather to raise to a simple imitation of truth—the kind of strong imagination that is as likely to be inspired by phantoms as by scenes from life.

In works whose primary characteristic is gaiety, we might miss Ariosto's delightful use of his ingenious fictions.[6] But there are no rules or goals in the good fortune that creates this kind of amusement. The impression it makes cannot be analyzed; reflection gets us nowhere. There is so little cause for gaiety in the true-to-life that works trying to inspire gaiety do sometimes need the marvelous. Nature and thought are inexhaustible sources of sentiment and meditation, but pleasantry is a kind of good luck in expression or insight whose twisting path is impossible to predict. Every idea that makes people laugh may well turn out to be the last anyone will ever find: there is no highway leading to this genre, no fountainhead from which to draw success. We know the result exists, because it happens again and again, but we know neither cause nor means: the gift of pleasantry is much closer to inspiration than even the loftiest enthusiasm. This kind of literary gaiety, which does not arise from a sensation of happiness, and is enjoyed by the reader much more than the writer, is a talent won and lost all at once, and all at a stroke. It can be controlled, but never replaced by any other faculty of even the greatest mind. If I have recognized an analogy between the marvelous and the lighthearted, it is because neither of them can really portray nature. Passion, destiny, truth, have no gaiety about them at all—and yet amusing contrasts only emerge from passing nuances of these positive ideas.

The comic talent is a far superior genre, though it too creates funny situations. The comic genre draws its strength from characters and passions in nature; like all serious works, it would be adulterated and weakened by a use of the marvelous. If the characters in *Gil Blas*, *Tartuffe*, or *The Misanthrope* were miraculous in any way, these masterpieces would be much less able to attract and impress our minds.[7]

Imitation of the truth always makes more of an effect than supernatural means. Higher metaphysics may let us assume the existence of thoughts, truths, and beings superior to human knowledge in things beyond the reach of our intelligence; but as we have no conception of these abstract realms, our use of the marvelous does not come anywhere near them, and remains beneath even our known reality. Our power of understanding is limited to the nature of things and men; what we call our creation is only an incoherent assemblage of the ideas we draw from the same natural world we are trying to escape. The stamp of divinity is on the truth. People associate the word "invention" with genius, but the only way for genius to merit the glory of being called creative is by retracing, reuniting, discovering what actually exists.

Allegories are a form of fiction whose effect seems to me inferior even to the effect of the marvelous. I think allegories weaken the idea, just as the marvelous spoils the tableau of passion. In the form of the apologue, allegories can sometimes popularize useful truths, but the very example shows that in giving this form to thought we think we are bringing it down to the level of the common people. The need of images to understand ideas is an intellectual weakness in the reader: any thought which can be perfectly apprehended this way necessarily lacks some degree of abstraction or subtlety. Abstract thought is superior to images, having a kind of geometric precision that lets us express it only in its own positive terms. The absolute delicacy of the mind escapes allegories. Nuances in tableaux are never so delicate as metaphysical insights; things that can be shown in relief are never the most ingenious, subtle part of what one is thinking.

Quite aside from the damage to the ideas it is trying to express, however, allegory is a genre that almost never gives anybody any kind of pleasure. Its aim is both to make some moral truth stand out and to attract us by the fable emblematic of it. Each usually fails because of the attempt to achieve the other: the abstract idea is represented vaguely and the tableau has no dramatic effect. Allegory is a fiction within a fiction. The events in an allegory can interest no one, since they exist only as the incarnation of philosophical conclusions, and understanding them is much more tiring than their pure metaphysical expression. We have to separate abstract from image, discover the ideas represented by the names of characters, and begin by guessing the riddle before we understand the thought. If we try to explain the cause of the monotony in the charming poem *Telemachus*, we realize that it is the character Mentor.[8] Being both marvelous and allegorical, Mentor has the disadvantages of two genres at once. Marvelous, Mentor keeps us from feeling any suspense as to Telemachus' fate as we grow certain of his triumph over any possible danger with the help of the goddess; allegorical, Mentor completely spoils the effect of the passions, which comes from their internal struggles. In Fénelon's poem, the two powers distinguished by moralists in the human heart exist as two characters: Mentor has no passion, Telemachus no control over himself. Man falls in between; our interest is unable to focus. Pointed allegories in which Willpower goes out to seek Happiness (as in *Thélème and Macare*),[9] or interminable allegories in which every stanza narrates the struggle between a chevalier who represents some virtue and his adversary vice (as in Spenser's *Faerie Queen*), these are boring no matter what sort of talent is decorating them.[10] We finish the poem so tired of the tale told by the allegory that we no longer have the strength to understand its philosophical meaning.

Fables with talking animals were first used as apologues whose meaning would be easier for the common people to grasp. Afterward they became a literary genre, practiced by many writers. One—La Fontaine—must have been unique in this line of work, as his completely natural manner kept him from ever repeating or imitating himself; he is able to make his animals speak as if they were some sort of thinking creatures who exist before the reign of prejudice and affectation.[11] His talent keeps one from thinking of allegory in connection with his work, because the character of each species is personified according to what is right and fitting for it. The comedy in his fables comes from the actual portrayal of the manners of the animals onstage, not from allusions. This success was necessarily a limited one, and the other fables people have written in various languages all fall back into the nuisances of allegory.

The Orientals made much use of allegories, no doubt primarily because of the despotism of their governments. They had to tell the truth under a veil, so that subjects could understand things escaping their master; even when they dared to wish that this truth might reach the throne, they thought that linking it to emblems drawn from the laws of physical nature could separate it from human influence and opinion, always dependent on the sultan's wishes. When this truth was presented as a story, the moral was never drawn by the author, who could therefore flatter himself that the sultan would be merciful to this conclusion, should he notice it, as if to a discovery of his own intelligence. But the devices to which we are condemned by despotism should be banished along with its power; they lose all their interest as soon as they are seen to be unnecessary.

Works of allusion are another kind of fiction that appeals only to contemporaries. Posterity judges such writings without reference to the application they might have had at some other time, or to an awareness of the difficulties their authors had to overcome. Whenever talent operates relatively, it loses its brilliance when it loses the circumstances that originally set if off. For example, people may call *Hudibras* a witty poem, but we have to hunt for the author's meaning through what he is saying, with innumerable notes to understand his jokes, and preliminary instruction on how to find it funny or interesting. The merit of this poem is therefore no longer generally appreciated.[12] A philosophical work may require research, but fiction can only produce a convincing effect when it contains within itself whatever the readers need for a complete impression of it at every moment. Actions are useful, and therefore immortal in glory, insofar as they are adapted to immediate circumstances; the written word, however, achieves greatness only by detaching itself from current events and rising to the unchanging nature of things. As Massillon says, whatever writers do for today is time wasted for eternity.[13]

Comparisons are a derivation of allegory, but they distract our attention less because they are shorter, and almost always a further development of the thought that precedes them. All the same, a feeling or an idea is rarely at full strength if it can be expressed by an image. The line "That he die!" in *Horace* would have been impossible to do as an image.[14] When we read the chapter where Montesquieu tries to give us some idea of despotism by comparing it to the acts of Louisiana savages, we might well prefer to this image a reflection of Tacitus—or of Montesquieu himself, who has so often outdone the best writers of antiquity.[15] We would be too severe if we rejected all such decorations: the mind often needs them as a relief from inventing new ideas, or to vary familiar ones. Images and tableaux constitute the charm of poetry and whatever resembles it. But everything relating to reflection gains greater power and more concentrated intensity when the expression of thought draws its power from itself alone.

We must now discuss allegories whose only aim is a combination of humor and philosophical ideas, such as Swift's *Tale of the Tub, Gulliver, Micromégas*, etc.[16] I could repeat what I said about marvelous fictions: if they make people laugh, the goal is achieved. But this sort of work has a higher goal—to set off some philosophical object—which it never really accomplishes. When an allegory is amusing in its own right, most people remember the fable rather than its result, more likely to be fond of Gulliver's story than taught anything by its moral. Allegory invariably falls between two stools. If the point is too clear, it bores us; if it is hidden, we forget it; and if an attempt is made to divide our attention, it no longer arouses any interest at all.

II

In this second part, as I said, I am going to talk about historical fictions: inventions with a basis of truth. Tragedies and poetry drawn from history cannot manage without fiction. History cannot provide an adequate model when all the emotions have to be evoked and concentrated in the course of twenty-four hours and five acts, or when a hero has to be kept up to the level of epic poetry. But the invention essential to historical fiction bears no resemblance to the marvelous. It does not involve another nature, but a choice in the framework of existing nature: the work of Apelles, who composed beauty by gathering together individual delightful details.[17] Granting that the language of poetry has its own distinguishing characteristics, all our emotions are involved when we judge beautiful situations and great epic or dramatic characters. These characters and situations are borrowed from history—not to disfigure them, but to detach them from mortality and consecrate their apotheosis. Nothing in such fiction goes beyond nature: the same pace is observed, the same proportions. If a man born for glory heard a masterpiece such as the *Henriad, Gengis Khan, Mithridate*, or *Tancred*, he would probably admire it unsurprised, enjoying it without ever thinking about the author, or suspecting that anything in these scenes of heroism had been created by talent.[18]

But I wish another kind of historical fiction were absolutely banned. This consists of novels grafted onto history, such as *Anecdotes of the Court of Philippe-Auguste*.[19] Such stories might be pretty enough, if we could detach them from proper names, but they put themselves between you and history, presenting you with details whose invention imitates the ordinary course of daily life and thus blends with the truth so closely that it becomes very difficult to separate the two.

This kind of historical fiction destroys the morality of history by loading the action with a lot of motives that never existed. Such fiction can never achieve the morality of the novel, either, because it has to fit onto a real canvas, so that the plan cannot be devised with the liberty and coherence which a work of pure invention can afford. The interest added to novels by famous names from history is offered by the advantages of allusion; as I have tried to show, fiction that depends on souvenirs instead of internal developments is never perfect in itself. Then too, it is dangerous to make such changes in truth. Such a novel never shows anything but love affairs, because every other event taking place at the time has already been related by historians. The author then tries to explain these other events by the influence of love, so as to make the subject of his novel look more important, and ends by giving us the falsest possible view of human life. These fictions weaken the effect that should be produced by history itself—that same history from which the original idea was borrowed—just as a bad copy of a painting can damage our impression of the original, which it brings to mind lamely, with a few random strokes.

III

The third and last part of this essay must deal with the usefulness of natural fictions, as I call them, where everything is both invented and imitated, so that nothing is true but everything looks true to life. Tragedies with completely imaginary subjects will not be included here; they portray a more lofty nature, an extraordinary situation at an extraordinary level. The verisimilitude of such plays depends on events that are extremely rare, and morally applicable to very few people. Comedies and other dramas are in the theater what novels are to other fiction: their plots are taken from private life and natural circumstances. However, the conventions of the theater deprive us of the commentary which gives examples of reflections their individuality. Dramas are allowed to choose their characters among people other than kings and heroes, but they can show only broadly defined situations, because there is no time for nuance. And life is not concentrated like that—does not happen in contrasts—is not really theatrical in the way plays have to be written. Dramatic art has different effects, advantages, and means which might well be discussed separately, but I think only the modern novel is capable of achieving the constant, accurate usefulness we can get from the picture of our ordinary, habitual feelings. People usually make a separate case of what they call philosophical novels; all novels should be philosophical, as they should all have a moral goal. Perhaps, however, we are not guided so inevitably toward this moral goal when all the episodes narrated are focused on one principal idea, exempting the author from all probability in the way one situation follows another. Each chapter then becomes a kind of allegory—its events are only there to illustrate the maxim at the end. The novels *Candide*, *Zadig*, and *Memnon*, while delightful in other respects, would be much more useful if they were not marvelous, if they offered an example instead of an emblem and if, as I say, the whole story did not have to relate to the same goal.[20] Such novels are at the same disadvantage as teachers: children never believe them, because they make everything that happens relate to the lesson at hand. Children unconsciously know already that there is less regularity than that in real life. Events are also invented in novels like Richardson's and Fielding's, where the author is trying to keep close to life by following with great accuracy the stages, developments, and inconsistencies of human history, and the way the results of experience always come down to the morality of actions and the advantages of virtue, nonetheless. In these novels, however, the feelings are so natural that the reader often believes he is being spoken to directly, with no artifice but the tactfulness of changing the names.

The art of novel-writing does not have the reputation it deserves because of a throng of bad writers overwhelming us with their colorless productions; in this genre, perfection may require the greatest genius, but mediocrity is well within everyone's grasp. This infinite number of colorless novels has almost used up the passion portrayed in them; one is terrified of finding the slightest resemblance in one's own life to the situations they describe. It has taken the very greatest masters to bring this genre back again, despite the writers who have degraded it. And others have dragged it even lower by including disgusting scenes of vice. Despite the fact that fiction's main advantage is to gather around man everything in nature that might be useful to him as a lesson or model, some writers supposed we might have some kind of use for these detestable paintings of evil habits. As if such fictions could ever leave a heart that rejected them in the same state of purity as a heart that had never known them! The novel as we conceive of it, however—as we have a few examples of it—is one of the most beautiful creations of the human mind, and one of the most influential on individual morality, which is what ultimately determines the morality of the public.

There is a very good reason why public opinion does not have enough respect for the writing of good novels, however. This is because novels are considered to be exclusively devoted to the portrayal of love—the most violent, universal, and true passion of them all, but also the passion which inspires no interest at any other time of life than youth, since youth is all it influences. We may well believe that all deep and tender feelings belong to the nature of love, and that hearts which have neither known nor pardoned love cannot feel enthusiasm in friendship, devotion in misery, worship of one's parents, passion for one's children. One can feel respect for one's duties, but no delight or self-surrender in their accomplishment, if one has not loved with all the strength of one's soul, ceasing to be one's self to live entirely in another. The destiny of women and the happiness of men who are not called upon to govern empires often depend for the rest of their lives on the role they gave to the influence of love in their youth. Nevertheless, when people reach a certain age, they completely forget the impression love made on them. Their character changes; they devote themselves to other goals, other passions; and these new interests are what we should extend the subjects of novels to include. A new career would then be open to authors who have the talent to paint all the emotions of the human heart, and are able to use their intimate knowledge of it to involve us. Ambition, pride, greed, vanity could be the primary topic of novels which would have situations as varied as those arising from love, and fresher plots. Will people object that such a tableau of men's passions exists in history, and that we should look for it there? History does not reach the lives of private men, feelings and characters that do not result in public events. History does not act on you with sustained moral interest. Reality often fails to make an effect; and the commentary needed to make a lasting impression would stop the essential quick narrative pace, and give dramatic form to a work that should have a very different sort of merit. And the moral of history can never be completely clear. This may be because one cannot always show with any degree of certainty the inner feelings that punish the wicked in their prosperity and reward the virtuous in their misery, or perhaps because man's destiny is not completed in this life. Practical morality is founded on the advantages of virtue, but the reading of history does not always put it in the limelight.

Great historians (especially Tacitus) do try to attach some moral to every event they relate, making us envy the dying Germanicus, and hate Tiberius at the pinnacle of his grandeur.[21] But they can still portray only those feelings certified by facts. What stays with us from a reading of history is more likely to be the influence of talent, the brilliance of glory, the advantages of power, than the quiet, subtle, gentle morality which is the basis of individual happiness and the relationship between individuals. Everyone would think me ridiculous if I said I set no value on history, and that I preferred fictions—as if fictions did not arise from experience, and as if the delicate nuances shown in novels did not come from the philosophical results and mother-ideas presented by the great panorama of public events! However, the morality of history only exists in bulk. History gives constant results by means of the recurrence of a certain number of chances: its lessons apply to nations, not individuals. Its examples always fit nations, because if one considers them in a general way they are invariable; but it never explains the exceptions. These exceptions can seduce each man as an individual; the exceptional circumstances consecrated by history leave vast empty spaces into which the miseries and wrongs that make up most private destinies could easily fall. On the other hand, novels can paint characters and feeling with such force and detail that they make more of an impression of hatred for vice and love for virtue than any other kind of reading. The morality of novels belongs more to the development of the internal emotions of the soul than to the events they relate. We do not draw a useful lesson from whatever arbitrary circumstance the author invents as punishment for the crime; what leaves its indelible mark on us comes from the truthful rendition of the scenes, the gradual process or sequence of wrongdoing, the enthusiasm for sacrifices, the sympathy for misfortune. Everything is so true to life in such novels that we have no trouble persuading ourselves that everything could happen just this way—not past history, but often, it seems, the history of the future.

Novels give a false idea of mankind, it has been said. This is true of bad novels, as it is true of paintings which imitate nature badly. When novels are good, however, nothing gives such an intimate knowledge of the human heart as these portrayals of the various circumstances of private life and the impressions they inspire. Nothing gives so much play to reflection, which finds much more to discover in details than in generalities. Memoirs would be able to do this if their only subjects were not, as in history, famous men and public events. If most men had the wit and good faith to give a truthful, clear account of what they had experienced in the course of their lives, novels would be useless—but even these sincere narratives would not have all the advantages of novels. We would still have to add a kind of dramatic effect to the truth; not deforming it, but condensing it to set it off. This is the art of the painter: far from distorting objects, it represents them in a way that makes them more immediately apprehended. Nature sometimes shows us things all on the same level, eliminating any contrasts; if we copy her too slavishly we become incapable of portraying her. The most truthful account is always an imitative truth: as a tableau, it demands a harmony of its own. However remarkable a true story may be for its nuances, feelings, and characters, it cannot interest us without the talent necessary for the composition of fiction. But despite our admiration for the genius that lets us penetrate the recesses of the human heart, it is impossible to bear all those minute details with which even the most famous novels are burdened. The author thinks they add to the picture's verisimilitude, blind to the fact that anything that slows down the interest destroys the only truth fiction has: the impression it produces. To put everything that happens in a room onstage is to destroy theatrical illusion completely. Novels have dramatic conventions also: the only thing necessary in an invention is what adds to the effect one is creating. If a glance, a movement, or an unnoticed circumstance helps paint a character or develop our understanding of a feeling, the simpler the means, the greater the merit in catching it—but a scrupulously detailed account of an ordinary event diminishes verisimilitude instead of increasing it. Thrown back on a positive notion of what is true by the kind of details that belong only to truth, you soon break out of the illusion, weary of being unable to find either the instruction of history or the interest of a novel.

The greatest power of fiction is its talent to touch us; almost all moral truths can be made tangible if they are shown in action. Virtue has so much influence on human happiness or misery that one can make most of life's situations depend on it. Some severe philosophers condemn all emotions, wanting moral authority to rule by a simple statement of moral duty. Nothing is less suited to human nature. Virtue must be brought to life if she is to fight the passions with any chance of winning; a sort of exaltation must be aroused for us to find any charm in sacrifice; misfortune must be embellished for us to prefer it to the great charm of guilty enticement; and the touching fictions which incite the soul to generous feelings make it unconsciously engage itself in a promise that it would be ashamed to retract in similar circumstances. But the more real power there is in fiction's talent for touching us, the more important it becomes to widen its influence to the passions of all ages, and the duties of all situations. The primary subject of novels is love, and characters who have nothing to do with it are present only as accessories. It would be possible to find a host of new subjects if one followed a different plan. *Tom Jones* has the most general moral of any novel: love appears in it as only one of many means of showing the philosophical result. The real aim of *Tom Jones* is to show the uncertainty of judgments founded on appearances, proving the superiority of natural and what we may call involuntary virtues over reputations based on mere respect for external etiquette. And this is one of the most useful, most deservedly famous of all novels. *Caleb Williams*, by Mr. Godwin, is a recent novel which, despite some tedious passages and oversights, seems to give a good idea of this inexhaustible genre.[22] Love plays no part in this fiction; the only motives for the action are the hero's unbridled passion for the world's respect and Caleb's overpowering curiosity, leading him to discover whether or not Falkland deserves the esteem he enjoys. We read this story with all the absorption inspired by romantic interest and the reflection commanded by the most philosophical tableau.

Some successful fictions do give pictures of life unrelated to love: several *Moral Tales* of Marmontel, a few chapters of *Sentimental Journey*, various anecdotes from the *Spectator* and other books on morality, some pieces taken from German literature, whose superiority is growing every day.[23] There is still, however, no new Richardson devoting himself to paint men's other passions in a novel completely exploring the progress and consequences of these passions. The success of such a work would come from the truth of its characters, the force of its contrasts and the energy of its situations, rather than from that feeling which is so easy to paint, so quick to arouse interest, pleasing women by what it makes them remember even if it cannot attract them by the greatness or novelty of the scenes it presents. What beautiful things we would find in the Lovelace of ambition![24] What philosophical developments, if we were eager to explain and analyze all the passions, as novels have already done for love! Let no one object that books on morality are enough to teach us a knowledge of our duties; such books cannot possibly go into all the nuances of delicacy, or detail the myriad resources of the passions. We can glean a morality purer and higher from novels than from any didactic work on virtue; didactic works are so dry that they have to be too indulgent. Maxims have to be generally applicable, so they never achieve that heroic delicacy we may offer as a model but cannot reasonably impose as a duty. Where is the moralist who could say: "If your whole family wants you to marry a detestable man, and you are prompted by their persecution to give a few signs of the most innocent interest to the man you find attractive, you are going to bring death and dishonor upon yourself"? This, however, is the plot of *Clarissa*; this is what we read with admiration, without a word of protest to the author who touches us and holds us captive. What moralist would claim that it is better to abandon oneself to deep despair, the sort of despair that threatens life and disturbs the mind, rather than marry the most virtuous man in the world if his religion is different from your own? Well, we need not approve of the superstitious opinions of *Clementina*,[25] but love struggling against a scruple of conscience and duty winning out over passion are a sight that moves and touches even loose-principled people who would have rejected such a conclusion disdainfully if it had been a maxim preceding the tableau instead of an effect that followed it. In novels of a less sublime genre, there are so many subtle rules for women's conduct! We could support this opinion by quoting from masterpieces like *The Princess of Clèves*, *The Count of Comminge*, *Paul and Virginia*, *Cecilia*, most of the writings of Madame Riccoboni, *Caroline*, whose charm is felt by everyone, the touching episode of Caliste, the letters of Camilla, in which the mistakes of a woman and their miserable consequences give a more moral and severe picture than the spectacle of virtue itself, and many other French, English, and German works.[26] Novels have the right to offer the severest morality without revolting our hearts; they have captured feeling, the only thing that can successfully plead for indulgence. Pity for misfortune or interest in passion often win the struggle against books of morality, but good novels have the art of putting this emotion itself on their side and using it for their own ends.

There is still one serious objection to love stories: that they paint love in such a way as to arouse it, and that there are moments in life when this danger wins out over every kind of advantage. This drawback could not exist in novels about any other human passion, however. By recognizing the most fleeting symptoms of a dangerous inclination from the very beginning, one could turn oneself as well as others away from it. Ambition, pride, and avarice often exist without the least consciousness on the part of those they rule. Love feeds on the portrait of its own feelings, but the best way to fight the other passions is to make them be recognized. If the features, tricks, means, and results of these passions were as fully shown and popularized by novels as the history of love, society would have more trustworthy rules and more scrupulous principles about all the transactions of life. Even if purely philosophical writings could predict and detail all the nuances of actions, as do novels, dramatic morality would still have the great advantage of arousing indignant impulses, an exaltation of soul, a sweet

melancholy—the various effects of fictional situations, and a sort of supplement to existence. This impression resembles the one we have of real facts
we might have witnessed, but it is less distracting for the mind than the
incoherent panorama of events around us, because it is always directed toward a single goal. Finally, there are men over whom duty has no influence,
and who could still be preserved from crime by developing within them
the ability to be moved. Characters capable of adopting humanity only
with the help of such a faculty of emotion, the physical pleasure of the soul,
would naturally not deserve much respect; nevertheless, if the effect of these
touching fictions became widespread enough among the people, it might
give us some assurance that we would no longer have in our country those
beings whose character poses the most incomprehensible moral problem
that has ever existed. The gradual steps from the known to the unknown
stop well before we reach any understanding of the emotions which rules
the executioners of France. Neither events nor books can have developed
in them the least trace of humanity, the memory of a single sensation of
pity, any mobility within the mind itself for them to remain capable of
that constant cruelty, so foreign to all the impulses of nature—a cruelty
which has given mankind its first limitless concept, the complete idea
of crime.

There are writings whose principal merit is the eloquence of passion,
such as the "Epistle of Abelard" by Pope, *Werther*, the *Portuguese Letters*, and
especially *The New Héloïse*.[27] The aim of such works is often moral, but
what remains with us more than anything else is the absolute power of the
heart. We cannot classify such novels. Every century has one soul and one
genius capable of achieving this—it cannot be a genre, it cannot be a goal.
Who would want to proscribe these miracles of the word, these deep impressions which satisfy all the emotions of the passionate? Readers enthusiastic about such talent are very few in number; these works always do
their admirers good. Let ardent, sensitive souls admire them; they cannot
make their language understood by anyone else. The feelings that disturb
such beings are rarely understood; constantly condemned, they would believe themselves alone in the world, they would soon hate their own nature
for isolating them, if a few passionate, melancholy works did not make them
hear a voice in the desert of life, letting them find in solitude a few rays of
the happiness that escapes them in the middle of society. The pleasure of
retreat is refreshing after the vain attempts of disappointed hope; far from
this unfortunate creature, the entire universe may be in motion, but such
eloquent, tender writing stays near him as his most faithful friend, the one
who understands him best. Yes, a book must be right if it offers even one

day's distraction from pain; it helps the best of men. Of course there are also sorrows that come from one's own character flaws, but so many of them come from superiority of mind or sensitivity of heart! and there are so many that would be easier to bear if one had fewer good qualities! I respect the suffering heart, even when it is unknown to me; I take pleasure in fictions whose only effect might be to comfort this heart by capturing its interest. In this life, which we pass through rather than feel, the distributor of the only real happiness of which human nature is capable would be some-one who distracts man from himself and others, suspending the action of the passions by substituting independent pleasures for them—if the influ-ence of his talent could only last.

From *On Literature* (1800)

OF THE TRAGEDIES OF SHAKSPEARE.

The English entertain as profound veneration and enthusiasm for Shak-speare, as any nation perhaps has ever felt for any writer.—A free people have a natural love for every thing that can do honour to their country; and this sentiment ought to exclude every species of criticism.

There are beauties of the first order to be found in Shakspeare, relating to every country and every period of time. His faults are those which be-longed to the times in which he lived; and the singularities then so prevalent among the English, are still represented with the greatest success upon their theatres. These beauties and eccentricities I shall proceed to examine, as connected with the national spirit of England, and the genius of the litera-ture of the North.

Shakspeare did not imitate the ancients; nor, like Racine, did he feed his genius upon the Grecian tragedies.[1] . . . When an author is solely pene-trated with the models of the dramatic art of antiquity, and when he imi-tates imitations, he must of course have less originality: he cannot have that genius which draws from Nature; that immediate genius, if I may so express myself, which so particularly characterizes Shakspeare. From the times of the Greeks, down to this time, we see every species of literature derived one from another, and all arising from the same source. Shakspeare opened a new field of literature: it was borrowed, without doubt, from the general spirit and colour of the North: but it was Shakspeare who gave to the En-glish literature its impulse, and to their dramatic art its character.

A nation which has carved out its liberty through the horrours of civil war, and whose passions have been strongly agitated, is much more suscep-tible of the emotion excited by Shakspeare, than that which is caused by

Racine. When misfortune lies heavy and for a long time upon a nation, it creates a character, which even succeeding prosperity can never entirely efface. Shakspeare, although he has since been equalled by both English and German authors, was the first who painted moral affliction in the highest degree: the bitterness of those sufferings of which he gives us the idea, might pass for the phantoms of imagination, if Nature did not recognize her own picture in them.

The ancients believed in a fatality, which came upon them with the rapidity of lightning, and destroyed them like a thunderbolt. The moderns, and more especially Shakspeare, found a much deeper source of emotion in a philosophical distress, which was often composed of irreparable misfortunes, of ineffectual exertions, and blighted hopes. But the ancients inhabited a world yet in its infancy; were in possession of but very few histories; and withal were so sanguine in respect to the future, that the scenes of distress painted by them, could never be so heart-rending as those in the English tragedies.

The terror of death was a sentiment, the effects of which, whether from religion or, from stoicism, was seldom displayed by the ancients. Shakspeare has represented it in every point of view: he makes us feel that dreadful emotion which chills the blood of him, who, in the full enjoyment of life and health, learns that death awaits him. In the Tragedies of Shakspeare, the criminal and the virtuous, infancy and old-age, are alike condemned to die, and express every emotion natural to such a situation. What tenderness do we feel, when we hear the complaints of Arthur, a child condemned to death by the order of King John; or when the assassin Tirrel comes to relate to Richard III the peaceful slumber of the children of Edward? When a hero is painted just going to be deprived of his existence, the grandeur of his character, and the recollection of his achievement, excite the greatest interest: but when men of weak minds, and doomed to an inglorious destiny, are represented as condemned to perish; such as Henry VI, Richard II, and King Lear; the great debates of Nature between existence and non-existence absorb the whole attention of the spectators. Shakspeare knew how to paint with genius that mixture of physical emotions and moral reflections which are inspired by the approach of death, when no intoxicating passion deprives man of his intellectual faculties.

Another sentiment which Shakspeare alone knew how to render theatrical, was pity unmixed with admiration for those who suffer;* pity for

*The death of Catherine of Arragon, in "Henry VIII."

an insignificant being,★ and sometimes for a contemptible one.† There must be an infinity of talent to be able to convey this sentiment from real life to the stage, and to preserve it in all its force: but when once it is accomplished, the effect which it produces is more nearly allied to reality than any other. It is for the man alone that we are interested, and not by sentiments which are often but a theatrical romance: it is by a sentiment so nearly approaching the impressions of life, that the illusion is still the greater.

Even when Shakspeare represents personages whose career has been illustrious, he draws the interest of the spectators towards them by sentiments purely natural. The circumstances are grand, but the men differ less from other men than those in the French tragedies. Shakspeare makes you penetrate entirely into the glory which he paints: in listening to him, you pass through all the different shades and gradations which lead to heroism; and you arrive at the height without perceiving any thing unnatural. . . .

In England, the troubles and civil commotions which preceded their liberty, and which were always occasioned by their spirit of independence, gave rise much oftener than in France to great crimes and great virtues. There are in the English history many more tragical situations than in that of the French; and nothing opposes their exercising their talents upon national subjects. . . .

Before it would be possible to judge of the effects of an English tragedy, which might be proper for the French stage; an examination remains to be made, which is, to distinguish in the pieces of Shakspeare, that which was written to please the people; the real faults which he committed; and those spirited beauties which the severe rules of the French tragedies exclude from their stage.

The crowd of spectators in England require that comic scenes should succeed tragic effects. The contrast of what is noble with that which is not, as I have observed before, always produces a disagreeable impression upon men of taste. A noble style must have shades; but a too glaring opposition is nothing more than fantasticalness. That play upon words, those licentious equivocations, popular tales, and that string of proverbs, which are handed down from generation to generation, and are, as one may say, the patrimonial ideas of the common people; all these are applauded by the multitude, and censured by reason. These have no connection with the sublime effects which Shakspeare drew from simple words and common circumstances art-

★The Duke of Clarence, in "Richard III."
†Cardinal Wolsey, in "Henry VIII."

fully arranged, which the French most absurdly would fear to bring upon their stage.

Shakspeare, when he wrote the parts of vulgar minds in his tragedies, sheltered himself from the judgment of taste by rendering himself the object of popular admiration: he then conducted himself like an able chief, but not like a good writer.

The people of the North existed during many centuries, in a state that was at once both social and barbarous; which left for a long time the vestiges of the *rude* and *ferocious*. Traces of this recollection are to be found in many of Shakspeare's characters, which are painted in the style that was most admired in those ages, in which they only lived for combats, physical power, and military courage.

We may also perceive in Shakspeare some of the ignorance of his century with regard to the principles of literature; his powers are superior to the Greek tragedies for the philosophy of the passions, and the knowledge of mankind:* but he was inferior to many with regard to the perfection of the art. Shakspeare may be reproached with incoherent images, prolixity, and useless repetitions: but the attention of the spectators in those days was too easily captivated, that the author should be very strict with himself. A dramatic poet, to attain all the perfection his talents will permit, must neither be judged by impaired age, nor by youth, who find the source of emotion within themselves.

The French have often condemned the scenes of horror represented by Shakspeare; not because they excited an emotion too strong, but because they sometimes destroyed the theatrical illusion. They certainly appear to me susceptible of criticism. In the first place, there are certain situations which are only frightful; and the bad imitators of Shakspeare wishing to represent them, produced nothing more than a disagreeable invention, without any of the pleasures which the tragedy ought to produce: and again,

---

*Among the great number of philosophical traits which are remarked even in the least celebrated works of Shakspeare, there is one with which I was singularly struck. In that piece intitled *Measure for Measure*, Lucien, the friend of Claudius, and brother to Isabella, presses her to go and sue for his pardon to the Governour Angelo, who had condemned this brother to die. Isabella, yound and timid, answers, that she fears it would be useless; that Angelo was too much irritated, and would be inflexible, &c. Lucien insists, and says to her,

—Our doubts are traitors,
And make us lose the good we might win
By fearing to attempt.

Who can have lived in a revolution and not be sensible of the truth of these words?

there are many situations really affecting in themselves, which nevertheless require stage effect to amuse the attention, and of course the interest.

When the Governour of the Tower, in which the young Arthur is confined, orders a red-hot iron to be brought, to put out his eyes; without speaking of the atrociousness of such a scene, there must pass upon the stage an action, the imitation of which is impossible, and the attention of the audience is so much taken up with the execution of it, that the moral effect is quite forgotten.

The character of Caliban, in the "Tempest," is singularly original: but the almost animal figure, which his dress must give him, turns the attention from all that is philosophical in the conception of this part.

In reading "Richard III," one of the beauties is what he himself says of his natural deformity. One can feel that the horror which he causes, ought to act reciprocally upon his own mind, and render it yet more atrocious.—Nevertheless, can there be any thing more difficult in an elevated style, or more nearly allied to ridicule, than the imitation of an ill-shaped man upon the stage? Every thing in nature may interest the mind; but upon the stage, the illusion of sight must be treated with the most scrupulous caution, or every serious effect will be irreparably destroyed.

Shakspeare also represented physical sufferings much too often. Philoctetes is the only example of any theatrical effect being produced by it; and in this instance, it was the heroic cause of his wounds that fixed the attention of the spectators. Physical sufferings may be related, but cannot be represented. It is not the author, but the actor, who cannot express himself with grandeur; it is not the ideas, but the senses, which refuse to lend their aid to this style of imitation.

In short, one of the greatest faults which Shakspeare can be accused of, is his want of simplicity in the intervals of his sublime passages. When he is not exalted, he is affected; he wanted the art of sustaining himself, that is to say, of being as natural in his scenes of transition, as he was in the grand movements of the soul. . . .

It may be a question, whether the theatre of republican France, like the English theatre, will now admit of their heroes being painted with all their foibles, the virtues with their inconclusiveness, and common circumstances connected with elevated situations? In short, will the tragic characters be taken from recollection, from human life, or from the *beautiful ideal?*—This is a question which I propose to discuss after having spoken of the tragedies of Racine and Voltaire. I shall also examine, in the second part of this work, the influence which the French revolution is likely to have upon literature.

Anne-Louise Germaine Necker de Staël (1766–1817)

OF TASTE AND URBANITY OF MANNERS;

AND OF THEIR INFLUENCE IN LITERATURE AND POLITICS.

It has for some time been a prevailing opinion in France, that a revolution in literature was necessary, and that the laws of taste in every department ought to be indulged with the greatest possible latitude. Nothing could be more inimical to the progress of literature,—that progress which so effectually promotes the diffusion of philosophical light, and consequently the support of liberty; nothing can be more fatal to refinement of manners, one of the first aims that republican institutions ought to have in view. The fastidious nicety of some societies of the ancient system have, undoubtedly, no connection with the true principles of taste, which are always in conformity with reason; but some prescribed laws might be abolished without subverting those barriers which point out the path of genius, and preserve both consistency and dignity in oratory as well as composition. The only motive alleged for an entire change in the style and forms which preserve respect and promote reflection, is the despotism which the aristocratic classes of a monarchy exercise over taste and customs. It is therefore useful to mark the defects which may be found in some of the pretensions, pleasantries, and exigencies of the societies of the ancient system, in order to shew afterwards with more effect what disgusting consequences, both in literature and politics, have arisen from the boundless audacity, the awkward gaiety, and the degrading vulgarity which it has been attempted to introduce in some periods of the revolution. From the opposition of these two extremes, from the factitious ideas of monarchy, and the gross systems of some individuals during the revolution, some just reflections must necessarily accrue respecting the noble simplicity which ought to characterize the oratory, the compositions, and the customs of a republican government.

The French nation was, in some respects, too much civilized; its institutions and social habits had usurped the place of natural affections. In the ancient republics, and above all at Lacedemon, the laws moulded the individual character of each citizen, formed them all upon the same model, and political sentiments absorbed all other sentiments. What Lycurgus effected by his laws in favour of the republican spirit, the French monarchy had done by its powerful prejudices in favour of the vanities of rank.[2]

This vanity engaged almost exclusively the minds of each class; the life of man seemed dedicated to the desire of making a conspicuous figure, to obtain an acknowledged superiority over his immediate rival, and to excite that envy in others, to which he himself in his turn became a prey. . . . This spirit of contention upon subjects totally frivolous, except in their influence over happiness; this ardent desire to succeed; this dread of offending; altered and often exaggerated the true principles of natural taste; there was a fashion of the day, a fashion of some particular class, in a word, that which must arise from the general opinion created by similar relations. Societies then existed, which could by allusions to their customs, their interests, or even their caprices, ennoble the most hacknied phrases, or proscribe the most simple beauties. If we shewed ourselves strangers to these manners in society, we publicly acknowledged ourselves to be of an inferior rank; and inferiority of rank is of itself an unsavoury mouthful in a country where a distinction of rank exists. Individuals ridicule individuals, where the people are strangers to an education of liberty; and in France, even with the most exalted mind, it would have been only an absurdity in him who should endeavour to emancipate himself from that prevailing style which was established by the ascendency of the highest class.

This despotism of opinion being carried too far, must eventually be prejudicial to real talents; the laws of taste and politeness became daily more refined; the manners were continually growing more dissimilar from the impression of nature. Ease of address existed without freedom of sentiments; politeness divided the people into classes instead of cementing a general union amongst them; and all that natural simplicity requisite to be perfectly graceful, did not prevent men from growing old either in a constant habit of attention, or a pretended inattention to the observance of the least marks of social distinction.

Nevertheless they wished to establish a sort of equality which placed all characters and all talents apparently upon the same level; an equality most undesirable to men of distinguished abilities, but at the same time most consoling to jealous mediocrity. It was necessary to speak and to be silent exactly like other people; to know the reigning customs that no innovation might be hazarded; and it was only an assiduous imitation of received habits, that it was possible to acquire a reputation peculiar to ourselves. . . .

[The] tyranny of ridicule, which particularly characterized the latter years of the ancient government, after having given a polish to taste, terminated in violent measures, and literature must necessarily have felt the effects of them. In order, therefore, to give more elevation of style to composition, and more energy to character, we find it requisite that taste should not be subordinate to the elegant and studied habits of aristocratical societies, however remarkable they may be for the perfection of grace; their despotism would produce the most serious ill-consequences to liberty, political equality, and even to the higher walks of literature: but how greatly would bad taste, carried even to grossness, be prejudicial to literary fame, to morality, to liberty, to all, in fact, of good and great that can exist in the relations and connections between man and man?

Since the revolution, a disgusting vulgarity of manners has often been found united to the exercise of the highest authorities. Now the defects of power are contagious; in France, above all, power not only influences the actions and conversations, but even the secret thoughts of the numerous flatterers who hover about men in power. . . .

Bad taste, such as we have seen it to prevail during some years of the revolution, is not only prejudicial to the relations of society and literature, but undermines morality: men indulge themselves in pleasantries upon their own baseness, their own vices, and shamelessly glory in them in order to ridicule those timid minds which still shrink from this degrading mirth. Those free-thinkers of a new description make a boast of their shame, and applaud themselves in proportion to the astonishment they have excited around them. . . .

An excellent law in England interdicts men, whose profession obliges them to shed the blood of animals, from the power of exercising judiciary functions. Indeed, independent of the morality which is founded upon reason, there is also that of natural instinct,—that, whose impressions are unforeseen and irresistible. When we accustom ourselves to see animals suffer, we in time overcome the natural repugnancy of the sense of anguish, we become less accessible to pity even for our fellow-creatures, at least we no longer involuntarily feel its impressions. Vulgar and ferocious expressions produce in some respects the same effect as the sight of blood, when we accustom ourselves to pronounce them the ideas which they excite become more familiar. Men in battle animate each other to those sentiments of revenge which ought to inspire them, by an incessant use of the grossest language. The justice and impartiality necessary for civil administration make it their duty to employ such forms and expressions as may calm both him who speaks and those who hear.

Good taste, in the language and in the manners of those who govern, by inspiring more respect, renders more terrific measures less necessary. A magistrate whose manners create disgust, can scarcely avoid having recourse to persecution in order to obtain obedience.

Kings are wrapt in a certain cloud of illusions and recollections: but deputies commanding in the name of their personal superiority, have need of all the exterior marks of that superiority: and what more evident mark can be found, than that good taste which, discovering itself in every word, gesture, accent, and even in every action, announces a peaceable and stately mind, which comprehends immediately whatever is brought before it, and which never loses sight of its own respectability nor of the respect due to others. It is thus that good taste exercises a real influence in political affairs.

It is a truth generally received, that a spirit of republicanism requires a revolution in the character of literature. I believe this idea true, but in a different acceptation from that generally allowed. A republican spirit requires more correctness in good taste, which is inseparable from sound morality: it also, undoubtedly, permits more energetic beauties in literature, a more philosophical and more affecting picture of the important events of life. Montesquieu, Rousseau, and Condillac, belonged by anticipation to the republican systems;[3] and they have commenced the so desirable revolution in the character of French writings:—this revolution must be completed. The republic necessarily drawing forth stronger passions, the art of portraying must improve, while the subject becomes more exalted; but, by a whimsical contrast, it is in the licentious and frivolous style that authors have most profited by the liberty which literature is supposed to have acquired. . . .

In a free country, society will be more engaged by political affairs than by attention to ceremony, or even the charms of pleasantry. In a nation where political equality shall subsist, all kinds of merit may gain admission: and there will no longer exist an exclusive society, dedicated only to bring itself to perfection, and uniting in itself all the ascendency of fortune and power. Now, unless such a tribunal constantly exists, the youthful mind cannot be formed to that delicacy of feeling, to those fine and correct shades which alone can give to the lighter kinds of writing that grace of conformity, and that finished taste so much admired in some French authors, and particularly in the fugitive pieces of Voltaire.[4]

Literature will disgrace itself completely in France, if we multiply those affected attempts at grace and taste which only serve to render us ridiculous: some genuine humour may, nevertheless, still be found in good comedy; but as to that playful gaiety with which we have been inundated even amidst all our calamities, if we except some individuals who can still remember the times that are past, all new attempts in this style corrupt the taste for literature in France, and place the French below the level of all the serious nations in Europe.

Before the revolution it had been frequently remarked, that a Frenchman, unaccustomed to the society of the first class, made known his inferiority of rank the instant he attempted pleasantry: whilst the Englishman, whose manners are always serious and simple, scarcely ever betrayed by his conversation to what rank in society he belonged. In spite of the distinctions which will long exist between the two nations, French writers must shortly perceive that they no longer have the same means of succeeding in the art of pleasantry; and far from believing that the revolution has given them greater latitude in this respect, they ought more than ever to pay an assiduous attention to good taste; since the confusions in society produced by a revolution, no longer offer any good models, and do not inspire those daily habits which render grace and taste natural to us without the aid of reflection to recall them.

The laws of taste, as applied to republican literature, are in their nature more simple, but not less strict than those which were adopted by the authors of the age of Louis XIV.[5] Under a monarchical government, a multitude of customs sometimes substituted conformity for reason, and the respect paid to society for the sentiments of the heart: but in a republic, taste ought to consist only in the perfect knowledge of all true and durable relations: to fail therefore in the principles of taste, would be nothing less than ignorance of the true nature of things.

In the time of the monarchy, it was frequently necessary to disguise a bold censure, to veil a new opinion under the form of received prejudices; and the taste which it was necessary to introduce in these different turns, required a singularly delicate ingenuity of mind: but the garb of truth, in a free country, accords with truth itself;—expression and sentiment ought to spring from the same source.

We are not obliged, where liberty reigns, to confine ourselves within the circle of the same opinions, neither is a variety of forms necessary to conceal a sameness of ideas. The interest of progression always exists, since prejudices do not limit the career of thought: the mind, therefore, having no longer to struggle against lassitude, acquires more simplicity, and does not hazard, in order to awaken attention, those studied graces which are repugnant to natural taste.

A bold and very difficult stratagem, allowed under the ancient government, was the art of offending against the manners without wounding taste, and to make a mockery of morality by proportioning delicacy of expressions to indecency of principles. Happily, however, this talent is as ill adapted to the virtue as to the genius of a republic: as soon as one barrier was overthrown, the rest would be disregarded, the relations of society would no longer have the power to curb those whom sacred ties could not restrain. . . .

The taste necessary for republican literature, in serious works as well as those of imagination, consists not merely in one talent, but in the perfection of all; and so far from being inimical to depth of sentiment or energy of expression, the simplicity it exacts, and the ease it inspires, are the only suitable ornaments to strength of mind.

Urbanity of manners, as well as good taste, (the former of which indeed constitutes a part of the latter,) are both very important in the literary and political world. Although literature may free itself, in a republic much more easily than in a monarchy, from the empire of any fashion generally received in society, yet it is not possible that the models of the greater number of works of imagination should be taken from other examples than from those which we see daily before our eyes. Now, what would become of those writings which necessarily bear the stamp of the manners of their time, if vulgarity, and that style of behaviour which displays the defects and disadvantages of every character, should continue to prevail? . . .

It will be said, perhaps, that politeness is so trifling an advantage, that even the privation of it would not in the least tarnish those great and valuable qualities which constitute strength and elevation of mind. If the ceremonies of gallantry in the age of Louis XIV. are called politeness, most certainly the first-rate men of antiquity had not the slightest idea of it . . . but if the politeness is in reality that just propriety of conduct which ought to be maintained by man to man; if it indicates what we think ourselves to be, and what we really are; if it teaches others what they are, or what they ought to be; a vast number of sentiments and reflections are allied to politeness. . . .

Politeness is that tie which society has established between men who are strangers to each other. Virtue attaches us to our families, to our friends, and to the unfortunate; but in all those relative connections which have not assumed the character of duty, urbanity of manners softens the affections, opens the way to conviction, and preserves to every man the rank which his merit ought to obtain for him in society.

It points out the degree of consideration to which each individual has raised himself; and viewed in that light, politeness becomes the dispenser of those rewards which it has been the object of a whole life to gain. . . .

In the course of the last ten years, we have frequently seen the enlightened governed by the ignorant; whose arrogance of tone, and vulgarity of manners, inspired more disgust than even the shallowness of their intellects. Many of these people confounded republican opinions with unfeeling speeches and gross pleasantries; and spontaneous affection was naturally banished from the republic.

Manners have a greater power of attracting or repelling, than opinions;

I will almost venture to assert, even than sentiments. Possessed of a certain liberality of mind, we may live agreeably in the midst of a society professedly devoted to a different party from that to which we ourselves belong: we may even forget serious injuries, or fears, perhaps, justly inspired by the immorality of a man, if the nobleness of his language lulls us into an illusion as to the purity of his mind. But it is impossible to endure that vulgarity of education which betrays itself in every expression, every gesture, in the tone of the voice, the attitude, in short, in all the involuntary marks of the general habits of life.

I do not here speak of the esteem which arises from reflection, but of that involuntary impression which is every moment renewed. In great events, sympathetic minds discover each other by the sentiments of the heart; but in the minutiæ of society, we are known to each other by our manners; and vulgarity, carried to a certain length, makes the unfortunate object or witness of it experience a feeling of embarrassment, and even of shame, which is altogether insupportable. . . .

We must not deceive ourselves as to the exterior marks of respect: to smother noble sentiments, or to dry the source of thought, is to produce only the ill-effects of fear; but to elevate the minds of others to the standard of our own, to give to the understanding its full play, to encourage that confidence which all generous minds feel in each other; such is the art of inspiring durable respect.

It is of importance to create in France some ties which may connect parties now at variance; and urbanity of manners is an efficacious means to attain this desirable end. It would unite all enlightened men; and this class so firmly connected, might form a tribunal of opinion, which could distribute praise or censure with some justice.

This tribunal might also exercise its influence over literature: authors would know where to find taste and national spirit, and would strenuously endeavour to describe and to aggrandize it. But of all confusion, the most fatal is that which blends all modes of education without distinction, and separates nothing but the spirit of party. Of what consequence is it to agree in our political opinions, if we differ in mind and sentiments? How lamentable is the effect of civil commotions to attach more importance to a similarity of our views in public affairs, than to all those which constitute the only system of fraternity, whose impressions are indelible!

Urbanity of manners can alone soften the asperities of party-spirit; it suffers us to see others long before we begin to esteem them, and to converse with them long before any acquaintance commences; and by degrees, that violent aversion which we might feel towards a man whom we had never accosted, grows weaker by the influence of respect and of esteem: hence a sympathy is created, and, in the event, we find our own sentiments inherent in the person whom we had been accustomed to consider as an enemy.

Notes

Essay on Fictions

1. Benjamin Constant (1767–1830), French man of letters, is best known for his novel *Adolphe* (1816) and for his political and philosophical works, including the work to which Staël refers, which was published beginning in 1824 as *De la Religion considérée dans sa source, ses formes, et ses développements.* Constant and Staël were lovers for many years.

2. Dido's ill-fated love for Aeneas is recounted in Virgil's *Aeneid.* The victories of Achilles are narrated in Homer's *Iliad.*

3. Staël refers here again to the *Iliad.*

4. I.e., in the Inferno of Dante's epic poem *The Divine Comedy,* completed in 1321.

5. John Milton's humanized Satan figures in *Paradise Lost* (1667); Rinaldo and Armida fall in love through the workings of magic in Torquato Tasso's *Jerusalem Delivered* (1581).

6. Lodovico Ariosto (1474–1533) is best known for his epic *Orlando Furioso* (1516, 1532), which makes ironic use of magic and enchantment.

7. *Gil Blas* is a picaresque novel by René Lesage published in the early seventeenth century; *Tartuffe* and *The Misanthrope* are plays by Molière (1622–1673), France's greatest classical comic dramatist.

8. *Télémaque* (1699), the best-known work of François de Fénelon, offers a sequel to Homer's *Odyssey.*

9. *Thélème et Macare* (1764) is by the French belle-lettrist and philosopher Voltaire (1694–1778).

10. *The Faerie Queene* (1590, 1596) is an allegorical epic by the English poet Edmund Spenser (1552?–1599).

11. Jean de La Fontaine (1621–1695) is best known for his extremely popular *Fables,* charming and witty verse narratives usually involving animals, based on classical sources but wearing lightly their moral purposes.

12. *Hudibras* is a long, satirical, mock-heroic poem by Samuel Butler (1612–1680).

13. Jean-Baptiste Massillon (1663–1742), bishop and orator, is noted for his sermons and funeral orations.

14. The reference is to a famous moment in the *Horace* of Pierre Corneille (1640), which recounts the Roman story in which two families battle for power. In the third act, when Horace is pitted alone against the three Curiaces, his father utters this line in response to the question "What would you have wished that he do against three?"

15. Cornelius Tacitus was a first-century Roman historian. Charles Louis de Montesquieu (1689–1775) was one of the earliest of the *philosophes* of the eighteenth-cen-

tury, a student of Roman law, and the author among other works of *Les Lettres persanes* (1721) and *L'Esprit des lois* (1748).

16. Jonathan Swift (1667–1745) was an English satirist best known for *Gulliver's Travels* (1726); his *Tale of a Tub* (1704) satirizes Christian dividedness. *Micromégas* (1752) is a satiric work by Voltaire.

17. Apelles was a Greek portraitist of the fourth century B.C.E.

18. Staël refers here to three works by Voltaire—the epic *Henriade* (1723), which recounts the struggles of Henry IV; the tragedy *Orphan of China* (1755), which is about Genghis Khan; and the tragedy *Tancred* (1760). *Mithridate* (1673) is a tragedy by the classical playwright Jean Racine (1639–1699).

19. The *Anecdotes* is by Marguerite de Lussan and the Abbé de Boismorand.

20. Three works by Voltaire, published respectively in 1759, 1747, and 1749.

21. The warrior Germanicus Julius Caesar was nephew of the emperor Tiberius. Tacitus recounts their history.

22. The radical philosopher William Godwin (1756–1836), husband of Mary Wollstonecraft and father of Mary Shelley, published *Caleb Williams* in 1794. Godwin is best known for *Enquiry concerning Political Justice* (1793).

23. Staël refers respectively to the tales of Jean-François Marmontel (1723–1799), to Laurence Sterne's satirical *Sentimental Journey* (1768), and to the *Spectator*, the British Journal published in 1711–1712 by Joseph Addison and Richard Steele.

24. Lovelace is the anti-hero of Richardson's *Clarissa* (1747–1778).

25. Clementina is a character in Richardson's *Sir Charles Grandison*; Prévost's French translation of the novel gives her name as the title. She renounces Grandison and paves the way for his marriage to Harriet Byron.

26. With only one exception, Staël here refers to works by women: *La Princesse de Clèves* (1678) by Madame de La Fayette, *Mémoirs du comte de Comminge* (1735) by Claudine de Tencin, *Paul et Virginie* (1787) by Bernardin de St.-Pierre, *Cecilia* (1782) by Frances Burney, *Caliste* by Isabelle de Charrière, *Caroline de Lichfield* (1785) by Isabelle de Montolieu. *Camilla* is the title of a novel by Frances Burney (1796), but it is not an epistolary text. Marie-Jeanne Riccoboni (1714–1792) was a highly regarded and prolific novelist.

27. Staël refers here to epistolary fictions: Pope's "Eloisa to Abelard" (1717), Johann Wolfgang von Goethe's *Die Leiden des jungen Werthers* (1774), the anonymous seventeenth-century *Lettres portuguaises*, and Rousseau's *Nouvelle Héloïse* (1761).

On Literature

1. Jean Racine (1639–1699) has remained the most revered playwright of seventeenth-century France, praised especially for the poetic qualities of his tragedies, which conform strictly to classical conventions. Debates about the relative merits of Racine and Shakespeare—and hence about adherence to the classical conventions— were common in the eighteenth and early nineteenth centuries.

2. Lycurgus is considered the founder of the Spartan constitution.

3. Charles-Louis de Montesquieu (1689–1775), Jean-Jacques Rousseau (1712–1778), and the Abbé de Condillac (1714–1780) were among the philosophers whose ideas were said to have inaugurated the spirit of republicanism that led to the Revolution.

4. Probably the preeminent French thinker of the eighteenth century, Voltaire

(pseudonym of François-Marie Arouet, 1694–1778) met with considerable censure—and even imprisonment and exile—for his writings.

5. Louis XIV reigned in France as an absolute monarch from 1643 to 1715. His support for literature and the arts helped to make the seventeenth century a period of greatness for French culture.

MARIA EDGEWORTH (1768–1849)

Maria Edgeworth, a member of the Anglo-Irish gentry, was born to the first of her father's four wives; her mother died when Maria was five. Richard Lovell Edgeworth, an energetic, conscientious, and progressive man, formed Maria's mind—educating her carefully, encouraging her writing, training her to help manage his estate, and urging her to take an interest in public affairs. Maria idolized her father, never married, and lived with her family all her life. As the eldest daughter among twenty-one children, she took a major role in educating younger siblings. This experience qualified her to collaborate with Richard Edgeworth on *Practical Education* (1798), a pioneering work of educational psychology, and to write engaging and authentic stories for children.

Edgeworth's first tale for adults was *Castle Rackrent* (1800), an innovative masterpiece set in Ireland. *Belinda* (1801), which centers on a young lady's entrance into the fashionable world, is a more typical eighteenth-century woman's novel. *The Absentee* (1812) and *Ormond* (1817) dramatize the problems of Ireland and the responsibilities of the landholding class. Almost all of Edgeworth's novels were critically acclaimed and highly profitable.

Entertaining, good-humored, and kindly, Maria Edgeworth was a great social success when she visited London in 1813. She knew many of the celebrities of the day, including Anna Laetitia Barbauld, to whom she proposed collaboration on a politically liberal women's journal. Barbauld declined on the grounds that the leading women writers were too ideologically dissimilar.

In the two letters presented here, Edgeworth generously praises Elizabeth Inchbald's *Simple Story* (1791), which sympathetically portrays a more unconventional heroine than Edgeworth ever ventured to draw.

Maria Edgeworth: Chosen Letters, ed. F. V. Barry (London: Jonathan Cape, 1931); James Boaden, *Memoirs of Mrs. Inchbald* (London: Richard Bentley, 1833).

From Letter to Miss Ruxton (1809)

I have just been reading, for the fourth time, I believe, *The Simple Story*, which I intended this time to read as a critic, that I might write to Mrs.

375

Inchbald about it: but I was so carried away by it that I was totally incapable of thinking of Mrs. Inchbald or anything but Miss Milner and Doriforth, who appeared to me real persons whom I saw and heard, and who had such power to interest me, that I cried my eyes almost out before I came to the end of the story: I think it the most pathetic and the most powerfully interesting tale I ever read.¹ I was obliged to go from it to correct *Belinda* for Mrs. Barbauld, who is going to insert it in her collection of novels, with a preface; and I really was so provoked with the cold tameness of that stick or stone *Belinda*, that I could have torn the pages to pieces: and really, I have not the heart or the patience to *correct* her. As the hackney coachman said, "Mend *you!* better make a new one".

From Letter to Elizabeth Inchbald (14 January 1810)

. . . I hope you will not suspect me of the common author practice of returning praise for praise, when I tell you that I have just been reading, for the third—I believe for the fourth time—the 'Simple Story.' Its effect upon my feelings was as powerful as at the first reading; I never read *any* novel—I except *none*—I never read any novel that affected me so strongly, or that so completely possessed me with the belief in the real existence of all the people it represents. I never once recollected the author whilst I was reading it; never said or thought, *that's a fine sentiment*—or, *that is well expressed*—or *that is well invented*. I believed all to be real, and was affected as I should be by the real scenes if they had passed before my eyes: it is truly and deeply pathetic. I determined, this time of reading, to read it as a critic—or rather, as an author, to try to find out the secret of its peculiar pathos. But I quite forgot my intention in the interest Miss Milner and Dorriforth excited: but *now it is all over*, and that I can coolly exercise my judgment, I am of opinion that it is by leaving more than most other writers to the imagination, that you succeed so eminently in affecting it. By the force that is necessary to repress feeling, we judge of the intensity of the feeling; and you always contrive to give us by intelligible but simple signs the measure of this force. Writers of inferior genius waste their words in *describing* feeling; in making those who pretend to be agitated by passion describe the effects of that passion, and talk of the *rending of their hearts, &c.* A gross blunder! as gross as any Irish blunder; for the heart cannot feel, and describe its own feelings, at the same moment. It is '*being like a bird in two places at once.*'

What a beautiful stroke is that of the child who exclaims, when Dorriforth lets go his hands, '*I had like to have been down.*'

I am glad I have never met with a Dorriforth, for I must inevitably have fallen desperately in love with him; and destitute of Miss Milner's powers of charming, I might have died in despair. Indeed I question, whether my being free from some of her faults would not have made my chance worse; for I have no doubt that, with all his wisdom and virtue, he loved her the better for keeping him in a continual panic by her coquetry. I am excessively sorry you made her end *naughtily*; though I believe this makes the story more moral. Your power as a pathetic writer is even more conspicuous in the second volume, however, than in the first: for notwithstanding the prodigious and painful effort you require from the reader to jump over, at the first page, eighteen years, and to behold at once Dorriforth old, and Miss Milner a disgraced and dying mother, with a grown-up daughter beside her; notwithstanding the reluctance we feel to seeing Dorriforth as an implacable tyrant, and Sandford degraded to a trembling dependent; yet against our will, and absolutely against our resolution to be unmoved, you master our hearts, and kindle a fresh interest, and force again our tears. Nothing can be finer than the scene upon the stairs, where Dorriforth meets his daughter, and cannot unclasp her hand, and when he cannot call her by any name but Miss Milner—dear Miss Milner.

I wish Rushbrooke had not been a liar. It degrades him too much for a hero. I think you sacrificed him too much to the principle of the pyramid. The mixture of the father's character in the daughter is beautiful. As to Miss Wordley, who can help loving her, and thinking she is like their best friend, whoever that may be?

Mrs. Horton is excellent comic. Her moving all the things about in the room, to lessen the embarrassment, and her wishing (without being ill-natured) to see a quarrel, that she might have some sensations, is admirable. Did you really draw the characters from life? or did you invent them? You excel, I think, peculiarly in avoiding what is commonly called *fine writing*— a sort of writing which I detest; which calls the attention away from the *thing* to the *manner*—from the feeling to the language; which sacrifices every thing to sound, to the mere rounding of a period; which mistakes *stage effect* for *nature*. All who are at all used to writing, know and detect the *trick of the trade* immediately; and, speaking for myself, I *know* that the writing which has least the appearance of literary *manufacture* almost always pleases me the best. It has more originality; in narration of fictitious events, it most surely succeeds in giving the idea of reality, and in making the biographer, for the time, pass for nothing. But there are few who can in this manner bear the *mortification* of staying behind the scenes. They peep out, eager for applause, and destroy all illusion by crying, '*I* said it; *I* wrote it; *I* invented it all! Call me on the stage and crown me directly.' . . .

Notes

1. Inchbald's novel relates the tragic marriage between upright, rigid Dorriforth and charming, light-minded Miss Milner. When she commits adultery, Dorriforth rejects both her and their daughter, although he cannot repress his love when he accidentally meets his daughter upon the stairs. The second part (vols. 3 and 4), set seventeen years after the first, tells the pathetic tale of this rejected daughter. Inchbald made her characters express their strong feelings through restrained speech and action, rather than describing them bombastically, as was usual at the time. A good example is Dorriforth's sudden release of a child he is holding on his lap, on realizing that it is the son of a sister he has disowned. Sandford, a Jesuit priest who originally appeared as Dorriforth's respected tutor, is dependent on him in the second part. Rushbrooke, Dorriforth's attractive and amiable heir, fears to tell him the truth. Edgeworth's own Belinda, though by no means a stick, is much less lively and touching than Miss Milner. Edgeworth was currently revising *Belinda* for Barbauld's *British Novelists*.

JANE AUSTEN (1775-1817)

Jane Austen is perhaps the best-known writer represented in this volume. Her six finished novels—*Sense and Sensibility* (1811), *Pride and Prejudice* (1813), *Mansfield Park* (1814), *Emma* (1816), and *Northanger Abbey* and *Persuasion* (both published posthumously in 1818)—are still enormously popular and have elicited intense critical interest. Born to Cassandra Leigh Austen and the Reverend George A. Austen, the author lived much of her life in the country villages of Steventon and Chawton, with brief sojourns in Bath and Southampton. Her secluded life, together with her own statements about her miniaturist style, have led some readers to believe that her concerns were provincial and her intellectual scope limited. Recent scholarship, however, has emphasized the range of her interests and knowledge as well as her engagement with the political and social debates of her time.

Austen also held firm opinions about writing. One of her earliest surviving works is a parody of Goldsmith's purportedly objective history of England: Austen's "A History of England by a partial, prejudiced & ignorant Historian" mocks not only the claim to impartiality, but also the historian's tone of judicious distance. This critical mockery continues through the juvenilia and *Lady Susan* and is perhaps best represented in *Northanger Abbey*, which parodies the excesses of sentimental and gothic fiction.

Nevertheless, as the famous defense of novels in *Northanger Abbey* testifies, Austen had a profound respect for other novelists, whose task was made more difficult by the aura of disrepute still associated with the genre. While critical of overtly didactic fiction (see her remarks on Jane West and Hannah More), she was fully aware that entertaining novels were suspect. Her light-hearted commentary about *Pride and Prejudice* ("too light and bright and sparkling") and her self-deprecating rejection of James Stanier Clarke's suggestions mask a real anxiety and annoyance about the status of novels. We cannot know if Austen ever recognized her own role in changing the perception and reception of novels; we do know that she was deeply conscious of the critical climate in which she read and wrote.

The Novels of Jane Austen, ed. R. W. Chapman, 5 vols. (Oxford: Clarendon Press, 1923); *Jane Austen's Letters to Her Sister Cassandra and Others*, ed. R. W. Chapman, 2d ed. (London: Oxford University Press, 1952).

Selected Letters (1809–1816)

I am gratified by her having pleasure in what I write—but I wish the knowledge of my being exposed to her discerning Criticism, may not hurt my stile, by inducing too great a solicitude. I begin already to weigh my words and sentences more than I did, and am looking about for a sentiment, an illustration or a metaphor in every corner of the room. Could my Ideas flow as fast as the rain in the Store closet it would be charming.—We have been in two or three dreadful states within the last week, from the melting of the snow &c.—and the contest between us and the Closet has now ended in our defeat; I have been obliged to move almost everything out of it, and leave it to splash itself as it likes.—You have by no means raised my curiosity after Caleb;[1]—My disinclination for it before was affected, but now it is real; I do not like the Evangelicals.—Of course I shall be delighted, when I read it, like other people, but till I do I dislike it.

Tuesday, 24 January 1809, to Cassandra Austen

My dear Cassandra

Your letter was truly welcome, and I am much obliged to you all for your praise; it came at a right time, for I had had some fits of disgust. Our second evening's reading [of *Pride and Prejudice*] to Miss Benn had not pleased me so well, but I believe something must be attributed to my mother's too rapid way of getting on: and though she perfectly understands the characters herself, she cannot speak as they ought. Upon the whole, however, I am quite vain enough and well satisfied enough. The work is rather too light, and bright, and sparkling; it wants shade; it wants to be stretched out here and there with a long chapter of sense, if it could be had; if not, of solemn specious nonsense, about something unconnected with the story; an essay on writing, a critique on Walter Scott, or the history of Buonaparte, or anything that would form a contrast, and bring the reader with increased delight to the playfulness and epigrammatism of the general style. I doubt your quite agreeing with me here. I know your starched notions.

Thursday, 4 February 1813, to Cassandra Austen

We quite run over with books. *She* [Austen's mother] has got Sir John Carr's Travels in Spain from Miss B. & *I* am reading a Society octavo, an Essay on the Military Police [*sic*] & Institutions of the British Empire by Capt Pasley of the Engineers,[2] a book I protested against at first, but which upon trial I find delightfully written & highly entertaining. I am as much in love with the author as ever I was with Clarkson or Buchanan, or even the two Mr Smiths of the city—the first soldier I ever sighed for—but he does write with extraordinary force & spirit. . . . The Miss Sibleys want to establish a Book Society in their side of the country, like ours. What can be a stronger proof of that superiority in ours over the Steventon & Manydown society, which I have always foreseen & felt? No emulation of the kind was ever inspired by *their* proceedings. No such wish of the Miss Sibleys was ever heard in the course of the many years of that Society's existence. And what are their Biglands & their Barrows, their Macartneys & Mackenzies to Capt Pasley's Essay on the Military police of the British Empire, & the rejected addresses? . . . Ladies who read those enormous great stupid thick quarto volumes which one always sees in the Breakfast parlour there, must be acquainted with everything in the world. I detest a quarto. Capt Pasley's book is too good for their Society. They will not understand a man who condenses his thoughts into an octavo.

Sunday, 24 January 1813, and Tuesday, 9 February 1813, to Cassandra Austen

My dear Anna[3]

We have been very much amused by your 3 books, but I have a good many criticisms to make—more than you will like.—We are not satisfied with Mrs. F.'s settling herself as Tenant & near Neighbour to such a Man as Sir T. H. without having some other inducement to go there; she ought to have some friend living thereabouts to tempt her. A woman, going with two girls just growing up, into a Neighbourhood where she knows nobody but one Man, of not very good character, is an awkwardness which so prudent a woman as Mrs. F. would not be likely to fall into. Remember, she is very prudent; you must not let her act inconsistently.—Give her a friend, & let that friend be invited to meet her at the Priory, & we shall have no objection to her dining there as she does; but otherwise, a woman in her situation would hardly go there, before she had been visited by other Families.—I like the scene itself, the Miss Lesleys, Lady Anne, & the Music, very much.—Lesley *is* a noble name.— Sir T. H. you always do very well; I have only taken the liberty of expunging one phrase of his, which would not be allowable. 'Bless my Heart'—It is too familiar & inelegant. Your G. M. is more disturbed at Mrs. F.'s not returning the Egertons visit sooner, than anything else. They ought to have called at the Parsonage before Sunday.— You describe a sweet place, but your descriptions are often more minute than will be liked. You give too many particulars of right hand & left.—Mrs. F. is not careful enough of Susan's health;—Susan ought not to be walking out so soon after Heavy rains, taking long walks in the dirt. An anxious Mother would not suffer it.—I like your Susan very much indeed, she is a sweet creature, her playfulness of fancy is very delightful. I like her as she is *now* exceedingly, but I am not so well satisfied with her behaviour to George R. At first she seemed all over attachment & feeling, & afterwards to have none at all; she is so extremely composed at the Ball, & so well-satisfied apparently with Mr. Morgan. She seems to have changed her Character.—You are now collecting your People delightfully, getting them exactly into such a spot as is the delight of my life;—3 or 4 Families in a Country Village is the very thing to work on—& I hope you will write a great deal more & make full use of them while they are so very favourably arranged. You are but *now* coming to the heart & beauty of your book; till the heroine grows up, the fun must be imperfect—but I expect a great deal of entertainment from the next 3 or 4 books, & I hope you will not resent these remarks by sending me no more.—We like the Egertons very well, we see no Blue Pantaloons, or Cocks & Hens;—there is nothing to *enchant* one certainly in Mr. L. L.—but we make no objection to him, & his inclination to like Susan is pleasing.—The Sister is a good contrast—but the name of Rachael is as much as I can bear.—They are not so much like the Papillons as I expected. Your last chapter is very entertaining—the conversation on Genius &c. Mr. St. J.—& Susan both talk in character & very well.—In some former parts, Cecilia is perhaps a little too solemn & good, but upon the whole, her disposition is very well opposed to Susan's—her want of Imagination is very natural.—I wish you could make Mrs. F. talk more, but she must be difficult to manage & make entertaining, because there is so much good common sense & propriety about her that nothing can be very *broad*. Her Economy and her Ambition must not be staring.— The Papers left by Mrs. Fisher is very good.—Of course, one guesses something.—I hope when you have written a great deal more you will be equal to scratching out some of the past. The scene with Mrs. Mellish, I should condemn; it is prosy & nothing to the purpose—& indeed, the more you can find in your heart to curtail between Dawlish & Newton Priors, the better I think it will be. One does not care for girls till they are grown up.—Your Aunt C. quite enters into the exquisiteness of that name. Newton Priors is really a Nonpareil.—Milton wd have given his eyes to have thought of it. Is not the Cottage taken from Tollard Royal?— . . .

I hope you do not depend on having your book back again immediately. I keep it that your G:Mama may hear it—for it has not been possible yet to have any public reading. I have read it to your Aunt Cassandra however—in our room at night, while we undressed—and with a great deal of pleasure. We like the first chapter extremely—with only a little doubt whether Ly Helena is not almost *too* foolish. The matrimonial Dialogue is very good certainly.—I like Susan as well as ever—& begin now not to care at all about Cecilia—she may stay at Easton Court as long as she likes.—Henry Mellish I am afraid will be too much in the common Novel style—a hand-some, amiable, unexceptionable Young Man (such as do not much abound in real Life) desperately in Love, & all in vain. But I have no business to judge him so early.—Jane Egerton is a very natural, comprehendable Girl—& the whole of her acquaintance with Susan, & Susan's Letter to Cecilia, very pleasing & quite in character.—But *Miss* Egerton does not entirely satisfy us. She is too formal & solemn, we think, in her advice to her Brother not to fall in love; & it is hardly like a sensible Woman; it is putting it into his head.—We should like a few hints from her better.—We feel really obliged to you for introducing a Lady Kenrick, it will remove the greatest fault in the work, & I give you credit for considerable forbearance as an Author in adopting so much of our opinion.—I expect high fun about Mrs. Fisher and Sir Thomas.—You have been perfectly right in telling Ben of your work, & I am very glad to hear how much he likes it. *His* encourage-ment & approbation must be quite 'beyond everything.'— I do not at all wonder at his not expecting to like anybody so well as Cecilia *at first*, but shall be surprised if he does not become a Susan-ite in time. Devereux Forester's being ruined by his Vanity is extremely good; but I wish you would not let him plunge into a 'vortex of Dissipation.' I do not object to the Thing, but I cannot bear the expression;—it is such thorough novel slang—and so old, that I dare say Adam met with it in the first novel he opened.—Indeed I did very much like to know Ben's opinion.—I hope he will continue to be pleased with it, I think he must—but I cannot flatter him with their being much Incident. We have no great right to wonder at his not valueing the name of Progillian. *That* is a source of delight which he hardly ever can be quite competent to.—Walter Scott has no business to write novels, especially good ones.—It is not fair.—He has Fame and Profit enough as a Poet, and should not be taking the bread out of other people's mouths.—I do not like him, & do not mean to like Waverley if I can help it.—but I fear I must.[4] I am quite determined however not to be pleased with Mrs. West's Alicia de Lacy,[5] should I ever meet with it, which I hope I may not.—I think I *can* be stout against anything written by Mrs. West.—I have made up my mind to like no Novels really, but Miss Edgeworth's, Yours & my own.—

What can you do with Egerton to increase the interest for him? I wish you cd contrive something, some family occurrence to draw out his good qualities more—some distress among Brothers or Sisters to relieve by the sale of his Curacy—something to [tak]e him mysteriously away, & then heard of at York or Edinburgh—in an old great coat.—I would not seriously recommend anything Improbable, but if you cd invent something spirited for him, it wd have a good effect.—He might lend all his Money to Captn Morris—but then he wd be a great fool if he did. Cannot the Morrises quarrel, & he reconcile them? Excuse the liberty I take in these suggestions.—

Friday, 9 September 1814, and Wednesday, 28 September 1814, to Anna Austen

I am honoured by the Prince's thanks and very much obliged to yourself for the kind manner in which you mention the work.[6] I have also to acknowledge a former letter forwarded to me from Hans Place. I assure you I felt very grateful for the friendly tenor of it, and hope my silence will have been considered, as it was truly meant, to proceed only from an unwillingness to tax your time with idle thanks. Under every interesting circumstance which your own talents and literary labours have placed you in, or the favour of the Regent bestowed, you have my best wishes. Your recent appointments I hope are a step to something still better. In my opinion, the service of a court can hardly be too well paid, for immense must be the sacrifice of time and feeling required by it.

You are very kind in your hints as to the sort of composition which might recommend me at present, and I am fully sensible that an historical romance, founded on the House of Saxe Cobourg, might be much more to the purpose of profit or popularity than such pictures of domestic life in country villages as I deal in. But I could no more write a romance than an epic poem. I could not sit seriously down to write a serious romance under any other motive than to save my life; and if it were indispensable for me to keep it up and never relax into laughing at myself or other people, I am sure I should be hung before I had finished the first chapter. No, I must keep to my own style and go on in my own way; and though I may never succeed again in that, I am convinced that I should totally fail in any other.

Monday, 1 April 1816, to James Stanier Clarke

—and how good Mrs. West cd have written such Books & collected so many hard words, with all her family cares, is still more a matter of astonishment! Composition seems to me Impossible, with a head full of Joints of Mutton and doses of rhubarb.

Sunday, 8 September 1816, to Cassandra Austen

By the bye, my dear Edward, I am quite concerned for the loss your Mother mentions in her Letter; two Chapters & a half to be missing is monstrous! It is well that *I* have not been at Steventon lately, & therefore cannot be suspected of purloining them;—two strong twigs & a half towards a Nest of my own, would have been something.—I do not think however that any theft of that sort would be really very useful to me. What should I do with your strong, manly, spirited Sketches, full of Variety and Glow?—How could I possible join them on to the little bit (two Inches wide) of Ivory on which I work with so fine a Brush, as produces little effect after much labour?

Monday, 16 December 1816, to J. Edward Austen

From *Northanger Abbey* (1818)

. . . and if a rainy morning deprived them[1] of other enjoyments, they were still resolute in meeting in defiance of wet and dirt, and shut themselves up, to read novels together. Yes, novels;—for I will not adopt that ungenerous and impolitic custom so common with novel writers, of degrading by their contemptuous censure the very performances, to the number of which they are themselves adding—joining with their greatest enemies in bestowing the harshest epithets on such works, and scarcely ever permitting them to be read by their own heroine, who, if she accidentally take up a novel, is sure to turn over its insipid pages with disgust. Alas! if the heroine of one novel be not patronized by the heroine of another, from whom can she expect protection and regard? I cannot approve of it. Let us leave it to the Reviewers to abuse such effusions of fancy at their leisure, and over every new novel to talk in threadbare strains of the trash with which the press now groans. Let us not desert one another; we are an injured body. Although our productions have afforded more extensive and unaffected pleasure than those of any other literary corporation in the world, no species of composition has been so much decried. From pride, ignorance, or fashion, our foes are almost as many as our readers. And while the abilities of the nine-hundredth abridger of the History of England, or of the man who collects and publishes in a volume some dozen lines of Milton, Pope, and Prior, with a paper from the Spectator, and a chapter from Sterne, are eulogized by a thousand pens,—there seems almost a general wish of decrying the capacity and undervaluing the labour of the novelist, and of slighting the performances which have only genius, wit, and taste to recommend them. "I am no novel reader—I seldom look into novels—Do not imagine that *I* often read novels—It is really very well for a novel."—Such is the common cant.—"And what are you reading, Miss ——?" "Oh! it is only a novel!" replies the young lady; while she lays down her book with affected indifference, or momentary shame.—"It is only Cecilia, or Camilla, or Belinda;"² or, in short, only some work in which the greatest powers of the mind are displayed, in which the most thorough knowledge of human nature, the happiest delineation of its varieties, the liveliest effusions of wit and humour are conveyed to the world in the best chosen language. Now, had the same young lady been engaged with a volume of the Spectator, instead of such a work, how proudly would she have produced the book, and told its name; though the chances must be against her being occupied by any part of that voluminous publication, of which either the matter or manner would not disgust a young person of taste: the substance of its papers so often consisting in the statement of improbable circumstances, unnatural characters, and topics of conversation, which no longer concern any one living; and their language, too, frequently so coarse as to give no very favourable idea of the age that could endure it.

. . . .

"That is, I can read poetry and plays, and things of that sort, and do not dislike travels. But history, real solemn history, I cannot be interested in. Can you?"

"Yes, I am fond of history."

"I wish I were too. I read it a little as a duty, but it tells me nothing that does not either vex or weary me. The quarrels of popes and kings, with wars or pestilences, in every page; the men all so good for nothing, and hardly any women at all—it is very tiresome: and yet I often think it odd that it should be so dull, for a great deal of it must be invention. The speeches that are put into the heroes' mouths, their thoughts and designs—the chief of all this must be invention, and invention is what delights me in other books."

"Historians, you think," said Miss Tilney, "are not happy in their flights of fancy. They display imagination without raising interest. I am fond of history—and am very well contented to take the false with the true. In the principal facts they have sources of intelligence in former histories and records, which may be as much depended on, I conclude, as any thing that does not actually pass under one's own observation; and as for the little embellishments you speak of, they are embellishments, and I like them as such. If a speech be well drawn up, I read it with pleasure, by whomsoever it may be made—and probably with much greater, if the production of Mr. Hume or Mr. Robertson, than if the genuine words of Caractacus, Agricola, or Alfred the Great."[3]

"You are fond of history!—and so are Mr. Allen and my father; and I have two brothers who do not dislike it. So many instances within my small circle of friends is remarkable! At this rate, I shall not pity the writers of history any longer. If people like to read their books, it is all very well, but to be at so much trouble in filling great volumes, which, as I used to think, nobody would willingly ever look into, to be labouring only for the torment of little boys and girls, always struck me as a hard fate; and though I know it is all very right and necessary, I have often wondered at the person's courage that could sit down on purpose to do it."

"That little boys and girls should be tormented," said Henry, "is what no one at all acquainted with human nature in a civilized state can deny; but in behalf of our most distinguished historians, I must observe, that they might well be offended at being supposed to have no higher aim; and that by their method and style, they are perfectly well qualified to torment readers of the most advanced reason and mature time of life. I use the verb 'to torment,' as I observed to be your own method, instead of 'to instruct,' supposing them to be now admitted as synonimous."

"You think me foolish to call instruction a torment, but if you had been as much used as myself to hear poor little children first learning their letters and then learning to spell, if you had ever seen how stupid they can be for a whole morning together, and how tired my poor mother is at the end of it, as I am in the habit of seeing almost every day of my life at home, you would allow that to *torment* and to *instruct* might sometimes be used as synonimous words."

"Very probably. But historians are not accountable for the difficulty of learning to read; and even you yourself, who do not altogether seem particularly friendly to very severe, very intense application, may perhaps be brought to acknowledge that it is very well worth while to be tormented for two or three years of one's life, for the sake of being able to read all the rest of it. Consider—if reading had not been taught, Mrs. Radcliffe would have written in vain—or perhaps might not have written at all."

From *Persuasion* (1818)

. . . He[1] was evidently a young man of considerable taste in reading, though principally in poetry; and besides the persuasion of having given him at least an evening's indulgence in the discussion of subjects, which his usual companions had probably no concern in, she had the hope of being of real use to him in some suggestions as to the duty and benefit of struggling against affliction, which had naturally grown out of their conversation. For, though shy, he did not seem reserved; it had rather the appearance of feelings glad to burst their usual restraints; and having talked of poetry, the richness of the present age, and gone through a brief comparison of opinion as to the first-rate poets, trying to ascertain whether *Marmion* or *The Lady of the Lake* were to be preferred, and how ranked the *Giaour* and *The Bride of Abydos*;[2] and moreover, how the *Giaour* was to be pronounced, he shewed himself so intimately acquainted with all the tenderest songs of the one poet, and all the impassioned descriptions of hopeless agony of the other; he repeated, with such tremulous feeling, the various lines which imaged a broken heart, or a mind destroyed by wretchedness, and looked so entirely as if he meant to be understood, that she ventured to hope he did not always read only poetry; and to say, that she thought it was the misfortune of poetry, to be seldom safely enjoyed by those who enjoyed it completely; and that the strong feelings which alone could estimate it truly, were the very feelings which ought to taste it but sparingly.

His looks shewing him not pained, but pleased with this allusion to his situation, she was emboldened to go on; and feeling in herself the right of seniority of mind, she ventured to recommend a larger allowance of prose in his daily study; and on being requested to particularize, mentioned such works of our best moralists, such collections of the finest letters, such memoirs of characters of worth and suffering, as occurred to her at the moment as calculated to rouse and fortify the mind by the highest precepts, and the strongest examples of moral and religious endurances.

Captain Benwick listened attentively, and seemed grateful for the interest implied; and though with a shake of the head, and sighs which declared his little faith in the efficacy of any books on grief like his, noted down the names of those she recommended, and promised to procure and read them.

When the evening was over, Anne could not but be amused at the idea of her coming to Lyme, to preach patience and resignation to a young man whom she had never seen before; nor could she help fearing, on more serious reflection, that, like many other great moralists and preachers, she had been eloquent on a point in which her own conduct would ill bear examination.

Notes

Selected Letters

1. Hannah More, *Coelebs in Search of a Wife* (1809). Many critics point out the apparent discrepancy between this criticism and Austen's later statement to Fanny Knight: "I am by no means convinced that we ought not all to be Evangelicals" (*Letters* 410).

2. Sir John Carr, *Descriptive Travels in the Southern and Eastern Parts of Spain and the Balearic Isles, in the Year 1809* (1811); Captain John Pasley, *Essay on the Military Policy and Institutions of the British Empire* (1810).

3. Jane Anna Elizabeth (1793–1872) was the oldest daughter of Austen's brother James (1765–1819). The novel in progress that Austen critiques here was never published.

4. *Waverly, or 'tis Sixty Years Since* (1814). Scott's phenomenal success as a novelist eclipsed Austen's growing reputation, although he himself was one of her earliest admirers, contrasting her subtle art with his own "Big Bow-wow strain."

5. Jane West, *Alicia de Lacy, an Historical Romance* (1814).

6. *Emma* was dedicated to the Prince Regent, the transaction being arranged through the Prince's librarian, the Reverend James Stanier Clarke. Clarke, having previously (and unsuccessfully) urged Austen to use her talents to depict a clergyman very much like himself, suggested that she write "any historical romance, illustrative of the history of the august House of Cobourg" (*Letters* 451). At the time he made the request, he had been appointed by the Prince Regent to serve as chaplain to Prince Leopold of Cobourg.

Northanger Abbey

1. The "they" refers to the heroine, Catherine Morland, and her bosom friend, Isabella Thorpe. The two share a passion for gothic novels.

2. Austen refers here to novels by other women: Frances Burney's *Cecilia; or, Memoirs of an Heiress* (1782) and *Camilla; or, a Picture of Youth* (1796) and Maria Edgeworth's *Belinda* (1801). Austen's name appears on the subscription list for Camilla.

3. David Hume, *The History of England: From the Invasion of Julius Caesar to the Revolution in 1688* (1754–1761). William Robertson's several histories include *The History of the Reign of Emperor Charles V: With a View of the Progress of Society in Europe, from the Subversion of the Roman Empire, to the Beginning of the Sixteenth Century* (1769) and *The History of America* (1777).

Persuasion

1. Captain Benwick's fiancée has died, and when Anne meets him, he seems to her to be feeding his grief by reading Romantic poetry.

2. Walter Scott's *Marmion* (1808) and *Lady of the Lake* (1810) and Byron's *Bride of Abydos* and *Giaour* (both 1813) were enormously popular poems. For Austen on Scott's shift from poet to novelist, see her letter of September 1814 to Anna Austen.

RACHEL MORDECAI LAZARUS
(1788–1838)

BORN TO a Jewish family whose forebears had emigrated to the United States earlier in the century, Rachel Mordecai was raised in North Carolina and lost her mother in 1796. In 1809, after suffering business reversals, Mordecai's father opened a school for girls based on principles espoused in the writings of Maria and Richard Lovell Edgeworth. The older Mordecai children made up its teaching staff, with Rachel most centrally involved. The school flourished until it was sold in 1818. Apparently with some reluctance, Rachel Mordecai married in 1821 Aaron Lazarus, a businessman and widower with seven children; four children were born to this union. In 1838, traveling to visit her dying father, to whom she had remained extremely close, Rachel herself died suddenly.

In 1815, Lazarus had initiated a correspondence with Maria Edgeworth prompted by her conflicted response to Edgeworth's work: strong admiration, tainted by distress at Edgeworth's negative representations of Jews. The correspondence flourished until Lazarus's death, and although there is a shade of ambivalence in Edgeworth's reference to Lazarus as "my American Jewess," the author considered Lazarus a close friend and confidante and deeply felt her loss. Their letters discussed subjects from literature to gardening, from international politics to slavery. Strikingly, a correspondence between women of the Edgeworth and Lazarus families continued for more than a century after Rachel's death: Rachel's sister Ellen Mordecai continued writing to Edgeworth, one of Edgeworth's sisters took up the exchange after the death of Maria, and so forth until the decease of Rachel's grandniece Rosina Mordecai in 1942.

The letters excerpted here, which initiated the correspondence, mark an extraordinary moment in literary history, for Edgeworth undertook her novel *Harrington* (1817) explicitly as "reparation" for the anti-Semitic representations made visible to her by Rachel Lazarus. Lazarus's intervention, itself an unusually direct critique of a pervasive cultural practice, thus inspires what is arguably the first explicit effort to expose and overturn Jewish stereotypes in English literature.

The Education of the Heart: The Correspondence of Rachel Mordecai Lazarus and Maria Edgeworth, ed. Edgar E. MacDonald (Chapel Hill: University of North Carolina Press, 1977).

From Correspondence with Maria Edgeworth (1815–1821)

Warrenton, North Carolina
U.S. of America
August 7th, 1815

A young American lady who has long felt towards Miss Edgeworth those sentiments of respect and admiration which superior talents exerted in the cause of virtue and morality never fail to excite, ventures, not without hesitation, to indulge a wish formed many months since of addressing her. If such temerity require more than an ordinary apology, it is to Practical Education[1] she must appeal as her intercessor; it is that, which by lately making her acquainted with the Edgeworth family, has gradually eradicated fear and in its stead implanted confidence.

With how much interest have I perused and re-perused the useful observations which those volumes contain. . . . [There follow several paragraphs praising Edgeworth's educational and moral writings.]

With all my confidence in the benignant goodness of Miss Edgeworth I tremble at having said so much, and trespassed so very greatly on her patience and indulgence; still must I entreat that they may be extended to me yet a little longer.

Relying on the good sense and candour of Miss Edgeworth I would ask, how it can be that she, who on all other subjects shows such justice and liberality, should on one alone appear biased by prejudice: should even instill that prejudice into the minds of youth! Can my allusion be mistaken? It is to the species of character which wherever a *Jew* is introduced is invariably attached to him. Can it be believed that this race of men are by nature mean, avaricious, and unprincipled? Forbid it, mercy. Yet this is more than insinuated by the stigma usually affixed to the *name*. In those parts of the world where these people are oppressed and made continually the subject of scorn and derision, they may in many instances deserve censure; but in this happy country, where religious distinctions are scarcely known, where character and talents are all sufficient to attain advancement, we find the Jews to form a respectable part of the community. They are in most instances liberally educated, many following the honourable professions of the Law, and Physick, with credit and ability, and associating with the best society our country affords. The penetration of Miss Edgeworth has already conjectured that it is a Jewess who addresses her; it is so, but one who thinks she does not flatter herself in believing that were she not, her opinion on this subject would be exactly what it is now. Living in a small village, her father's the only family of Israelites who reside in or near it, all her juvenile friendships and attachments have been formed with those of persuasions different from her own; yet each has looked upon the variations of the other as things of course—differences which take place in every society. Again and again I beg pardon for thus intruding myself on Miss Edgeworth's notice; yet even now is my temerity about to appear in a new form while I give utterance to a very imperfect hope, that these lines may be honoured with a reply, and their author thus taught to believe herself not wholly unpardonable, in the liberty she takes in writing them. Should she be thus highly favoured, Miss Edgeworth will have the goodness to direct the letter according to the address, which a brother of the writer's, now in England, will annex.

With sentiments of admiration, esteem, and gratitude, Miss Edgeworth's

> most respectful and obedient servant
> [Rachel Mordecai]

> Edgeworthstown, Ireland
> [August 1816]

Dear Madam,

Your polite, benevolent and touching letter has given me much pleasure, and much pain. As to the pain I hope you will sometime see that it has excited me to make all the atonement and reparation in my power for the past. It was impossible to remonstrate with more gentleness or in a more convincing as well as persuasive manner than you have done. Your own letter is the very best evidence that could have been offered of the truth of all you urge in favor of those of your own religious persuasion. And the candor and spirit of tolerance and benevolence you shew, you have a right to expect from others.

Will you be so kind to tell me how I can send you what I am now preparing for the press?[2] It probably will not be published till the end of the year, so that I shall have time for your answer. Is there any person in London to whom I can consign the book? Though you did not sign any name to your letter and though it seems an extraordinary coincidence that your brother's name should happen to be *Mordecai* (absentee),[3] yet I am persuaded from the tone of truth throughout the letter that you are a real living person and that you think and feel all you say. Perhaps I am credulously vain in believing all the gratifying things you say about Practical Education, but I own that they have given me great pleasure. Nothing can be more agreeable to my father and to me than to think that what we have written on education has been practically useful, especially to one so amiably intent upon the education of a family as you appear to be. . . .

> I am Dear Madam
> Your obliged and grateful
> Maria Edgeworth

> Warrenton, North Carolina,
> 25 September 1816

The twenty-fifth of September, if I kept a diary, should be noted as one of the most agreeable days I have ever known, and for its pleasurable sensations I am indebted to Mr. and Miss Edgeworth. . . .

With Mr. Edgeworth's flattering request that I will make you better acquainted with my real self, I readily comply. It was not indeed in the first instance my intention to conceal my name, and it was signed at full length to my letter but Rachel, as well as Mordecai, formed so striking a coincidence,[4] that believing it would give an idea of my character being an assumed one, my brother erased both. . . .

I must confess that I was rather gratified than surprised at Miss Edgeworth's frank admission of my charge (shall I call it) against her. It was my conviction of her being capable of a conduct so noble that first encouraged me to touch on so delicate a subject, but that she should immediately set about making what she calls 'atonement and reparation' was more than I could have hoped. Still do I rejoice at it, as it raises her character still higher in my estimation. We are told that authors at home and authors on our shelves are quite different persons; this assertion has often been a source of mortification to me, and I rejoice to find that in some instances at least it is erroneous. . . .

[R. Mordecai]

Warrenton, October 28th, 1817

. . . .

We have read both Harrington and Ormond[5] with much satisfaction; the former will, I hope by asserting the cause of toleration, reward the benevolent intentions of its author. In England, where from circumstances related in that work, we must believe prejudices carried to an excess, hardly conceivable by us in America, it will doubtless be productive of much good. If by scrutinizing the conduct of Jews, they are proved to fulfill in common with other men every moral and social duty, it is to be hoped that the stigma which habit has associated with the name will lose its influence. The eagerness with which Miss Edgeworth has sought for such characters, and such incidents, as were honourable to our unfortunate nation, evinces the sincerity with which she undertook their defence. It is impossible to feel otherwise than gratified by the confidence so strongly, yet so delicately manifested, by the insertion of a passage from the letter in which I had endeavoured to give an idea of their general standing in this country.[6] I say *in this country*, tho' I acknowledge myself but imperfectly acquainted with the opinions entertained in some parts of it. So far as regards some of the Southern States, I speak with confidence. The Northern might, I think, be included; the Eastern[7] are perhaps somewhat less liberal, but of this, I am not certain; and as for the Western they are yet in their infancy and have no determinate character.

To return to Harrington. The portrait of Mr. Montenero is rendered the more gratifying by its contrast with even the very few of those Israelites who have, in fictitious writings, been represented as estimable. I have met with none, that I recollect, but Cumberland's Shever.[8] And in Shever, tho' we find much to approve, there is still a want of respectability. He was a benevolent man; but in the profession of a *userer*, there is something against which correct principle revolts. Mr. Montenero is a good man, a man of science, and a gentleman whose acquaintance and intimacy anyone may covet. It is difficult duly to appreciate the greatness of mind which can relinquish opinions long indulged and avowed, and which has courage to recant when convinced that justice calls for recantation. The passage, page

30, beginning, "I have met with authors, professing candour and toleration, etc.," I read with peculiar satisfaction; such an instance of the candour, the superiority of Miss Edgeworth's mind and heart, I dwell on with a degree of pleasure, I may venture to say it, nearly equal to that which the reflection of having written it must yield herself. Many other remarks on this volume present themselves, but if I attempt to tell of all I found in it to give me pleasure, I shall say both too much and too little. Let me therefore, without dwelling longer on its many excellences, confess with frankness that in one event I was disappointed. Berenice was not a Jewess.[9] I have endeavoured to discover Miss Edgeworth's motive for not suffering her to remain such; it appeared that there must be another, besides that of the obstacle it presented to her union with Harrington; and I have at length adopted an opinion suggested by my dear father, that this circumstance was intended as an additional proof of the united liberality and firmness of Mr. Montenero's principles. He had married a lady of different religious persuasion, without being inclined to swerve in the least from his own; and he had brought up his daughter in the belief of her mother, but with an equal regard for both religions; inculcating thereby the principle that, provided the heart is sincere in its adoration, the conduct governed by justice, benevolence, and morality, the modes of faith and forms of worship are immaterial; all equally acceptable to that Almighty Being, who looks down on all his creatures with an eye of mercy and forgiveness. It is not wonderful that I should, in the present instance, have adopted this opinion, for it is that in which all my father's children have been educated: we regard our own faith as sacred, but we respect that of others, and believe it equally capable of conducting them to the Throne of Grace. It would be gratifying to us to know how far our impressions respecting Berenice are correct. . . .

With every wish for Miss Edgeworth's prosperity and happiness, I have the honour of subscribing myself,

> her very grateful friend and servant
> R. Mordecai

Edgeworthstown, June 21, 1821

I have never, I believe, written to you since I received a very kind letter from you about Harrington and Ormond. It came to my hands when I was so unhappy that I could not write any answer.[10] The feeling that my Father would have been so much gratified by it and that it came when he could no longer sympathise with me as he had done for so many happy years was dreadful. I have since read your letter again lately, after an interval of near four years, and feel grateful now for not having thanked you. I wish you would thank your kindhearted father for the reason he gave for my making Berenice turn out to be a Christian. It was a better reason than I own I had ever thought up. I really should be gratified if I could have any testimony even were it ever so slight from those of your persuasion that they were pleased with my attempt to do them justice. But except from you, my dear Madam, and one or two other individuals in England, I have never heard that any of the Jewish persuasion received Harrington as it was intended. A book or merely a print of any celebrated Jew or Jewess or a *note* expressing their satisfaction with my endeavors or with my intentions would have pleased—I will not say my vanity—but my heart. . . .

> Believe me, Dear Madam, your grateful
> Maria Edgeworth

Notes

1. Coauthored by Maria Edgeworth and her father, Richard Lovell Edgeworth (1744–1817), *Practical Education* (1798) sets forth a theory and practice for modern education based on modified Rousseauian principles of sympathy, utility, and intellectual experiment. The work was widely read and avidly debated both within and beyond Great Britain. It contains, however, at least one negative reference to Jews in which they are described as avaricious extortionists of "knavish propensity" (I, 248).

2. I.e., *Harrington* (1817), undertaken, according to both Maria and Richard Edgeworth, specifically in "reparation" for anti-Semitism in Edgeworth's earlier works.

3. Mordecai is the name of the Jewish coachmaker in Maria Edgeworth's *Absentee* (1812) whose wily and exploitative business practices suggest those of Shakespeare's Shylock (in *The Merchant of Venice*).

4. Rachel is the name of a character in Edgeworth's *Belinda* (1801), another novel that includes a sharply negative representation of a Jewish usurer (see esp. chap. 29). Although Edgeworth's Rachel is not Jewish, the Jewish resonances of her name may explain the extraordinary (and uncriticized) act of her "rescuer" Clarence Hervey, who renames her Virginia because he "could not endure" the name Rachel (chap. 26).

5. *Ormond*, a novel of Irish life partly set in eighteenth-century Paris, was published together with *Harrington* in 1817.

6. See *Harrington*, chap. 8.

7. By Eastern, Lazarus means specifically the New England states.

8. Richard Cumberland's play *The Jew* (1794) creates in Sheva the moneylender a benevolent antithesis to Shylock.

9. At the end of *Harrington* it is revealed that although Berenice's father is a Jew,

her late mother was a Christian who raised Berenice in that faith. Harrington, the Christian narrator who loves Berenice, does not, therefore, actually end up having to marry a Jew as he, his family, and the reader have been led to believe.

10. Edgeworth refers here to the death of her father in June 1817, just two weeks after he wrote the preface to *Harrington*.

BIOGRAPHICAL AND BIBLIOGRAPHICAL SOURCES

General Works

Dictionary of Literary Biography.
Dictionary of National Biography.
Dictionnaire des lettres françaises.
Dictionnaire des littératures de langue française.
Battestin, Martin C., ed. *British Novelists 1660–1800.* Detroit: Gale, 1985.
Blackwell, Jeannine, and Susanne Zantop. *Bitter Healing: German Women Writers 1700–1830.* Lincoln: University of Nebraska Press, 1990.
Blain, Virginia, Patricia Clements, and Isobel Grundy, eds. *The Feminist Companion to Literature in English: Women Writers from the Middle Ages to the Present.* New Haven: Yale University Press, 1990.
Sartori, Eva, and Dorothy Wynne Zimmerman. *French Women Writers: A Bio-Bibliographical Source Book.* Westport: Greenwood Press, 1991.
Todd, Janet, ed. *A Dictionary of British and American Women Writers, 1660–1800.* Totowa: Rowman and Allanheld, 1985.
Todd, Janet, ed. *British Women Writers: A Critical Reference Guide.* New York: Ungar/Continuum, 1989.
Williamson, Marilyn L. *Raising Their Voices: British Women Writers 1650–1750.* Detroit: Wayne State University Press, 1990.

Works about Individual Authors

Argyros, Ellen. " 'Intruding Herself into the Chair of Criticism': Elizabeth Griffith and *The Morality of Shakespeare's Drama Illustrated.*" In *Eighteenth-Century Women and the Arts,* ed. Frederick M. Keener and Susan E. Lorsch (New York: Greenwood Press, 1988), 283–289.
Beauchamp, Virginia Walcott. "Pioneer Linguist: Elizabeth Elstob." *University of Michigan Papers in Women's Studies* 1, no. 3 (October 1974), 9–19.
Birch, Thomas. "The Life of Mrs. Catherine Cockburn" in *The Works of Mrs. Catherine Cockburn,* 2 vols. London, 1751.
Britt, Christa Baguss. Introduction to *The History of Lady Sophia Sternheim.* Albany: SUNY Press, 1991, 3–36.
Elliott, Emory, ed. *American Writers of the Early Republic.* Detroit: Gale, 1985.
Farnham, Fern. *Madame Dacier: Scholar and Humanist.* Monterey: Angel Press, 1976.

Biographical and Bibliographical Sources

Flexner, Eleanor. *Mary Wollstonecraft: A Biography*. New York: Coward, McCann & Geoghegan, 1972.

Goldberger, Ariel H. Introduction to Germaine de Staël's *Corinne, or Italy*. Trans. Ariel H. Goldberger. New Brunswick: Rutgers University Press, 1987.

Gutwirth, Madelyn. *Madame de Staël, Novelist*. Urbana: University of Illinois Press, 1978.

Hays, Mary. "Charlotte Smith" in *Public Characters for the Year 1800–1801*. London: Richard Phillips, 1800.

Heidenreich, Bernd. *Sophie von LaRoche: eine Werkbiographie*. Frankfurt: Peter Lang, 1986.

Heiland, Donna. "Swan Songs: The Correspondence of Anna Seward and James Boswell." *Modern Philology* 90, no. 3 (February 1993): 381–391.

Hutner, Heidi, ed. *Re-reading Alpha Behn: History, Theory, and Criticism*. Charlottesville: University Press of Virginia, 1993.

Isles, Duncan. "The Lennox Collection." *Harvard Library Bulletin* 18 (1970), 326–328.

Kamm, Josephine Mary. *Hope Deferred: Girl's Education in English History*. London: Methuen, 1965, 60–61.

King, Kathryn R. "Female Desire in Jane Barker's *A Patchwork Screen for the Ladies*." *Tulsa Studies in Women's Literature* 14 (1995): 75-91.

Laborde, Alice M. *L'Oeuvre de Madame de Genlis*. Paris: A. G. Nizet, 1966.

Reynolds, Myra. *The Learned Lady in England, 1650–1760*. Boston: Houghton Mifflin, 1921, 169–185.

Rogers, Katharine M. "Britain's First Woman Drama Critic: Elizabeth Inchbald," in *Curtain Calls: British and American Women and the Theater, 1660–1820*, ed. Mary Anne Schofield and Cecilia Macheski (Athens: Ohio University Press, 1991), 277–90.

Rogers, Katharine M. "Anna Barbauld's Criticism of Fiction—Johnsonian Mode, Female Vision," *Studies in Eighteenth-Century Culture* 21 (1991), 27–41.

Saje, Natasha. "Artful Artlessness: Reading the Coquette in the American Novel 1797–1913." Ph.D. dissertation, University of Maryland, 1995.

Séjourné, Philippe. *The Mystery of Charlotte Lennox: First Novelist of Colonial America (1727?–1804)*. Aix-en-Provence: Publications des Annales de la Faculté des Lettres, Nouvelle Série no. 62, 1967.

Shields, John C. "Phillis Wheatley's Struggle for Freedom," in *The Collected Works of Phillis Wheatley*, ed. Shields. New York: Oxford University Press, 1988, 252–267.

Small, Miriam Rossiter. *Charlotte Ramsay Lennox: An Eighteenth Century Lady of Letters*. New Haven: Yale University Press, 1935.

Spencer, Jane. "Creating the Woman Writer: The Autobiographical Works of Jane Barker." *Tulsa Studies in Women's Literature* 2 (Fall 1983): 165–181.

Spender, Dale. "Charlotte Lennox and North America." *Mothers of the Novel*. New York: Pandora, 1986, 194–205.

Stanton, Judith. Preface to Charlotte Smith, *The Old Manor House*, ed. Anne K. Ehrenpreis. New York: Oxford University Press, 1989.

Stanton, Judith, ed. *The Letters of Charlotte Smith*. Bloomington: Indiana University Press, forthcoming.

Steegmuller, Francis. *A Man, a Woman, and Two Kingdoms: The Story of Madame d'Epinay and the Abbé Galiani*. New York: Knopf, 1991.

Tomalin, Claire. *The Life and Death of Mary Wollstonecraft*. New York: Harcourt Brace Jovanovich, 1974.

Wardle, Ralph Martin. *Mary Wollstonecraft: A Critical Biography*. Lincoln: University of Nebraska Press, 1966.

Wiede-Behrendt, Ingrid. *Lehrerin des Schönen, Wahren, Guten: Literatur und Frauenbildung im ausgehenden 18. Jahrhundert am Beispiel Sophie von LaRoche*. Frankfurt: Peter Lang, 1987.

Weinreb, Ruth Plaut. *Eagle in a Gauze Cage: Louise d'Epinay, femme de lettres*. New York: AMS Press, 1992.

Wyndham, Violet. *Madame de Genlis: A biography*. New York: Roy, 1958.

MEMBERS OF
THE FOLGER COLLECTIVE
ON EARLY WOMEN CRITICS

Virginia Walcott Beauchamp, Associate Professor Emerita of English at the University of Maryland, has written widely on English Renaissance writers and on women's diaries and letters. She edited *A Private War: Letters and Diaries of Madge Preston, 1862–1867* (Rutgers University Press, 1987) and is a Coordinating Editor for *Vives and His "Instruction of a Christen Woman,"* an edition of Richard Hyrde's 1529 English translation of the work by the Spanish humanist Juan Luis Vives.

Matthew Bray recently completed a dissertation at the University of Maryland on Charlotte Smith, Helen Maria Williams, and the ideology of Romanticism. He is Director of Product Engineering at NISC, Baltimore, a publisher of CD-ROM bibliographic databases.

Susan Green is an Assistant Professor of English at the University of Oklahoma and an editor of *Genre*. She has published articles on early women critics and writers and is working on a book-length critical study of the writings of seventeenth-century Englishwomen entitled *Blank Events: Reading Mary Wroth, Margaret Cavendish and Aphra Behn in Postmodern Time.*

Susan Sniader Lanser is Professor of Comparative Literature and English at the University of Maryland. She is the author of *The Narrative Act* (Princeton University Press, 1981), *Fictions of Authority: Women Writers and Narrative Voice* (Cornell University Press, 1992), and numerous essays in publications that include *Eighteenth-Century Life* and *Eighteenth-Century Women in the Arts*. Her newest project explores eighteenth-century representations of spinsters, Sapphists, and romantic friends.

Katherine Larsen is a Ph.D. candidate in English at the University of Maryland. She has written on early women novelists and is completing a critical edition of John Dunton's *Voyage Round the World*. Her next project is a study of the cultural constructions of domestic and commercial textile production in the late seventeenth and eighteenth centuries.

Judith Pascoe is Assistant Professor of English at the University of Iowa. She is completing a book on the theatricality of literary culture in the 1790s with a focus on the work of British women poets. Her essays "Female Botanists and the Poetry of Charlotte Smith" and "Mary Robinson and the Literary Marketplace" appear in collections of essays on Romantic women writers. She is also at work on an edition of Mary Robinson's poetry.

Katharine M. Rogers, Professor Emerita at the City University of New York, has written *The Troublesome Helpmate* (University of Washington Press, 1966), *Feminism in Eighteenth-Century England* (University of Illinois Press, 1982), and many articles on eighteenth-century women writers. Her latest book is *Frances Burney: The World of "Female Difficulties"* (Harvester, 1990). She has edited Meridian anthologies of early British and American women writers, including, most recently, *The Meridian Anthology of Restoration and Eighteenth-Century Plays by Women.*

Ruth Salvaggio, Professor in the Department of American Studies at the University of New Mexico, is the author of *Dryden's Dualities* (University of Victoria, 1983) and *Enlightened Absence: Neoclassical Configurations of the Feminine* (University of Illinois Press, 1988). She teaches and publishes in the fields of eighteenth-century studies, critical theory, and cultural studies.

Amy Cohen Simowitz holds a Ph.D. in French from Yale University and was Professor of French at the University of the District of Columbia from 1972 until 1987. She is the author of *Theory of Art in the Encyclopédie*, issued in 1984 by University Microfilms International.

Tara Ghoshal Wallace is Associate Professor of English at George Washington University. She is the editor of Frances Burney's *A Busy Day* (Rutgers University Press, 1984) and the author of *Jane Austen and Narrative Authority* (Macmillan, 1995). She has written articles on Jane Austen, Walter Scott, and Samuel Johnson and is writing a book on Pope, Swift, Thomson, and Johnson.

INDEX

Addison, Joseph, xxi, 63, 83, 274; *Tragedy of Cato,* 82; Hamilton on, 275–77; and Steele, 227; *Spectator,* xxi, 275, 357, 386

Adventurer, 227

Aeschylus, 103, 149, 153

Alcock, Mary, xix; life and works, 161; "A Receipt for Writing a Novel," *162–64*

Ambrose, St., 13

Arabian Nights, 139–40, 176

Architecture: Charrière on, xxii, 151–52, 157–58

Ariosto, 348

Aristophanes, 225

Aristotle, 13, 36, 37, 40, 49, 93, 103, 105

Aubin, Penelope, xxv

Augustine, St., 13

Austen, Jane, xvii, 330; life and works, 379; *Selected Letters, 380–85;* "From *Northanger Abbey,*" *385–88,* xix; "From *Persuasion,*" *388–89*

Bacon, Francis, 74

Baillie, Joanna, xiv, xx, 273; life and works, 301; "From 'Introductory Discourse,' *Plays on the Passions,*" *302–22,* xx; "From 'To the Reader,' from *A Series of Plays,*" *322–29*

Barbauld, Anna Laetitia, xiv, xxii, 301, 375; life and works, 174; "From 'On the Origin and Progress of Novel-Writing,' " *175–86;* "From Preface to Richardson, in *The British Novelists,*" *186–98,* xix, 376, 378*n1*

Barclay, John, 75

Barker, Jane, xxi; life and works, 29; "From *A Patchwork Screen for the Ladies,*" *30–32*

Beattie, James, 337

Beaumont, Sir Francis, 47

Behn, Aphra, xiv, xvi–xvii, xx, xxii, 142; life and works, 17–18; "Epistle to the Reader from *The Dutch Lover,*" *18–21,* xx; "Preface to *The Lucky Chance,*" *21–25;* "Translator's Preface to *A Discovery of New Worlds,*" *25–26; Oroonoko,* 142, 250–51

Benger, Elizabeth, xxv; *Memoirs of the Late Mrs. Elizabeth Hamilton,* 273

Bentley, Thomas, 330

Blackwell, Thomas, 137

Blood, Fanny, 284

Blunt, Sir Thomas Pope, 77

Boileau Despreaux, Nicolas, 50

Boyle, Roger, Earl of Orrery, 62

Brooke, Arthur, 247

Brooke, Frances, xxv

Brooke, Henry: *Fool of Quality,* 181

Burke, Edmund, 236, 335–36; *Philosophical Inquiry into the Origin of Our Ideas of the Sublime and the Beautiful,* 330; *Reflections on the Revolution in France,* 284

Burney, Frances (D'Arblay), xxiii, 181, 185; life and works, 231–32; parody of, 158–59; "From *Journal,*" *232–33;* "Author's Preface to *Evelina,*" *233–35;* "Letter to Samuel Crisp," 235; "From Dedication to *The Wanderer,*" *236–39,* xix, xxiii; *Camilla,* xvii, xxiii, 358, 386; *Cecilia,* 180, 235, 358, 386; *Witlings,* xvii

Burton, Robert: *Anatomy of Melancholy,* 179

Butler, Samuel: *Hudibras,* 330

Byron, George Gordon, Lord, 301; *Bride of Abydos,* 388; *Giaour,* 388

Carew, Thomas, 76

Carter, Elizabeth, xxv

Cato, 40

Cavendish, Margaret, Duchess of Newcastle, xiii, 178; life and works, 9–10; "Preface to *The World's Olio,*" *10–11,* xxi; "From *Sociable Letters,*" *11–13;* "Preface to *Observations upon Experimental Philosophy,*" 13, xxiv; "Preface and Epilogue to *The Description of a New World, called the Blazing-World,*" *14–15*

Centlivre, Susannah, 213

Cervantes, Miguel de, 177

Chapone, Hester, 279

Charles II, 250, 254

Charrière, Isabelle, xvii, xxii; life and works, 148–49; "Is Genius Above all Rules?" *149–58; Camilla, or, The New Novel, 158–59; Caliste,* 358

Chaucer, Geoffrey, 59–60, 64, 75, 76, 178

Chezy, Helmina von, xxv
Cibber, Colley, 252–54; *The Careless Husband,*
253–54
Cibber, Susannah Maria, 248
Cicero, 13, 277
Clark, James Stanier, 379
Cockburn, Catherine Trotter, xxiii; life and
works, 54; "Dedication to *The Unhappy
Penitent A Tragedy,*" 55–57
Coleridge, Samuel Taylor, xx
Collins, William, 271; *Passions. An Ode for Mu-
sic,* 337
Comedy: Baillie on, 314–20; Genlis on, 212–
13. *See also* Drama; Theater; Tragedy
Condillac, Abbé de, 368
Congreve, William, 55, 83, 212, 258–59
Cooper, Elizabeth, xiv, xviii, xxii; life and
works, 72; "Preface to *The Muses Library,*"
73–78
Corbet, Richard, 76
Corneille, Pierre, 107, 154, 210, 249; *Clitandre,*
107; *Horace,* 351
Cottin, Sophie, xvii, xxv
Cowley, Abraham, 62, 63
Cowley, Hannah, xvii, xxi; life and works,
199–200; " 'An Address' from *A School for
Greybeards,*" 200–202
Cowper, William, 270
Cromwell, Oliver, 250
Crowne, John: *The City Politicks,* 23; *Sir
Courtly Nice,* 23
Cruz, Sor Juana de la, xxv
Cumberland, Richard, 185, 395; *The Jew,*
xxiii, 259–61

Dacier, Anne Lefèvre, xviii, 50; life and
works, 34–35; "Translator's Preface to *The
Odyssey,*" 35–43
Daniel, Samuel: *Musophilus,* 74
Davenant, Sir William, 22, 27n3, 76, 248. *See
also* Dryden, John
Davies, John, 76
Davys, Mary, xxv
Defoe, Daniel, 178, 287–88
Demosthenes, 277
Denham, John, 49
Diderot, Denis, xx; Epinay on, 112–14
Dobson, Susanna, 139; *Life of Petrarch,* 299
Donellan, Ann, xxv
Donne, John, 76
Douglas, Gavin, 59
Drama: Baillie on, 304–29; Behn on, 18–21;
Charrière on, 153–55; Cowley on, 201–202;

Epinay on, 112–14; Inchbald on, 247–63;
Montagu on, 103–109; Murray on, 222–26;
early women critics on, xiv, xx. *See also*
Comedy; Morality; Theater; Tragedy
Drayton, Michael, 60
Dryden, John, 20, 27n3, 50, 55, 59, 63, 77, 83,
167, 250, 336; *Alexander's Feast,* 337; *All for
Love,* 249–50; *Don Sebastian,* 82; *Mac
Flecknoe,* xxiii; and Lee, *Oedipus,* 23; and
Davenant, *Tempest,* 337
Duns Scotus, John, 13
D'Urfy, Thomas, 83

Edgeworth, Maria, xvii, xviii, xxi, xxiii, 181,
185, 273, 384, 391–97; life and works, 375;
"From Letter to Miss Ruxton," 375–76;
"From Letter to Elizabeth Inchbald," 376–
77; *Belinda,* xviii, 386, 394, 397n4; *Har-
rington,* xviii, 391, 394–97; *Ormond,* 395;
and Edgeworth, Richard Lovell, *Practical
Education,* 392
Education, for women: Foster on, 279–83;
Lazarus on, 392–94; More on, 204–206;
Reeve on, 134; Smith on, 217
Elstob, Elizabeth, xviii, xxii, xxiii; life and
works, 58–59; "From *The Rudiments of
Grammar for the English-Saxon Tongue,*"
59–65
English Language: Cooper on, 73; Elstob on,
59–65
Epic: Dacier on, 35–43; Reeve on, 135–41. *See
also* Poetry; Romance
Epinay, Louise D': life and works, 111–12;
"Review of Diderot's *Le Fils naturel* from
the *Correspondance littéraire,*" 112–14, xx
Euclid, 13
Euripedes, 104

Fairfax, Edward, 75, 78
Fénelon, François de: *Télémaque,* 175, 349
Fenton, Elijah, 170
Fenwick, Eliza, 296
Fiction: Scudéry on, 2–8; Staël on, 344–60;
Wollstonecraft on, 285. *See also* Novel
Fielding, Henry, 102, 177, 178, 185, 233, 235,
353; *Tom Jones,* 184, 193–96, 357; *Amelia,*
184, 195–96
Fielding, Sarah, xxii; life and works, 80–81;
"From *The Adventures of David Simple,*" 81–
84, xvii; "From *Remarks on Clarissa,*" 84–
88; "From *The Cry,*" 88–93; "From Preface
to *The History of the Countess of Dellwyn,*"
93–95

Finch, Anne, xvi, 65; life and works, 45–46; "The Introduction," *46–47*; "The Preface," *47–52*; "To the Nightingale," *52–53*

Fletcher, Andrew, 186

Fletcher, John, 47

Foster, Hannah Webster, xxii; life and works, 279; "From *The Boarding School*," *279–83*

French Revolution, xiii–xiv, xx, xxii; Burney on, xxiii, 237; Staël on, 365–72

Galen, 13

Garrick, David, 248, 259, 267, 326

Genius: Charrière on, 149–58

Genlis, Stephanie-Félicité Ducrest, Comtesse de, xvii; life and works, 207–208; "From 'Preliminary Reflections' to *The Influence of Women on French Literature*," *208–11*, xiii; "Reflections on Comedies of Character," *212–13*

George, First Baron Lyttleton, 290

Gleim, Betty, xxv

Godwin, William, 273, 284; *Caleb Williams*, 185, 357; *Political Justice*, 296

Goethe, Johann Wolfgang von: *Sorrows of Young Werther*, *294n6*, 298, 359

Goldsmith, Oliver, 172, 379; *Vicar of Wakefield*, 181, 232–33

Gottsched, Luise, xxv

Gower, John, 59

Granville, George, First Baron Lansdowne, 63

Gray, Thomas, 172, 251; *Bard*, 337

Greville, Sir Fulke, First Baron Brook, 76

Griffith, Elizabeth, xiv, xviii; life and works, 116–17; "From *The Morality of Shakespeare's Drama Illustrated*," *117–23*, xx; and Griffith, Richard, *Letters*, 232–33

Habermas, Jürgen, xv

Hamilton, Elizabeth, xxi; life and works, 273; "From 'The Breakfast Table,' " *274–78*; *The Modern Philosophers*, 185

Harrington, Sir John, 78

Hawkesworth, John: *Adventurer*, 276

Hawkins, Laetitia, xxv

Hays, Mary, xvi, 289–90; life and works, 296; "From *Letters and Essays, Moral, and Miscellaneous*," *297–300*, xix

Haywood, Eliza, xv, xxi; life and works, 67; "From *The Female Spectator*," *68–71*, xiv

Herz, Henriette, xxv

Hippocrates, 13

Hobbes, Thomas: "Doctor of Malmsbury," 18

Holcroft, Thomas, 185

Homer, xviii, 4, 13, 35–43, 58, 93, 106, 137–39, 229, 264, 346

Horace, 37, 49, 64, 93; *Ars Poetica, 39*

Howard, James, 248

Hume, David, 387

Imagination: and the supernatural, Radcliffe on, 331–38; Wheatley on, 243–44

Inchbald, Elizabeth, xiv, xvii, xx, xxi, xxiii, 185; life and works, 246; "Selected *Remarks* from *The British Theatre*," *247–63*, xviii; "Letter to George Colman, the Younger," *263–64*; *Lovers' Vows*, 261–63; *Simple Story*, xvii, 375–77

Jacob, Giles, 77

Johnson, Samuel, xxi, 117, 135, 166, 233, 235, 236, 238, 258, 260, 269, 273, 288, 290; Hamilton on, 274–77; *Rambler*, xix, 275

Jones, David, 139

Jonson, Ben, 20, 61, 78; *Alchemist, 20*

Karsch, Anna, xxv

Kemble, John, 259, 301

Killigrew, Thomas, 22

La Calprenède, Gautier de Costes de, 37; *Cassandre*, 35–36; *Cléopâtre*, 36

La Fayette, Madame de: *Princess of Clèves*, 209, 358

La Fontaine, Jean de, 350

Langland, William, 75

LaRoche, Sophie, xxi; life and works, 144–45; "On Reading," *145–47*; *Pomona*, xv

La Rochefoucaul, François, 94

Lazarus, Rachel Mordecai, xviii, xxi, xxiii; life and works, 391–92; "From Correspondence with Maria Edgeworth," *392–97*

Leapor, Mary, xxv

Le Bossu, René, *43n2*, 93

Lee, Nathaniel, 55. See also Dryden, John

Lennox, Charlotte, xviii, xx, 285–86; life and works, 125–26; "From *Shakespear Illustrated*," *126–33*, xiv; *Euphemia*, xvii; *Female Quixote*, xvii; *Lady's Museum*, xv

Lesage, René: *Gil Blas*, 184, 209–10, 348

L'Estrange, Sir Roger, 22

Letters: Burney on, 232–35; letter writing, Foster on, 282–83

Lettres Péruviennes, 209

Lillo, George: *George Barnes*, 82; *Fatal Curiosity*, 82

Longinius, 41

Lucian, 14
Lussan, Marguerite de: *Anecdotes of the Court of Philippe-Auguste,* 352
Lydgate, John, 60

Mackenzie, Henry, 301
Maintenon, Mme. de, 209
Malone, Edmond, 247
Manley, Delarivier, xxv
Marivaux, Pierre, 102, 177, 233
Marmontel, Jean-François: *Belisaire,* 175; *Moral Tales,* 357
Massillon, Jean-Baptiste, 350
Milton, John, 76, 92, 238, 268, 269, 271, 287, 330, 335–37, 386; *Paradise Lost,* 208
Molière, 212–13; *Tartuffe,* 348; *Misanthrope,* 348
Montagu, Charles, Earl of Halifax, xxiii, 63
Montagu, Elizabeth, xviii, xxii, 330; life and works, 96–97; "From *Dialogues of the Dead,*" *97–102*; "From *An Essay on the Writings and Genius of Shakespear,*" *103–109*
Montague, Mary Wortley, 139
Montesquieu, Charles-Louis de, 351, 368
Montolieu, Isabelle de: *Caroline,* 358
Moore, John: *Zeluco,* 184
Morality: Dacier on, 35–43; Griffith on, 117–23; Hays on, 297–99; Lennox on, 126–27, 132–33; Robinson on, 274–75; Schlegel on, 341–42; Scudéry on, 5–7; Staël on, 356–59; early women critics on, xix–xx. *See also* Drama; Novel; Reading
More, Hannah, xiv, xix, 379; life and works, 203; "From *Strictures on the Modern System of Female Education,*" *204–206; Coelebs in Search of a Wife,* 380
More, Sir Thomas: *History of King Richard the Third,* 106
Murray, Judith Sargent, xiv, xxii; life and works, 221–22; "From *The Gleaner,*" *222–30*

Napoleon Bonaparte, 343, 380
National literature, English: Cooper on, 73–78; Elstob on, 59–65; Staël on, 360–64
Novel: Alcock on, 162–64; Austen on, 380–86; Baillie on, 302–303; Barbauld on, 175–96; Barker on, 30–32; Burney on, 232–39; Charrière on, 158–59; Edgeworth on, 376–77; Foster on, 280–81; Hays on, 297–99; More on, 204–206; Murray on, 226–30; Reeve on, 141–42; Schlegel on, 341–42; Wollstonecraft on, 285–86, 293–94; early

women critics on, xviii–xx. *See also* Morality; Reading

Oldys, William, 77
Opie, Amelia, 185
Otway, Thomas, 55, 83, 87, 247, 254, 256; *The Orphan,* 87; *Venice Preserved,* xx, 255–56
Ovid, 13, 137

Painting: Charrière on, 149, 152; Montagu on, 105–106; Wheatley on, 244–45
Paracelsus, 13
Percy, Thomas, 137
Petrarch, 268, 271; *Life of Petrarch,* 299
Phillips, Edward, 77, 78
Phillips, Katherine, 50, 62, 64; "Orinda," 48, 51
Pickering, Amelia: *Sorrows of Werter, a Poem,* 289
Pliny, 13
Plutarch, 13, 97–102
Poetry: Baillie on, 303–304; Finch on, 46–53; Robinson on, 268–72; Wheatley on, 241–45; Wollstonecraft on, 290–93; early women critics on, xxi. *See also* Epic
Pope, Alexander, xvii, xviii, 83, 86, 105, 138, 168, 171, 182, 227, 250, 251, 252, 254, 279, 386; "Essay on Criticism," 73; *Dunciad,* xxi, xxiii; *Eloisa to Abelard,* 283, 359
Portuguese Letters, 359
Priestley, Joseph, 290
Prior, Matthew, 64, 83, 386

Race, and aesthetics: Wheatley on, 244–45; early women critics on, xxii–xxiii; Jewish stereotypes, Lazarus on, 392–97; *Othello,* Fielding on, xxii–xxiii, 81
Racine, 154, 360, 364; *Mithridate,* 352
Radcliffe, Ann Ward, xxi, xxii, 185; life and works, 330–31; *On the Supernatural in Poetry,* *331–38*
Rapin, René, 50
Ravenscroft, Edward: *The London Cuckolds,* 23
Reading: Barker on, 30–31; Haywood on, 68; Foster on, 279–81; LaRoche on, 145–47; biography and history, Hays on, 299; early women critics on, xiv–xv, xxi; history, Austen on, 386–88, Foster on, 281; readers, Cavendish on, 10–11; poetry, Austen on, 388–89. *See also* Morality; Novel
Reeve, Clara, xvii, xviii, xix, 166–72; life and works, 134; "From *The Progress of Ro-*

mance," *135–142,* xiv, 166; *English Baron,* 166–69, 171

Reynolds, Sir Joshua, 236; *Discourses on Art,* 330

Riccoboni, Marie-Jeanne, xxv, 358

Richardson, Samuel, xvii, xviii, 166–72, 177, 178, 185–93, 233, 235, 279, 353, 357; *Clarissa,* 84–88, 101–102, 178, 180, 183, 186–93, 219, 228–30, 294*n1,* 298–99, 358; *Sir Charles Grandison,* 102, 183, 192–93, 294*n1,* 358, 373*n25*

Robertson, William, 387

Robinson, Mary, xiv, xvi; life and works, 267; "Preface to *Sappho and Phaon,*" *268–72*

Rollin, Charles: *History of Cyrus,* 299; *Life of Alexander the Great,* 299

Romance: Austen on, 384; Baillie on, 302; Barbauld on, 176–78; Burney on, 234; Dacier on, 36–43; Fielding on, 88; Foster on, 280; Hays on, 297–99; Reeve on, 135–42; early women critics on, xviii–xx. *See also* Epic; Fiction; Novel

Roscommon, Wentworth Dillon, Fourth Earl of, 50, 62

Rousseau, Jean-Jacques, xviii, 167–68, 170, 177–78, 182, 204, 233, 235, 368; *Emile,* 294*n1,* 343; *Julie, or the New Heloise,* 299, 359

Rowe, Elizabeth, xxv, 232

Rowson, Susanna, xxv

Sackville, Charles, Lord Buckhurst, 75

Sackville, Thomas, First Earl of Dorset, 78

Schlegel, Dorothea Mendelssohn Veit, xix, xx; life and works, 339–40; "From 'A Conversation about the Latest Novels by French Women Writers,'" *340–42*

Schlegel, Friedrich, 339

Schlegel-Schelling, Caroline, xxv

Scott, Mary, xxv

Scott, Sir Walter, 301, 380; *Lady of the Lake,* 388; *Marmion,* 388; *Waverley,* 383

Scudéry, Madeleine de, xviii, 43*n4,* 58, 100–101, 110*n7*; life and works, 1–2; "From *Clelia,*" *2–8*; *Artamène ou le Grand Cyrus,* 36, 100; *Clelia,* 36, 85

Seneca, 13

Sévigné, Madame de, xvii, xxv, 209, 279

Seward, Anna, xvii, xxiii; life and works, 165; "Correspondence between Anna Seward and Clara Reeve from the *Gentleman's Magazine,*" *166–72*

Shaftsbury, Anthony Ashly Cooper, Third Earl of, 74

Shakespeare, William, xvii, xviii, xx, xxii, 20, 56, 81–82, 83, 90, 92, 153–55, 167, 169, 172, 219, 226, 262, 287, 305, 306, 324, 330, 336–37, 343; Cavendish on, 11–13; Griffith on, 117–23; Lennox on, 126–33; Montagu on, 103–109; Staël on, 360–64; *Cymbeline,* 332; *Hamlet,* 334–35, 338; *Henry IV,* 20, 103–104; *Julius Caesar,* 331–32, *King Lear,* xxiii, 81, 107–108; *Macbeth,* 332–33; *Measure for Measure,* xx, 126–33, 363; *Merchant of Venice,* 119; *Midsummer Night's Dream,* 295*n3*; *Othello,* xxii–xxiii, 81, 119–22; *Richard III,* 364; *Romeo and Juliet,* 247–49; *Tempest,* 364; *Winter's Tale,* 267

Sheffield, John, Duke of Buckingham, 63

Shelley, Mary, 284

Sheridan, Frances, xxv, 179

Sheridan, Thomas, 179, 256

Siddons, Sarah, 259, 301, 324, 333

Sidney, Sir Philip, 59, 74, 78, 178

Skelton, John, 75

Smith, Charlotte, xvi; life and works, 216; "Preface to *Desmond,*" *217–19,* xxiii; "From *Marchmont,*" 219; *Elegaic Sonnets,* 267; *Old Manor House,* xvii

Smollett, Tobias, 178, 233, 235

Socrates, 40

Sophocles, 40, 103, 153, 155

Southerne, Thomas, 142, 252; *Oroonoko,* 250–52

Spenser, Edmund, 61, 64, 75, 76, 90, 271; *Faerie Queen,* 349

Staël, Germaine de, xiv, xix, xxii, 182, 340; life and works, 343–44; *Essay on Fictions, 344–60;* "From *On Literature,*" *360–72*; *Corinne,* 339

Steele, Richard, 275. *See also* Addison, Joseph

Sterne, Laurence, 178, 299, 386; *Sentimental Journey,* 357

St.-Pierre, Bernardin de: *Paul and Virginia,* 358

Stuart, Gilbert: *History of Scotland,* 299

Sully, Maximilian de Bethume, Duke of: *Memoirs,* 299

Surry, Henry Howard, Earl of, 60, 75

Swift, Jonathan, xviii, 58, 175, 186, 287; *Battel of the Books,* xxiii; *Gulliver's Travels,* 175, 351; *Tale of a Tub,* 351

Tacitus, 13, 106, 355

Talbot, Catherine, xxv

Tasso, 50; *Jerusalem Delivered,* 209
Taylor, Ann, xxv
Taylor, Jane, xxv
Tencin, Claudine de: *Count of Comminge,* 358
Theater: Baillie on, 322–29; Charrière on, 156–57; Cowley on, 200–202; American theater, Murray on, 222–24. *See also* Comedy; Drama; Tragedy
Thomson, James, 168, 171, 337
Thrale, Hester, xxv, 330
Tragedy: Baillie on, 306–14; Cockburn on, 56–57; Montagu on, 105; tragicomedy, Inchbald on, 249–50. *See also* Comedy; Drama; Theater
Translation: Behn on, 25–26

Virgil, 13, 40, 59, 138, 168, 171; *The Aeneid,* 40; Maro, 242, 346
Voltaire, 107, 175, 212, 364, 368; *Age of Louis XV,* 299; *Babone,* 175; *Candide,* 175, 353; *Henriade,* 352; *History of Charles XII, King of Sweden,* 299; *History of the Russian Empire under Peter the Great,* 299; *Mahomet,* 256–58; *Memnon,* 353; *Micromégas,* 351; *Orphan of China,* 352, 373n18; *Tancred,* 352; *Thélème et Macare,* 349; *Zadig,* 353

Waller, Edmund, 51, 62, 63, 76, 270
Warren, Mercy Otis, xxv
West, Jane, xxv, 185, 379; *Alicia de Lacy,* 384
Wharton, Anne, 65

Wheatley, Phillis, xxiii; life and works, 241; "On Recollection," *241–43;* "On Imagination," *243–44;* "To S. M. a young *African* Painter, on seeing his Works," *244–45*
Williams, Helen Maria, xxv
Winstanley, William, 77
Wollstonecraft, Mary, xiii, xvi, xvii, xxi, 273, 296; life and works, 284; "Advertisement to *Mary, a Fiction,*" *285;* "Selected Reviews from *The Analytical Review,*" *285–89;* "From Letter to Mary Hays," *289–90;* "On Poetry and our Relish for the Beauties of Nature," *290–93;* "Preface to *The Wrongs of Woman: or, Maria,*" *293–94*
Women critics: Fielding on, 81–84; Inchbald on, 263–64; Reeve on, 135; early women critics on, xvii–xviii
Women writers: Behn on, 22–24; Cavendish on, 13; Finch on, 46–47, 48–50; Genlis on, 208–11; Robinson on, 272; Schlegel on, 340–42; Smith on, 217–18; Staël on, 358; Wollstonecraft on, 289–90; early women critics on, xvii
Wood, Anthony, 62, 77
Wordsworth, William, xx, 301; *Lyrical Ballads,* 267
Wraxall, Sir Nathaniel William: *Memoirs of the Kings of France,* 299

Yearsley, Ann, xxv